LEIGH HUNT

Leigh Hunt.

ÆTAT. 20

ENGRAVED BY H. MEYER

From an unpublished Miniature by Joseph Severn.

LEIGH HUNT

A BIOGRAPHY

BY

EDMUND BLUNDEN

ARCHON BOOKS
1970

First published 1930
Reprinted 1970 with permission
in an unaltered and unabridged edition

SBN: 208 00846 2
Library of Congress Catalog Card Number: 74-95020
[Reproduced from a copy in the Yale University Library]
Printed in the United States of America

CONTENTS

ILLUSTRATIONS

PREFACE

A CAREFUL life of Leigh Hunt should have been written many years ago, when some who had known him were alive, and when the documents were still mainly assembled. It was reported that the family of his friend William Smith Williams had made the necessary preparations for an authoritative biography. Nevertheless, the plan was given up, and among the papers which I have not seen I regret that those are included.

But anyone who begins to explore manuscript and printed sources of information, or at all events words, touching Leigh Hunt, will not complain that "the materials are scanty." Through my mind, at many stages of my enquiry, the Latin poet's phrase has sounded, *Inopem me copia fecit.* The list of authorities set out at the end of the book by no means expresses the great confusion of references and notes with which I have necessarily surrounded myself, and it will not be judged a serious offence, I believe, when I admit that the search for Leigh Hunt might still go on—

> And longer had I mused, but with a frown
> Old Time impatient rose.

Manuscript and newspaper evidence about this man of letters with his sixty years of literary life and his countless friends, acquaintances, and endeavours is naturally plentiful, but it is scattered. Mr P. J. Dobell alone has issued more than one catalogue of autographs almost wholly relating to Hunt.

Besides my indebtedness to the British Museum, and the Dyce and Forster collection, for access to valuable letters and other papers, I acknowledge the great generosity of Lady Butterworth, who, several years ago, placed in my hands a large collection preserved by the late Miss Alice Bird.

These papers are more often associated with Hunt's eldest son than with Hunt, on whom however they throw many sidelights. Lady Butterworth also enabled me to bring out new portraits of Leigh Hunt. Another benefactor to me and readers of this work is the Rt Hon. Sir William Bull, so many years M.P. for Hammersmith. It will be recalled that he assisted the youngest daughter of Leigh Hunt in the difficulties of her old age,—she lived almost to see the Great War. From the series of curious silhouettes by Mrs Leigh Hunt in his possession, Sir William invited me to publish which I would; and his cordial permission will not be forgotten.

Since the first proceedings of my book, ten years have passed. The catalogue of those who have at one time or another sent me a suggestion, a name, or a date is a long one. I do not attempt here to thank so many well-wishers individually; but there are several to whom I am obliged for more than occasional help. It was Mr S. L. Sassoon who placed on my shelves several of the scarcer works of my author, which he had successfully hunted for. Others came to me from Mrs G. A. Anderson, who should have been living to-day to discuss with her wonted candour and cheerfulness this and any other work in which Charles Lamb is encountered, and to apply her unique learning to the errors and omissions. Mr H. S. Milford, the editor of Hunt's *Poetical Works*, has not ceased to encourage me, and his reading of the proofs has strengthened the text with touches of the fine scholarship seen in full in his *Hunt*, or his *Cowper*. Mr Frederick Page, who persists in giving others the benefit of his genius for biographical research, has answered my questions, transmitted quotations, and read the proofs. From Cedar Rapids, Ohio, Mr Luther A. Brewer has presented me with some transcripts of letters, and with two of his highly informative books on Hunt, privately printed; he is, I believe,

the ablest collector of Leigh Hunt in the world, and will forgive
me for mentioning his promise to bring out a great bibliography
of the treasury of original papers and books in his hands.
When it appears, it will illustrate the extreme difficulty that a
one-volume biographer has in recording all Hunt's ramifi-
cations, though, perhaps, the *aureus ramus* is the best object
for a work of medium compass. From New York, Mr Frank
Monaghan sent me his biographical discoveries concerning
Isaac Hunt. I must mention, too, the faithful and clever
industry of Miss Aki Hayashi, who has undertaken much dry
labour among periodicals and autographs on my behalf.
Another friend of the book and the writer will, I am sure,
accept the dedication as a testimony; nor can I fail to reflect
that the book's existence commemorates many instances of the
invincible companionship at every point of Richard Cobden-
Sanderson.

One word more. A considerable proportion of the passages
quoted are new to print, or else to a biography of Hunt, but I
have preferred not to interrupt the reader (who will, as it is,
find quite enough footnotes) with a researcher's specifications,
and bristling references.

E. B.

April 1930

I

Parentalia

SOME day, perhaps, one of our historians will add to our understanding and pleasure by producing a retrospective study of minor emigrations, and the benefit which England has received from these in music, literature, the arts and sciences, and public enterprise and character. Our traditions of freedom and (in spite of the ancient "'Eave 'arf a brick at 'im" story) equity towards the stranger have been rewarded by the talent, genius, and personal quality of many foreign families settling among us, and uniting with us. If the chronicle of this fortunate hospitality proper to England comes to be written, a passage should not be omitted in which particularly the re-migration of distinguished men and women from America in the colonial days and the earlier period of independence would be gratefully set forth. And in that chapter, if our recorder is of a sociable and generous turn of mind, possibly more than a footnote will commemorate one gentleman who really ought to have flourished for ever in some standard novel, but having been in fact born, educated, married, ordained, imprisoned and buried, is qualified for material memoirs such as the present. This was Isaac Hunt, who deserves some remembrance both on account of his career and individuality and because he was the father of men eminent in the shaping of English thought and feeling during the nineteenth century. The descendants of this ex-American have been numerous, and his family tree has not yet disappeared from the land which it has adorned and advantaged; yet had Isaac Hunt been only the father of John and Leigh Hunt and grandfather of that good journalist Thornton Hunt, he would have earned his place among successful progenitors. He has it in the new *Dictionary of American Biography*.

Isaac Hunt himself was the son of another Isaac Hunt, vicar of Bridgetown, Barbados, at the middle of the eighteenth century. We may take a glance at Barbados as Mr Salmon the geographer depicted it at that time: "It produces Sugar, Rum, Molosses, Cotton, Indigo, Ginger, Pine-Apples, Guava's, Plantains, Oranges, Citrons, and other Tropical Fruits. A College is erected here with a Revenue for Professors in the several Sciences: Colonel *Codrington* was the principal Benefactor. The Number of white Inhabitants are computed to be 20,000, and of their Negroe Slaves 100,000. They receive their Corn, Cattle, Flour, Flesh, and salted Fish, from *Pennsylvania*, and other *British* Northern Countries, or from *Ireland*; and their Furniture and Cloathing from *Old England*." It is apprehended, in the light of subsequent events, that the Rev. Isaac Hunt's son Isaac found his early sensibilities not un-soothed with the local product of rum and pineapples, and Leigh Hunt (agreeably balancing the cause of respectability and the charm of good fellowship) reports that this younger Isaac, being sent to college at Philadelphia in 1757, "became the scapegrace who smuggled in the wine, and bore the brunt of the tutors." Further, he issued "scurrilous and scandalous pieces" against certain persons of importance. However, the young man's capacities carried him through his undergraduateship to the degree (as appears in a subscription list prefixed to Leigh Hunt's earliest book) of "M.A. of the Universities of Philadelphia and New York." Accepting the same authority, published many years later, one may observe that Isaac Hunt Junior made an impression on a number of men conspicuous in American university life and public affairs. The exact terms in which these worthies are complimented, probably by Isaac himself, in the subscription list, throw light on the inherited temperament of Leigh Hunt, and the family characteristic of being confidential with the world at large: "Hon. J. Dickenson, the celebrated author of the Farmer's Letters—member of the American congress—good as well as great." "Rev. John Ewing, D.D. Provost of the University of Pennsylvania—one of the first mathematicians and philosophers in the United States." "Governor Franklin, formerly the able and faithful governor of New Jersey—Son of the late ingenious Benjamin Franklin, *prime conductor* of the American revolution, and principal *founder* of the United States of America—without his *type* in our days." "Hon. Robert Livingston—Plenipotentiary of the United States of America to the French Republic." "D. Rittenhouse, esq. of Philadelphia, one of the greatest philosophers of the present age." "Benjamin Rush, M.D. Professor of Chemistry in the University of Pennsylvania—whose tender care of the lives of his fellow citizens, at the risque of his own, when the yellow fever raged, endears his name to every philanthropist in the Old, as well as the New World." "Rev. William Smith, D.D. Provost of the University of Pennsylvania on its first establishment—one of the first who diffused the light of science over the new world." "Nicholas Waln—in his youth an eminent Barrister, at Philadelphia, and for some years past as eminent a Preacher in the Society of Friends—a people simple, yet for the most part subtle." All these gentlemen and many more had the pleasure of recalling their old friend Isaac Hunt as they read his prospectus and parted with the price of his son's "Juvenilia."

While they had been marching steadily onwards and upwards, their old friend or pupil had found life more precipitous. In admitting this we do not imply any cynical comment on an event quickly succeeding his departure from the University— his marriage; although even in that matter Isaac Hunt was faced with a problem, for, "when he spoke the final oration on leaving

college, two young ladies fell in love with him." It was a case
of choosing between Mary Shewell, daughter of a Philadelphia
merchant, and her sister who was of about the same age. Isaac
Hunt found that Mary was his choice; and, although Stephen
Shewell differed from him, the suitor read the English poets
with so handsome a presence, so tuneable a voice, that not only
was Mary's fascination completed, but also Mary's mother
thoroughly agreed with Isaac. Mr Shewell could only retreat; it
is not known whether his taste for English poetry underwent any
change on the occasion. The marriage took place in 1767.

Apparently Isaac Hunt had some slender allowance or independent income from Barbados; but he intended to make his
livelihood as a lawyer, and began to be favourably known in his
profession. That eager assertiveness of political principle, however, which was to shape the life and shatter the worldly prospects of his son, under the tremendous influences of that
period, interfered with his practical plans. His knack of publishing ironical tracts for the times drew friendly and hostile
attention to him. In the combat of opinions leading to and
following on the American War of Independence, his lively
expressions of loyalty to George III resulted in his being
harried by the crowd and shut in a prison, whence, by paying
the sentry, he obtained his midnight escape to a merchantman
belonging to Stephen Shewell, just then leaving the Delaware
for the West Indies. His wife was left behind in Philadelphia
with those of her children who survived; it is difficult to make
out, in the hazily disposed recollections of Leigh Hunt and the
other scanty evidence, exactly what her young family was, but
here is the place to give as precise a list of names as we can.
Before leaving America, Isaac and Mary Hunt had lost a son,
Benjamin, and a daughter, Eliza; four boys remained, Stephen
Shewell, later on an attorney; Robert, apprenticed to art; John,

destined to be a publisher, editor, and Liberal man of action; Horatio, who presumably (his name almost proves it) is the one who ran away to sea and was not heard of again. In England were born Mary, who died a child, and James Henry Leigh, the central figure of these pages following.

How long Isaac Hunt remained in Barbados, and what degree of public activity he showed there, is forgotten, but presently he left the island again, and this time for ever. "He should have been kept at home," his famous son declares. "He was a true exotic, and ought not to have been transplanted." Through the operations of destiny, however inept, the exotic crossed the Atlantic, and found that his professional chances in London were almost as unpromising as they had latterly been in Philadelphia; whereon, declining a recommendation to go on the stage, he turned his dramatic sense and manner to another purpose by becoming ordained and attracting large congregations to his artfully delivered sermons. "He had crowds of carriages at the door," and these were not the only sign of approval; for a lady who had been among his hearers bequeathed to him the sum of £500. The sermons, or some of them, were printed in 1778, 1781, 1782, 1784, and 1786; the date of the earliest is a clue to the period which had passed since Hunt's flight from the Philadelphians, as its occasion is a proof of his loyalty—"Preached before the Laudable Association of Anti-gallicans." What he had urged under the sounding-board, he continued in private to selected Britons, "and when the bottle was to circulate it did not stand with him." Such Christianity seldom fails to charm some sort of flock, but it also brought this shepherd a crop of bills which his fees did not meet. His wife and children arrived from America in time to watch the one-sided battle between Cr and Dr reaching a decisive point, and their new home was temporarily broken up. The boys were sent forth to the care of schoolmasters or friends, while the preacher and his wife found a refuge in the house of another remarkable man from America—Benjamin West, R.A. This painter had married the other sister who fell in love with Isaac Hunt as he evolved his declamation in the University of Pennsylvania. Let me make a present of this general situation to any dramatist with a pretty taste in sentimental atmosphere. In memory of West's exemplary benevolence to his parents and himself, Leigh Hunt did not fail to be one of the company of rank and talent who attended the painter's funeral in 1820.

Preaching when and where he could, the distressed Isaac Hunt chanced to address a congregation at the village of Southgate, near which was the seat of the Duke of Chandos. The Duke, "grandson," as Leigh Hunt gladly mentions, "of Pope and Swift's Duke of Chandos," heard the preacher, liked him, and appointed him tutor to his nephew, James Henry Leigh. We cannot doubt that this engagement, besides being a present help in trouble, harmonised sweetly with the tutor's disposition, for in 1790 the pupil took his place among the quarto poets with his *Poems on Several Occasions*. Isaac Hunt duly removed to Southgate, and there in a house classically graceful and pastorally embowered his youngest son was born on October 19th, 1784; the newcomer received the names of his father's amiable and devoted pupil. It is sad to pursue the story of Isaac Hunt at this stage, for it leads us through mismanaged generosities and procrastinations to the debtor's prison which provided the setting of Leigh Hunt's earliest memories (somewhere round 1789); yet, since his difficulties appear to have been due in part to his candour and sympathy with other struggling men, there is a gleam of light from his cell. At length, thanks to the appeals of Benjamin West to George III, Isaac Hunt was granted a Loyalist Pension of £100. This useful recognition may have inspired him to put forth, in 1791, his *Rights of Englishmen: an Antidote to the Poison now vending by the Transatlantic Republican, Thomas Paine.* With this counterblast Isaac Hunt's bibliography probably came to a close, and at this point we may leave him awhile with his Bible, glass, churchwarden and (behind the pantry door) "pressing" accounts in infallible copperplate, in order to attempt a better acquaintance with the sharer of his chances, Leigh Hunt's mother.

Mary Hunt had exchanged a home of golden security and plenty for her husband's perpetual improvidence. Tall, black-haired, with fine eyes, she "had no accomplishments but the two best of all, a love of nature and of books." She had embarked with her four small sons, valiant to join her husband in London, on the *Earl of Effingham*, and, as has been seen, she had to endure many years of anxiety from the time she arrived. The pathetic and cloistered beauty created round her by Leigh Hunt in his *Autobiography*, as he looks back from his old age to hers, cannot be imitated. If marriage never brought any other grace into being, it might be justified by the pattern of so mild a consistency, so faultless an acquiescence. She combined the most exacting principles with a delightful leniency in practice, and in this paradoxical spirit her youngest son must remind us of her, never allowing what should have been done to shut out what should be. "She had the highest notions of chastity; yet when a servant came to her, who could get no place because she had had an illegitimate child, my mother took her into her family upon the strength of her candour and her destitute condition, and was served during the remainder of the mistress's life with an affectionate gratitude." Leigh Hunt also printed in one of his political essays in *The Examiner* and elsewhere an anecdote of this excellent mother, displaying that rare courage which dares all misconstruction or ridicule. Being asked for help by a destitute woman in Blackfriars Road, one bleak London day, she turned into a gateway, took off her flannel petticoat, and gave it to the one whose need was greater. No sequel could make that almsgiving much finer, but there is one: Mary Hunt took cold on her way home and became an invalid for the rest of her life.

A peculiar tenderness accompanied the childhood of Leigh Hunt, partly because of his own happy and sensitive nature, but more, no doubt, because he was so decidedly the youngest in the house, nine years separating him from his next older brother John. The other boys had been assigned to various employments before he was sent to school; Stephen was on the way to becoming a "solicitor and secretary to the society for prosecuting felons," Robert endeavouring to emulate his relative Benjamin West and groping out the art of engraving, John apprenticed to Carew Reynell, a notable printer at Pimlico. Mary Hunt still had her little Leigh and the daughter Mary to dote upon, but Mary the younger died very early. Then it was to Leigh more and more that the patient, fading mother looked and spoke, to him she sang her favourite songs, impressing them for ever on his memory; the "Hardy Tar" was one, with its refrain, "He'll show his daring spirit," which she could not but love him to hear, although it brought to her mind that other son on some unknown sea; and she would encourage Leigh to sing too. With transforming emotion, he came upon a copy of one of his childhood songs on a stall in Wardour Street nearly sixty years afterwards, and in the simple verse (the music was by Hook, the words by John Logan) one may discern some reflection of the solitary sweetness of his mother:

> The day is departed, and round from the cloud
> The moon in her beauty appears;

LEIGH HUNT, AGED ABOUT 7 YEARS

FROM A MINIATURE

The voice of the nightingale warbles aloud
　　The music of love in our ears:
Maria, appear! now the season so sweet
　　With the beat of the heart is in tune;
The tune is so tender for lovers to meet,
　　Alone by the light of the moon,—
　　Alone by the light of the moon.

Throughout Leigh Hunt's long and careworn life, one
pleasure never lost the intimacy which it had for him in his
earliest experience—the pleasure of singing to the piano; and
when he picked up that piece of Hook's in Wardour Street, all
his adventures resolved themselves into a sequestered melody:
"The universe itself was nothing but a poor sitting-room in the
year '89 or '90, with my mother in it bidding me sing, Miss C.
at the pianoforte—harpsichord more likely, and my little sister,
Mary, with her round cheeks and blue eyes, wishing me to
begin."

Pleasures like these, though not utterly set beyond reach,
were seriously interrupted when the necessities of Isaac Hunt,
and surely his genuine desire to give his sons a fair beginning
in the market of life, induced him to send the youngest to
school. Accordingly he submitted (on the usual form) his
Petition "To the Right Honourable, Right Worshipful, and
Worshipful the Governors of CHRIST'S-HOSPITAL, LONDON,"
on April 1st, 1791, from the parish of St Pancras. Pleading "a
wife and five Children," the applicant duly proceeded, "Therefore he humbly beseeches your Worships, in your usual Pity
and Charity to distressed Men, poor Widows, and Fatherless
Children, to grant the Admission of his said Child into CHRIST'S-
HOSPITAL, named James Henry Leigh Hunt, of the Age of
Seven Years & upwards, there to be Educated and brought up
among other poor Children." To the petition was added the

requisite certificate of honest origin and poverty, and agreement "to leave the said Child to the Disposal of the Governors of the said Hospital, to bind him an Apprentice to such Trade or Calling, whether for Land or Sea Employments, as they shall judge the said Child most fit and proper for," as well as the promise "to discharge the said Hospital of the said Child, at the age of fifteen Years" or at any other time if the Governors required it. The signatures of the minister, churchwardens and three householders of St Pancras, and that of Isaac Hunt (gay, supple, clear, very like his son's), completed the document. The Governors treated the appeal favourably, and on October 30th, 1791, Leigh Hunt was baptised according to their requirements; perhaps his father's imprisonment had caused this event to be deferred so long. On November 24th, 1791, he was "clothed" at Christ's Hospital, and walked a Bluecoat boy.

II

The Fortunate Bluecoat Boy

MUCH more than a century has passed since Leigh Hunt found himself parted from the world by the monastic walls of Christ's Hospital, but the school was even then a redoubtable piece of antiquity; since Edward VI signed its charter, almost two hundred and fifty years had created and coloured its tradition. Founded with the immediate object of reducing the vagabondage and destitution which disgraced London in the sixteenth century, Christ's Hospital had from the first years of its existence commended itself to the imagination and affection of the City as being much more than a refuge and a poorhouse. The wisdom and long view of its earliest administrators modelled it as a means not simply of feeding the hungry and correcting the vicious, but, far more, of assisting England with a succession of hardy, well-mannered and skilled apprentices, both in the spheres of commerce and of culture, for ever. The Hospital had fulfilled the warm desires of its ancient and recent benefactors. Even in its infancy it had sent out boys who rose to mercantile power and dignity and some others who live on in the spiritual story of their country—George Peele the poet and dramatist, Father Baker the Catholic mystic, and Edmund Campian the martyr. Later on, while its devotion to the Church and Universities did not fall by the way, the Hospital was above all famous for its Writing School, commanded by astonishingly able quillmen themselves educated in it, to whom the great trading houses would send for recruits; and for the Navigation School (called the Mathematical), founded by Charles II and shaped by Samuel Pepys, to equip the Navy and the Merchant Service with youths of trained ability. At the end of the eighteenth century the reputation of Christ's Hospital was, in the words of "Public Characters," "a most excellent institution, which has furnished the universities with admirable scholars, the church with many learned divines, the navy with able officers; and what, in a commercial nation like this, is no small praise, the exchange, with enterprising and successful merchants."

The school stood in Newgate Street, with its entrance against Christ Church—which is, now that the last relics of the other buildings known to Hunt have been effaced, the best place to which a dreamer, wishing to call up from the deeps the presence of Hunt's generation of Blues, can address himself. The interior geography of Christ's Hospital at that time need not detain us, but one may remark that it was within easy reach of St Paul's Cathedral, the Tower (to which Bluecoat boys are admitted free), West Smithfield, and also the Fleet and Newgate Prisons. Here was no sounding cataract nor savage rock to impress the Wordsworthian mystery upon the minds of the young Blues—

> who were reared
> In the great city, pent 'mid cloisters dim,
> And saw nought lovely but the sky and stars;

yet in those cloisters dwelt an influence powerful to arouse a romantic terror. "And here lies Isabella, wife of Edward the Second—

> She-wolf of France, with unrelenting fangs,
> Who tore the bowels of her mangled mate.

It is well we did not know of her presence when at school, otherwise, after reading one of Shakespeare's tragedies, we should have run twice as fast round the cloisters at night-time as we used." And Hunt lost no time on that journey, urged by the legends of the school and his own readings of phantasmal passages in literature. At less supernatural hours, he luxuriated in a different mood with the same grey precincts for setting:

> Talking away the hours, my friend belov'd,
> Beneath the lamp's dull flame, that palely shed
> Its feeble light along the cloister'd walks,
> Where oft we'd ramble! o'er our youthful heads
> The gloomy arch, that favour'd converse sweet
> Of whisper'd vows of friendship, heav'd on high
> Its massy vault, along whose time-worn roof
> Soft murmurs ran of breathing constancy.

In the same walks, once paced by the Grey Friars, Hunt hurried towards his mother, whenever she approached "with that weary hang of the head on one side, and that melancholy smile."

The Bluecoat boys lived in twelve wards, each of which was in charge of a "nurse," usually "the widow of some decent liveryman of London," seconded by a daughter whose smile or frown played a considerable part in the education of the elder boys. Coleridge is said to have written his early lyrics in honour of one of these young ladies, and Hunt would not coldly reject his agreeable remembrance of another who, when he was recovering from an accident, "brought him tea and buttered toast, and encouraged him to play the flute." Moreover, Lamb tells us that the hero who smuggled in a donkey as a pet, and managed to keep him comfortably for weeks on the leads of his ward, was indebted for the miracle to the connivance of his nurse's daughter. No apology, therefore, is required for referring prominently to those who enlivened the tedium of the incarcerated Blues. The number of these in the London school (for there was a separate school for girls and younger boys at Hertford) was between six and seven hundred. The wards were their dormitories, places of private study, and homes. From these retreats the boys went forth to their schoolrooms, meals in the Great Hall, religious services (very frequently), public ceremonies, games, and "leaves" or clever escapades into the town whose motley pageant swept noisily by the ancient seclusion of the Hospital.

The system of education was simpler than what has been attempted in later days without more convincing results. A Blue either spent his school life in the Writing School, where he would normally become a master of counting-house rules and fearsomely fine longhand; or in the Mathematical School, there to vanquish the ogres of latitude, longitude, azimuth, parallax; or in the Grammar School, with "insolent Greece and haughty Rome." To this policy of segregation Leigh Hunt, who was bred in the Grammar School, was accustomed to attribute his inability to add figures, and further, by an easy transition, his clumsiness with money; but probably Christ's Hospital had less to do with that than he fancied. On the other hand, the school gave him an accurate, extensive and lasting control of Latin and Greek, which continued to supply dignity of image and graciousness of allusion to his style through his over-busy literary career. It is not common among journalists to have Apollonius Rhodius or Strabo at their elbow as he had; not that such authors were entertained in the Christ's Hospital *agenda*, which comprised principally what the present biographer endured in his day, Homer, Demosthenes and Cicero. English exercises (and this dispensation remained much the same until a recent reform) were scanty, being either essays to be composed on "a given subject, such as Ambition or the Love of Money," or abridgements to be made "of some paper in the *Spectator*." On rare occasions English verses were prescribed.

The two masters whom Leigh Hunt was chiefly expected to serve were made the subject of some of the most pleasing and perfect character-writing in the language, not only by Coleridge, Lamb and Hunt but also by a forgotten novelist named W. P. Scargill in his rare *Recollections of a Blue-Coat Boy* (1829), dedicated to Elia. They formed a contrast worthy of the comedy of Goldsmith. The Rev. James Boyer, who hurled forth the lightnings, had been Upper Grammar Master since 1776; and the Rev. Matthew Field, mild as that "season atwixt June and May," had reigned over the Lower Grammar School for the same length of time. Examples of the contrariety of these two preceptors may be enjoyed by any curious person who traces copies of Boyer's Easter Anthems for the use of the school, and the songs of Field's unlucky trifle *Vertumnus and Pomona* (on the stage production of which, some professor in the gallery suited the action to the word by pelting Pomona with apples). The grim, curt severity of Boyer's metre seems to suit with all that is recorded of his disciplinary measures by his talented young observers, of whom Leigh Hunt is the most drastic. Before turning to Boyer's effect on Leigh Hunt, it is just to speak of his effect on the school. Under his leadership a remarkable succession of scholars proceeded to the Universities and carried off many distinctions there and in their after-lives. These men chiefly became classical experts and divines, but one of them became an ambassador, and one was Coleridge, who delighted to counterbalance his memories of Boyer's violence with estimates of his critical wisdom. "At School I enjoyed the inestimable advantage of a very sensible, though at the same time a very severe master, the Reverend James Bowyer. He early moulded my taste to the preference of Demosthenes to Cicero, of Homer and Theocritus to Virgil, and again of Virgil to Ovid. ... At the same time that we were studying the Greek tragic poets, he made us read Shakespeare and Milton as lessons: and they were the lessons, too, which required most time and trouble to *bring up*, so as to escape his censure. I learned from him that poetry, even that of the loftiest and, seemingly, that of the wildest odes, had a logic of its own, as severe as that of science; and more difficult, because more subtle, more complex, and dependent on more, and more fugitive, causes. In the truly great poets, he would say, there is a reason assignable, not only for every word, but for the position of every word. . . ." By this testimony, Boyer's agency appears to his eternal glory in that gleaming poetic translucency which Leigh Hunt found in Coleridge's verse. Coleridge's school friend Middleton, first Bishop of Calcutta, in his *Country Spectator*, "doubted not to compare Boyer with the ablest teachers of antiquity." George Richards, Vicar of St Martin's-in-the-Fields, and author of a prize poem, *The Aboriginal Britons*, praised by Byron and Lamb, dedicated his composition *The Christian* to Boyer "as a small testimony of respect and gratitude" from "his former pupil and most affectionate friend."

But we do not find Leigh Hunt inscribing any of his performances to James Boyer, nor does that potent name occur among the numerous subscribers to Hunt's first poetry-book. Instead, we are taught to see Hunt's schooldays in the form of a verdant and flowery landscape, subject to the lurid onslaughts of a bloodthirsty dragon. "He was a short stout man, inclining to punchiness, with large face and hands, an aquiline nose, long upper lip, and a sharp mouth. His eye was close and cruel. The spectacles threw a balm over it. Being a clergyman, he dressed in black, with a powdered wig. His clothes were cut short; his hands hung out of the sleeves, with tight wristbands, as if ready for execution. . . . The only merits of this man consisted in his being a good verbal scholar, and acting up to the letter of time and attention. I have seen him nod at the close of the long summer school-hours, perfectly wearied out; and should have pitied him, if he had taught us to do any thing but fear. Though a clergyman, very orthodox, and of rigid morals, he indulged himself in an oath, which was 'God's-my-life!' When you were out in your lesson, he turned upon you with an eye like a fish; and he had a trick of pinching you under the chin, and by the lobes of the ears, till he would make the blood come." In the *Autobiography* Hunt tells with wonderful freshness several anecdotes of Boyer *versus* Blues, blending the fierce with the comical, and illustrating particularly the mark made on a delicate, glowing and unusual spirit by this dry Boreal gale of law and order.

Boyer had one grace, even in Hunt's eyes, and one which has made him a person of interest to several literary investigators. He kept a *Liber Aureus*, in which he caused his boys to copy such English essays or verses as they had written to his particular liking. Coleridge was honoured with his master's invitation to a severely limited anthology on four occasions, Lamb (who left school much younger) once, and many of Hunt's rivals and friends on occasion; but Hunt himself, never succeeding in charming his old Serpent, "thenceforward dragged a maiméd life." Not only did he fail to write a word in that extraordinary Book; he would probably have failed had he stayed twenty years in the Grammar School. For Boyer had detected in the habits and expressions of this dark stripling with the American look, and the subtle understanding with his neighbours, a suggestion of Jacobinism. Hunt's essays were crumpled up and thrown to youths of obvious loyalty and rectitude with a "Here, children, there is something to amuse you." Luckily for English prose, the victim of this sublime contempt had a relish for the value of a situation imaginatively considered, even though it was immediately damaging to himself; and besides, his thoughts were mostly beyond the bounds of the Hospital, at the circulating library or with the band in St James's Park.

When Matthew Field was taking his class, the relief of
Hunt and others of his temper came like a peep into the
Elysian fields. One recalls Lamb's fond lingering over this part
of the subject; Hunt tallies with Elia; and Field was like the
Lamb of common legend, for "he came late of a morning;
went away soon in the afternoon; and used to walk up and
down, languidly bearing his cane, as if it was a lily, and hearing
our eternal *Dominuses* and *As in praesenti's* with an air of
ineffable endurance. Often, he did not hear at all. It was a joke
with us, when any of our friends came to the door, and we
asked his permission to go to them, to address him with some
preposterous question wide of the mark; to which he used to
assent. We would say, for instance, 'Are you not a great fool,
sir?' or 'Isn't your daughter a pretty girl?' to which he would
reply, 'Yes, child.' When he condescended to hit us with the
cane, he made a face as if he was taking physic." Field was
an elegant classic, admired by his boys and "the ladies" for
his gentlemanly presence and style of dress. He had just "obtained preferment in the Church of St Paul's" when he died in
1796, leaving his young friends to the unmitigated benefits of
Boyer. It is rumoured that the Fields are being superseded and
deposed from our modern schools, but they will return. Their
importance lies less in the syntax of learning than in the cultivation of the graces; "Grow old along with me" comes from them
with a charm that outlives tuition of the colder, readier kind.
Was it not worth while that Lamb and Hunt should early have
an example of that genius for fancy, holiday and unconventional
humanity which in their lives and works smiles with perennial
benediction? Their successors in our classrooms should not be
deprived of their "delightful guide."

Here let us glance through the gateway of Hunt's Christ's
Hospital, and identify some of the other senior figures who,

through his extended course of acquaintance with great and famous men, always moved through his inward scene in their old state, power and dress. William Wales, mathematical master, although his contributions to the published knowledge of astronomy, population, and determinate sections never stirred Leigh Hunt's enthusiasm, was one of the heroes of the place; for he had received his Hospital appointment after one voyage to Hudson's Bay and two with Captain Cook. During the Gordon Riots he had confronted and silenced an angry crowd who arrived with intent to break into the Hospital. The cheerful intrepidity of which such actions were the index obtained for Wales not merely the obedience of his pupils (that lawless group, with their idolatry of Henry Morgan the buccaneer) but the veneration of the whole school. Once, and only once, was Wales understood to have been discomfited. "When he was in Otaheite, the natives played him a trick while bathing, and stole his small-clothes; which we used to think an enormous liberty, scarcely credible." In remembering Wales with his "plain simple manners, heavy large person and benign countenance," Hunt passes naturally to "a thin stiff man of invincible formality of demeanour, admirably fitted to render encroachment impossible"—Matthias Hathaway, the Steward. The boys, with the talent for nicknames which no Boyers could extinguish, thought of Shakespeare's father-in-law, the "substantial yeoman" of the same name as their Steward, who duly became "The Yeoman." There was one time-honoured means by which the school could take its revenge on this gentleman for his baffling aloofness. When in the services at Christ Church the parable of the Unjust Steward chanced to be read, the whole multitude, gleefully waiting their moment, at the words "thou unjust steward" fastened their eyes on Hathaway in his separate post of observation. His marble sufficiency did not falter, but, Hunt says, "we persuaded ourselves that the more unconscious he looked, the more he was acting." No change of fashion could greatly reduce the Hathawayan austerity, as Hunt notices in one of his essays, speaking of hats: "We remember when our steward at school . . . left off his cocked-hat for a round one; there was, undoubtedly, though we dared only half confess it to our minds, a sort of diminished majesty about him. His infinite self-possession began to look remotely finite. His Crown Imperial was a little blighted. It was like divesting a column of its capital. But the native stateliness was there, informing the new hat. He

> had not yet lost
> *All* his original beaver; nor appeared
> Less than arch-steward ruined, and the excess
> Of glory obscured."

We should assemble with these gentlemen a great many more, from "little Hudson" the music-master, who composed so many hymns for the school, to "Monk" the pieman whose works in another medium were not less popular; from Treasurer and Governors, to Beadles and Cobbler.

It is recorded that S. T. Coleridge was once almost apprenticed to a cobbler, the only obstacle being the raised right hand of Boyer. When Leigh Hunt arrived at Christ's Hospital, Coleridge had received Boyer's last blessings and warnings and gone to Cambridge, leaving behind him a personal reputation for fantastic intellectual endowments, and strong general curiosity about poetry. Hunt also missed Lamb, already the delight and the familiar but sensitively respected friend of many; yet he sometimes saw Lamb revisiting the cloisters, and retained the first impression of "his fine intelligent face." Occasionally one of Lamb's greatest friends, and probably the one whom through Elia we love most, George Dyer, passed quiet as dreams through his old schoolroom on his way to the library. It must have been on one of these occasions that the Muse of Dyer was animated by the grateful sentiments towards Christ's Hospital extant in the 23rd Ode of his *Poetics*. During Leigh Hunt's eight years of Bluecoat life the literary tradition was borne on by several youths who afterwards published esteemed works in various subjects, and kept up their friendship with him by fits and starts. These early companions included John Rogers Pitman, "ever remarkable for his dry humour and great good-nature," subsequently a preacher of admired fluency and force and author or editor of numerous books; Thomas Mitchell, one of the most natural, Attic and luminous translators of Aristophanes, and a "Quarterly Reviewer" in the days when that title made strong men tremble; Thomas Barnes, athlete, scholar, wit, fighting journalist of theatre and forum, and ultimately editor of *The Times*; James Scholefield, Greek Professor, theologian and classic—another "Quarterly Reviewer"; William Stephen Gilly, long respected by the reading public for his works on the Piedmont mountains and the Waldenses; William Pitt Scargill, a clever but anonymous novelist, whose bold-thinking essays in *The Athenæum* helped to establish the excellence of that wonderful journal; and still others. With these names there should occur, in reference to Leigh Hunt's works and days, that of Barron Field, son of the Apothecary to Christ's Hospital, intimate with Hunt and Lamb and a pleasant occasionalist in the world of authorship between 1800 and 1830.

Among the schoolfellows named, Hunt's most conspicuous attachments were with those nearest to himself in school rank—Pitman, Mitchell and Barnes. With these and similar fortunate friends he often converted business into pleasure, and united the happy liberty of escape from London, into the fields or along

unchartered streams, with jubilant adorning of the solemn
studies prescribed by authority. "What pleasant days have I
not passed with Barnes, and other schoolfellows, bathing in the
New River, and boating on the Thames! He and I began to learn
Italian together; and anybody not within the pale of the enthusiastic might have thought us mad, as we went shouting the
beginning of Metastasio's Ode to Venus, as loud as we could
bawl, over the Hornsey fields." And the retrospector, by one
of those sparkling aptitudes like sunbeams that endear his
writings, proceeds to complete the grace which the mind-sight
of those merry young scholars awoke in him, with a quotation
from the Ode: "I can repeat it to this day, from those first
lessons,

> Scendi propizia
>   Col tuo splendore,
> O bella Venere,
>   Madre d' Amore;
> Madre d' Amore,
>   Che sola sei
> Piacer degli uomini,
>   E degli dei."

Not less acceptable is his remembrance of other happy days—
Leigh Hunt was not to have an excess of these, a fact which
mingles a sadness with the sweet—at Richmond, where the boys
gave a demonstration of the spell cast by William Collins'
poetry over the last part of the eighteenth century, loudly
saluting the last home of Thomson of *The Seasons* with the
verses of his friend:

> Remembrance oft shall haunt the Shore,
>   When Thames in Summer-wreaths is drest,
> And oft suspend the dashing Oar
>   To bid his gentle Spirit rest!

Thomson's father had some reputation for laying spirits, but these young visitors did their best to call up that of the peaceful poet.

Besides the associations now touched upon, there was much in Hunt's young life to make him a contrast to the "poor friendless boy" whose difficult solitariness in Christ's Hospital was so intimately described in Lamb's essay. We have seen him out and away in the green freedoms of Middlesex, with books and simple luxuries, careless of anything but the sun's decline; he had no need to yearn, like other Blues, for the Peerless Pool to which of a summer's afternoon they went in columns of sixty or so, headed by their beadles, some eagerly pulling off their coats and shirts on the way, all in a glory at the prospect of the pleasure-bath. Few could afford, as Hunt could, to keep up the credit of the school on the river, and to patronise that artful ancient with boats for hire: "How used old Roberts of Lambeth to gratify the aspiring modesty of our school-coats, when he welcomed us down to his wherries on a holiday, and said 'Blue against Black at any time,' meaning the Westminster boys!" And, though Cooke's editions of the poets then appearing cost only sixpence a number, and though not a few Blues longed for pretty books and immortal verse, was not Hunt supremely lucky that he could record, "I bought them over and over again, and used to get up select sets which disappeared like buttered crumpets; for I could resist neither giving them away, nor possessing them"? Opulence like this naturally depended on the fortune of the Hunt family as a whole, or on some stroke of luck such as the surprising half-guineas given to the irresistible Bluecoat boy by rich relations newly come from Barbados. Hunt moreover is seen to have kept his heart free throughout to enjoy life, even when he had an empty pocket and a rather empty body—the school tables in those days were not overladen; and together with all the more elegant and expensive recreations and excursions of his boyhood, he afterwards reckoned in a spirit of equal exhilaration the simplest and hardiest. No one who has an imaginative acquaintance with Christ's Hospital in London (for now a quarter of a century has passed since its exodus into Sussex) forgets the fame of the Pump, nor did Hunt: "The food was poorer than the learning; but the monks had lived in its cloisters; and left us a spring of delicious water. Hence we have the pleasure of enjoying a crust of bread and a draught of water to this day." Indeed, Hunt in after-life scarcely asked more of heaven. Then, too, he counted himself blessed in the carol-singing of his ward at Christmas "round huge fires, fit to roast an ox, making inconceivable bliss out of cakes and sour oranges"; and he enjoyed in his own rapturous way the art which afterwards gave him ethereal escapes from all burdens. "Many a holiday morning have we hastened from our cloisters in the city to go and hear 'the music in the park,' delighted to make one in the motley crowd, and attending upon the last flourish of the hautboys and clarionets. There we first became acquainted with feelings which we afterwards put into verse (if the recollection be not thought an impertinence); and there, without knowing what it was called, or who it was that wrote it, we carried back with us to school the theme of a glorious composition, which afterwards became a favourite with opera-goers under the title of *Non più andrai*, the delightful march in *Figaro*." Hunt must have been one of the first Englishmen to write general appreciation of Mozart.

In his holidays this boy had the good luck to be welcome in the luxurious homes of Benjamin West, "Historical Painter to his Majesty," and Godfrey Thornton, "Russia-merchant." West's gallery of classic episodes in patriotism and nobility of conduct added its influence to that of Isaac Hunt's magnanimous allusions, and the painter's serenity of countenance and solemnity of artistic immolation also shaped the Bluecoat boy's view of human desire. The noiseless house with its statues and mezzotints and spacious canvases, its kind-hearted mistress, its old Academician in his white woollen gown, was one part of an imaginative education, to which the complement was provided by the home of the Thorntons. "There was cordiality, and there was music, and a family brimful of hospitality and good nature, and dear Almeria T. turning over for the hundredth time the books in her library."

In school, notwithstanding his points of difference or misery, Hunt distinguished himself so far as to become head of the form of Deputy Grecians, above whom stood only a few Olympian spirits, the Grecians, chosen for a University and then a church career. Hunt was of opinion that, like Lamb, he missed their final advancement because he stammered, and so could not make a public oration; but Boyer had other competitors, their characteristics and necessities to weigh in his austere scale. So the youth, at the age of fifteen, and at the close of 1799, was sent out from the old half-monastery—was "with sighing sent." We take a last look at him in his Bluecoat glory— "Ill befall thee, if we ever dislike anything about thee, old nurse of our childhood! How independent of the weather used we to feel in our friar's dress—our thick shoes, yellow worsted stockings, and coarse long coat or gown! Our cap was oftener in our hand than on our head, let the weather be what it would. We felt a pride as well as pleasure, when every body else was hurrying through the streets, in receiving the full summer showers with uncovered poll, sleeking our glad hair like the feathers of a bird." It is almost as though Keats were expressing an enjoyment, nor could Keats have wept more affectionate tears than did Hunt that day when his town clothes had come, been put on, scanned with traditional omniscience by his still blue-coated companions; when his father had called at the Counting-House for the final instructions of our dear Christ's Hospital; and one more Old Blue was free to startle the universe as and where he might.

III

Ver et Venus

THE first part of the course, if not of startling the universe, of telling England, was manœuvred by Isaac Hunt, who in consequence incurred his son's disapproval before many years went by. He hastened on the publication by subscription of "*Juvenilia*; or, A Collection of Poems. Written between the Ages of Twelve and Sixteen, By J. H. L. Hunt, Late of the Grammar School of Christ's Hospital. Dedicated, by permission, to James Henry Leigh, Esq., Nephew to the late Duke of Chandos." The old-fashioned lists of subscribers did good to penniless versemen, but they pleasantly detain posterity from attending to those aspirants' verses by reason of the personal curiosities twinkling in them. This is remarkably the fact with Hunt's first production, from which we already borrowed some information on the old acquaintance of his father. *Juvenilia*, dedicated on May 17th, 1800, issued in 1801 (hardly in time to admit a hasty "Anthem on the Death of an Amiable and Accomplished Young Lady"), was so fashionable as to arrive at a fourth edition in 1803; and the roll of subscribers (with critical and biographical interlinings) was revised with each edition. Of it Isaac Hunt could say, with the madman in Webster, "It was my masterpiece"; and even after the fourth edition he was still marching breast forward, as his manuscript insertion of the additional name "J. Upward Esqre. Throgmorton Street No. 20" in the present biographer's copy avouches. Who, then, were the auriferous ones to whom Leigh Hunt's rhyming recreations were offered between 1800 and 1803?

Something has been said of the American contingent, and I shall not extend that subject, which does not deeply concern

Leigh Hunt. It is comfortable to arrange the others in groups, much as, one of these days, the sheep will be disposed on the right hand and goats and biographers on the left. We may begin with the aristocrats (not in allusion to the sheep and goats), and need not muster them all. The Earl of Aylesbury, the late Duke of Bedford ("the friend of man"), the Duke of Bedford, the Earls of Cardigan, Carlisle, Carysfort, the Duchess of Devonshire (poets usually collected this lady's guinea), Earls of Dartmouth and Digby, Marquis of Exeter, Earl of Fauconberg, Lord Viscount Falmouth, Duke of Grafton, of Gordon, Earl of Guilford, Lord Glenbervie, Duke of Hamilton, Marquis of Headfort, Earl of Harrington, Lord Holland, Lord Hawke, Earl of Kinnoul, Marquis of Lansdowne, of Lorne, Earl of Leicester, of Liverpool, Duke of Marlborough, Earl of Mansfield, Earl of Moira, Lord Montague, Lord Mulgrave, Lady Milbanke—but the rest of this noble army may be left to the reader's imagination or mathematical skill. Next we may assemble the Bishops—of St Asaph, Bath and Wells (two, the late, and the reigning), Chester, Chichester, Durham, Ely, Lincoln, Llandaff, London, Rochester, Salisbury, Winchester; the Archbishop of Canterbury took his copy, but the Archbishop of York unaccountably refrained. Among the statesmen, the Chancellor (Henry Addington), George Canning, Charles James Fox (saluted as "the British Demosthenes"), William Huskisson, the Home Secretary (Pelham) and William Wilberforce were perhaps the most conspicuous supporters. The law relaxed its severe front and conferred shillings if not laurels. But among its names were some who presently had a very different effect on Leigh Hunt, as, Sir Simon le Blanc, who pronounced sentence on him in 1813; Lord Eldon, who deprived Shelley of his children; and Lord Ellenborough, who also took part in sending the proprietors of *The Examiner* to gaol.

Mrs Benjamin West had been very industrious in enlisting the Royal Academicians, of whom Bartolozzi—he gave an engraving for the book—Beechey, Copley, Cosway, Downman, Fuseli, Hoppner, Thomas Lawrence, George Stubbs, Stothard, Westall, and of course West compose a sufficient representation. All his life Hunt was friendly with eminent medical men, and his early welfare did not lack their attention; here were named the humorous I. Lettsom, old Batty who gave the poet his lock of Milton's hair, John Aikin who contributed later to Hunt's *Reflector*, Edward Jenner "author of the most ingenious Discovery of the Eighteenth Century," and several Royal physicians and surgeons. The literary camp was exemplified chiefly by those authors with a touch of public gilding on their names, as Payne Knight of virtuoso renown, Thomas Hope the "gentleman of sphinxes," the incomparable Sheridan, Richard Cumberland, Edward Jerningham, and Poet Laureate Pye. Friends of liberty came to the rout, as Cobbett (twelve copies), Horne Tooke (who had patted the bard on the head in real life), and one of the earlier Thomas Hardys. From Christ's Hospital or its associations came another pleasing crop of subscriptions, among them one or two with a passing hint of Charles Lamb. George Dyer for once had not forgotten an engagement; "J. Lamb, South-Sea House" remembered his brother's school in a practical way. His colleague Richard Plumer, whose noisy cheerfulness sounds on in Elia's *South-Sea House*, subscribed also.

In bringing forward this brief catalogue of names with the aim of illustrating the cultured world of that time and the glittering illusion of fame and substance thrust upon young Leigh Hunt, I have deliberately detained two or three gentlemen for whom I have a special kindness. One was the "Rev. Wm Vidler—the catholic and worthy successor in Artillery-

Street Chapel, of the late eminent, eloquent preacher of the love
of God to man, Elkanan Winchester—the powerful maintainer
of the sovereignty of Jesus Christ over Satan and the kingdom
of darkness—the savage Calvinist and hard-hearted Pre-
destinarian." It is possible that Mrs Hunt obtained this clergyman's co-operation. Next, but probably canvassed by Isaac
Hunt, is "Mr Prince, a favourite victualler of the London
citizens in St Mary Axe." Next—a weighty name—"Mr
Daniel Lambert." He was now about to turn the scale at
eighty-seven stone, and to attract a more numerous share of the
ton than even the poet of *Juvenilia*. And, last, in the fourth
edition, comes one who would scarcely have been anticipated
in this galley more than Lambert: "Right hon. Lord Nelson,
Duke of Brontë, &c." Did he read his copy?

It is time to look from these matters to the other contents of
Juvenilia, though to do so is like passing under a triumphal arch
into a schoolboy's study. If there had been any accomplished
poetry in it we should have heard as much by this time, for
copies of the book are easily found. Boyer was perversely
right in not purchasing one. Yet there is no reasonable call for
artillery when youth is taking its pleasure among the devices
of phrase and cadence and stanza. The best poetical promise in
Juvenilia was an occasional floweriness of colouring and
personal fancy, as when the weeping willow is imaged

> green as spring,
> And silent as the rev'rence of an angel,

or we are given

> hearts-ease rich
> Purpl'd with gold-dropt velvet.

But even in its most juvenile passages the collection informs us
of Hunt's boyish attainments and natural tastes, anticipating

his later characteristics in several tendencies. The inclination to gossip by way of preface already shows itself in two pages prefixed to the Spenserian composition *The Palace of Pleasure*; there too appears Hunt's quality, for good or bad, of seeing life through the medium of high art and heroic instance, for he designates himself "a Muse, who is entering into public in her sixteenth year, bashful on her first exhibition, and listening with trembling expectation, as she passes, to the shouts of disapprobation or applause that burst from the surrounding multitude." We discern the man of explorative and spirited reading, the cosmopolitan of the library, in the versions and mentions of Anacreon, Horace, Lope de Vega, and "the Italian"; we welcome the international humanist in the little ballad of *The Negro-Boy*, the lines on Swiss independence, and occasional sentiments. Friendship is everywhere hailed with rapture, casting its blessed light over the stony cloister or the sedgy Thames. The love poems are not so natural or securely founded. To Hunt women were to be ever "the ladies," and not (so far as such secrets may be divined) mysteries troubling the deep waters of instinct and idea. Of his tastes in English literature, the *Juvenilia* bears witness to a regard for Spenser, prophetic of a life's devotion; a slight knowledge of Shakespeare and Milton; and a much stronger concern with eighteenth-century poetry. Hunt copies Pope's early work ("Hyblaean Pope"), acknowledges stately Dryden and gentle Gay, placates Thomson's blushing Muse, fits out Ossian's Evening Star with rhymes, and pays a left-handed compliment to his schoolmaster, who had in a rare mood lent him Johnson's Poetical Works, by imitating the Doctor's glum ridicule of "Hermit hoar"—and that only. But the idol of *Juvenilia* is William Collins, whose delicate variety of style and union of intellect with sensibility had won him in the closing decades of his

century an intense and ubiquitous admiration, embodied in new
editions, in constant quotations and in attempts to walk in his
paths. Hunt's book is one of many signs of that quiet hero-
worship; it is strewn with reminiscences of Collins' perfect
expressions, would-be assumptions of his poetic forms and
tones, and eulogistic invocations of his name.

Before quitting the contents of *Juvenilia*, it is also necessary
to touch on the enthusiasm for painting there displayed,
kindled no doubt in West's studio. One of the Collins exercises
is an Ode, *The Progress of Painting*, introducing amid mountains with blue foreheads, prattling runnels, murmuring groves,
blue-eyed Naiads, and panting Pleasures, the unequal forms of
Raphael, Barry, Fuseli, West, the late T. Kirk, R. K. Porter
("He comes!") and Michael Angelo. Elsewhere the index to
our author's pictorial preference runs,

> he that shone
> The star of Italy, expressive Raphael,
> The strict Correggio, Titian's glowing hand,
> Fus'li's gigantic fancy, or the fire
> Of Britain's fav'rite West.

These selections are not unsignificant, for they accord with the
larger manifesto of art and its masters reverberated later by
Hunt's newspaper. Not the least agreeable item in most copies
of *Juvenilia* is the oval engraving of a miniature of Hunt by R.
Bowyer, showing the boy poet in his town clothes—dark-
complexioned, his black hair enjoying emancipation from the
school barber, his large eyes looking compassion with something of fear, his lip seeming to reveal a patient reflection,
a shy resolution to be of use to his fellows.

The only really harsh interruption to the ensuing season of
flattery and parties came from old Stephen Shewell in America,
who had read the poetry perhaps with mercantile exactitude;

he wrote inviting his grandson to Philadelphia where he declared "he would make a man of him." But Leigh Hunt was thoroughly though transiently comfortable with his visits to Oxford, and Cambridge, and Windsor in the company of old school friends. A boat, a flute, a few pocket editions and his harmonious Papendieck and Barnes were not gifts of fortune to be traded away on so hard-headed a proposal. In town, moreover, his sudden reputation as a "young Roscius" gave him many opportunities of exciting conversations with public characters. At the British Museum he could present himself like an old intimate at the rooms of Thomas Maurice[1], author of the *History of Hindostan* and formerly encouraged and assisted in his plaster poetry by Dr Johnson; there the formula for Maurice's colds and Hunt's hunger was roast fowl, claret, and all about authors and books, of which the old librarian was an amusing observer. Now, too, Hunt could go to the theatre, so long inaccessible to him by Christ's Hospital decree. "The first time I ever saw a play," he records, "was in March 1800; it was the *Egyptian Festival* of one Mr Franklin: the scenery enchanted me, and I went home with the hearty jollity of Mr Bannister laughing all the way before me. After that I was present at the comedies of Mr Reynolds and of Mr Dibdin, and I laughed very heartily at the grimaces of the actors; but somehow I never recollected a word of the dialogue." This last negative was presently worked up into a sparkling critical campaign against contemporary dramatists, the journalists who flattered them, and many of the actors as well. Meanwhile Hunt thought, as often in later years and less genial circumstances he was to think, that he might himself give the theatre a play or two not unworthy the nation of Shakespeare—in fact, farces, a comedy, a tragedy. *The Poetical Register*, in which his

---

[1] Educated at Christ's Hospital.

new poems were printed, announced the tragedy as *The Earl of Surrey*, but despite this fortunate choice of an unfortunate hero the tragedy never reached the stage. One of the farces was put in the hands of Michael Kelly of Drury Lane, but obtains no word in Kelly's *Reminiscences*.

At this period of his life, Hunt was not the recluse and studious prisoner which he became in time. The age of "Tours," with Pennant and Gilpin and Grose and Ireland among its most popular delegates, was not over; the railway had yet to arrive and dispel the "wildness" and "solemn fantastic windings" of unmetropolitan scenery. An excursion to Box Hill was still something like visions. We see young Hunt going here and there by the coach, reporting what and whom he had encountered with grave exactness and a sense of danger so far eluded. While his poems were passing into fresh boudoirs, he and a friend named John Robertson went off to Margate on the *Methodist hoy*, which was advertised circumspectly as sailing "by Divine Providence"; and on landing they walked along the coasts of Kent and Sussex as far as Brighton—a distance of 112 miles on foot in four days. The instance is worth giving, to temper the notion that Hunt was a listless hothouse plant; although no doubt the little club of "Elders" of which he and his brother tourist were members poured out the elderberry a little too heroically after the explorers' safe return to Westminster.

The coasts along which they had taken their picturesque walk were beginning to be haunted with the menaces of Napoleon, and though Hunt was one of those who did not insist much on his chances of invading us, still there was a gusty glory in the air, a prospect of honour in action, with wit and pun in attendance. The newspapers, then produced rather for reasons of faith and conviction than of commerce, were riotous with pleasantries on the subject, of which the reader may care to see one:

IN REHEARSAL.

Theatre Royal of the United Kingdom.

Some dark, foggy night, about November next, will be *attempted*, by a Strolling Company of French Vagrants, an old Pantomimic Farce, called

HARLEQUIN's INVASION,

OR, THE

DISAPPOINTED BANDITTI.

With new Machinery, Music, Dresses, and Decorations.

Harlequin Butcher, by Mr. BONAPARTE, from Corsica.
(Who performed that character in *Egypt, Italy, Switzerland, Holland,* &c.)

THE OTHER PARTS BY

Messrs. Sieyes, Le Brun, Talleyrand, Murat, Augereau, Massena, and THE REST OF THE GANG.

In the course of the piece will be introduced a distant view of
Harlequin's Flat-bottomed Boats

WARMLY ENGAGED BY THE

WOODEN WALLS OF OLD ENGLAND.

To which will be added (*by Command of his Majesty*, and at the particular request of all good Citizens) the favourite Comic-tragic Uproar of

THE REPULSE;

Or, Britons Triumphant.

The parts of John Bull, Paddy Whack, Sawney MacSneish, and Shon-ap-Morgan, by Messrs. NELSON, MOIRA, ST. VINCENT, GARDNER, HUTCHINSON, WARREN, PELLEW, S. SMITH, &c.

The Chorus of "*Hearts of Oak*" by the JOLLY TARS and
ARMY of OLD ENGLAND,
Assisted by a numerous Company of provincial Performers,

WHO HAVE

VOLUNTEERED their services on this occasion.

** No room for Lobby Loungers.

Vivant Rex et Regina.

In this bill Leigh Hunt was figuring among the Volunteers, the St James's Regiment, evidently answering in the type of its men to the Public Schools Battalions of 1914. Hunt's service must have been during 1803 and 1804. He was rewarded with one incident which at the later period would have been considered "priceless"; the regiment had waited long months for a colonel, a colonel was at length gazetted; he was a nobleman, politically powerful, and related to General Wolfe. The ceremonial of his first review was organised: "Our parade was the court-yard of Burlington House. The whole regiment attended. We occupied three sides of the ground. In front of us were the great gates, longing to be opened. Suddenly the word is given, 'My lord is at hand!' Open burst the gates—up strikes the music. 'Present arms!' vociferates the major.

"In dashes his lordship, and is pitched right over his horse's head to the ground."

Under this chieftain the volunteers conscientiously drilled and marched, with many a joke at the expense of the inevitable Lieutenant "Molly" with his girlish colouring and Major Downs for his undertaker's business at 15 Piccadilly and the size in coffins he would require himself. Their battle-field was often the neighbourhood of Turnham Green, once indeed the last halting-place of six hundred cavaliers and many of their opponents; but in Leigh Hunt's campaign the casualties were confined to bakers' baskets and innkeepers' cellars. After these dusty exploits, Hunt might solace himself at the play, or the Elders' Club, or at a club of young lawyers anxious to perfect themselves in public speaking, to whose circle he had been introduced by his friend Barron Field, subsequently a judge in Gibraltar and in New South Wales. Here came such men as Thomas Wilde, a future Lord Chancellor, and Frederick Pollock, twice Attorney-General. Both these gentlemen, though their course of activity soon diverged from Hunt's, were among his readers in later days.

The question now arises, what Hunt was reading in this desultory phase of youth and sociability. Since he was addicted to bookstalls, no complete answer can be given, but he has reviewed the subject himself with a fond delay. When the literary appreciations scattered through his *Juvenilia* were assembled above, it was plain that prose writers had not captivated him before he left school; and yet Boyer had made him read the *Spectator*, fruitful in his mind when his antipathy to all things Boyerian had ceased to be militant. He passed on to other eighteenth-century periodicals, particularly the *Connoisseur* of Colman and Thornton, which appeared to him a canon of "animal spirits, humour and wit." Goldsmith, Fielding and Smollett, Ann Radcliffe with her vizored mysteries, and the popular "sensibility" novelists all pleased him. He sauntered whistling his rude non-proven through the grand historians, Herodotus, Villani, Froissart and Gibbon. He even invaded the grim earthworks of Blackstone on the laws and de Lolme on the constitution of Britain. Above all, he had gone farther than most of his contemporaries into Voltaire's works; they talked about Voltaire, Hunt "was transported" with his books; and the young man, instinctively impelled against the inherited rubbish of society, though none too certain in his discrimination of the rubbish from the necessary workshop makeshifts of man, found "an abridgment of the *Philosophical Dictionary* [1802] for a long while his text-book, both for opinion and style."

As for poetry at this time, he was being slowly weaned from the adoration of Pope's limited dexterity to Dryden's broader sweep of guns; he was venturing further into the Italian anthologies; he answered every nod and wink of Horace. By fits and starts he showed these likings in the verses which he printed in fugitive publications, and among those we duly find *The Shade of Collins*, an Ode, which was admired for a few months, but in style and statement was dead and buried forty years before. If the bibliographical list so far available does not mislead us, we must conclude that for some ten years after the production of *Juvenilia* Hunt's poetical growth, in reading and in writing, was retarded; in part because the good old *Gentleman's Magazine* versifiers, to whom he had become known at once, awed him with their admired names and approbations, and yet did not seem to illuminate life's trampled crossroads or the zigzags of Parnassus with their carriage candles, though patented and warranted as the genuine article.

More momentous than any other affairs of this doubtful interim, Leigh Hunt's courtship must now reveal its odd and none too hopeful elements. John Robertson, the friend noticed above, introduced Hunt upon their return from hoys and lighthouses to a family named Kent. Mrs Kent, a widow, had been a court milliner. (It may save confusion presently if we say at once that she soon married Rowland Hunter, bookseller in St Paul's Churchyard.) Mrs Kent had two daughters, Marianne and Elizabeth, then children; but Elizabeth was already a bluestocking, and ambitious of being published with other budding authors in a magazine called *The Monthly Preceptor*. But, seeing in that paper a most superior essay by Leigh Hunt, Bessy owned herself outclassed; and then John Robertson offered to bring Leigh Hunt to the house! The celebrity came, was admired, perhaps—but why speculate? Poor Bessy saw his regard directed away to Marianne. As Hunt was attacked with an illness on one of his visits, Mrs Kent gave him rooms and a place in the family circle; the regard for Marianne became an engagement, though she was a little young—"about thirteen," as Thornton Hunt observes. The pretty black eyes, however, could express obstinacy, and presently she broke off the engagement. Here the patient reader was expecting news of Bessy, but there is none; the engagement with Marianne was renewed some time in 1803, and led to marriage. Elizabeth Kent was never married. She was sometimes the housemate of her brother-in-law, almost always in his confidence; she kept her secret, and was in some degree recompensed by the friendship of Shelley and others of Hunt's intimacy. Calumny did not miss her, but only a hypocrite and knave would blot out the beauty in her difficult devotion to the man who, passing her by, seems to have been the loser by the decision through half a century of an unequal compact.

IV

The Three Brothers

FEELING that his business was to write sketches, descriptive but satirical of the ways of the world, Leigh Hunt at length attempted to transfer himself from the now weather-worn pavilions of *Juvenilia* into the newspaper offices. Journalism was his real flame, although for simple reasons he had to affect some other employment. It was first found in "that gloomiest of all 'darkness palpable,' a lawyer's office"—under his brother Stephen. This experiment collapsed, and Hunt for a period gave himself up to a laborious indolence, whence in 1805 he was called by the friendly action of Henry Addington, a recent Prime Minister, in response to Isaac Hunt's applications. For the next three years the pacific Leigh was an unpunctual clerk in the War Office. These movements I bring in without elaboration, because they did not leave any deep impress on Hunt's character or chronicles. Trollope is your only office autobiographer. Leigh Hunt's unofficial life now began to put forth its blossoms of eloquence (*The Connoisseur* variety) in an evening paper called *The Traveller*—if he has not misrecorded the title. His pay was probably adequate, "five or six copies of the paper"—at any rate he had not expected even that remuneration. In May 1805 his brother John, when he established *The News*, invited Leigh to share house with him, and to act as his theatrical critic. Early in 1806 John made another beginning with *The Statesman*, again commanding Leigh's pen. While these periodical performances were going on, to which it will be necessary to look again, John Hunt joined his old master Carew Reynell in the issue of a pretty set of volumes containing *Classic Tales, Serious and Lively*, of which Leigh Hunt was the general editor and Robert Hunt the chief illustrator.

Classic Tales tells us indirectly something of these three brothers. The total responsibility and the sober typography are signs of John Hunt's mode of action. The stiff, slightly ridiculous, classically servile embellishments denote the honest obtuseness of Robert Hunt, to whom a bandbox and a murderess presented much the same problem in comprehension and delineation; at the same time, his glimmerings of more luminous impression cause him to admit the freer recognitions of Wilkie and Uwins. Then Leigh Hunt hurries into the ring. He has been reading *Rasselas*, and is delighted with the possibilities of rendering experience in that sort of literary algebra. "All nations," he begins, "have been delighted with fictitious story, for it suits all men." "The knowledge of private life is the foundation of wisdom, that of public life is the superstructure: let us study ourselves first as *men*, and we may study ourselves afterwards as public characters." "Hear, hear" and applause: a voice, "Physician!—" But nothing is more difficult and rare than the consciousness of imperfect knowledge of life. On the literary ground, Leigh Hunt in this work shows his quickness of discernment and his resources of ornament. The selections to which his verdicts are attached are taken from Henry Mackenzie, whose Addisonian labours he despises, while he acclaims the short stories; from Goldsmith, with considerations on his verse as well as his comedies and miscellaneous prose; from Henry Brooke, author of *The Fool of Quality*; Voltaire, very copiously displayed; Johnson, his *Rasselas*, which "for a model of grave and majestic language will claim perhaps the first place in English composition." (Other little papers accompanying extracts from Marmontel, Hawkesworth and Sterne were by one of the Reynells.) Most revealing of these essays is that on Goldsmith, for Hunt makes the topic of the *Enquiry into the State of Polite Learning in* 1759 an excuse for a similar enquiry by himself in 1806. By that time one might have conjectured that a young ardent soul would have been aware of the Romantic sun, arisen in all the hues of a new day. *Lyrical Ballads* was almost ten years old. But Hunt, though he runs over the names of the German Romantics, had not perceived the genius of his own country, seeing only an "elegant mediocrity" around him. He selects Southey and Cowper as the outstanding poets "of our age"; he admits that Charlotte Smith has "managed" the sonnet with tenderness, and that Joanna Baillie is the nearest contemporary approach to a tragic writer. These and a few other exceptions piece out his literary tableau for that date, when Wordsworth, Landor, Coleridge, Lamb, Rogers, Moore, Crabbe, Campbell, Scott, Godwin, Blake and "Dante" Cary were all in action.

But his dominant concern was with the plays and players of the moment. John Hunt had determined on an unusual independence of speech in his journals, whether the subject were Napoleon or Kemble; and as he delegated the sanguine Leigh to attend to the Kembles, it was not long before Leigh Hunt and the theatre managers, dramatists and actors were at variance. William Archer's account of the state of British drama as Hunt found it may be read in the volume of Hunt's theatrical criticism published in 1894, and it is a gloomy picture. "These were certainly not the palmy days of English dramatic authorship." The three busiest purveyors of comedy were Frederick Reynolds, Thomas Dibdin, and Andrew Cherry ("Merry-Andrew"), and these were the targets of Hunt's nimble archery from the office of *The News*. No longer, the omens seemed to say, would the green-room be able to obtain critical bouquets by an arrangement with the box-office. Good plays and bad plays, inspired acting and humbug would now be judged by Liberty paying for his own seat and dinner. This new

style, of course, involved Hunt in many adjectival disputes, and
obtained for him from one eminent actor the title "the damned
boy"; yet it let the fresh air so briskly into the dusty lumber-
room that it won its battle. Charles Mathews, for instance, was
happy when in 1808 his Sir Fretful Plagiary was admired (we
quote Mrs Mathews) "by the greatest dramatic critic of that
day, Mr Leigh Hunt, whose judgment was universally sought
and received as infallible by all actors and lovers of the drama."
For modern readers, it is not so much Hunt's punishment of
contemporary plays worth a pig-nut, as his entertaining
precision in describing the habits, voices and faces of celebrated
actors, which attracts and rewards attention.

Early in 1808 a selection of his *Critical Essays on the Performers of the London Theatres, including General Observations
on the Practice and Genius of the Stage,* was brought out by
John Hunt, "at whose suggestion it was attempted" and to
whom it was inscribed. It is extremely lively, not so pugnacious
and overbearing as might have been feared, and written with
respect for the natural meanings and most pleasing or com-
pelling arrangements of words. The opinions are heartily definite, and must have been startling to a public accustomed to
cushioned indiscrimination and the aesthetic philanthropy of
"the second bottle." In the first paper, Kemble's stage personality is analysed; he is allowed to have great judgment, and
forceful conception of "the more majestic passions"; his
Roman appearance is brought before us as on a medallion.
"He excels in soliloquies." In "exact knowledge of every stage
artifice local and temporal," in byplay, he is called a master.
But "I have known him make an eternal groan upon the inter-
jection *Oh!* as if he were determined to shew that his misery
had not affected his lungs," and there is the painful question of
his delivery. Instead of "To *err* is human," he says, "To *air*

is human," "*fair*" is "*fay-er-r-r*" and he is liable to bring off such a line as "*Ojus, insijjus, hijjus,* and *perfijjus.*" Leigh Hunt sticks to his man and his dialect with grimness and presently contrives a Kemble Lexicon to be printed on the play-bill. Throughout his book there is the same observant earnestness, zeal for excellences, resistance to vanity and pedantry, and a sustaining calmness which, had it remained with our author, might have enabled him to model his large lifework of criticism in a more permanent and consistent way. *Critical Essays*, as it is a scarce little volume, is a notable one, and probably nothing more eloquent, definite, and influential[1] was ever done in this branch of literature by a writer twenty years of age.

At Rowland Hunter the bookseller's—he succeeded John Johnson who published Blake and Cowper—Hunt was now familiar, and there could meet almost outmoded figures whose singularity charmed him. To those Friday dinners came together (as they would afterwards depart) old Fuseli the painter and Bonnycastle the mathematician, Godwin occasionally, and Kinnaird the magistrate. The last-named would merit immortality if only because he listened to the National Anthem "as if his soul had taken its hat off." Of Godwin Hunt says nothing, although they were acquainted for many years, and on good terms. Little swearing Fuseli and gaunt horse-like Bonnycastle ("I have often thought that a bag of corn would have hung well on him," says Hunt) amused themselves and all present with their skirmishing, which equalled Leech's rival omnibus drivers. At another house, that of Thomas Hill, of *The Monthly Mirror*, literary practitioners, skilful in merry impromptu, used to gather to plain dinners and good

---

[1] "A Farce in two Acts, entitled *Antiquity*, is in the Press, written upon the dramatic principles inculcated by the author of the theatrical criticisms in the *News*, to whom it is dedicated." January 1808.

wine, and Hunt, his brother John, his schoolfellow Barnes, and his "dearest friend" Barron Field, were of that party. Horace Smith, one of the revellers, calls Hill's villa the "Sydenham Tusculum," and hospitable Hill "a retired elderly Cupid" who had not lost the business manner of a drysalter. Hill was good sport in debate. Having propounded some terrific extravagance of fact or theory, he would defend it with goggling eyes and outstretched hands and fingers and these remarks in order—

"Sir, I happen to *know* it . . . ."

"Sir, I affirm it with all the solemnity of a death-bed utterance, a sacramental oath."

Round this philosopher assembled Thomas Campbell—who also lived at Sydenham, and whose poetical genius and appearance of primness with hilarity punctually intervening fascinated Hunt—Theodore Hook, Mathews imitating everything and everybody, and the two Smiths, of whom *Rejected Addresses* remains the best memorial. It may be, as Keats was to write presently of this very group of late departers, that "these men said things which made one start without making one feel; they all knew fashionables; they had all a mannerism in their very eating and drinking, in their mere handling of a decanter." (He did not know that Hill had sent over to Smith's for the meeting thus summed up a dozen "of Keats' favourite beverage, some quite undeniable Château Margaux.") But one risks saying, one would have liked to be of the circle; where are its similars now? It was only one of the many social sets enjoyed and enriched by Leigh Hunt between 1802 and 1859.

At the end of his *Critical Essays* two announcements were printed. One reads:

◆

SATIRES,
EPISTLES, AND LYRIC PIECES.
By LEIGH HUNT.

◆

THE VARIOUS
POEMS OF HORACE
That have been happily
TRANSLATED OR IMITATED
BY OUR BEST POETS,
*With an attempt to supply the more translatable
of what remain;*
AND,
AN ESSAY
ON HIS GENIUS AND WRITINGS
By LEIGH HUNT.

These volumes would have been hailed with a magnum at the Sydenham Tusculum, but they failed to take shape, and I do not hear of any surviving manuscripts. The other advertisement was an exhibition of fine writing headed

PROSPECTUS
OF
THE EXAMINER
A NEW SUNDAY PAPER
Upon Politics, Domestic Economy, and Theatricals.
PRICE 7½d.

It was dated from John Hunt's office at 15, Beaufort Buildings, Strand, in October 1807, but a note corrected that by reporting, "The first number of this Paper appeared on the 3d. January 1808."

V

"*The Examiner*" *in Action*

JOHN HUNT was a reformist no less courageous though less conspicuous than Cobbett and that other Hunt, Henry Hunt, who is so frequently mistaken for a relative of Leigh: and now, having tried his hand here and there in the art of training the public spirit by newspaper, he was ready for his major attempt. One of the best judges of men, he recognised in his brother Leigh a brilliant opportunist who had now had his journalistic initiation, who understood some of the ups and downs which happen to a public writer, and would provide a fresh and optimistic profusion of persuasive comment on affairs. Besides inventing political parables and social studies, this young man seemed capable of enlivening an audience with the literary and dramatic news presented in a style of confidence and vitality. His friends, Barnes, Mitchell, Field, seemed fitted by nature, education and association to supplement his vivid *pros* and *cons* in the arbitration of elegances. Then, Robert Hunt was technically prepared to write of the fine arts, and, if not brilliant, at least had caught up some of the audacious notions of the circle, and might be relied upon to attend to his work without artistic delinquency. John Hunt knew what he himself was commissioned to do; to select the news—in those days of Continental rumour no child's play: to control the office and combine his assistants: to urge the gradual advance of Englishmen against a social and political convention which he thought in many points tyrannical. With his precarious capital and small team of youthful journalists, he set out to change the thought of England, and he soon succeeded in making *The Examiner* a presence and an inspiration up and down the country.

As a minute review of this journal under John Hunt's

guidance has been offered in a companion volume to the present work, I do not propose entering into full details of it now. But the characteristics of *The Examiner* are not to be passed over. Its foundation stone was impartiality, the Hunts refusing "either Pittite or Foxite, Windhamite, Wilberforcite, or Burdettite" leanings. Its theatrical department would "be in the same spirit of opinion and manner with the *present* theatrical observations in the *News*." In promising fair play to the fine arts, *The Examiner* plumed itself on unusual enterprise, and set out to illuminate the British School from West's tragedy to Wilkie's comedy. (Here poor Robert Hunt was put up with no false eulogy—"if he does not promise for his taste, he promises for his industry.") The section of domestic economy was to be none too lavish with adultery, seduction, racing, prize-fighting, and religious admonition. No advertisements; not much about the market; and no quarter to quacks.—While the brothers were thus settling the public side of domestic economy, it is uncertain how strictly they settled the private side—the contract between John and Leigh. Apparently they shared the proprietorship and the profits equally. In November 1808 Leigh Hunt wrote to his Marianne: "The paper gets on gloriously indeed: our regular sale is now two thousand two hundred, and by Christmas, or a few weeks after, I have little doubt we shall be three; and what is best of all, we shall now keep it to ourselves. My brother told me the other day that he had no doubt but we should be getting eight or ten guineas *apiece* every week in a year's time."

With this help to the study of matrimony Leigh Hunt joined his "hundred a year from the War Office (for I rose ten pounds the other day)," and it must now appear a fantastic tale that a man could edit a powerful Sunday newspaper and serve regularly as a Government clerk at the same time.

Having almost completed a year of the double occupation, Hunt resigned his War Office post, not injudiciously calling it in his letter to the Secretary-at-War "a situation in which a sound freedom of thinking and speaking is liable to mistrust and misrepresentation." The letter was dated December 26th, 1808, and was probably written at that moment in order to solve a somewhat puzzling turn of affairs; for *The Examiner* was already in dispute with the Government on military subjects, and had undergone one prosecution. The occasion of this first brush with the law had been the publication of a pamphlet, *Appeal to the Public, and a Farewell Address to the Army*, by an artillery major named Hogan, whom Hunt has described as "a furious but honest Irishman." Hogan's irruption into print was due to a grievance on the subject of promotion; he assailed the Commander-in-Chief, the Duke of York, and not only rejected hush-money of £500 but accompanied his remonstrance with a disclosure of the attempted bribe. Grateful for an easy reformist opportunity, *The Examiner* aired the whole matter, and was prosecuted; but soon the action of a member of Parliament, Colonel Wardle ("a native of North Wales"), who was determined to expose the Duke by bringing his mistress and messenger Mary Anne Clarke before the House of Commons, drew off the legal offensive. Preparations to meet the trial, nevertheless, had made heavy demands on the purse of the Hunts, and for Leigh it was distinctly awkward and hazardous to be simultaneously holding an employment at the War Office and inveighing against the Duke. Even £100 a year and a chance of marrying had to be set aside.

The young man's self-sculpturing yet honest zeal for independence soon took occasion to fling away another chance of income. In 1809 John Murray founded the *Quarterly Review*, with William Gifford as its editor. At what date Leigh Hunt discovered this stony-minded man to be intolerable is not clear, for he had previously made public references to him of a complimentary sort; but by 1809 he did not like Gifford. I have before me a little book called *Beauties of Gifford*, but not, alas, Hunt's comments on it. To proceed—Murray applied to Hunt on March 31st, 1809, desiring him to write theatrical criticisms for the *Quarterly*; and the reformer declined to do so. Presently he was to realise the effects of this aloofness; but now his mind was full of immediate interests, particularly Marianne. The days were soon coming when it would be unnecessary for his Aunt West to keep a motherly eye on him and send him such recommendations as even the greatest of political Messiahs do not despise. "Mrs West's affec^e. regards attend Mr Leigh Hunt & is sorry to find that He is confined to his Chamber, wrapped up she hopes in *Flannel* & that he will gargle his throat with Port Wine, or Brandy & water, or camphorated spirit, and rub the outside of the throat with the camphorated spirit. I always do so when a sore throat is coming and find the greatest benefit from this practice." So apparently did her nephew, who married Marianne, under the sharp eye of Mrs Hunter, on July 3rd, 1809. For the first months of their new life the couple went into a cottage "out of the road of coaches" at Beckenham, apparently built on the Japanese plan, for Hunt described it to the agent as "a box of paper."

His literary performances were temporarily retarded, but there are one or two ephemeral examples worth annotation. Isaac Hunt[1] did not live quite long enough to mix with his

---

[1] Leigh Hunt does not often write of his father, but there is a kind of epitaph for him in the essay *Coffee-Houses and Smoking* (1826): "The last smoker I recollect among those of the old school, was a clergyman. He had seen the best society, and was a man of the most polished behaviour. This did not hinder him from taking his pipe every evening before he went to bed. He sat in his arm-chair, his back gently bending, his knees

Hardham's Best and his madeira the laudation of his son's *Attempt to Shew the Folly and Danger of Methodism*—a tract assembling a series of lay sermons from *The Examiner*, with additions. The unconquered Methodists registered Hunt for future destruction. Kindlier memories were to be associated with some of Hunt's sentimental lyrics, thin and tinselled as they were; such celebrated ballad composers as William Horsley and John Whitaker came forward to provide the musical settings, and one at least of Whitaker's melodies gave to the words "Mary, Mary, list, awake!" half a century of occasional feminine "interpretation." Yet, even here, the fate of Leigh Hunt was to discover the unexpected serpent under the roses more helplessly than most men. The plot of "Mary" was that, as the watchdog was silent and her father asleep, she should come in the moonlight to her lover, who was urging his kind desires in terms like these:

> And, O! could my kisses like stream-circles rise,
> To dip in thy dimples, and spread round thine eyes!
> And, O! to be lost, in a night such as this,
>   In the arms of an angel like thee!

(The poem is apparently imitated by Keats in one of the sickliest of his uninspired pieces.) In 1815 Whitaker brought an action against one Hime for infringing the copyright of this serenade to Mary, and to Hunt's astonishment and alarm the counsel for the defence assailed the impropriety of his lyrics. More fusillades from *The Examiner*; another pamphlet of "proceedings," "to which are subjoined observations on the extra-

---

a little apart, his eyes placidly inclined towards the fire; and delighted, in the intervals of puff, to recount anecdotes of the Marquis of Rockingham, and 'my Lord North.' The end of his recreation was announced to those who had gone to bed, by the tapping of the bowl of his pipe upon the hob, for the purpose of emptying it of its ashes. Ashes to ashes; head to bed. It is a pity that the long day of life cannot always terminate as pleasantly."

ordinary defence made by Mr Serjeant Joy, by Leigh Hunt Esq."

At the close of 1809 *The Examiner* was in a very healthy way, but once more its progress was due to be greatly affected by a libel action. This time the pretext on which its editors were to be reduced was an article called "Change of Ministry," though indeed they had been ingeniously ridiculing the Government in many articles; and now the Attorney-General selected the following not very objectionable animadversion: "Of all monarchs since the revolution, the successor of George the Third will have the finest opportunity of becoming nobly popular." As it happened, James Perry reprinted the paragraph in his excellent *Morning Chronicle*, was prosecuted for it, and, his trial coming on first, defended himself so skilfully that even Lord Ellenborough "charged the Jury in his favour." Perry's acquittal secured the cancelling of the action against the Hunts. Their lives at this period, however, must have been an emotional ordeal, for almost immediately—in the autumn of 1810—they gave the wide currency of their journal to a protest from *The Stamford News*, entitled "One Thousand Lashes!!" Military flogging was almost a sacred subject, and the year 1810 ended with a new prosecution hanging over John and Leigh Hunt, for profanely discussing it. We look away from the now familiar preparations of justice to what is visible of the social existence of Leigh Hunt at about the age of twenty-five.

His marriage did not at once embarrass those ardent friendships which he had kindled at school and soon afterwards. Up to this point, and for some years beyond it, Hunt was a conspicuous proof of Charles Lamb's declaration (1813), "The Christ's Hospital boy's friends at school are commonly his intimates through life." His group were men of unusual

literary powers and deep classical reading—a scholarship which
he emulated; we notice Scholefield offering him bibliographical
hints "while you are making up a classical Library." At the
beginning of 1811 Hunt travelled to Cambridge across a
"wilderness covered with snow, diversified with streams of ink
and ready-stuck pincushions fixed on posts," to sit at Scholefield's fireside and be a guest in Trinity College. His feelings
on the occasion were very much the same with Lamb's on taking
similar University holidays. Both men, having been senior
Deputy Grecians at Christ's Hospital, had missed the congenial
perfections of a liberal education by a touch. Hunt too "walked
gownéd" in fancy, and wrote to Marianne, after an exploration
of the rarities of Trinity, "So much for *our* chapel and library,
for I am already a Trinity man in my likings as well as my
lodgings." In 1812 Scholefield pictures Hunt blessing the first
of his great academic distinctions—the Craven Scholarship;
and knows how he will rejoice with him over the piece of plate
presented to him by the Governors of their old school, as well
as over another Blue's good fortune—the election of "Owen,
our last importation, whom perhaps you do not know, to one
of those magnificent scholarships on Dr Bell's Establishment."
Through Scholefield's letters we see that George Dyer was one
of the circle, and regarded as especially Leigh Hunt's friend.
The splendid abilities and hearty sympathies of Thomas Barnes
appear in several surviving letters from him; Thomas Mitchell's
preciseness and candour are preserved in the same way. This
companion does not shrink from the endeavour to make Hunt
a little less dangerous to his own cause: "Your opinions are
delivered a little ex cathedrâ examinantis"; and he trusts that
"the Friendship between you and me is not of an every-day
kind." An even more eternal friendship (for eternity is oddly
defined), subsisting between Hunt and Barron Field, was sub-

ject to an obscure erosion. On August 31st, 1812, Field is writing, "I never saw Mrs Hunt look better; her complexion clear and healthy, set off by her beautifully black hair"; but on December 3rd the writer is obliged to play on another stop. "Some of the charges which you make against me are so utterly frivolous and unworthy of you, that I cannot believe they originate with you, and should not have supposed that you would have adopted them." They partly referred to Marianne, and Field protests, "*I have never called her by her Christian name* (to descend to just contradiction at once) except in jocose imitation of Thornton, for the nonce." The letter names "our closest friends, Mitchell and Barnes," and concludes with the prediction, "You shall one day acknowledge, Leigh, that I am not a trifler." Another prediction of Field's a year afterwards is not quite so confident, "There may come a time, when you will trust more to your own discernment than that of the ladies around you."

Who was Thornton whom Field had imitated with misunderstood jocosity? Thornton was the eldest child of Leigh and Marianne, and he plays a precocious, mature, and later on a much maligned part in the narrative; in introducing him, we have the cue for introducing a friend of Leigh Hunt's who scattered happiness and unhappiness at random through the lives of himself, his family, his friends—a variously vociferous, combative gentleman—a heroic painter whom nobody loves—the hugeous Benjamin Haydon. Thornton was born on September 10th, 1810. Haydon hears of it, and writes:

My dear Hunt,

I congratulate you with all my soul on the safety of an amiable wife and the birth of a son. It is a grand thing to have occasioned the existence of a thinking being, one, who *may* be

HUNT IN THEATRICAL COSTUME
FROM AN OIL PAINTING PROBABLY BY B.R.HAYDON

famous in this World, and immortal in the next—I feel my
heart expand at the fancy—

Most affectionately yours

My dear Hunt

41 Great Marl. Street   B. R. Haydon.
Thursday morning

Haydon had known Hunt, through their common acquaintance
Wilkie, for about two years already, and *The Examiner* was
hopefully applauding his enormous journey over the canvas
destined to create a season of wonderment among the con-
noisseurs. Besides giving Wilkie their public blessing, the
Hunts went so far as to buy one of his best pictures.

Another personage attracted by the fearlessness and pioneer
activity of the proprietors of *The Examiner* was Henry
Brougham, of whose grim hieroglyphs of letters very creditable
transcripts are given plentifully enough in the first volume of
Leigh Hunt's *Correspondence*. "The gigantic Brougham" was
building up his power in the law and the state with magnificent
rapidity, and when the Hunts were brought to trial for their
hatred of military flogging, in 1811, Brougham defended them
with success and came through his first great crisis in reputation
with glory. It was not only as a Whig politician that Brougham
enjoyed his contact with Leigh Hunt. He read Hunt's poetry
in the making, and sought for literature which might prosper
the work; he exercised his elegance in private reviews of
Hunt's renderings of Catullus, and his larger discrimination in
discussing Voltaire; he softened so much as to request that Hunt
would not risk his health "by going to hot theatres." These
friendly relations were maintained on the whole as long as the
journalist lived.

The chronicle might be more generally admired if I could
trace the early acquaintance of Charles Lamb with Leigh Hunt

as plainly. "That is to us unknown." By 1810, as will be seen, these men were friends; and yet the earliest allusion in the manuscript papers seen by the present enquirer is contained in a letter from Mitchell dated November 20th, 1813: "Do you see anything of Lambe at present? Did he write the Sonnet to Miss K. in the Chronicle?" (It was indeed Lamb's; and shows that he was enchanted by Miss Kelly long before his biographers have realised.) A similar mysteriousness conceals from us the circumstances of another friend's arrival in the life of Hunt, one who is equally desired to stand forth in the light of day. We have at least the letter in which Shelley addressed Hunt first from Oxford, on March 2nd, 1811, the news of the Hunts' escape from the Crown lawyers and Lord Ellenborough's direction. to the jury having aroused the writer's ardour. "Permit me," he wrote, "although a stranger, to offer my sincerest congratulations on the occasion of that triumph so highly to be prized by men of liberality; permit me also to submit to your consideration, as one of the most fearless enlighteners of the public mind at the present time, a scheme of mutual safety and mutual indemnification for men of public spirit and principle.... Of the scheme, the enclosed is an address to the public, the proposal for a meeting ... of such enlightened, unprejudiced members of the community, whose independent principles expose them to evils which might thus become alleviated; and to form a methodical society, which should be organized so as to resist the coalition of the enemies of liberty, which at present renders any expression of opinion on matters of policy dangerous to individuals." If Leigh Hunt did not take up this project (we have no evidence either way), it is no matter for amazement, since the letter-box of *The Examiner* was overflowing with radical invocations and panaceas. Before that March was out, Shelley, expelled from Oxford, was mewing his mighty youth in the back sitting-room at 15 Poland Street; that August he went north; probably, then, it is to the spring and summer of 1811 that we should ascribe all that is recorded of his further encounters with Hunt at this period. "I first saw Shelley," Hunt states in his *Autobiography*, "during the early period of the *Examiner*, before its indictment on account of the Regent; but it was only for a few short visits, which did not produce intimacy." Thornton Hunt lightens this darkness a little: "It was indeed Mr Rowland Hunter who first brought Leigh Hunt and his most valued friend personally together. Shelley had brought a manuscript poem which proved by no means suited to the publishing house in St Paul's Churchyard. But Mr Hunter sent the young reformer to seek the counsel of Leigh Hunt." This information was given by old Hunter, then in the Charterhouse; Hunter also wrote to Thornton Hunt in 1859 on the characteristics of Edward Copleston, D.D. (*alias* "Gobblestone"), who procured Shelley's expulsion from Oxford: "He was a short man with a protuberant stomack, which convinced me that he played a good knife and fork . . . N.B. A complete cheap edition of your dear father's works would sell very well." I can do no more in illustration of this part of Shelley's relations with Leigh Hunt than quote Hunt's first impression from the *Autobiography*: "He was then a youth, not come to his full growth; very gentlemanly, earnestly gazing at every object that interested him, and quoting the Greek dramatists." Hunt candidly recommended him not to publish the poems which he brought with him, and Shelley accepted the dissuasion.

The man who was to become Shelley's publisher, Charles Ollier, of Huguenot family, had already begun his half-century of affectionate friendship with Leigh Hunt. "Similarity in age, in pursuits, in charity, in love for the quaint byways of literature, supplied plenty of common ground for their friendship to thrive on." It was in 1810 that they met at the office of *The Examiner*, where Ollier, then employed in Coutts' bank, went to offer a manuscript of theatrical criticism; and from this meeting it chiefly came about that when Ollier left the bank in 1817 and set up, with his younger brother, a publishing house, he had the honour of issuing as choice a series of great writers as will readily be imagined. By the end of 1818 his "list" included Keats, Shelley, Lamb and Hunt. His account-books did not in consequence show any special advantage. Incidentally, Ollier delighted Hunt by his excellence as a flutist and as a reader of Shakespeare.

Being armed with so many literary friendships, and himself fresh and anticipative, Hunt experimented with a quarterly of his own, called *The Reflector*. The publisher was not hard to find—John Hunt; the types were the unlovely ones of *The Examiner*, with nothing of Baskerville or Bulmer about them. A prospectus was of course circulated, a form of literature in which Leigh Hunt was very handy and which his visionary aptitude delighted to variegate. This *Reflector* was called for, he argued, because "reform of periodical writing is as much wanted in Magazines, as it formerly was in Reviews, and still is in Newspapers." He made play with the usual farrago of the Magazines; said that the old ones "were in their dotage; and as to the new ones, that have lately appeared, they have returned to the infancy of their species—to pattern-drawing, doll-dressing, and a song about Phillis." After many unkind flourishes of this style, he promised as the more meritorious contents of *his* Magazine broad political reports—"Its opinions will be exactly those of the *Examiner*"—luminous with con-stitutional yet liberal creed; "comparative and didactic criticism" of the drama; an uncommon ardour for the British school of painting, to take away the reproach of Winckelmann; and more

than all these, a variety of essays characterising and estimating
men and manners, past and present literature, wit, morals, and
"a true refinement." *The Reflector* would endeavour to por-
tray "the *mind*" of the age. For this purpose, it would content
itself with "not more than 240 pages in each Number"—a
moderation which in our tabloid times has a strange sound.
The first number, of 248 pages, was brought out in October
1810. It was at once learned, animated and diverse. The editor's
contributions display, among other qualities, a surprising
familiarity with the fine arts, in their whole range. Blake is not
there, but we must wonder whether he would have been comprehended at any period by a youthful critic; and Hunt may not
have seen his work. Turner is acknowledged: "Our first land-
scape-painter is Mr Turner, who has the same fault in drawing
as Sir Joshua, that of indistinctness of outline; but this fault,
which is so obnoxious in human subjects, and baffles Mr Turner's
ragged attempts at history, becomes very different in the mists
and distances of landscape; and he knows how to convert it into
a shadowy sublimity." Like Mr J. C. Squire in our own day,
who has refreshed a rather drouthy decade with an editorial
zest and observancy resembling *The Reflector's*, Hunt watched
metropolitan improvements with a jealous eye. "Somerset
House is light and elegant, but it is said to be ill built, and in a
word, what beauty has it that is new? Mr Soane, a theoretical
master of his art, wished to be original when he repaired the
Bank; and how did he effect his purpose? Merely by giving his
edifice the look of a different object—merely by giving us a
title-page contradictory to the contents of the book; the Bank
has the air of a mausoleum, as if its builder intended to be
ironical on our departed gold—

> To shew by one satiric touch,
> No nation wanted it so much."

The critic catalogues the architects, only to ask where their invention is; one hopes that his troubled spirit has since been permitted to gaze in gratitude at the water-front of New York, or the airy wonder of Hong Kong when uncounted lights through the dusk begin to identify invention with fairy-land.

Notwithstanding the restless liberties and sprightly imagery of Hunt and his first assistants, *The Reflector's* glory dwells in its association with Charles Lamb, who frolicked in the second number with such grave figures as "The Inconveniences Resulting from being Hanged" and "The Danger of Confounding Moral with Personal Deformity." In the third number he gave several papers, of which that "On the Genius and Character of Hogarth" was a bold and intense revelation of his critical originality, immediately discerned by progressive tastes as the definitive appreciation of Hogarth. Lamb appears to have been highly pleased with the latitude given him in *The Reflector*, which did not merely consist in liberality of space. In his Hogarth essay he ridiculed "the late Mr Barry," whom the editor had praised as "one of the fathers of the historical school," and whose memory had been vindicated with warmth, detail, and classic comparison, "from the aspersions of the *Edinburgh Review*." Lamb was not unobservant of such generous candour, and in the fourth number at least seven articles came from his pen, one among which was a critical masterpiece even more beautiful and illuminating than that on Hogarth. Its title was "*Theatralia*. No. 1.—On Garrick and Acting; and the Plays of Shakespeare, considered with reference to their fitness for Stage Representation." (As one rejoices in what has been achieved, one laments for what was only intended; and had *The Reflector* lasted Lamb proposed to add to his realisations of Shakespearean tragedy a demonstration "why Falstaff, Shallow, Sir Hugh Evans, and the rest, are equally incompatible

with stage representation.") Some twenty years later Leigh
Hunt's magazine had a successor, *The Reflector* of Edward
Moxon, and it is a remarkable instance of Lamb's inveteracy
and sense of journalistic suitability that in writing for it he re-
verted both for tone and type of theme and discrimination to
his *Reflector* character of 1811: his new essay being on the
"Barrenness of the Imaginative Faculty in the Productions of
Modern Art." On the great benefit received by him from Leigh
Hunt's magazine, Mr Lucas is the best spokesman: "The
Reflector gave Lamb his first encouragement to spread his
wings with some of the freedom that an essayist demands. . . .
It is not too much to say that had he lacked the preliminary
training which his *Reflector* exercises gave him his *Elia* essays
would have been the poorer."

The other friends of Hunt entered into the spirit of the work
without reserve. Perhaps he sometimes felt the awkwardness
of such pen-driving enthusiasm, as when Mitchell wrote:
"Being something of a Botanist, I have (with an eye to the
same Reflector) been turning the whole terms of English
Botany in their respective Classes and Orders into Latin verse.
Of course it is a barbarous work, but I think will be of great
use to Botanists in enabling them to retain the names and
classes of Plants." The nearest approach to botany in *The
Reflector* appears to have been Lamb's *Farewell to Tobacco*;
but Mitchell found other means of collaborating; Barnes,
Scholefield, Dyer, Barron Field were all eager contributors—
"a set of Persons educated in one School, and valuable to each
other for their friendship and congenial tastes." Old Dr Aikin,
one of the many medical men who have served literature with
grace and truth, and Octavius Gilchrist, who had just announced
his poetic insight by editing Bishop Corbet, also lent a hand.
At the end of 1811, upon the publication of the fourth number,

there seemed no apprehension of *The Reflector's* decease, and an editorial notice promised that "with the commencement of 1812, the *Reflector* will put on more staid and quarterly habits," and hinted at "fresh and valuable Correspondence." But it had run its race. No more was printed. The obituary paragraph inserted in the collected volumes, which are significantly called "Essays originally published as the commencement of a quarterly magazine," is in the well-known Hunt manner of taking the reader into the office. "As far as the limited means of the Proprietors could give it publicity, it met with the most promising encouragement, and it was discontinued, partly by reason of the Editor's uneditorial want of attention to regularity of publication, but *chiefly* on account of those limited means. The Proprietors still think that a Work of the kind would succeed, and have not given up the hope of reviving it some future day, though perhaps in a smaller form and with more select materials; but proper Contributors must be well paid, both out of policy and justice; and they plainly confess that they were unable to bear the expense."

To many readers Leigh Hunt is known as the author of an Autobiography—it has been called his only real book; it is faintly foreshadowed in the vague memoir which he published in *The Monthly Mirror* for April 1810, at the request of his friend the editor, to accompany his portrait by John Jackson, one of Haydon's companions. The memoir contains very little bread to a great deal of sack, and is an example of that paradoxical expressiveness of Hunt's which leaves us after all vainly asking important questions. In the course of it he makes one of many admiring elegiac allusions to his mother. "No rigid economy could hide the native generosity of her heart, no sophistical and skulking example injure her fine sense or her contempt of worldly-mindedness, no unmerited sorrow convert her resignation into bitterness. But let me not hurt the noble simplicity of her character by a declamation, however involuntary." By contrast with this and more written in the same mood, his laconic mention of his father and the puffing of *Juvenilia* acquires a harshness. There is a comment on his vacating his clerkship at the War Office: "This I voluntarily gave up, not only from habitual disinclination, but from certain hints, futile enough in themselves yet sufficiently annoying, respecting the feelings of the higher orders, who could not contemplate with pleasure a new paper called the *Examiner*." Of that paper he says, "With constitutional reform for its object, and a stubborn consistency for its merit, it promises, in spite of the wretched efforts of the wretched men in power, to procure for me all that I wish to acquire, a good name and a decent competency." This man knows his Horace. He proceeds, by way of an apologia for his theatrical criticism, after advising the temporary playwrights to use their talents in fitting up baby-theatres, into an *Examiner* peroration: "I am not conscious of having given praise for policy's sake, or blame for malignity's; and I never will. A strict adherence to truth, and a recurrence to first principles, are the only things calculated to bring back the happier times of our literature and constitution; and however humble as an individual, I have found myself formidable as a lover of truth, and shall never cease to exert myself in its cause, as long as the sensible will endure my writings, and the honest appreciate my intentions." We perceive also that he knows his Johnson. Certainly Leigh Hunt enjoyed writing these manifestoes, but let it be well known that he did not only write them; he acted them too.

VI

The Wit in the Dungeon

LITERARY historians have not lingered over the close of the eighteenth and beginning of the nineteenth century as a time of great satirical activity and not a little masterly design and point on the part of the versifying wits. Without presuming to reveal this extensive province of literature, I may remark how rapidly the volunteer censorship of taste and personality produced its declarations; how in 1809 Byron stirred society with *English Bards and Scotch Reviewers*, of which the fourth edition appeared in 1811; how the *Rejected Addresses* made everyone laugh in 1812, though *Horace in London* by the same brothers Smith, already seen in these pages, followed less triumphantly in 1813; how in 1812 T. J. Mathias brought out the magnificent sixteenth edition of his *Pursuits of Literature*, and Moore's *Two-Penny Post-Bag* against the ministers, appearing that year, passed through fourteen editions within a twelvemonth. With these admired carabineers would naturally be catalogued Leigh Hunt, who in the fourth and final number of *The Reflector* revived the old-fashioned scheme of holding, or causing Apollo to hold, a Session of the Poets; in prefacing this ingenuity, he spoke of Suckling, Rochester and Sheffield as his principal predecessors in the "sessional" device of provocation. From *The Reflector* Hunt's exercise in familiar verse and audacious criticism was transferred into a volume published in 1814 and republished in 1815. Its ultimate shape conveys a suggestion of Mandeville's *Fable of the Bees*, where a few hundred lines of verse usher in a few hundred pages of prose disquisitions arising from them; Hunt's satire in the 1815 book occupies 25 pages and the Notes on it 125. *The Feast of the Poets* and its history may be considered at this point with some leisurely attention, seeing that the effusion discloses Hunt's second poetical period definitely opened and his ambition and effort moving away from political and dramatic contest to the literary arena; it records his principles and tastes in development; and it was one of his many pugnacious feats for the furtherance of what he thought truth and light. Such challenges at once secured attention and involved him in obvious as well as subterraneous troubles.

The Feast of the Poets in its 1811 state was mainly verse and not yet a miscellany. The style was jaunty, uncertainly swinging between great brilliance and slovenly makeshift, and it showed through all its inequalities the impress of a personality. In the machinery and costume of the Session, apart from fault and failure, a gift for the marvellous and for the human touch was readily observable. We shall render our account of the fable very briefly: Apollo is discovered "twiddling a sunbeam, as I may my pen," and noticing that it is time for him to descend and hold a meeting of the English poets. He reflects how little has been achieved since Dryden and Milton, and how there has recently been some show of poetical renaissance:

> I'll e'en go and give them a lesson or two,
> And as nothing's done there nowadays without eating,
> See how many souls I can muster worth treating.

The god arrives in "the Shakespeare," Russell Street, and has hardly had time to ring for the landlord when a troop of Hunt's old villains, the contemporary playwrights, wait expectantly on him. Apollo mistakes them for the waiters, and they leave. After the exit of these displeasing callers, three cards are handed in.

> Apollo just gave them a glance with his eye—
> "Spencer,—Rogers,—Montgom'ry"—and putting them by,
> Begg'd the landlord to give his respects to all three,
> And say he'd be happy to see them to tea.

The waiter now informed him

> That a person nam'd Crabbe has been waiting below;
> He's been looking about him this hour, I dare say;

to which Apollo replied by requesting that Crabbe should be entertained—"down stairs." Next appeared a "sour little gentleman" named Gifford, who was lectured and sent about his business; then Scott, who was bidden to stay but advised to "study more, scribble less." (A note assailed the "innate and trusting reverence for thrones" displayed in his edition of Dryden.) Campbell was more eagerly welcomed:

> How have you been
> Since the last time I saw you on Sydenham Green?

Moore also was made welcome, and complimented on an improvement in his morals:

> There are very few poets, whose caps or whose curls
> Have obtain'd such a laurel by hunting the girls.
> So it gives me, dear Tom, a delight beyond measure
> To find how you've mended your notions of pleasure.

After this, there was a hubbub on the stairs, "but 'twas only Bob Southey and three or four others"—the Lake Poets; "Were there ever such asses on earth?" as Bob, Billy and Sam? Their tenets were reduced to the absurdity

> That poetry lies, not in something select,
> But in gath'ring the refuse that others reject.

The offended god assumed all his glory in order to drive them out to the tune of chiming spheres and celestial choirs; yet Southey escaped from the expulsion, and remained to dinner. "Laurels for four!" called Apollo, and at once the accepted poets were wearing garlands:

> Tom Campbell's with willow and poplar was twin'd,
> And Southey's with mountain-ash, pluck'd in the wind;
> And Scott's with a heath from his old garden stores,
> And with vine-leaves and Jump-up-and-kiss-me, Tom Moore's.

The dinner was sumptuous and fanciful, and only interrupted by such slips as Southey desiring to give the toast "A great genius—one Mr Landor." In the course of the poem, Hunt only once hinted that he had a design of being himself among Apollo's guests—"a poem I've by me" is the earliest portent of *The Story of Rimini.*

The whole performance was received with envious curiosity and elegant applause. We see Crabb Robinson the ubiquitous, who already knew Hunt and disliked him, taking the poem with him to read to his friends. On the other hand, Hunt's fluency in brushing aside profound and patient literary enterprise, like a dandy flicking a speck of dust from his sleeve, offended many well-established men of letters, and put him in an inconvenient position; for he soon became aware of his fragmentary acquaintance with new poetry, and especially he perceived his natural response to the real achievements of Wordsworth and Coleridge when he met with those. Politically incensed against those recanting reformers, he had made himself appear sadly antiquated in not proclaiming their orient poetic genius. Moreover, he had irritated most cultured readers by his rudeness towards the "cuckoo-song" of Pope, who was still high in the firmament. When, therefore, he converted his magazine item into a book, he attempted to straighten his position in those main sectors of unsoundness, and in general to round and adjust his decisions. The profuse "Notes" in 1814—meant "to shew that he had at least considered the subjects of which he talked"—contained detailed essays on the bad versification of Pope; on the mediaeval costumery of Scott; on the poetic dogmas and characteristics of the Lake Poets; and on the advantages and disadvantages in the situation of an added figure at Apollo's feast, Lord Byron. In the text and notes now appeared an attack on the inoffensive William Hayley, whose

Triumphs of Temper had gone through more than a dozen editions. In 1815 Hunt reissued his pasquinade with new matter in prose and verse, greatly transforming his previously published attitude to contemporary poets.

There was now no kicking Wordsworth and Coleridge downstairs. In the verse, it is true, they came in for several caustic remarks: Coleridge still vexed Apollo

> By his idling, and gabbling, and muddling in prose,

and Wordsworth

>   one day made his very hairs bristle
> By going and changing his harp for a whistle.

But they now stayed to dinner, and the god ordered "Laurels for eight," which will epitomise Hunt's imaginative evolution and personal graduation in the school of sympathy rather than intolerance:

> Lord Byron's with turk's cap and cypress was mixed,
> And Scott's with a thistle, with creeper betwixt;
> And Wordsworth's with celandin, aloe, and pine;
> And, Bob, penny-royal and blow-ball with thine;
> Then Sam's with mandragoras, fearful to wear;
> With willow Tom Campbell's, and oak here and there;
> And lastly, with shamrock from tear-bedew'd shores,
> And with vine-leaves and Jump-up-and-kiss-me, Tom Moore's.

Above all, the new preface made the confession that Hunt had already esteemed Wordsworth "the first poet of the day," and "his admiration of him had become greater and greater between every publication of *The Feast of the Poets*"; which naive, recantatory satire we now lay aside in order to attend to a controversial history of larger scope and more painful consequences to our author. For this we must accompany him to the editor's room at the *Examiner* office, behind the round window invented by John Hunt in Brydges Street.

At the beginning of 1812, three attempts had been made to

silence John and Leigh Hunt with the rigours of the law; three had failed. The two brothers, borne on by a burning sense of the difference between Englishmen like King Alfred and John Hampden and Englishmen like the Prince Regent and Sheridan, had continued to throw their torchlight on the decadence of the country's governors, and they used their effigy of the Regent at once as a figure of fun and a public scandal. Even *The Reflector*, despite its guaranteed neutrality, had been pressed into this service of sarcastic reform. The adulation of ministerial papers like the *Morning Post* was habitually countered by the daring disgust of this youthful *Examiner*. A final battle between the Regent's protectors and the insistent reformists could not be long delayed. Again and again the Hunts took the risk, and it was not only in consequence of the celebrated *Examiner* leader of March 22nd, 1812, "Princely Qualities," that they were sent to their prisons; that article merely summed up their campaign and served as a convenient opportunity for bringing them to trial. Enough is said of the article and its libellous passage[1] in a separate work on *The Examiner*, while every writer on Hunt's life has with more or less accuracy discoursed on its rendering of the *Morning Post's* "Adonis in Loveliness" as a "corpulent man of fifty," who is also qualified as "a violator of his word, a libertine over head and ears in disgrace, a despiser of domestic ties, the companion of gamblers and demireps" and other unorthodox things. Before this catalogue of royal vices appeared, its challenge and appeal to the authorities were anticipated. At a party at Lamb's on March 16th, 1812, Crabb Robinson found its writer with Barnes and Field, "prepared for the worst. Hunt said, pleasantly enough, 'No one can

---

[1] The libel, Hunt said afterwards, "originated in my sympathies with the sufferings of the people of Ireland," and was precipitated "by my indignation at the Regent's breaking his promises to the Irish." O'Connell told him subsequently that he had read the article with delight, but with no doubt of the penalty which its author would incur.

accuse me of not writing a libel. Everything is a libel, as the law is now declared, and our security lies only in their shame.'" The momentous article was published, and on March 26th Robinson "stepped late to Barron Field's chambers. Barnes, Lamb, J. Collier. We talked about Hunt whose indiscreet article about the Prince even his friends censure." Lamb however had amused himself, probably caring less for the main theme than for the humour of it, in supporting Hunt's anti-Regentiana with wicked epigrams[1]. A month later *The Examiner* was discussing, with unabated candour, the charge for libel formulated against the proprietors.

While this ominous case was being prepared, Leigh Hunt does not seem to have been an unhappy man. The birth of his second son, John, doomed to be one of his worst sources of discomfort in years to come, added present hope and sweetness to his home. There were honours of a private kind, such as the amicable correspondence of the already illustrious Brougham, friendly invitations from Jeremy Bentham, and even visits from him. There was a summer holiday in Somersetshire, and Glastonbury—"I did not know, till I left Glastonbury, that it was said to be the burial-place of King Arthur, or I should have had a hundred poetical reveries and recollections for that 'president of chivalry'; but I am afraid the truth is, that he was buried in the same place in which he was born and lived—the brain of a poet." Hunt's condemnation of Tom Moore's *Blue-Stocking*, again, had brought that Irish musician to the *Examiner* office, and Hunt thought him then "as delightful a person as one could imagine," a spirit from whom reform

---

[1] Something of Lamb's share is shown by a letter of Monk Lewis with a transcript of "The Triumph of the Whale": "I send you some verses which I read in the *Examiner*; I think them very witty, although very abominable." (*Diary of the Times of George IV*, 1838, i. 130. In the same work we see that the Princess of Wales was a reader of *The Examiner*.)

would receive the blessings of wit and fancy. Above all, Hunt had now fallen in love with Hampstead, about whose little hills Defoe had written so contemptuously a century before. In the autumn of 1812 Marianne and he went to live there, and we find him writing to Brougham on September 27th, that he was "about to move to a cottage at West-end, Hampstead, where I do not despair of seeing you sit down with me to a plain joint and a pudding, some day on your return. The cottage is really and *bonâ fide* a cottage, with most humble ceilings and unsophisticated staircases; but there is green about it, and a little garden with laurel: and I can put you into a room where there will be a little library of poets, and an original portrait of Milton to overlook us as we sit drinking our glass of wine." The portrait of Milton was that by Janssen. Within a few days Hunt had hurried his books and pictures into the cottage in West End Lane and could command his garden, "on the gate of which is my name on a fair plate of brass." For the adverse side of Hunt's private life in 1812, we may begin with his frequent bad health, his disputes with the most comprehensive reformers of the race over trivial affairs of their small sphere, and debts which that July amounted to over five hundred pounds.

On November 25th, 1812, Brougham, who was retained for the defence of the Hunts, wrote to Earl Grey: "Hunt's trial comes on about the middle of the week after next, and they are in some consternation at Carlton House. Two several attempts have been made to buy him off, but of course in vain; one of them came almost directly from Macmahon soon *after* the trial, put off last July. I feel somewhat anxious about the verdict, but am full of confidence as to the defence and its effects all over the country—It will be a thousand times more unpleasant than the libel." The same day Leigh Hunt wrote peacefully to Haydon, whom he had been befriending with his best domestic openness: "Mrs Hunt is going to her modelling again, and wishes for a good original bust, not so large as life, in order that she may be able to work at it easily and on the table of an evening. Do you know anybody who could lend her such a one for two or three months, and a small bust of Apollo, for instance, or any other that has a good poetical head of hair? I am getting better, just in time for those legal rogues, and am preparing my next Sunday's lash for that poor creature at Carlton House, whom I really commiserate all the while. I hope 'Solomon' goes on well (what a transition!), but pray don't forget your 'Mercury' as an occasional refreshment. It is an exquisite little conception, and dipped in poetry."

A fortnight afterwards the defendants took their stand in court before Lord Ellenborough, and answered the charge of libelling His Royal Highness the Prince of Wales, Regent of the United Kingdom. The arguments of Brougham did not result in an acquittal, but there was an interval between the verdict and the sentence, lasting so long that on January 29th, 1813, Haydon was still able to visit the cheerful editor at Hampstead: "Spent the evening with Leigh Hunt at West-end— walked out and in furiously after dinner, which did me great good. Leigh Hunt's society is always delightful: I do not know a purer, a more virtuous character, or a more witty, funny, or enlivening man. We talked of his approaching imprisonment. He said it would be a great pleasure to him if he were certain to be sent to Newgate, because he should be in the midst of his friends [his old school was very near that prison]—and then we both laughed heartily at the idea of his being in the midst of his friends at Newgate, and his being reduced to say it would be a great pleasure to be sent there." On February 3rd the Hunts attended to hear their sentence. Leigh was determined to adorn the sacrifice with flowers in some way or other; so he

wore his best suit, new hat and gloves, and carried a little book
to banish the spectre of the day—"the *Comus* of Erycius
Puteanus," a Dutch poet. John we may picture not from
any sketch in the dock but from his having been painted by
West in the character of a Roman Centurion. The sentence
certainly was one to test the gaiety of Leigh and the inflexibility
of John. Each must go to a separate prison for two years, and
pay a fine of £500, and find security at the end of the two years
of £500 apiece for their good behaviour during the next five
years—or remain imprisoned. "My brother and myself instinctively pressed each other's arm. It was a heavy blow; but
the pressure that acknowledged it, encouraged the resolution
to bear it; and I do not believe either of us interchanged a word
afterwards on the subject." Without delay they were driven
off by hackney-coach to their different prisons, John to Cold-
bath Fields and Leigh to Horsemonger Lane; the younger
brother was accompanied by Barron Field, and years later he
remembered the circumstance with ironical glee, when Field
had grown into a complete Judge and no friend of such lawless
types as Hunt.

The shutting up of the two Hunts was a gift to Liberal
opinion, and Tom Moore commented on the situation in some
fluent yet emotional verses.

> Go to your prisons—though the air of spring
> No mountain coolness to your cheeks shall bring;
> Though summer flowers shall pass unseen away,
> And all your portion of the glorious day
> May be some solitary beam that falls
> At morn and eve upon your dreary walls—
> Some beam that enters, trembling as if awed,
> To tell how gay the young world smiles abroad!
> Yet go—for thoughts, as blessed as the air
> Of spring or summer flowers, await you there;

Thoughts such as he, who feeds his courtly crew
In rich conservatories, *never* knew!
Pure self-esteem—the smiles that light within—
The zeal whose circling charities begin
With the few lov'd ones Heaven has placed it near,
Nor cease till all mankind are in its sphere!—
The pride that suffers without vaunt or plea,
And the fresh spirit that can warble free,
Through prison bars, its hymn of liberty.

With these tunes of militancy to assist him in combating illness of body, Leigh Hunt came in sight of the gate and high wall of the prison, and after waiting in the yard "as long as if it had been the anteroom of a Minister," was taken into the presence of his gaoler—a solemn man with a scarlet face and a white night-cap on, whose first remark was, "Mister, I'd ha' given a matter of a hundred pounds, that you had not come to this place—a hundred pounds!" This unusual altruist, however, did not propose any immediate softening of the hardship, and Hunt perceived that the sum mentioned was the essential condition. But the hopeful gaoler was being circumvented by the activities of Hunt's friends, and after a little while the prisoner was made moderately comfortable. On February 5th, 1813, he submitted a paper of requests, first, that he might have his wife and children living with him, or that they might spend the daytime with him, and second, that his friends might be allowed to visit him in the day. This petition ends with a sort of "Political Examiner" in brief. In a week or so Hunt was given the privileges which he sought, and he and Marianne set themselves to transform the Surrey Gaol into a new home—a piece of colonisation rendered much easier by the thoughtfulness of the prison doctor, who secured for Hunt two rooms on the south side of the infirmary. Those rooms, into which the little family moved on March 16th, became famous. John Hunt meanwhile found the governor of his prison at Clerkenwell considerate and agreeable; two rooms were prepared and fresh-painted for him, and he was invited to take his walks in the governor's garden.

The eyes of the town were on the dramatical Leigh rather than on the stoic John, and Leigh quickly made his imprisonment the subject of pleased and wondering conversation. The wit and fancy which so often chased realities away from him now enabled him to look like a modern Prospero. His larger room, disguised with wallpaper and distemper, became a bower of roses under a Florentine heaven; the bower of course sheltered a pianoforte, a lute, and busts of the great poets, with bookcases in which Chaucer, Spenser, Milton and Dryden were seldom left to rest. Above the mantelpiece hung the inspiring portrait of John Hunt. This Shenstonian alcove must have been prepared with good design and well-chosen trappings, or Charles Lamb would not have "declared there was no other such room except in a fairy tale." Hunt himself says, "Perhaps there was not a handsomer room on that side the water," and no partisan of the Surrey side has yet arisen to contradict him. The magic casements were nevertheless (wearisome condition!) haunted by plain, mundane considerations. They cost money; and Hunt meditated later, "I had not yet learned to think of money." In addition to his bower, Hunt had another Arcadian vignette for his visitors; he could lead them into what had been a yard of the gaol, but was now a garden thronged with those flowers he loved for their intenser glow—the pansies, and the trellised scarlet runners. Sweetbriar also perfumed the bunches of flowers which he triumphantly gave to his visitors.

The gaoler, astonished by all this conjuring, appeased with gifts, and apprehensive of the powers of Mr *Examiner* elsewhere, now trimmed his sails the better way; he began to demand his share of the applause, and to permit his prisoner a kind of Gray's Inn prestige. "My friends," says Hunt, "were allowed to be with me till ten o'clock at night, when the under-turnkey, a young man, with his lantern, and much ambitious gentility of deportment, came to see them out." It was a famous victory. The prison became the scene of many gatherings of intellect and personality. Perhaps Charles and Mary Lamb were the most regular of Hunt's visitors. No storms or yellow fogs could keep them from their promises, and firelight sessions in honour of Lamb's Elizabethans, of Chapman's *Homer* (that unmeasured source of so much in Romantic literature), of Sir Thomas Browne, or the patriot Marvell. Lamb's umbrella and greatcoat became almost a part of Hunt's equipment. Here Hazlitt came, overcoming a diffidence; and Barnes arriving like a character out of Fielding brought Alsager, the financial editor of *The Times*, who was as deep in Chapman's *Homer* as any of them. When, in April 1813, Marianne Hunt took the two little boys to Brighton for the sea air, the number of visitors increased, Bessie Kent attending to their entertainment, if more entertainment than the circumstances of the place gave were needed. Even the best idealists perhaps required some support beyond what Hunt's talk and flowers offered that May; when "the yellow globes were out and full, the Persian lilac hung with delicate bunches of blue, the daisies stood up quite swelling and proud, the broom shot out a profusion of snowy blossoms along its rods, and the left-hand rhododendron threw up the promise of a most splendid flower."

Maria Edgeworth came—"and Marianne, the Edgeworthian, not in town"; Bentham came, and played battledore and shuttlecock, immediately proposing "an amendment in the constitution of shuttlecocks"; James Mill appeared; Haydon (we must resort to the only exact expression) "blew in" before Hunt was out of bed, and ordered breakfast; Brougham gave the gaoler a chance to air his importance—"I find that they calls him *Broom*; but, Mister, *I* calls him *Bruffam*." Keats's country schoolmaster, Cowden Clarke, sent in baskets of fruit and vegetables and new-laid eggs (Hunt's Eden including no hens), and in July 1813 showed himself in that family circle where he was afterwards an ever welcome figure. Sir John Swinburne, Hunt's benefactor, dined with the others; already middle-aged, he went on to survive even Hunt, and just missed his century, as he has missed Hunt's full acknowledgement of his benevolence and love of liberty. But the roll of Hunt's prison visitors must be shortened in order to make room for an acquaintance of wider reverberations, that of Lord Byron. The meeting was brought about by Thomas Moore, although Byron's taste for the inner history of the moment would have led to one sooner or later, and he had had a curiosity about Hunt from the time at Harrow when *Juvenilia* had pointed the way to *Hours of Idleness*. Moore called at the prison, spoke of Byron's sympathies with *The Examiner* and *The Feast of the Poets*; a dinner was arranged, it being agreed that there should be "plenty of fish and vegetables for the noble bard"; and on May 18th, 1813, Byron flung off some anticipatory atmospherics for Moore:

> Tomorrow be with me, as soon as you can, sir,
> All ready and dress'd for proceeding to spunge on
> (According to compact) the wit in the dungeon—
> Pray Phoebus at length our political malice
> May not get us lodgings within the same palace . . .
> But tomorrow, at four, we will both play the *Scurra*,
> And you'll be Catullus, the Regent Mamurra.

The author of *Childe Harold* kept his hour, and the afternoon passed in the most easy and discoursing manner. Moore, however, objected to some friends who "dropped in." Next time, only three or four days having intervened, Byron came alone; he brought with him a present of books, "with the air of one who did not seem to think himself conferring the least obligation." So Hunt wrote to Marianne,. proceeding, "This will please you. It strikes me that he and I shall become *friends*, literally and cordially speaking: there is something in the texture of his mind and feelings that seems to resemble mine to a thread; I think we are cut out of the same piece, only a different wear may have altered our respective naps a little." The letter goes on with a serene forecast of a happy meeting between Byron and Marianne.

But Marianne was not so confident. She had "heard something" about Byron, and it was necessary for her husband to use further persuasions: "You must make allowances for the early vagaries of Lord B. Bess (who, by-the-by, you do not seem aware, is with me always as well as Henry) likes him very much. I am persuaded that his heart is an excellent one, and I am sure that his understanding is." Bess's approval was perhaps an unfortunate part of this communication. Byron's visits appear to have ceased after Marianne's return. His regard for Hunt was not diminished, for in December 1813 the occasion of sending Hunt his new poems moved him to set down in his Diary a well-known sketch of the recipient. "An extraordinary character, and not exactly of the present age. He reminds me more of the Pym and Hampden times—much talent, great independence of spirit, and an austere yet not repulsive aspect. If he goes on *qualis ab incepto*, I know few men who will deserve more praise or obtain it. I must go to see him again. . . ." In these last words, the value that Byron in 1813 had for Hunt is unmistakable, and easily overcomes the additional comments on Hunt's opinionated position as the leader of a set.

A relic of Byron's early zeal for Hunt has been communicated to the public through the liberality of Mr Wise and the scholarliness of Mr Milford. The longer Hunt was in prison, the more poetical his intentions became; and in particular he endeavoured to apply all his originality and reading to a proposed masterpiece, which had already allured him in 1811. The two quarto volumes which Byron carried into Surrey Gaol on his second visit were meant to nourish this growing narrative poem; they were "the last new Travels in Italy," and the poem was *The Story of Rimini*. Hunt announced it at the beginning of 1814 as "a piece of some length, with which he is varying less agreeable studies, and in which he would attempt to reduce to practice his own ideas of what is natural in style, and of the various and legitimate harmony of the English heroic." Byron did Hunt the honour to pencil his opinions on this poem while it was being composed, and they were in the most soothing tones of approval, with some interjections of discord, and hints for revision. "Very very good," "The whole passage is very fine and original," "Superlative," "Many more beauties than there is time or place to express here"—such are some of the eulogistic marginalia of Byron on the manuscript of *Rimini*. It was probably through Byron's introduction that the publisher James Cawthorn joined the pilgrimage to the Surrey Gaol, and early in 1814 brought out the first separate edition of *The Feast of the Poets*. Dedicated to Thomas Mitchell, who was now becoming more Quarterly in his opinions and would soon drift away from Hunt's flowery symposia, this edition contained among its crowd of notes a long advisory criticism on Byron. "I feel a more than ordinary interest in his fame, and have had some chords about me so touched by his poetry, as to speak whether I will or not." The advice was sufficiently paternal: "That, in the first place, he would habituate his thoughts as much as possible to the company of those recorded spirits and lofty countenances of public virtue, which elevate an Englishman's recollections, and are the true household deities of his country—or to descend from my epithets, that he would study politics more and appear oftener in Parliament;—secondly, that he would study society, not only in its existing brilliance or its departed grandeur, but in those middle walks of life, where he may find the most cordial sum of its happiness, as well as the soundest concentration of its intelligence;—and thirdly, that though he has done a good deal already, he would consider it as little until he could fully satisfy himself—or if this be difficult, perhaps impossible—that he would consider what he has done as too full of promise to warrant his resorting at any time to a common property in style, or his use of such ordinary expedients in composition, as a diligent student of our great poets will be too proud to adopt." Advice is frequently in need of simplification, and Hunt's involved recommendations may be simplified: Share *Examiner* principles; come to dinner when you like; and drop the Works of Alexander Pope.

Byron thanked Hunt for a copy of the book on February 9th, 1814, and for his "very handsome note. . . . Of myself, you speak only too highly—and you must think me strangely spoiled, or perversely peevish, even to suspect that any remarks of yours, in the spirit of candid criticism, could possibly prove unpalatable." If, then, Hunt's "dear Byron" manner is to be condemned as tactless and artificial, Byron himself is partly to blame for it; clearly he did not choose to be irritated by it until other persons had educated him into that feeling. "I shall break in upon you in a day or two—distance has hitherto detained me; and I hope to find you well and myself welcome. Ever your obliged and sincere, BYRON."

VII

The Descent of Liberty

THE appearance of Hunt's satire as a book marked the end of half his imprisonment, a time of less privation than his friend Moore had anticipated, of enlarged personal influence, of leisure for books and music, but of poor health. Horse-riding had been strongly recommended to the invalid, but his situation afforded only skipping, top-whipping and marbles as convenient athletics. There is an incongruous aspect in the fate of a man who, recently busy scourging a mighty Government with his wit, must now use a simpler lash on a schoolboy's "beehive." Yet the contrast is not in entire accordance with the facts, for Hunt had been editing *The Examiner* throughout the twelvemonth with much the same strokes of opinion and irony as if he were at Hampstead or in Covent Garden. The weight of his sentence was relieved by the human readjustments which seldom fail to take the worst terrors from any systematic imposition; it is astonishing that a political prisoner at such a time could edit his journal every week, but it is true. Through 1813 Barnes and Lamb gave the best proofs of their loyalty to their friend by writing finely and frequently for *The Examiner*, and at the year's close the circulation of that journal was as regular as ever. There were many determined patriots in England, from Shelley with his "princely offer" to solve Hunt's money problem, to "a Rev. Mr Morris, who called to urge some kind things about a subscription," all believing in the necessity and the ultimate victory of this keen instrument of liberty. In 1814 Hazlitt united his powers of reasoning and invective with that of the Hunts, and *The Examiner* went on in a more formidable candour.

The Feast of the Poets, cordially received by the public and at least not unnoticed by the leading judges, headed a series of books of verse by Hunt, of which as a whole the first appearances suggest a much deeper imaginative refreshment than is felt in the end. After *The Feast*, the studious author attempted a higher flight in an unusual form. On July 10th, 1814, he inscribed his *Descent of Liberty: A Mask* to Thomas Barnes. He has thus associated two schoolfellows with his two first products of riper verse—a happy instance of his gift for friendship. 'I dedicated the first poetical attempt of my maturer years to a man of wit and scholarship, who stood the next above me at school:—allow me to present the second to another, who stood the next below. How far he was my superior in general knowledge, and the anticipation of a manly judgment, I well remember." It was a little ceremony *de amicitia*, a poetic unity. Passing to the question of the Mask, we find that it was thought out in his seclusion upon the news of Napoleon's abdication, and was an expansion and embellishment of an "Ode for the Spring of 1814" printed in *The Examiner* of April 17th. It was an idealisation of the world's political drama, and at the same time the dream and fancied escape of a captive, whose wall

> If wrongly round him, like a curtain flies;
> The green and laughing world he sees,
> Waters, and plains, and waving trees.

Prefixed to it stood an account of the "Origin and Nature of Masks," revealing how the Elizabethans were now recapturing the English imagination, and closing in a witty defence of the theory that much drama is not meant for stage representation. "When a storm blows on the stage without disturbing the philosophy of the trees,—when instead of boiling up a waste of waters it sets in painful motion a dozen asthmatic pieces of tin,—when Ariel, instead of breaking out of the atmosphere with ready eagerness at his master's ear, comes walking in with his wand like a premature common-councilman,—in short, when the lightning lingers, the rain leaves dry, and one flat piece of carpeted board performs the eternal part of lawn, meadow, and lea, of overgrown wild and finished garden, who, that has any fancy at all, does not feel that he can raise much better pictures in his own mind than he finds in the theatre?" The passage may be taken as an index to Hunt's critical rank, for Lamb had already discussed Shakespeare's plays as seen on the stage; and whereas Hunt has a twinkling sprightliness which Lamb had not, the argument of the one is temporary, of the other permanent; Hunt's physical, Lamb's metaphysical. The literary courage of Hunt may be recognised in the simple fact of his resuscitating the ingenuities of the Mask, which, except for such isolated exhibitions as Thomson and Mallet's *Alfred* in 1740—complete with *Rule Britannia*—had slept since the court of Charles the Second. But there was, as Hazlitt perceived, an affinity between Leigh Hunt and the vivid Cavaliers.

Distinguished in its retrospective congeniality, the *Descent of Liberty* is singular in its anticipatory coincidence; it is the principal poetic vision of Napoleonic Europe before Mr Hardy's overwhelming *Dynasts*. One catches an odd superficial likeness to that work in Hunt's stage directions: "Another cloud, similar to that over the city, emerges from the north after the light, and begins to come slowly onward, the latter meantime shifting its place a little towards it, and leaving the spires of the city whitening up into the air." But Hunt's superhuman intelligences are not the race that Mr Hardy portrayed: "To the sound of distant and grand music, the other cloud, turning to a silvery hue, moves into the former's place over the city, and separates into four bright globes, on each of which sits a Genius, with one hand holding a thunderbolt carelessly on the thigh, and in the other lifting an olive-branch. They descend gradually into the city, amidst the far-off sound of bells and artillery." Among the dramatic presences whom, so far as I remember, Mr Hardy did not include in his giant morality, Hunt (descended from West Indian slave-owners) calls in "a Sable Genius, with fetter-rings at his wrists, a few of the links not broken off," to whom Liberty:

> What, again
> The Southern Genius troubled! What has caused
> This evil fear in thee, unhappy spirit? ...

The Sable Genius replies, and tells her his dreams, in one of the loftiest and most Shelleian passages outside Shelley; the reader will gladly receive a fragment of it:

> That I too rose bewildered, and stood staring
> Till the foul vision to the shore came nigh;
> With human voice it came, and cried aloud,
> "Twice are ye sold, ye wretches, twice are sold
> To me and mine: fresh compact has been made,
> Now that your fellow-creatures have grown happier,
> Shaking all off in their own loose from care,
> And I am here again:—bring out your wives,
> Bring out your wives, ye husbands,—youths, your loves,
> Mothers, your children—that I may select
> My victims, and with their united agonies
> O'er the far sea return, leaving your eyes
> And hearts to burst on the impossible shore."

Mastery in poetry consists largely in the instinct for not ruining or smothering or tinkering with moments of vision. Hunt had his moments, but not the instinct. His public felt some thrilling possibility in *The Descent of Liberty*, which led to its being reprinted[1].

---

[1] "We met in solemn council, divested we are convinced of any blind partiality arising from our knowledge of the author, and with our limited

Of the poet's prison domesticities in 1814, the records are not numerous. The rosy bower, the mignonette, the sunflowers and the martyr, like all novelties, could not remain sensational. A savage winter opened the year, but failed to deter the Lambs, nor did unkinder ingratitude deflect Cowden Clarke's weekly basket (sometimes even supplying the ingredients for Roast Pig) from Hunt and his family. Byron remembered him in the shooting season. Haydon in Paris bought Dante and Ariosto for him, and caused his large picture, the *Judgment of Solomon*, to be carried into the prison for Hunt's inspection. There were now three children round the table. The eldest, Thornton, was an extraordinary little boy, to whom at the age of three his father wrote: "Pray tell me what is the Greek for a horse, and a man, and a woman; a boy, a girl, the moon, and a flower; and as many others of your fifty words as mamma chooses to ask you. You ought now to learn the Greek for the sea, as you are in the habit of seeing it;— it is *thalassa*, and *kuma* is a wave;—a ship you know already." This year Lamb, the childless, wrote the pretty and expressive lines on the model of Ambrose Phillips to *Thornton Hunt, my*

judgment considered it for its intrinsic merit, with a minute attention that might be alike observant of its faults and its beauties. Of the former we only agreed in two or three instances, and those were respecting points in the allegorical Representations, of very trivial importance. In our admiration of its abundant beauties we were unanimous, whether we viewed it for its fancy, for the fine human feelings that it excites, or for the grand abstractions that abound particularly towards the close of the poem. Our hearts and imaginations were alike delighted, and we found the true ends of Poetry answered, as they are laid down in the noble passage you have quoted from Bacon. When we had concluded we felt such an impression of excellence on our minds, and were left in so pleasant an absorption of fancies by the magic of your pen, that we resolved thus to address you. . . . We are, Dear Sir, very truly yours, Henry Robertson, William Havell, Charles Ollier." January 22nd, 1815.

Favourite Child. Like his father's, this child's earliest memories
were those of a prisoner:

> Gates that close with iron roar
> Have been to thee thy nursery door;
> Chains that chink in cheerless cells
> Have been thy rattles and thy bells;
> Walls contrived for giant sin
> Have hemmed thy faultless weakness in;
> Near thy sinless bed black Guilt
> Her discordant house hath built
> And filled it with her monstrous brood—
> Sights, by thee not understood,
> Sights of fear, and of distress,
> That pass a harmless infant's guess.

The verses recall us to a sense of the dismal dens amidst which,
after all, Hunt's boudoir was a heroic counterfeit. Presently
Thornton's father wrote a similar but less poetical piece in
praise of the younger John; nobody seems to have sung Mary
Florimel, who was born in the prison, but in the *Autobiography*
Hunt says of her what many poets would have said at greater
length—"She was beautiful."

The grimly toilsome Brougham did not forget the political
friend whose advocate he had been, and through these months
he sent him notes and letters serviceable for *Examiner* harangues;
restoratives to Hunt's political fervour, descriptive of "the
hissing, groaning, &c., with which the Prince is received
wherever he goes," and "fright and signs of capitulation" at
Carlton House. On September 21st, 1814, Brougham proffered a larger service. "Soon after your sentence, a hint was
conveyed to me that a very honest and amiable man, who had
been on the jury, having never ceased since the trial to lament
his joining in the verdict, was anxious to satisfy his mind, as
far as was then possible, by paying the fine imposed, and it was

said that the sum would be deposited in my hands in trust for that purpose. I did not feel authorized to propose this to you then, but I said that my opinion being very clear that you should avail yourself of it, if you found it suited your feelings and your convenience jointly, I should certainly have an eye towards the matter when the day of payment approached. My principal reason for the delay was that you might avail yourself of the possibility of a remission, which events that have *not* happened would have produced.

"The period of your liberation now drawing near, I felt it to be my duty to renew the negotiation, and I at the same time let your entire ignorance of what was going on be quite distinctly known. I found the most decided and anxious desire continued on the part of the excellent man above mentioned—a feeling the more honourable because its duration clearly shows it not to be a momentary ebullition, or the result of what might be termed a compunctious visiting, but a sense of duty and principle. You have but to say the word, and the matter is settled; and that, in the course of a post.... If you will suffer me to indulge the idea that my opinion has any value in your eyes, I am sure of your favourable answer, for I think very decidedly upon this subject. But oblige me (before you make up your mind) so far as to consult with two persons beside your brother, and let Mrs Hunt be one."

The inner intonation with which Brougham brought in the last five words will remain a mystery and occasion for guesswork, but nothing could be clearer than the glory of that anonymous juryman who desired to pay the fine. Such sturdy works of principle flourished in the English character at that time, and still they are seen to originate similar acts of natural nobility, but the cheapening and adulteration of our traditions have threatened to supersede them. The sequel was as magnanimous as the offer. "We declined it, with proper thanks," says Hunt; "and it became us to do so. But, as far as my own feelings were concerned, I have no merit; for I was destitute, at that time, of a proper instinct with regard to money. It was not long afterwards that I was forced to call upon friendship for its assistance; and nobly was it afforded me!" Supposing this abnegation to be correct, we still admire its spirit, and we must discern in John Hunt, who understood, if Leigh did not, the status of pounds and pence in the community, "that iron philosophy" which sets itself to cross all the whirlpools without even the company of St Christopher.

At Clerkenwell Prison, John Hunt was peacefully working out his sentence—an experience which he was to repeat later in the cause of liberty of opinion. The governor, Townsend, was friendly, and enabled him to walk in his garden two hours a day; his room was airy and well furnished. John Hunt also received his visitors, and was pleased if they would play chess with him; he read deeply, but passed most of his time in reflection and in close consideration of the problems of the age. Cowden Clarke sent him his market baskets from Enfield, and we find Leigh Hunt writing: "Let me thank you for your very acceptable present of apples to my brother John. If you had ransacked the garden of the Hesperides, you could not have made him, I am sure, a more welcome one. I believe his notion of the highest point of the sensual in eating is an apple, hard, juicy and fresh." John Hunt's imprisonment, and that of Leigh, ended on February 2nd, 1815.

John Hunt resumed his life in the house at Maida Vale and the *Examiner* office without difficulty. The return to freedom and its bondage, however, operated on Leigh Hunt's less Roman make of mind with peculiar pain. At school he had been trained like "a young monk," in a kind of friary, where the

conflicting demands of the struggle for existence were seldom
heard except as an aesthetically agreeable murmur; he wept
when he had to leave the cloisters of Christ's Hospital, Boyer
and all. In his prison he again found something like a hermitage,
a home for the abstractions, a pause from the clamours of the
outer world, and when he came out he did not remember Lot's
wife. "It was thought that I should dart out of my cage like a
bird, and feel no end in the delight of ranging. But partly from
ill health, and partly from habit, the day of my liberation brought
a good deal of pain with it. An illness of a long standing, which
required very different treatment, had by this time been burnt
in upon me by the iron that enters into the soul of the captive,
wrap it in flowers as he may; and I am ashamed to say, that
after stopping a little at the house of my friend A., I had not
the courage to continue looking at the shoals of people passing
to and fro, as the coach drove up the Strand. The whole
business of life appeared to me a hideous impertinence. The
first pleasant sensation I experienced was when the coach turned
into the New-road, and I beheld the old hills of my affection
standing where they used to do, and breathing me a welcome."

A. was Alsager of *The Times*, to whom Hunt now presented
a miniature of himself as a "grateful trifle," supplementing it
with a sonnet in praise of Alsager's cordial companionship
throughout the past two years. There was another sonnet
written that day in praise of Hunt by one who worshipped him
at a distance—John Keats. Versed in *The Examiner*, and in
Cowden Clarke's talk, Keats could readily bring to his mind a
picture of the man he most eagerly wished to see.

> What though, for showing truth to flatter'd state,
>   Kind Hunt was shut in prison? yet has he,
>   In his immortal spirit, been as free
> As the sky-searching lark, and as elate.

Minion of grandeur! think you he did wait?
  Think you he naught but prison walls did see,
  Till, so unwilling, thou unturn'dst the key?
Ah, no! far happier, nobler was his fate!
In Spenser's halls he stray'd, and bowers fair,
  Culling enchanted flowers; and he flew
With daring Milton through the fields of air:
  To regions of his own his genius true
Took happy flights. Who shall his fame impair
  When thou art dead, and all thy wretched crew?

Whatever else Hunt was, he was a poet; and it was a kindness of fortune that permitted his entering his cell to be celebrated by one known poetic voice, his leaving it to be hailed by another and a greater. Fate in our days has surely departed from these elegances.

A few days after his liberation, Leigh Hunt was encouraged by the arrival of some books by Wordsworth, from the Author; together with a letter "in the third person." This thoughtful if stately act on the part of the Lake Poet brings us back to the evolution of Hunt's character as a literary critic in *The Feast of the Poets*, which we shall now conveniently glance at again, in the new edition of 1815. It resolved itself into a laureation of Wordsworth, and no doubt Hunt's maturing preference of that poet was quickened by the courtesy mentioned just now and by Wordsworth's calling on him as soon as he came to London. Hunt was living at the time in the Edgware Road, in order to be near his brother. The day of the visit, June 11th, 1815, was unfortunate, or threatened to be so; since that day's *Examiner* took a slash at Wordsworth's political record. The pen that did this was Hazlitt's, but his authorship was concealed. On Wordsworth's arrival, Hunt asked him "in a very manly way" whether he had seen the morning's paper, saying that, if he had seen it, his visit conferred a higher honour. Hunt added that he was not the author of the attack. He further showed that his appreciation of William Wordsworth was not verbal only, for, although the visit was unexpected, there on the shelves stood Wordsworth's Poems alongside Milton's. Whatever Words-worth felt about his neighbour, at least this was something. Hunt asked the bard whether he would take any refreshment; and, as he put the question, his eye was on a cart outside passing through the archway underneath their room. Wordsworth replied "Anything which is *going forward*" with such gravity that Hunt felt like asking him to take a piece of the cart. But the monumental Presence forbade the quip. The meeting was, we see, rather a ceremony than a festivity. One month later Hunt wrote his new preface for *The Feast of the Poets*, which was speedily published by Gale and Fenner with the announce-ment, "Shortly will be published, In one volume 4to, THE STORY OF RIMINI: a Poem. By Leigh Hunt."

The 1815 edition of *The Feast of the Poets* entertained Words-worth most hospitably in preface, text and notes, as "a noble poet, who has so many beauties that you are only apt now and then, perhaps with no very great wisdom, to grow impatient at his faults." Apollo had grown Byronically affable:

Come, my dear Will,—imperfections apart,—
Let us have a true taste of our exquisite art;
You know very well you've the key to my heart.

The notes expressed this more finely and carefully, with an elaborate meditation on Wordsworth's theory of poetry and the question how far he had acted upon it. Hunt's opposition to his views was formidable; he argued that the simplicities selected by Wordsworth were out of the way of the poet's function, "delight and utility," and that the glorification of the primitive was not so healthy as that mental labour and appetite of the metropolitan era which it endeavoured to counteract.

"That eremitical vagueness of sensation,—that making a business of reverie," struck the social Hunt as being of small service to society. And yet, he again and again drew attention to the executive felicity of Wordsworth's genius. To Coleridge he was at that stage much less just. The *Ancient Mariner* was catalogued among the crazy herd—"Idiot Boys, Mad Mothers, Wandering Jews, Visitations of Ague, Indian Women left to die on the road, and Frenzied Mariners, who are fated to accost us with tales that almost make one's faculties topple over." Hunt could nevertheless acknowledge Coleridge's "congeniality with Mr Wordsworth in point of real powers," and after all Coleridge himself was to blame for much of the misconstruction of his achievement. He had now been writing poetry for almost a quarter of a century, some of it quite wildly bad, the best of it still in manuscript and drifting from hand to hand— and it was necessary for an intelligent adversary to ask him to do himself justice. "It is a pity that all the poems written by Mr Coleridge are not collected in one publication."

Wordsworth was not wholly unuplifted by the suffrages of Hunt. When Haydon wrote to him in December 1815 that "Leigh Hunt's respect for you seems to increase daily; his brother it is who has had your bust made," the poet replied, with a gentle malice, "It may be agreeable to Mr Leigh Hunt to learn that his 'Mask' has been read with great pleasure by my wife and her sister under this peaceful roof. They commend the style in strong terms; and though it would not become *me* to say that their taste is correct, I have often witnessed with pleasure and entire sympathy the disgust with which in this particular they are affected by the main part of contemporary productions."

VIII

Young Poets

HUNT applied himself to his former duties and recreations with a trembling slowness, and, having been so ingenious in making one unpromising place his happy haven day in and day out, now found it difficult to go here and there and call on his friends in London. Byron invited him with kindly insistings to the theatre, but Hunt remained at home. "I have the alternate weeks of a private box at Drury Lane Theatre: this is my week, and I send you an admission to it for Kean's nights." Hunt had seen Kean in the earliest days of his release, and had been disappointed; he did not feel capable of visiting the theatre in his old spirit of ardent seriousness. Byron's letter of June 1st, 1815, just now quoted, called Hunt to Piccadilly Terrace when he was at liberty: "I shall be happy to make you acquainted with Lady Byron, whom you will find anything but a fine lady—a species of animal which you probably do not affect more than myself." But Hunt missed the opportunity, and only saw Lady Byron in her carriage waiting for her capricious husband, while he loitered genially in his friend's modest study. Byron in that mood awoke all Hunt's artistic if not personal admiration. "His appearance at that time was the finest I ever saw it. . . . He was fatter than before his marriage, but only just enough so to complete the manliness of his person; and the turn of his head and countenance had a spirit and elevation in it, which, though not unmixed with disquiet, gave him altogether a nobler look, than I ever knew him to have, before or since. His dress, which was black, with white trowsers, and which he wore buttoned close over the body, completed the succinctness and gentlemanliness of his appearance." When Hunt at length reached 13, Terrace,

Piccadilly, Lady Byron had parted from this noble creature, and Hunt missed another meeting too; for Byron had come from hearing Coleridge, in another room, recite *Kubla Khan* with a voice of dreams.

This belated visit must have been paid early in 1816. Meanwhile Byron had treated his acquaintance with Hunt sensitively, even heartily. In October 1815 he made him a present of a copy of *English Bards and Scotch Reviewers*, with manuscript revision, as a rarity: "it is the only gift of the kind I have made this many a day." At the same date Byron was reading the later parts of *The Story of Rimini* with an eye to correcting its "occasional quaintness and obscurity" before it should be sent to press. Hunt sent him copies of other poems—*The Descent of Liberty* was just now reprinted—and Byron seems to have had them finely bound before returning them. Again he beckoned the once insatiable judge of the drama to Drury Lane: "Will you come to the Theatre and see our new management? You shall cut it up to your heart's content, root and branch, afterwards, if you like; but come and see it! If not, I must come and see you." In return for these marks of esteem, Hunt endeavoured to assist Byron, at a time when opinion ran hard against him in his domestic position, with a defence in *The Examiner*.

All these personal occurrences fell under the shadow of irrelevance and unreality because of the titanic situation over the Channel. The Child of Destiny was out of prison at much the same time as the harmless "Libertas," and the Gazettes of that spring were scanned with inconceivable anxiety. This time, there was less anti-Gallican wit abroad in England than in Hunt's volunteering days. At length the *London Gazette Extraordinary*, of June 22nd, informed the British public that there had been a battle at Waterloo on June 18th, which had ended in the rout of Napoleon. In those easier days British headquarters did not conceal main facts from the public, and Wellington's magnificent account of his victory includes the plain words: "Your lordship will observe, that such a desperate action could not be fought, and such advantages could not be gained, without great loss; and I am sorry to add that ours has been immense." This was the colour in the rainbow of victory which most vividly awakened Hunt's feelings, and it explains the comments of *The Examiner* on war rather than a triumph, or equally it introduces the following careless entry in the Journals of Haydon: "June 25.—Read the *Gazette* again, till I now know it actually by heart. Dined with Hunt. I give myself great credit for not worrying him to death at this news: he was quiet for some time, but knowing it must come by-and-by, and putting on an air of indifference, he said, 'Terrible battle this, Haydon.' 'A glorious one, Hunt.' 'Oh yes, certainly,' and to it we went."

Wherever Haydon's enthusiasm for public events could go, his propositions for the employment of historical painters could go also; and ten days later he was writing to Hunt requesting him to give the muscles of *The Political Examiner* a little exercise with the wicked Ministry that had voted £500,000 for a Waterloo Memorial without a word about painting but with many on "all these monuments and pillars." "It is in your power to assist our great object, my dear Hunt." But even historical painting was finding Leigh Hunt a disappointingly abstracted spectator. Nor was *The Examiner* quite so far-reaching and kindling as it had been. The miracle of its survival during the imprisonment of the proprietors did not empower it to hold its own against the wave of Tory sentiment in the country, neither did it accord with the harder mood of the industrial reformists who now began to rise with the rising factories and slums. It became, in the hands of Leigh Hunt, a journal for the poets and amateurs of literature, as far as John Hunt would concur; the change was gradual, and gradual the decline in the newspaper's influence, for Leigh Hunt did his best at all seasons to serve his brother genuinely with political rhetoric and dissertation. But his heart was not often in that business. Another contrary influence to *The Examiner* was a journal of much the same pattern, independent politics and intellectual substance, recently established in London—John Scott's *Champion*. Scott was an acquaintance of Hunt's[1] and is somewhat obscurely spoken of as having received considerable benefits from the fact, but as returning evil for good. This may mean no more than that *The Champion* successfully contested with *The Examiner* for the support of Hazlitt, Wordsworth, Keats and J. H. Reynolds; and that, though Leigh Hunt himself contributed at least one article to his competitor's pages, Scott presently affirmed in those pages that *The Examiner* was "a grossly anti-English publication."

In October 1815 Hunt left the neighbourhood of Maida Vale and realised one ambition by living at Hampstead. No rhapsodist ever loved a mountain solitude, not even John Clare loved Helpstone's molehilly heath, more than Hunt loved that place. From time to time since his imprisonment he had been publishing little poems in honour of it; even in the winter of 1814 he had longed to be climbing with the wanderer there who

sees
The cold sky whitening through the wiry trees.

---

[1] John Scott was one of those who, to T. Moore's annoyance, "dropped in" at Horsemonger Lane gaol when Byron was on his first visit to Hunt. He also enraged Moore by subsequently assailing Byron, though Moore does not give Hunt the credit for having defended Byron at that time.

G. Shepherd.

S. Lacey.

THE VALE OF HEALTH, HAMPSTEAD

SHOWING HUNT'S HOUSE. FROM AN ENGRAVING OF 1827

In May, the first May of his unprisoning, he had gone there in the early morning, and gazed deeply

> To see how sweet and self-same she appears.

And that autumn he drew the portrait of the favourite village and her region, not so well as Constable, but with skill in the now little practised art of giving a definite view of a beautiful scene in verse. We must brighten our paragraphs with this sonnet in water-colours:

> A steeple issuing from a leafy rise,
>   With farmy fields in front, and sloping green,
>   Dear Hampstead, is thy southern face serene,
> Silently smiling on approaching eyes.
> Within, thine ever-shifting looks surprise,—
>   Streets, hills, and dells, trees overhead now seen,
>   Now down below, with smoking roofs between,—
> A village revelling in varieties.
> Then northward what a range,—with heath and pond,
>   Nature's own ground; woods that let mansions through,
> And cottaged vales with pillowy fields beyond,
>   And clump of darkening pines, and prospects blue,
> And that clear path through all, where daily meet
> Cool cheeks, and brilliant eyes, and morn-elastic feet.

Strange, that the easy unity and natural onset of this poem from nature to humanity should not have been reckoned of sufficient merit to outweigh the faulty and indeterminate touches; but stranger, that a man could not pay so kind a tribute to a suburban amenity without being assailed by anger and indecency. The subject and the air of these Hampstead sonnets were received by Hunt's political haters with all the horse-laughs of malice. So this daisy-gatherer was the scourge of tyrants and standard-bearer of Freedom!

During the last months of 1815 Hunt was completing his long considered poem, *The Story of Rimini*, in the surroundings of the Heath which gave him sketchbook hints for its landscape interludes. Byron sedulously acted as consultant, and cheered the author with anticipatory verdicts. "You have two excellent points in that poem—originality and Italianism. I will back you as a bard against half the fellows on whom you have thrown away much good criticism and eulogy: but don't let your bookseller publish in *quarto*; it is the worst size possible for circulation. I say this on bibliopolical authority." On January 29th, 1816, Byron wrote: "I hope you are by this time on the verge of publication. My pencil-marks on the margin of your former MSS. I never thought worth the trouble of decyphering, but I had no such meaning as you imagine for their being withheld from Murray, from whom I differ entirely as to the terms of your agreement; nor do I think you asked a piastre too much for the poem. However, I doubt not he will deal fairly by you on the whole: he is really a very good fellow." Murray sent Hunt £50 for the first edition. Hunt had asked for £450 to begin with. It was the day when narrative poems, by Scott or Crabbe or Byron, had a prodigious sale, and *Rimini* must have seemed to the fond eye of Hunt the householder to promise a not wholly dissimilar credit account. The same date as that of Byron's letter stands in the poetry-book at the foot of a dedication to the Right Honourable Lord Byron: "My dear Byron, You see what you have brought yourself to by liking my verses. It is taking you unawares, I allow; but you yourself have set example now-a-days of poet's dedicating to poet; and it is under that nobler title, as well as the still nobler one of friend, that I now address you." So begins one of the too numerous failures of Hunt to address Byron in print without palaver, jauntiness and self-deception.

The poem was published in duodecimo, by Murray in London and W. Blackwood in Edinburgh. It almost became fashionable.

Sam Rogers, who quoted it tastefully at his breakfasts, assured the author, on a momentary meeting, that he had seen a beautiful woman in tears over it; but in the end it by no means challenged the poetico-commercial achievements of Rogers himself. Hunt's friends offered him all the eulogy that he could desire. Barron Field congratulated him on "the poetical philosophy with which you have found out the soul of goodness in things evil"; Hazlitt, one of those right-minded persons who avoid correspondence, nevertheless sent two pages of extracts and expressions of pleasure to the Vale of Health. Charles and Mary Lamb congratulated him "most sincerely on the treat of your prison fruit"—and Lamb singled out the third canto as most to his liking. Mitchell defined the piece as "the progress of a new mind," though he added a hint of borrowings from other new minds. Moore, who had lately received £3000 for a poem, observed, "In short, it is poetry"; Brougham liked his copy, but had not had time to read it with attention. Byron reported the satisfaction of Sir Henry Englefield, Augusta Leigh, J. H. Frere, and other distinguished persons; he was judicious in his allusion to the dedication: "I accepted [it] as it was meant—as a public compliment and a private kindness. I am only sorry that it may perhaps operate against you as an inducement, and, with some, a pretext, for attack on the part of the political and personal enemies of both:—not that this can be of much consequence, for in the end the work must be judged by its merits and in that respect you are well armed." But we must not fail to bring to light the agonising ecstasy of B. R. Haydon: "I have read, and re-read your exquisite pathetic tale, till my Soul is cut in two—and every nerve about me pierced with trembling needles—I can say no more till we meet—but that it is the sweetest thing of the time, and that the World must think so—you shall find when we do meet, that not the most secret touch of humanity in it, has been passed without shaking me to the core—Adieu, it will establish your genius."

Such critical rightness deserved a reward, and Hunt volunteered a sonnet on Haydon. The painter was indeed willing: "My dear Hunt, nothing would give me greater delight than a sonnet from you, and when you write me a sonnet I'll paint a Picture from your Poem—a bargain—do not forget that *your* Portrait is the only one I have painted or probably ever will. I can't say enough to you about your tale; if every body be affected as I have been there will not be a heart without a pang, or an eye without a tear, in the Kingdom. . . ." The sonnet was now a certainty, and Haydon greeted it—"Very, very fine. God grant I may deserve it," followed the next day with "The more I reflect on your sonnet, the more I am convinced it is the very best thing you have done." Such were those prime of days. But let us resume the history of *Rimini*.

What was the result of five years' labour in the collection and embodiment of Italianisms, and the study of reviving the English rhyming couplet in its earlier resourcefulness? A poem, "founded on a passage in Dante"— the episode told with so eloquent a quietness by the Italian in the conclusion of Canto II of the *Inferno*. It had recently been brought into the consciousness of unlearned English readers in the translation of H. F. Cary, which merely set out with the purpose "of affording an easy introduction to such as are desirous of forming an acquaintance with the Italian poet himself," and ended as a standard work. Hunt chose a love tragedy, then, which in subject would instantly set all the profitable prudery of his enemies in array—the adultery of Francesca, wife of Lanciotto, with his brother Paolo. The treatment also could not hope to win much respect except from the more enquiring and futurist

minds. Hunt showed himself as the man who thought Pope—
the traditional model of versification—a bad versifier when
put beside Dryden, Milton, Ariosto, Shakespeare, and
Chaucer; he desired to reform the narrative measure according
to true liberty, and, at the same time, he aimed at "a free and
idiomatic use of language." His theory was that there was a
poetic cant, adverse to the spirit of poetry, and his remedy was
the fellow to Wordsworth's—"like, but oh! how different"
—the use of "an actual, existing language—omitting of course
mere vulgarisms and fugitive phrases, which are the cant of
ordinary discourse." Hunt failed to omit a leaven of these,
lacking the instinct for what is perishable, or ludicrous, or
otiose in phrase, although he possessed an imagination for
verbal tones and impressions.

The first canto of *Rimini* opens, true to Hunt's philosophy,
with a May morning, and the pageantry preceding Francesca's
departure from Ravenna as a bride. The second describes her
journey in the evening and moonlight to Rimini; the third,
the scenes and moods culminating in Francesca's unfaithful-
ness; and the fourth, the discovery and death of the lovers. All
the cantos contain matter and impertinency mixed, the excellence usually dwelling in the setting, the irritating nonsense
in the characterisation and conversation. The splendours of
the bridal ceremony are enacted with a fresh feeling of holiday
surprise, and a chivalric emotion, sustained with a liveliness of
accent, making one seem a spectator in the rejoicing crowd.
The ride through the forest is a ride and not a natural-history
selection or a talk about futility or reactions. The garden at
Rimini is a prince's garden, with a delectable pavilion in it,
and a brook beside

> Whose low sweet talking seemed as if it said
> Something eternal to that happy shade.

In short, there are many

> Places of nestling green, for poets made,

if you persist through *The Story of Rimini,* but Hunt has done
his best to prevent you. You must listen to tragic figures
talking, or talked about, with the looseness of a novelette: to
some of those mysterious lines of verse which compete for the
wooden spoon of Apollo—as

> Nor, to say truly, was he slow in common
> To accept the attentions of this lovely woman,

and the still more exhausted, yet immortal couplet[1],

> The two divinest things this world has got,
> A lovely woman in a rural spot.

Through this patchwork of fineness and flippancy, one emerging
merit is felt; there is personality here. The composition is
stamped with the author's image, though not in any deliberate
sense introspective; and, though poetry must contain more, a
presence that is clearly recognisable is unusual. The intelligence
of Hunt dictated this enterprise in longer poetry; the inex-
perience of his mind was incapable of staying the course. We
know the position, comprehend the frequent lapses, and wish
him a more congenial opportunity.

What Hunt was talented to touch upon, not to seize and
appropriate, others were impelled by his poem to attempt with
power. *Rimini* has the honour of having opened more than one
poetical prospect to those who read it. It pointed the way to a
flexibility of style in verse, and the necessity for the poets of a
strongly advancing race to acquire expression through the
medium of significant daily speech. It showed that the epi-
grammatic couplet of Pope and his long line of followers was

---

[1] Patmore's parody is remembered too,

> The two divinest things this world can grab,
> A handsome woman in a hansom cab.

But Hunt could have had his revenge on C. P.'s glasshouse.

a metrical tyranny, and that the couplet might become flowing and even labyrinthine without loss of direction and with great joy of sound and interpretation. It brought into the Northern air a welcome Southern warmth and vinous brilliance, urging the senses of poets to triumph over a bleak environment and to irradiate it with the sunshine and azure of Ariosto's country. I shall not impede my readers with a technical review of its effects on Romantic poetry, but merely point out that the wonderful graces of Shelley and Keats in the heroic couplet arrived in the days after *Rimini* had revealed the matter to the literary public, and that Hunt anticipated Keats in frankly admitting the "luxuries" to verse—the colours, perfumes, clothing, food, drink, and physical experiences at large, so often judged foreign to the austerities of poetry. *Rimini* had other effects, not on poetry but on critics and on the lives of Hunt and Keats, of which much must be said shortly. Apart from its quality, status, share in the history of verse, and its massacre by the old Jack Ketches of criticism, the poem was a favourite with its author, and like other faded *heroica* of the nineteenth century —Horne's *Orion*, Bailey's *Festus*—it became an exercise-ground in which, edition by edition, its author tried fresh evolutions.

As the agoraphobia of Leigh Hunt wore itself out, he became a particularly admired and expected friend of the family of Vincent Novello, the organist at the Portuguese Embassy's Chapel in Grosvenor Square, and the father of musical publications for everybody in this country. The friendship was one of the happiest, gayest, fullest and least disturbed of Hunt's numerous associations with remarkable men; there were assignable reasons for this. Novello was half English, half Italian; he had been educated in France; he married a lady of German family. Here was obviously a cosmopolitan, easy-going and attractive assemblage of social qualities. It is also clear that music would be a great feature of the Novellos' home. Hunt was himself an imported flower, an exotic; he too was a musician, adoring Novello's demigods, Haydn, Mozart, Purcell. We must record Hunt's music in our memories as a constant theme through his biography, together with his Spenser and his Italian poets; his son's pen-portrait of him in this aspect may accompany us from this point, although it was written for the *Cornhill* over forty years afterwards. "Nature had gifted him with an intense dramatic perception," says Thornton; "an exquisite ear for music, and a voice of extraordinary compass, power, flexibility and beauty. It extended from the C below the line to the F sharp above: there were no 'passages' that he could not execute; the quality was sweet, clear, and ringing: he would equally have sung the music of *Don Giovanni* or *Sarastro*, of *Oroveso* or *Maometto Secondo*. Yet nature had not endowed him with some of the qualities needed for the practical musician,—he had no aptitude for mechanical contrivance, but faint enjoyment of power for its own sake." The poems of Hunt testify that he enjoyed the action of that power with an amazing bliss; his is the finest concert poetry, fragmentary as it is and very little read, in English.

As early as May 13th, 1815, he had written verses, in forgetfulness of all literary ambition, on the infinite awakenings of spirit caused by "a private concert." This was given by Charles Ollier at his house to celebrate the first return of his weddingday. Other musical friends were Harry Robertson of the Covent Garden Theatre—

who, full of tasteful glee,
Had music all about him, heart and lips—

and John Gattie—

whose voice was like a rill that slips
Over the sunny pebbles breathingly.

But above all Novello ruled the harmonious hours:

And Vincent, you, who with like mastery
Could chase the notes with fluttering finger-tips,
Or sway the organ with firm royalty.

The home of Novello had been 240, Oxford Street for over
thirty years. It overlooked Hyde Park. Its small drawing-room
was converted into a "little heaven below" with much the same
Arcadian fancy as Hunt's in his prison pastoral. "The walls
simply coloured of a delicate rose tint, and hung with a few
choice water-colour drawings by Varley, Copley Fielding,
Havell and Cristall (who were also personally known to
Vincent Novello); the floor covered with a plain grey drugget
bordered by a tastefully-designed garland of vine-leaves, drawn
and embroidered by Mrs Novello; towards the centre of the
room a sofa-table strewed with books and prints; and at one
end, a fine-toned chamber-organ, on which the host preluded
and played to his listening friends, when they would have him
give them 'such delights, and spare to interpose them oft'
between the pauses of their animated conversation." The party
at one time or another included the Lambs (see *A Chapter on
Ears*), Shelley and Keats. Supper was by common consent
bread and cheese, with "true Lutheran beer"; but Novello
thought that the author of *Rimini* deserved some Italian reward
for his labours, and for him, instead of single Gloucester or
Stilton, Parmesan was procured. In return for these musical,
social and dietetic arrangements, the Hunts would entertain the
Novellos among the buttercups at Hampstead, or round the
piano in the cottage at the Vale of Health.

While *Rimini* was still new, and Hunt had the temporary
attention of most poetry-readers, two young men of extreme
distinction of spirit, both his admirers, established themselves
among his familiar friends. Of Shelley he had already had a
glimpse or two. Of Keats he was aware through Cowden

Clarke, who took him some of that poet's manuscripts in the spring of 1816. Hunt was impressed with these, and his friends Hazlitt, Horace Smith, even Basil Montagu and William Godwin, to whom he read them, agreed with him. On May 5th, 1816, *The Examiner* made itself especially valuable to our retrospect by printing a sonnet on "Solitude" signed J. K. By December 1st of that year, Hunt had dipped into the future so delphically as to publish the hurried article announcing three "Young Poets" who would do great things—Shelley, J. H. Reynolds, and Keats. The admission of Reynolds, which now appears to have been a false alarm, was not at that date unintelligent, for he was writing verse of a sylvan, sad, melodious kind, which might have developed a new individuality; and even in proclaiming Reynolds, Hunt used less instant and assured phrase than for Shelley and Keats.

Shelley had recently lost sight of his first wife Harriet, and was with Mary Godwin at Bath. In what way he heard that Hunt was in difficulties with his debts, originated no doubt years before but massed against him through his imprisonment, legal expenses and heavy fine, I have failed to ascertain; I am inclined to think that Shelley, who read his *Examiner* religiously, caught the signal of distress in Hunt's remarks on *Timon of Athens*, printed on November 3rd—the hint that the tragedy contained "representations of pecuniary difficulty, and friendship put to the test" answering to the writer's circumstances. An offer was made by Shelley, accepted by Hunt; a large sum of money was sent to the Vale of Health, and an affectionate correspondence began. Shelley, on his side, thought of his money as merely the means of doing his duty. He was young and modest enough as a poet to be excited over the salutation of his powers in *The Examiner*; as the number containing it failed to reach him, he enquired at several houses for

a copy, and at length heard of one "at a village five miles off."
About December 6th Shelley went to Hampstead, and was
accepted without the least embarrassment as a member of
Hunt's household. *The Story of Rimini* had not been ignored
by the guest, willing as he was to see the world grow more outspoken and unconventional in regard to dilemmas like that of
Paolo and Francesca. The mutual enthusiasm of the two friends
of liberty had hardly been interrupted by Shelley's departure
when the young hierophant received the news of what looked
a little like a result of his own matrimonial philosophy.
Harriet had found the way out of prostitution by drowning
herself in the Serpentine.

Keats, at this time a medical student, was as fresh in poetical
yearnings as Shelley, and (so far as I am able to decide from the
contradictory evidences) he was so warmly pleased with the
praises of *The Examiner* of Sunday morning, December 1st,
1816, that he called on Hunt the same day with all the radiance
of one admiring and admired. Cowden Clarke accompanied
him. It might be winter without; it was high summer within.
Hunt was instantly delighted with his new friend, who had the
eagle eyes of his own imagined Cortez, staring at the intellectual
Pacific—"The character and expression of Keats's features
would arrest even the casual passenger in the street," says
Clarke. And this ardent being was a disciple of Hunt, a
student of *Examiner* democracy, a friend of *Rimini*. Hunt's
usual ceremony crowned the occasion—a new sonnet, beginning

> 'Tis well you truly think me one of those
> Whose sense discerns the loveliness of things;

not forgetting the benign Clarke,

> And such a heart as Charles's, wise and warm;

and concluding with the generous confidence,

> As surely as all this, I see, ev'n now,
> Young Keats, a flowering laurel on your brow.

There can be little doubt of the account I give of Keats's first meeting with Hunt, although the late Sir Sidney Colvin imagined it to have occurred in the spring of 1816; for Hunt's sonnet is dated in the manuscript, December 1st, 1816. Cowden Clarke distinguishes the sonnet by Keats which alludes to his reception at Hunt's home, and indeed it plainly speaks of a new experience and of winter-time. The friends parted, and Keats had to walk back to his rooms in Cheapside; "keen, fitful gusts," dead leaves and icy stars were his company—"And I have many miles on foot to fare";—but it had been a day of luck and charm from first to last.

> For I am brimfull of the friendliness
>   That in a little cottage I have found;
> Of fair-hair'd Milton's eloquent distress
>   And all his love for gentle Lycid drown'd;
> Of lovely Laura in her light green dress
>   And faithful Petrarch gloriously crown'd.

The adjective for Milton possibly sounds a note of gratitude to Hunt for showing Keats his lock of Milton's hair.

Consolation and benediction in the hour of his wretchedness were assured to Shelley at Hunt's cottage that December, as often as he could reach it; and Keats gladly frequented the same unconventional, musical fireside. The two immortals met, as is fitting to historical design, in the room of their first and best critic. Horace Smith describes them there: Shelley with the blue eyes, the stooping tallness, the earnest unmusical voice; Keats shy, embarrassed as unused to society, speaking little. Keats was not entirely at his best with Shelley, whether the cause was different birth and aspect, or that their creeds of poetic purpose clashed, or accidental misapprehension. Hunt was aware of a subdued dissatisfaction on the part of Keats, but his own talented amiability prevailed, and the meetings of the three were marked by pleasant discussion. Sometimes the cottage was the scene of poetical competitions, one of the indoor recreations of Hunt, much sneered at by those who cheer their leisure in other pastimes. Shelley was prevented, by the fact that he was marrying Mary the same day, from joining in the contest of sonnet-making on *The Grasshopper and the Cricket*, December 30th, 1816. Both Keats and Hunt wrote impromptus of lively spirit, and each thought the other's lines excellent.

Hunt was a little fantastic in his promotion of pleasure, but such divagation from commonly specified modes of behaviour had nothing in it calling for solemn reproof. His crime might consist in celebrating the birthdays of men of genius with appropriate flower-arrangements or other niceties. Once this led to a serious trouble. The commemoration of Josef Haydn was proposed, and agreed upon. Word reached Benjamin Haydon, who assumed that he was the genius being acclaimed, and dashed up to the Vale of Health all ready to pour forth his self-denying speech of althoughs and superlatives. Draw the veil on the disaster. Then, one day in the spring of 1817, Hunt crowned Keats with "two bending laurel sprigs," and in return accepted a "crown of ivy"; the event was concluded with two sonnets apiece. Bessy Kent, who was probably present, was a botanist, and as such finds fault with Hunt's verses in her *Sylvan Sketches*: "A heavy charge indeed may be made against a poet of our own times, for some lines which may tend to mislead posterity as to the true poetical Ivy. And unless the matter be here explained, it were hard to say how many quartos would be necessary to make this matter clear in after times. It has been observed that the leaves of the Poet's Ivy are egg-shaped; yet here is one poet receives an Ivy crown from another poet, and he remarks

> —How they spread
> With their broad angles, like a nodding shed
> Over both eyes!

Now this does not describe the Poet's Ivy, yet he assures us it was with that Ivy he was crowned, and from its luxuriance we might well believe it; probably the two kinds were intertwined." That is the spirit in which Hunt's harmless little rites ought to be annotated. Keats was not the man to be tragically misled by a diversion.

Whatever might be Hunt's "too much" of domesticity, affability and playfulness, whatever his debit account in money matters, or his immersion in literary engagements, his home was open to his friends day and night; and thanks to this fact we are enabled to see the picture of his little study at the Vale of Health in the verse of Keats and of Shelley. Keats, his imagination refusing him sleep, enumerated the busts and the prints round his sofa—and these Sir Sidney Colvin has identified; it was a little gallery of Raphael, Poussin, and Stothard, and from these nooks of art Keats saw his way down the long and gleaming vistas of myth and antiquity with more imaginative delight than he had ever done.

The third of Hunt's "Young Poets," the least, and least warranted by the prophetic critic, also came to the cottage, but never perfected his standing in Hunt's circle any more than in Hunt's view of poetry. Hamilton Reynolds, son of the old writing-master at Christ's Hospital ("Spongy"), and Keats's jealous friend, had set out with high ideas of Hunt as politician and poet. He had written him pages of panegyric. Early in 1816 Reynolds published, in *The Champion*, a parallel to Hunt's

Feast of the Poets; it was "The Pilgrimage of Living Poets to the Stream of Castaly," and Hunt was among the favourites[1]. Almost immediately *The Champion* quarrelled with *The Examiner* over Byron, but, though Reynolds was probably concerned in that dispute, Hunt watched his verses unalteringly through the year until he brought out the "Young Poets" article. Reynolds now joined the evening pilgrimage to the Vale of Health, but not for long. Shelley did not like him, and Reynolds, then and always, had a curious feeling of monopoly towards Keats as friend and as poet. On March 9th, 1817, *The Examiner* published two sonnets by Keats, but on the same day *The Champion* published the same two pieces and a page on Keats's *Poems*. In August 1817 Keats's sonnet *On the Sea* was printed—in *The Champion*, and Hunt must have felt hurt by the circumstance, since he had been the original means of Keats's poetical appearance in public, and still remained most eager to support the young genius in private and in print. Hunt replied with a pretty, and a pathetic reminder of friendship; he took from Keats's volume the sonnet *On the Grasshopper and Cricket*, reprinted it in *The Examiner*, and accompanied it with his own which had not appeared until then. The gesture may have been misunderstood. Reynolds had brought to Hampstead a commendatory poem on *Rimini*, to which Hunt had risen with the customary responsive sonnet; this exchange was insufficient to preserve the friendship through the petty disturbances of daily fact, and later we see nothing of Reynolds in Hunt's neighbourhood, though more in the Garrick Club.

[1] "Next came *Hunt* with a rich fanciful goblet in his hand, finely enamelled with Italian landscapes; he held the cup to his breast as he approached and his eyes sparkled with frank delight. After catching a wave, in which a sunbeam seemed freshly melted, he intimated that he should water heartsease and many favourite flowers with it. The sky appeared of a deep blue as he was retiring."

IX

With Shelley

No extravagance is risked when we say that the libel on the Regent and the penalty exacted had led to a great change in Leigh Hunt's mode of action. Inclined formerly to drive in frontal attack at the insincerities of society, and political injustice, he had been constrained by his serious casualties to try other methods of promoting liberty. Incapable of preparing a scheme of reform which should require years of calm influence and careful construction in *The Examiner,* he was also saved from the disaster of a new forlorn hope and crushing prosecution by the facts, those butts of our detached moods, those grinning commissioners of our actions. Involved in debt, reduced in nervous reserve, and diminished in popular curiosity, Leigh Hunt was compelled to avoid fresh raids into the country of his no longer anxious enemies. Then, too, his prison silences had made more of a bookman of him than ever, and had suggested to him that his own powers of spreading the opinions which he indulged could operate at once most enjoyably and fervently through a minority of private men of genius or position, gathered in fraternal colloquy. His rapid enlightenment as to the nature, potency, and mysterious paths of poetry in "the general heart of man," made him attend more and more to that art and its envoys. These are the considerations which produce a view of Leigh Hunt, personal and poetical, at the beginning of 1817—a man in some respects incomparably happy, with the simultaneous affection and even veneration of the two young poets whose abundant genius he perceived, Shelley and Keats.

It was at this time that Hunt's friend Ollier opened his publishing business; and the circle of idealists believed that a man of such aesthetic attainment, himself a sonnetteer and novelist, would do well. No publisher could have set out with books and authors less likely to sell, or more sought and illustrious after the passage of a century. Shelley gave Ollier his pamphlet, *A Proposal for putting Reform to the Vote*, by "the Hermit of Marlow," with instructions for sending out a number of copies, including twenty for Hunt to dispose of. The Hermit for all his oracular prescience did not guess at the future equivalent in bank-notes of these little adventurers. *A Proposal* was published before March 14th, 1817, and seconded by Hunt in his newspaper. Keats's *Poems* were ready at Ollier's office before March 9th. The volume was dedicated, in a sonnet written at the last moment, to Hunt, and Keats concluded it thus:

> And I shall ever bless my destiny
> That in a time, when under pleasant trees
> Pan is no longer sought, I feel a free,
> A leafy luxury, seeing I could please
> With these poor offerings, a man like thee.

(In passing, let me say that Buxton Forman is for once unsafe when he assumes that Hunt's sonnet to Keats is in return for this dedication; Hunt's piece is dated December 1st, 1816, and Keats's final proof-sheets would have been sent up in February.) Most unfortunately the issue of these *Poems* by Ollier, intended to strengthen the attachments of the Vale of Health optimists, had the effect of introducing speedy dissension. A first book of verse is not a perfect means of making Britain tremble and subscribe, but its author generally thinks that it might do so, and when it fails he is apt to blame the publisher. Keats may have felt that way, but his brother George, who had the poet's self-confidence and haste without much besides, was so indignant over the non-success of *Poems* that during John's absence from

London he sent Ollier his opinion of him. Ollier replied in substance that Keats had requested him to be his publisher, that those who had bought the book were usually caustic about it, that George Keats was no gentleman, and that the remaining copies should be transferred to the author, or his representative, with great willingness. This exchange of compliments preceded Leigh Hunt's extensive and laudatory essay on the *Poems* in *The Examiner*, which may have done something to appease the unrewarded poet and impoverished publisher, and to allure both together to the Vale of Health.

But the friendship of Keats and Hunt, after the excess of lustre observable in its first expansion, was damaged by other conditions. Reynolds, that dark horse, was eager to capture Keats for other company, and other aspects of life and art; Haydon too, unwilling to give up the pride of place in Keats's feelings, and offended by some characteristics of Hunt's household gods, allowed his jealousy to play at the poet's weaker moments. Beyond these amiable competitive movements, there was the daring, unchecked, and hungry spirit of Keats, quickly comprehending the ever-repeated projects of Hunt, seizing on the inexperienced vanities of the projector, and demanding a harder, a less operatic, a more bachelorial society than that of Hunt's female-haunted drawing-room. We entirely agree with Keats except in one passage of this transition: he seems to have expressed himself bitterly against Hunt, but to have concealed this attitude altogether from the now tarnished figure of his former imagining. These impressions may now be explored more particularly.

Keats's *Letters* supply the means. On April 17th, 1817, he writes to Reynolds, "Let me know particularly about Haydon, ask him to write to me about Hunt, if it be only ten lines— I hope all is well." On May 10th, he answers a letter from Hunt with apparent cordiality and touches of approval. "I am upon a horrid subject—what a horrid one you were upon last sunday and well you handled it. The last Examiner was a Battering-Ram against Christianity, blasphemy, Tertullian, Erasmus, Sr Philip Sidney. And then the dreadful Petzelians and their expiation by Blood—and do Christians shudder at the same thing in a Newspaper which they attribute to their God in its most aggravated form? What is to be the end of this?" Keats signs himself in the witty and affectionate nickname hit on by Hunt, "John Keats alias Junkets." But the next day Keats was addressing Haydon: "I wrote to Hunt yesterday—scarcely know what I said in it. I could not talk about Poetry in the way I should have liked for I was not in humor either with his or mine. His self delusions are very lamentable—they have inticed him into a Situation which I should be less eager after than that of a galley Slave—what you observe thereon is very true must be in time. Perhaps it is a self delusion to say so—but I think I could not be deceived in the manner that Hunt is—may I die tomorrow if I am to be. There is no greater Sin after the seven deadly than to flatter oneself into an idea of being a great Poet—or one of those beings who are privileged to wear out their Lives in the pursuit of Honor." In September Keats, having become more comfortable about Hunt's poetics, exclaims to Reynolds: "I think I see you and Hunt meeting in the Pit.—What a very pleasant fellow he is, if he would give up the sovereignty of a room pro bono. What evenings we might pass with him, could we have him from Mrs H. Failings I am always rather rejoiced to find in a man than sorry for; they bring us to a Level. He has them, but then his makes-up are very good."

At this point we may turn aside to obtain Haydon's statement of the part he played in Keats's disaffection. When this new planet of poetry first surprised him, he could spend some thought and time in telling (for instance) David Wilkie how meritorious Hunt was. "27th October 1816. I have been at Hampstead this fortnight for my eyes, and shall return with my body much stronger for application. The greater part of my time has been spent in Leigh Hunt's society, who is certainly one of the most delightful companions. Full of poetry and art, and amiable humour, we argue always with full hearts on everything but religion and Buonaparte, and we have resolved never to talk of these.... Though Leigh Hunt is not deep in knowledge, moral, metaphysical, or classical, yet he is intense in feeling, and has an intellect for ever on the alert. He is like one of those instruments on three legs, which, throw it how you will, always pitches on two, and has a spike sticking for ever up and ever ready for you. He 'sets' at a subject with a scent like a pointer.... As a poet, I think him full of the genuine feeling. His third canto in 'Rimini' is equal to anything in any language in that sweet sort.... As a man, I know none with such an affectionate heart, if never opposed in his opinions. He has defects, of course: one of his great defects is getting inferior people about him to listen, too fond of shining at any expense in society, and a love of approbation from the darling sex bordering on weakness." Now, Haydon and Hunt might swear to omit the topic of religion, but both were bursting to put their friends right about it. Haydon's stern vociferation proclaimed The Truth of the Bible, and it became necessary for men like John Scott to propose pre-Darwinian enigmas to him: "Did God make the world in the way and at the time said in Genesis?" Hunt was a Deist, in whom the orthodox eye readily detected an Atheist. Hence, Haydon presently served his Jehovah by warning the other friends of Hunt. To Wordsworth he sent word, on April 15th, 1817, that Hunt originally was "a delightful fellow, ardent in virtue, and perceiving the right thing in everything but religion," but now, how fallen, how changed! Hunt even objected to Haydon's including a hideous sneering Voltaire in the *Entry to Jerusalem*! "I never saw anything like the irritation of the Deists about this head," remarks Haydon.

Discussion, temporarily censored, became more and more painful and unavoidable. "It was singular," Haydon notes, "to watch the fiend that had seized Hunt's soul, trying with the most accomplished artifices to catch those of his friends. Often, when all discussion had ceased, and the wine had gone freely round—when long talk of poetry and painting had, as it were, opened our hearts—Hunt would suddenly (touching my arm with the most friendly pressure) show me a passage in the Bible and Testament, and say, as if appealing to my superiority of understanding, 'Haydon, do you believe this?' 'Yes,' I would instantly answer, with a look he will remember. He would then get up, close the book, and ejaculate, 'By heavens, is it possible!' This was another mode of appeal to my vanity. He would then look out of window with an affected indifference, as if he pitied my shallow mind; and, going jauntily to the piano, strike up, '*Cosi fan tutti*,' or '*Addio mi cuore*' with a 'Ring the bell for tea.'" These murmurs of storm in the Vale of Health loudened into clangour one day, when Shelley arrived for dinner, and broke into a tirade on worldly Christianity. All parties (including the ladies, Horace Smith and Keats) kept the matter waiting until the servant had gone—we should like the name of that awe-inspiring servant; but then the case of Shelley and Hunt *versus* Haydon was brought on with energy. "Haydon is fierce," said someone. He was; he had been asked to *think* about his Bible. That May he gave Keats his warning. With "*Trust in God*," he summed up his theological defence. "I love you like my own brother. Beware, for God's sake, of the delusions and sophistications that are ripping up the talents and morality of our friend! He will go out of the world the victim of his own weakness and the dupe of his own self-delusions, with the contempt of his enemies and the sorrow of his friends, and the cause he undertook to support injured by his own neglect of character."

There was one little listener who knew which side he was on. "Perhaps the first subject on which I can remember," says Thornton Hunt, "to have had a distinctive opinion was religion. I was in the habit of hearing the subject discussed by many who visited my father's house—Shelley, Jefferson Hogg, Keats, Charles Brown, not forgetting my father himself; and when quite a child I used to answer questions on the point by saying, 'We are Deists.' I had conversations innumerable with 'serious' people who tried to convert me, and used very bad arguments, which I answered as Prometheus Unbound would —that if God was the avenger they represented, I did not venerate him." Haydon was indeed "up against it" on the Hampstead front.

Moreover, Keats was no very literal student of the Bible. When (in October) he returned to London, he found Haydon and Hunt living as "jealous neighbours," but did not trouble himself afresh over the heresies of Hunt. The following January he noted, "The quarrel with Hunt I understand thus far. Mrs H. was in the habit of borrowing silver of Haydon— the last time she did so, Haydon asked her to return it at a certain time—she did not—Haydon sent for it—Hunt went to expostulate on the indelicacy, &c.—they got to words and parted for ever. All I hope is at some time to bring them all together again." The next world was no longer the cause of troubles in this, and Keats grew more cheerful about Hunt. But now another cloud appeared. Keats was aware—through

Reynolds—that Hunt doubted the soundness of his new long poem, *Endymion*, and when he showed him the manuscript of the first Book, Hunt frankly said it was "unnatural, and made ten objections to it in the mere skimming over." Shelley too was suspected of being adverse. It is to the credit of these three men that, however *Endymion* might win or lose, they could be meeting in a poetical match on February 4th, 1818. The subject was. *The Nile*, congenial with that on which Shelley and H. Smith tried conclusions that winter—*Ozymandias*. It was the period when Egypt was even more in the fashion in London than during the raid on Tutankhamen. A wit in *The Morning Chronicle*, possibly Lamb, posing as "Priscilla Plainstitch," thus pictured the effect: "My eldest boy rides on a sphynx instead of a rocking-horse, and my youngest has a pap-boat in the shape of a crocodile. My husband has built a water-closet in the form of a pyramid, and has his shirts marked with a lotus. He talks in his sleep of Ibis, Apis, and *Sir* Apis, and God knows what other heathen names, who, he tells me, were more celebrated in Egypt than Lord Nelson or Sir Sydney Smith. My eldest girl's music-master is turned away, because he could not teach her to play on the sistrum, a thing like a horse-shoe." The same source which produced these nonsensical phenomena set Shelley, Keats and Hunt writing their "Nile" sonnets.

Hunt's is in versification the finest of these, and the largest and best proportioned in imagination. That it should be so, in view of his inferior endowment, is odd, but it was his luck. He never came nearer the shadowy infinitudes of Blake than in the solemn opening with its originalities of stress and movement:

> It flows through old hush'd Egypt and its sands
> Like some grave mighty thought threading a dream;
> And times and things, as in that vision, seem
> Keeping along it their eternal stands,—

Caves, pillars, pyramids, the shepherd bands
That roam'd through the young world, the glory extreme
Of high Sesostris, and that southern beam,
The laughing queen that caught the world's great hands.

The enigma of Africa, of time when it blends with eternity, as in our inherited feelings of Egypt or China; the desert, the architectural solitudes, the lords of the desert, the bright immediate portrait of Cleopatra merry in her majesty—these presences were in Hunt's reach, nor should it be forgotten when his range of spirit is being belittled by those whose Egyptian association is chiefly defined in cigarettes.

It is time to see what serene companionship had been shared by Hunt and Shelley during 1817, and by their families. At the opening of that period, Shelley was in the toils of the Chancery proceedings which deprived him of his children by Harriet. Such pleasure as he could feel under a burden like that came chiefly from Hunt's sympathy and many-sided sociability; the two reformists and their womenfolk forgot the outrages of fortune round "Hunt's music," at the play or opera. The two households joined forces. The scene was not always Hampstead; the banks of the Thames were frequented that year by these intellectual and domestic allies; Millfield Lane, or West Street, Marlow, resounded to the voices of the excellent heretics. Their friendship was of a constancy superior to all misadventures. At Hampstead one snowy night Hunt was making his way home from the opera when he heard "strange and alarming shrieks, mixed with the voice of a man," in the vicinity of his cottage. It was Shelley endeavouring to rescue a poor woman in fits from a lodging on the cold ground. Hunt's cottage was quickly made the further scene of this Samaritan exploit. On the other hand, at Marlow, Hunt was amusing himself among Shelley's books when he hit on one of the skeletons in his friend's literary cupboard—a most incredible novel, *Zastrozzi*. Shelley was seized with "horror and shame"; "He snatched it out of my hands," said Hunt to Browning; but friendship survived without a scratch. The two men survived also many discussions, including that settled by the doctor at Marlow—a sort of joint testimonial by Shelley and Hunt to suicide. The doctor placed his instruments on the table and remarked that he was quite willing to lend them at once for any practical experiment. Shelley's dark angel could be ominous even when the poet was delighting Thornton Hunt's young intelligence with sailing paper boats on the Vale of Health pond. "The wind carried some of them over, or swamped most of them before they had surmounted many billows; and Shelley then playfully said how much he should like it, if we could get into one of the boats and be shipwrecked—it was a death he should like better than any other." Thornton, that young intellectual, could encompass this proposal with metaphysical calm.

Letters exist to give an unfaded impression of the friendship during 1817. It appears that Hunt looked up to Shelley as a sure guide in the wilderness of this world, for the younger man reflects: "You write accounts of your good behaviour to me as if I were some antient and wrinkled, but rather good-natured grand-uncle. Now this is a new feeling for me. I have been accustomed to consider myself as the most imprudent and [un]accountable of mankind." Shelley regarded Hunt as the sure guide to a good piano, at all events, and Marianne as equally competent to scrape Apollo and Venus into a whiteness suitable to his library. Mary Shelley (Marina) was a little inclined to think Hunt "contrary," and Marianne uneconomical, but these were minor matters. "I have written to Hunt," she tells Shelley, then quartering at Hunt's new house in Lisson Grove; "but tell him, over and above, that our piano is in tune, and that I wish he would come down by Monday's coach to play me a few tunes. He will think I jest, but it would really give me the greatest pleasure. I would make love to him *pour passer le temps*, that he might not regret the company of his Marianne and Thornton." The other "piping babes" with Bessy Kent to look after them—John, Mary, and Swinburne—were at Marlow, adding to the bewilderment of the inhabitants who were unused to such Bohemian combines, and wagged their heads and tongues to the old tune of "Nice Goings On." At a later date, Shelley's house was restored to respectability and decency; his drawing-room was advanced to the status of a tap-room, and his library consecrated a chapel, in which his tenets might be quite inconceivable. And yet, according to a visitor in 1860, the truth about him duly outweighed the scandal in Marlow. "During Shelley's residence, he was ever seeking to aid and benefit others, mingling with the poor, giving kind words of consolation—prized by them as much as by the rich —aiding and cheering them, and being to all a friend and confidant, and is even now spoken of by those who knew him with respect and admiration, for he has left behind him, at Marlow, a heritage of kind words and kinder deeds that are not forgotten by those who know but little of his fame."

In whatever rumours there were of Shelley's "keeping a seraglio" at Marlow, Hunt as his dearest friend and closest companion was accused as well, and the circumstance in a manner pleased him; it was a form of martyrdom, necessary to his spiritual health. Undoubtedly Hunt would have gone to prison or the scaffold for Shelley's sake. A friendship more sensitive, more intrepid, has not existed. From the slightest details, to the most serious human problems—from the pleasure of dropping down on a wayside to eat a dry crust or two, to the principles of love, and faith, and life, and death—in giving and in receiving, in proposal and in counter-proposal, there was a radiant agreement. I shall transcribe some typical evidences of this—on Hunt's side, from his preface in 1832 to *The Masque of Anarchy*.

"Mankind, and their interests, were scarcely ever out of Shelley's thoughts. It was a moot point, when he entered your room, whether he would begin with some half-pleasant, half-pensive joke, or quote something Greek, or ask some question about public affairs. I remember his coming upon me when I had not seen him for a long time, and after grappling my hands with both his, in his usual fervent manner, sitting down and looking at me very earnestly, with a deep though not melancholy interest in his face. We were sitting in a cottage study, with our knees to the fire, to which we had been getting nearer and nearer in the comfort of finding ourselves together; the pleasure of seeing him was my only feeling at the moment; and the air of domesticity about us was so complete, that I thought he was going to speak of some family matter—either his or my own; when he asked me, at the close of an intensity of pause, what was 'the amount of the National Debt.'

"I used to rally him on the apparent inconsequentiality of his manner upon these occasions; and he was always ready to carry on the joke, because he said that my laughter did not hinder me from being in earnest. With deepest love and admiration was my laughter mixed, or I should not have ventured upon paying him the compliment of it.

"I have now before me his corrected proof of... 'A Proposal for Putting Reform to the vote through the Country.'... The title-page of the proof is scrawled over with sketches of trees and foliage, which was a habit of his in the intervals of thinking, whenever he had pen or pencil in hand. He would indulge in it while waiting for you at an inn, or in a doorway, scratching his elms and oak-trees on the walls. He did them very spiritedly, and with what the painters call a gusto, particularly in point of grace. If he had room, he would add a cottage and a piece of water, with a sailing boat mooring among the trees. This was his *beau idéal* of a life, the repose of which was to be earned by zeal for his species, and warranted by the common good. What else the image of a boat brings to the memory of those who have lost him, I will not say, especially as he is still with us in his writings. But it is worth observing how agreeably this habit of sketching trees and bowers evinced the gentleness of my friend's nature, the longing he had for rest, and the smallness of his personal desires. . . .

"It was finely said one day in my hearing by Mr Hazlitt, when asked why he could not temporize a little now and then, or make a compromise with an untruth, that it was 'not worth his while.' It was not worth Mr Shelley's while to be an aristocrat. His spirit was large enough to take ten aristocracies into the hollow of his hand, and look at them as I have seen him look at insects from a tree, certainly with no thought of superiority or the reverse, but with a curious interest.

"The quintessence of gentlemanly demeanour which was observable in Mr Shelley, in drawing-rooms, when he was not over-thoughtful, was nothing but an exquisite combination of sense, moral grace, and habitual sympathy. It was more dignified than what is called dignity in others, because it was the heart of the thing itself, or intrinsic worth, graced by the sincerest idealism. . . .

"If ever there was a man upon earth, of a more spiritual nature than ordinary, partaking of the errors and perturbations of his species, but seeing and working through them with a seraphical purpose of good, such an one was Percy Bysshe Shelley."

There remain a host of memorials of Shelley by Leigh Hunt

in this tone of high faith; we are not disappointed when we enquire for Shelley's answering faith in Hunt. It is extant in famous phrase in the *Letter to Maria Gisborne*, the dedication of *The Cenci*, and *Adonais*; we shall save ourselves much petty bewilderment among wool-gathering cynical commentators on the affairs of Hunt and Shelley by reading these testaments as Shelley wrote them. After over two years of absence, Shelley exhorts Mrs Gisborne:

> You will see Hunt—one of those happy souls
> Which are the salt of the earth, and without whom
> This world would smell like what it is—a tomb;
> Who is, what others seem; his room no doubt
> Is still adorned with many a cast from Shout,
> With graceful flowers tastefully placed about;
> And coronals of bay from ribbons hung,
> And brighter wreaths in neat disorder flung;
> The gifts of the most learned among some dozens
> Of female friends, sisters-in-law, and cousins.
> And there he is with his eternal puns,
> Which beat the dullest brain for smiles, like duns
> Thundering for money at a poet's door;
> Alas! it is no use to say, "I'm poor!"
> Or oft in graver mood, when he will look
> Things wiser than were ever read in book,
> Except in Shakespeare's wisest tenderness.

That is a private sketch of Hunt the signor of Hampstead; for Shelley's public portrait of him as a man of the time, we pass to the dedication of *The Cenci* published in 1820. "Had I known a person more highly endowed than yourself with all that it becomes a man to possess, I had solicited for this work the ornament of his name. One more gentle, honourable, innocent and brave; one of more exalted toleration for all who do and think evil, and yet himself more free from evil; one who knows better how to receive, and how to confer a benefit, though he must ever confer far more than he can receive; one of simpler, and, in the highest sense of the word, of purer life and manners I never knew: and I had already been fortunate in friendships when your name was added to the list. In that patient and irreconcilable enmity with domestic and political tyranny and imposture which the tenor of your life has illustrated, and which, had I health and talents, should illustrate mine, let us, comforting each other in our task, live and die."

The year 1817, from the enchantments of which these mutual gratitudes sprang, hastened away; the warm days of loitering by "Cleveland's proud alcove, the bower of wanton Shrewsbury and love," or round Medmenham Abbey with its even more wanton *numina*, or writing and fal-lalling in Shelley's garden on the mound with its prospect of cornfields and drifting flocks and advancing haymakers, sank into twilight; and Platonic dialogues, water frolics, hospitalities and Mozartian selections were all interrupted. "I am strongly impelled to doubt," wrote Shelley to Godwin on December 1st, "whether Italy might not decide in my frame the contest between disease and youth in favour of life." The conjecture became a resolve, of which the execution was not long delayed; in February 1818 the worldly goods of Shelley were removed from Marlow, and he passed a few last weeks in London with Hunt as his frequent companion at dinner, or the play, or music and discourse. On March 10th, 1818, Shelley's last day in England, Leigh and Marianne Hunt were with him and Mary, the women no doubt solving the impossibilities of packing, the men blending all the colours of their sympathies into an evening rainbow; Mary Lamb came in, and the packing continued under more powerful direction than ever; at last Shelley fell asleep, and the Hunts found their hats and departed without waking him. Shelley and his wife were on the Dover road early next day, and as one link with their friends they read on their travels southward Hunt's newly published poems, *Foliage*; reporting on it a few days later, "When shall I see you again? Oh, that it might be in Italy!" The wish was to be granted; the Spirit of Irony had made a note of it.

X

Music and Discord

W E now leave for a time the remembrance of Shelley's nimbus for a region of chaotic howls and sulphurous flames. Leigh Hunt, though still a young man, had been vilified by many persons and journals, principally on account of his dramatic and political criticism. In 1817, his ambitious activities were no longer chiefly dramatic or political, but poetical; he had brought out several volumes of verse, culminating in *Rimini*; and he made no secret of assembling round him and his doctrines young men of accordant views in life, literature, above all, verse. Of these, Keats had the most obvious likeness to Hunt in the background, figures, and manner of his poetry, published in 1817; and observers who resented Hunt's principles and personality feared, or affected to fear, that he would be the ruin of taste and order, unless he was stopped. Even Byron showed signs of becoming corrupted! The clans gathered to repel the Italian invasion. Up in classic Edinburgh John Gibson Lockhart, aged twenty-three, prepared to exterminate the wickedness and vice spreading from Hampstead, his gunpit being the new Tory *Blackwood's Magazine*; which began to fulminate against "The Cockney School of Poetry" in October 1817.

Considered as Billingsgate, with a mixture of Sir Oran Haut Ton, these essays are the most remarkable ever written. No display of ferocity, superiority, and the metaphors of abuse could excel them. The genius of hate armed their author, who signed himself Z., with every kind of insult, and empowered him to pick out from Hunt's affable writings those personal glimpses which a little distortion, a falsification of colour, and disconnected exhibition would transform into a portrait of silliness and immorality. Z. was a liar to whom Munchausen would have yielded the crown, and mingled truth with his lying so vividly that bystanders could hardly do other than believe him to speak of intimate realities. Z. further knew where the wedge could be driven between Hunt and his associates. Let us call up Z. to run over specimens of his declamation.

He begins with his ungodly baptismal parody: "This school [of poetry] has not, I believe, as yet received any name; but if I may be permitted to have the honour of christening it, it may henceforth be referred to by the designation of THE COCKNEY SCHOOL." He affects to reprove the *Quarterly Review* for a "very illiberal attack on Rimini," and then shows how it should have treated that work: "One feels the same disgust at the idea of opening Rimini, that impresses itself on the mind of a man of fashion, when he is invited to enter, for a second time, the gilded drawing-room of a little mincing boarding-school mistress, who would fain have an *At Home* in her house. . . . The extreme moral depravity of the Cockney School is another thing which is for ever thrusting itself upon the public attention, and convincing every man of sense who looks into their productions, that they who sport with such sentiments can never be great poets. How could any man of high original genius ever stoop publicly, at the present day, to dip his fingers in the least of those glittering and rancid obscenities which float on the surface of Mr Hunt's Hippocrene? His poetry resembles that of a man who has kept company with kept-mistresses. His muse talks indelicately like a tea-sipping milliner girl. Some excuse for her there might have been, had she been hurried away by imagination or passion; but with her, indecency seems a disease, she appears to speak unclean things from perfect inanition." And this is the second version of the review, for Mr Blackwood "thought proper to soften some expressions" of its first state, among which occurred the least favourable criticism yet passed on a poetry-book: "The very Concubine of so impure a wretch as Leigh Hunt would be to be pitied, but alas! for the Wife of such a Husband! For him there is no charm in simple Seduction; and he gloats over it only when accompanied with Adultery and Incest." There were milder touches. "He would fain be always tripping and waltzing, and is sorry that he cannot be allowed to walk about in the morning with yellow breeches and flesh-coloured silk-stockings. He sticks an artificial rosebud into his button hole in the middle of winter. He wears no neckcloth, and cuts his hair in imitation of the Prints of Petrarch."

The melancholy Z., having done his best to make the public stand clear of Hunt's writings, then turned his talent to the work of sapping at Hunt's most influential literary acquaintances. "The Founder of the Cockney School would fain claim poetical kindred with Lord Byron and Thomas Moore. Such a connexion would be as unsuitable for them as for William Wordsworth. The days of Mr Moore's follies are long since over; and, as he is a thorough gentleman, he must necessarily entertain the greatest contempt for such an underbred person as Mr Leigh Hunt. But Lord Byron! How must the haughty spirit of Lara and Harold contemn the subaltern sneaking of our modern tuft-hunter. The insult which he offered to Lord Byron in the dedication of Rimini,—in which he, a paltry cockney newspaper scribbler, had the assurance to address one of the most nobly-born of English Patricians, and one of the first geniuses whom the world ever produced, as 'My dear Byron,' although it may have been forgotten and despised by the illustrious person whom it most nearly concerned,—excited a feeling of utter loathing and disgust in the public mind, which will always be remembered whenever the name of Leigh Hunt is mentioned." From this contrived appeal and warning to those two servants of reputation, Moore and Byron, the worst damage to Hunt was presently to come.

John Hunt at once demanded that Z. should send his name to the *Examiner* office. Z. preferred to remain *incog.*[1], and in November his second "Cockney School" diversion appeared, in which the lecture to Byron on his touching the unclean thing was continued—*Rimini* and *Parisina* were brought into one view, "the difference between the incest of Leigh Hunt and the incest of Byron" certified. Beneath the compliments to Byron lay the threat and the stiletto. He should read his fate in this language of flowers: Z. may be compelled to expose even Byron as a Cockney, unless there is a distinct arrangement. But Z. knew better than to expose his own name and address, and at length, in January 1818, he published a Letter to Leigh Hunt, affecting to be the resigned victim of Hunt's defamatory assault, an idealist innocently bewildered at the misunderstanding of his own purely literary observations: "a lover of virtue has poured out his bitter indignation against the husband and the father who had dared to be the apologist of adultery and incest"—what of it? Must he sign for it? Z. catalogued his charges against Hunt, and persisted, "I mean to handle each of these topics in its turn, and now and then to relieve my main attack upon you, by a diversion against some of your younger and less important auxiliaries, the Keateses, the Shellys, and the Webbes." Cornelius Webbe had been seen at the Vale of Health. John and Leigh Hunt decided not to waste the very

---

[1] Z. even sent Hunt a letter, signed "John Graham Dalyell," pretending to be a confession of authorship. Hunt wrote in reply. Sir J. G. Dalyell "was perhaps of all men then in Edinburgh the one who, as a good Whig, regarded *Blackwood's Magazine* with most intolerance." He went to a friend, with Hunt's letter, in violent agitation, exclaiming "Oh, the villainy of these fellows!"

limited funds of *The Examiner* in prosecuting *Blackwood's* for libel, and the "hooded terror" continued his monkey-tricks, arranging for August 1818 a special orgy on the subject of Keats and Hazlitt; "And so, like many other romances, terminates the 'Poetic Romance' of Johnny Keats, in a patched-up wedding." Keats was not deeply troubled; "pimpled Hazlitt" put a stop to the most ugly misuse of his name and personality by preparing an action at law, from which Blackwood saved himself by paying damages and expenses. The guying of Hunt, Keats, Haydon and the others went jovially on, year after year. In London, Gifford and his *Quarterly* carried out a similar, though less malodorous, campaign.

But these dandified desperadoes North and South did not escape a swift punishment. Hunt, except in defence of Keats and Shelley, refrained from retaliation: Z.'s failure to answer *The Examiner's* challenge by coming into the open had indeed been the failure of his whole filibustering. *The Pamphleteer* and *Critic* had already replied for Hunt to the tirades about perversion and illiteracy. The final reply was made by John Scott in the *London Magazine* of 1820 and 1821, and it was the verdict of intellect, justice and culture contemplating knavery and pretence. He found a good title for *Blackwood's*—the Reekie Magazine: "*Reekie* is an expressive Scotch word for SMOKED. It also means the capital of Scotland." Next month he found a better, the Mohock Magazine. He obtained accurate information on the secret history of the Mohocks, and convicted them not merely of personal slanders but of literary forgeries too. The game was up. Scott went further; and out of buffoonery's antics, as not infrequently happens, the sudden form of tragedy emerged. Incensed by some public expressions by Lockhart's friend Christie, arising from the quarrel about Keats, Scott challenged him, and in the duel was fatally wounded. Z. survived.

Undeterred by the opening of this long course of calumnia-

tion, Hunt continued his series of poetry-books for the pocket
with *Foliage*, 1818. It was originally planned that the contents
should form two separate publications, one of Hunt's own
poems, and one of translated pieces. Hunt's quick-handed fancy
hit on the happy idea of entitling the first part "Greenwoods"
and the second "Evergreens"; his gratitude inspired a dedication to Sir John Swinburne, "you who visit the sick and the
prisoner"; his garrulous bookmanship hurried in with a "Preface including Cursory Observations on Poetry and Cheerfulness." In that paper he did not eulogise his young friends, but
he declared his feelings about the older poets, and now at
length his instinct for the essence of poetry was deflecting him
from Wordsworth to Coleridge. He spoke of Wordsworth as
"the most prominent ornament" of the new school, of Coleridge as "the inner priest of the temple—a man who has been
the real oracle of the time in more than one respect." He added,
what most of us could add now, "Between these two for
natural powers, and superior to both in what renders wisdom
amiable and useful, which is social sentiment, I should place
Charles Lamb...." Of his own book he wrote: "I do not
write for the sake of a moral only, nor even for that purpose
principally:—I write to enjoy myself; but I have learnt in the
course of it to write for others also; and my poetical tendencies
luckily fall in with my moral theories. The main features of the
book are a love of sociality, of the country, and of the fine
imagination of the Greeks."

The first poem in *Foliage* was Hunt's parallel to Keats's
Endymion, composed at the same period, largely under the
same conditions of literary, artistic, and scenic experience, and
in honour of the same antique creation of immortal shapes and
mysteries. It was called *The Nymphs*, and is a frieze of graceful
imagery and "fair attitude," finer than any of Hunt's previous
poetry, and though free and easy in form yet sustained by a

strong philosophical design. Coleridge had struck the note for both Keats and Hunt in his sublime interpolation to *Wallenstein*, defending the imaginative worship of

> The intelligible forms of ancient poets,
> The fair humanities of old religion,
> The Power, the Beauty, and the Majesty
> That had their haunts in dale, or piny mountain,
> Or forest by slow stream, or pebbly spring,
> Or chasms and wat'ry depths.

Hunt elaborated this in a setting as sunny and leafy with his pleasures of life as he could create, and of course under the limitations of his experience and temper. He gave his local habitation to Dryads, Hamadryads, Napeads, Limniads, Oreads, Ephydriads, Naiads, Nereids, and last and most luxuriously to the Nepheliads. These beings were his addition to the classical mythology: "This poet was the first," says Bessy Kent in her prim way, "and has hitherto been the only mortal, who has been honoured with the sight of the Nepheliads in person." In this personifying vision of clouds, Hunt was verging on the realms of Shelley's genius, and the musical flow of his poem had a Shelleian newness (without that other's rapidity). In other points of feeling and allusion, *The Nymphs* shows a kinship with Keats at that time, not due to one's imitating the other, but to conversation and independent curiosity in the same fields of romance.

> *Hunt.*   And these are the kind terrors, that with sounds
>   Of groans about the air, or earthly quaking,
>   Or great gigantic shadows, that stand making
>   Gestures upon the fog, warn the low grounds
>   Against the dreadful snow-rocks . . . .
> *Keats.* Strange ministrant of undescribed sounds,
>   That come a swooning over hollow grounds,
>   And wither drearily on barren moors . . . .

Hunt. Now you might see
    One with grave settled look, as with sweet vaunt,
    Riding in front with an upgathered knee,
    Like the dusk Indian with his elephant . . . .
Keats. The cloudy rack slow journeying in the west,
    Like herded elephants . . . .

Shelley's opinion of Hunt's *Nymphs* is just: "What a delightful
poem 'The Nymphs' is—especially the second part! It is truly
poetical, in the intense and emphatic sense of the word. If six
hundred miles were not between us, I should say what pity
that *glib* was not omitted, and that the poem is not as faultless
as it is beautiful." *Glib* was a typical instance of Hunt's in-
felicities of touch. In "the rounder murmur, glib and flush,"
it might pass as brook-like, but Hunt quickly attempts "glib
flakes" of water, and then "glib sea flowers." And yet his error
of style is not glibness, but haste, rambling and restlessness.

The miscellaneous part of *Foliage* was largely a tribute to
love and friendship. There were such family pieces as a birthday address to Marianne, describing the autumn on the river
Avon by which she first saw the light; the well-known lyric of
fatherly solicitude during the illness of Thornton; a piece of
sing-song for "little ranting Johnny," which the parodists
promptly traduced with suggestions of Johnny's depravity and
its consequences. The Epistle to Byron reappeared, in case the
Northern and the *Quarterly* wits should care to refer to it again.
Tom Moore received two Epistles, which he may not have liked
overmuch, seeing that he had recently reproved Hunt for being
too expressive on religion and morality. Lamb, Hazlitt, Shelley,
Keats, Horace Smith, Haydon—the list of Hunt's admirations
included these and several more. Music was heard in the
allusions to Novello and his visitors, and in a sprightly appreciation of a musical box, the pleasantness of which nobody could

deny who has heard one of them as they were made at that period. "Epithet-exhausting toy," said Hunt at length, showing that he had caught Lamb's way of describing things. His reflective and interpretative nature shone well in the group of translations from Greek and Latin poets. Even the strengths and bold outlines of the *Iliad* were rendered without the intrusion of "glib eyes," and "busts and flowers," in good scriptural English. As a translator adept in all the kinds of poetry, Leigh Hunt is our master; he has not left an English Dante like Cary, or a Virgil like Dryden, but the anthology of European lyrics in our tongue which should be published from his poetical works is unrivalled for spirit, for that actual originality which springs from true devotion, for bringing the foreign beauty home to us without spoiling its native difference.

Hunt was now a healthier man than he had been for years, and his letters to Shelley in Italy during 1818 and 1819 give forth a zest and jollity, the air of self-portraiture without fear and without pomp. A biographer, toiling back through the shadow of a century in search of a Boswellian distinctness somewhere, feels that he has got upon good ground when he meets with such rare results of candid affection, lively hope, and the survival of documents. It is now only needful to choose our statements from Hunt's reports and the other remnants of the correspondence. In April 1818 Hunt asks for impressions of Venice, "as I am writing a comedy, mixed with quieter matter, the scene of which is laid there. I am in the second act, and am introducing the most beautiful of the Venetian airs." These were the more pleasing to Hunt because Hazlitt was pleased with them. Hunt goes on to say, "We go to plays, to operas, and even to concerts, not forgetting a sort of conversazione at Lamb's, with whom, and Alsager, I have renewed the intercourse, with infinite delight, which sickness interrupted. One of the best consequences of this is that Lamb's writings are being collected for publication by Ollier, and are now, indeed, going through the press. So we still have proof-sheets fluttering about us. As to myself in particular, I walk out quite a buck again, with my blue frock coat and new hat, waving my (orange) lily hands." It reminds us of *Blackwood's* against our will, and the no neckcloth, yellow breeches, flesh-tinted stockings, and artificial rosebud. In August, Marianne announces a change of address to 8, York Buildings, and a portrait of her husband by Wildman, Thornton's drawing master—"one of the most astonishing likenesses that ever was seen; you would almost think that it was going to speak to you; and the execution, as a drawing, equals the likeness." Hunt impulsively adds that he is sending Shelley a copy from this drawing in chalk: "Can you manage to carry the head about with you, like the pot of Basil in Boccaccio?" Hunt's love for tales of romance and chivalry appears in other recommendations of Boccaccio, and in the mention of his literary projects: "I have not gone on with my Coventry story yet, though I most assuredly mean to do so; but it must wait for this drama of mine: and this drama, you must know, in a great Shelleian fit, I have turned from a comedy to a tragedy, or rather serious play, and made the famous Cid the subject of it, moved thereto, not by any sympathies or emulations with Master Corneille, but by an account of his Spanish original, Don Evillen de Castro, in Lord Holland's Lives of him and Lopé." This play, one of Hunt's numerous dramatic hopes, was never acted, nor published as a volume.

"I have been writing a *Pocket-Book*," Hunt announced in November 1818; "the booksellers tell me it will do exceedingly well; and Shelley will be at once pleased and surprised to hear that it is my own property." This characteristic little invention was the now unprocurable *Literary Pocket-Book*, from the surviving sets of which it is to be wished that a facsimile might be published. It was at once practical and vacational, supplying the names and addresses of contemporary European authors, artists, and musicians, of medical lecturers, actors, print-sellers, booksellers, teachers of languages; various annotated calendars and rolls of honour; lists of libraries and reading-rooms, institutions, private art collections; original and selected verse and prose recreations. There were five issues[1], for the years 1819 to 1823. The price was half-a-crown, the binding usually Spanish morocco. A great part of the original writing was reprinted by the contributors elsewhere—in *The Examiner* or in separate volumes; hence came Hunt's short and sweet pageant of *The Months*, published by Ollier in 1821, while Shelley, Keats, and their elegant but watery imitator B. W. Procter either took their verses again or found editors who did so. It must be concluded that this little Pocket-Book, for all Hunt's protests, "Oh Diva Pecunia," "Let my Morocco blushes speak for me," for all Keats's harsh comments on "the most sickening stuff you can imagine," was a respectable worker in the cause of making the quality of Shelley and Keats known. In *The Months*, which was only one of its various series of diversions, and was received with liking and asked for with eagerness, Hunt quotes Shelley's *Skylark* as "what Shakespeare might have said to the lark," Wordsworth's *Cuckoo* as a song as genuine as any by the ancient Greeks, Keats's *Grasshopper* and *Autumn*, Lamb's *Woodvil*, and other beautiful and now familiar passages. It could be dreamed that there was a new England in which Leigh Hunt might for ever be employed in

---

[1] *The Literary Pocket-Book* was revived in 1827, but I have seen no copy, nor anything to show whether Leigh Hunt was concerned in it at that date.

making Literary Pocket-Books for use, delight, and ornament, so that no frightful knocks on the door and final demand-notes might break upon his flowery and serene work of national importance. Such knocks, however, disturbed him as the world was constituted in 1819, and the terms of his announcement to Shelley had to be modified. In July 1819 Ollier, who was no man of business, offered to buy the copyright for £200, and to continue minor payments to Hunt as editor and as contributor. This liberal arrangement was accepted.

"I am now," writes Hunt after the news of the Pocket-Book, "resuming my drama; and am going to propose to Constable, that when I have done it I will undertake specimens of the Italian poets from Dante to Metastasio." Something like that scheme matured almost thirty years later; again, one fancies a state of human economy wherein Hunt might have completed his design in peace according to his talents. But not only the treadmill of profit and loss damaged his fair intents; the thought of Italy, and Shelley in Italy, inviting him with his own magical intensity, made him close his desk and pace his room, under the cool stare of Raphael and Alfred done in plaster; the Italian message seemed clearer still as he turned from his Milton's minor poems to the countenance of Milton who had seen and embraced that warm South. But the lure seemed only more difficult, too; for now that John Hunt had gone into Somerset-shire in order to give his sons a better start in life, immediate *Examiner* business required Leigh to be attending at his office more and more. In these circumstances, Hunt felt the desire at least to have Shelley's friends about him. "Hogg and Peacock," he reports in March 1819, "generally live here over Sunday, when the former is not on the circuit; and we pass very pleasant afternoons, talking of mythology, and the Greeks, and our old friends. Hogg, I think, has a good heart as well as wit. You have heard, of course, of Peacock's appointment in the India House; we joke him upon his new oriental grandeur, his Brahminical learning, and his inevitable tendencies to be one of the corrupt, upon which he seems to apprehend Shelleian objurgation. It is an honour to him that 'prosperity' sits on him well." Hunt was not in prospect of aspiring to that sort of honour, for when he writes in July 1819, it is to record the misadventures of his play. "I can do nothing with my tragedy. ... Kean returned me a very polite answer, in which he said that his hands were full. I then sent it to Covent Garden. ... I had the honour to be rejected." At the same time Hunt mentions the publication of still another poetry-book by himself, containing his unequally written narratives *Hero and Leander* and *Bacchus and Ariadne*. This letter also yields some of Hunt's noblest thoughts: "I do not know that a soul is born with us; but we seem, to me, to *attain* to a soul, some later, some earlier; and when we have got that, there is a look in our eye, a sympathy in our cheerfulness, and a yearning and grave beauty in our thoughtfulness that seems to say, 'Our mortal dress may fall off when it will; our trunk and our leaves may go; we have shot up our blossom into an immortal air.'" And again, on the subject of Shelley's new poems: "You will see in the *Examiner* what I have said about your lovely poem of *Rosalind and Helen*, which is a great favourite of mine. I was rejoiced to find also that Charles Lamb was full of it. Your reputation is certainly rising greatly in your native country, in spite of its honest Promethean chains; and I have no doubt it will be universally recognized on its proper eminence. I long, by-the-by, to see Prometheus himself. I have no doubt you have handled his 'wearied virtue' nobly. It is curious, but I had thought a little while ago of writing a poem myself, entitled *Prometheus Throned*; in which I intended to have

described him as having lately taken possession of Jupiter's seat.
But the subject, on every account, is in better hands. I am rather
the son of one of Atlas's daughters, than of Atlas himself."

Following Hunt's own account of his affairs in 1819, we
find him happy, and on the balance more than satisfied with his
friends and acquaintance: "Peacock has been reasoned by some
mathematician out of his love for the opera, and is to read
Greek, they say, instead, on Saturday nights—the Dithyrambic,
of course—to begin at seven precisely. What do you think of
this début of mine in scandal? But he glories in doing nothing
except upon theory. He falls in love, as it were, upon a gravi-
tating principle. His passion, literally as well as metaphorically,
is quite problematical. Let b be Miss Jenkins, &c. I see a good
deal of Lamb, Hazlitt, Coulson, the Novellos, &c., but as much
at their own houses as at mine, or rather more just now. We
give no dinners as we used." The autumn found him reading
Donne and commending him to Shelley as being "as free and
deep a speculator in morals as yourself." At the same time he
was preparing to issue his excellent little journal called *The
Indicator*, which first appeared on October 13th, 1819. "They
tell me I am at my best at this work, which succeeds beyond all
expectation."

The friendship with Shelley in this way, betokened by a
series of beautiful impulses and mementoes, easily triumphed
over distance, distraction, and the passage of time. That with
Keats, which had so early threatened to collapse, is next to be
considered, and the letters of Keats during 1818 and 1819 afford
the means. Their evidence is sometimes of no very genial kind.
"Hunt has damned Hampstead and masks and sonnets and
Italian tales." It was in an unhappy mood about Hunt that
Keats went on his Scotch adventure, and when he returned he
was at first little less derogatory. "Hunt keeps on in his old

way—I am completely tired of it all. He has lately publish'd a Pocket-Book called the literary Pocket-Book—full of the most sickening stuff you can imagine." This annoyance finds further voice in the same letter to George Keats at the end of 1818. "The Night we went to Novello's there was a complete set-to of Mozart and punning. I was so completely tired of it that if I were to follow my own inclinations I should never meet any one of that set again, not even Hunt who is certainly a pleasant fellow in the main when you are with him—but in reality he is vain, egotistical, and disgusting in matters of taste and in morals. He understands many a beautiful thing; but then, instead of giving other minds credit for the same degree of perception as he himself professes—he begins an explanation in such a curious manner that our taste and self-love is offended continually. Hunt does one harm by making fine things petty and beautiful things hateful. Through him I am indifferent to Mozart, I care not for white Busts—and many a glorious thing when associated with him becomes a nothing." At length Keats winds up a series of bad-tempered personalities, intended to please the conceited and irascible George, with that brilliant moment of characterisation which makes one feel what graphic novels he might have lived to write. "I shall insinuate some of these Creatures into a Comedy some day—and perhaps have Hunt among them.—Scene, a little Parlour—Enter Hunt—Gattie—Hazlitt—Mrs Novello—Ollier. *Gattie:*—Ha! Hunt, got into your new house? Ha! Mrs Novello: seen Alt[h]am and his wife? *Mrs N.* Yes (with a grin), it's Mr Hunt's isn't it? *Gattie:* Hunt's? no, ha! Mr Ollier, I congratulate you upon the highest compliment I ever heard paid to the Book. Mr Hazlitt, I hope you are well. *Hazlitt:*—Yes Sir, no Sir— *Mr Hunt* (at the Music) 'La Biondina' &c.—Hazlitt, did you ever hear this? 'La Biondina' &c. *Hazlitt:*—O no Sir—I never—

Ollier:—Do Hunt give it us over again—divine— *Gattie:* divino—Hunt, when does your Pocket-Book come out— *Hunt:*—'What is this absorbs me quite?' O we are spinning on a little, we shall floridize soon I hope. Such a thing was very much wanting—people think of nothing but money getting— now for me I am rather inclined to the liberal side of things. I am reckoned lax in my christian principles &c. &c. &c. &c."

Here we see in a sharp light the worse or weaker side of Hunt's personality, and the foppery that we regret in Hunt's writings is marked out in indelible black by an intense observer. The only objection to be made, since Hunt's natural predominance of fine qualities reasserted itself with Keats and must arise from his biography without rhetorical cultivation, is that Hunt was not given the chance to know what Keats was feeling towards him. Thirty years later, on the production of Lord Houghton's memoirs of Keats, the tattered "Libertas" seems to have had his first hint of that, to have been taken by surprise and not a little hurt, and then to have perceived that illness and inward grief had given fair criticism an edge of bitterness. During 1819 the bitterness went away. Keats was touched, if we read the matter right, by Hunt's money troubles and hard work; he became aware that all but the rarest friends have their uncongenial elements; he saw that Hunt was impressively loyal, without effort or claim. *The Examiner* remained Keats's newspaper, and when he had read his copies they crossed the Atlantic.

The Examiner may be invoked to fill in our sketch of Hunt in 1819: "On Tuesday last (September 28th) Mrs Leigh Hunt of her sixth child—a boy." He was named Swinburne, after Hunt's benefactor, and that is almost all that we know of him.

We may conclude this part of the story with some miscellaneous effects, illustrating the extremes of feeling through which Hunt's personality was viewed. Here is Cowden Clarke: "I had hoped, my dear friend, to have paid you my congratulations in person today upon the appearance of your 'Foliage.' I am indeed delighted with it; and so I am with every thing which may be the means of increasing your present popularity and future renown. The preface is to my taste a piece of perfection for simplicity and elegance. And the pieces which most please me after the Nymphs"—one may omit a passage of eulogy—"But I will notice no more—suffice it to say, that I have scored every page. You may suppose how delighted and gratified I was to meet with the sonnet to Keats in which my obscure self was noticed. Who will the commentators of 2818 decide C. C. C. to have been?" Here is Crabb Robinson, at Lamb's in April 1818: "There was a large party,—the greater part of those who are usually there, but also Leigh Hunt and his wife. He has improved in manliness and healthfulness since I saw him last, some years ago. There was a glee about him which evinced high spirits, if not perfect health, and I envied his vivacity. He imitated Hazlitt capitally: Wordsworth not so well. Talfourd was there. He does not appreciate Wordsworth's fine lines on 'Scorners.' Hunt did not sympathize with Talfourd, but opposed him playfully, and that I liked him for." In Hazlitt's imperishable chronicle of the debate, at Lamb's, "Of Persons one would wish to have Seen," Hunt is envisaged in this mood, no haze of pretence but the genuine tenacity of colloquy; he "turns an eye on Lamb like a wild Indian, but cordial and full of smothered glee," when Lamb prepares to elect Guy Fawkes and Judas. In 1819 Hunt receives Shelley's splendid mark of esteem at the forefront of *The Cenci*. In 1819 he also receives among other slings and arrows an angry pamphlet: "A Theatrical Critique, and an essay (being no. 999 of the Pretender) on sonnet-writing, and sonnet-writers in general, including a sonnet on Myself; attributed to the editor of the *Ex-m-n-r*. Preceded by proofs of their authenticity, founded upon the authority of internal evidence." And *Blackwood's* duly mingled groans and horseplay with the woodnotes of *Foliage* and *The Literary Pocket-Book*, and the compliments and musical parties and bookbinder's bills that these works called forth.

XI

The Friend of Keats

UNDER the influence of time and change, the proprietors of *The Examiner* had begun to find some natural divergence of talents and concerns, which both expressed not by division in their old and beloved journal but by excursions from it. John Hunt gave Hazlitt's political force and his own indomitable but undramatic liberalism a new medium of appeal in the *Yellow Dwarf*, a small weekly journal begun and ended in 1818. Leigh adapted his various and cheerful reading, his poetical principles, his faith in a better world through better literature for the common reader, to his *Indicator*. It was the literary supplement to his Sunday newspaper, and perhaps the originator of this now indispensable type of periodical. It began on October 13th, 1819, and ended on March 21st, 1821, amounting to a volume of about six hundred pages, and good pages. At the outset the demand for *The Indicator* was vigorous. The first number went into four editions, if not more; and of the next dozen, reprints were instantly called for. One supposes that so very pretty an imitation of success must have revived the editor's occasional thoughts of paying his debts, and for the time supported his home in comfort; from surviving accounts, it appears that his half-share in the profits of *The Examiner* also during 1820 came to £443. 1s. 2¾d. Yet, as the price of *The Indicator* was two-pence, it may not have produced a large addition to his income.

The Indicator's dominant position in the history of Leigh Hunt was instantly realised and comprehensively defined by Lamb in a sonnet which the recipient delighted to repeat and laboured to justify.

> Your easy Essays indicate a flow,
> Dear Friend, of brain, which we may elsewhere seek;

And to their pages I, and hundreds, owe,
That Wednesday is the sweetest of the week.
Such observation, wit, and sense, are shewn,
We think the days of Bickerstaff returned;
And that a portion of that oil you own
In his undying midnight lamp which burned.
I would not lightly bruise old Priscian's head,
Or wrong the rules of grammar understood;
But, with the leave of Priscian be it said,
The *Indicative* is your *Potential Mood.*
Wit, poet, prose-man, party-man, translator—
H—, your best title yet is INDICATOR.

Criticism could hardly improve on this exact and artful description of Hunt's reorganisation of his powers in prose. These had indeed done their work in the formation and continuance of *The Examiner*, but never had they seemed perfectly fluent and "easy," as now they began to be. It was as though Hunt recognised that his usefulness in verse, which was likewise indicative and preliminary, had been for that time completed, and now he could relax his aims, change his music and range other heaths. The resignation caused him some natural tears. Writing in 1828, he still suspects a dimness in the inward eye: "I reaped more honour than profit; and the Indicator (*I fear*) is the best of my works:—so hard is it for one who has grown up in the hope of being a poet, to confess that the best things he has done have been in prose. The popularity of that work, however, evinced by the use made of it in others, and, above all, the good opinion expressed of it by such men as Mr Lamb and Mr Hazlitt, have long served to reconcile me to this discovery."

Seeing that the chief life of Leigh Hunt is in the wealth of his friendships, and that he truly lived less upon even the fabulous sums alleged to have been lent him than on the quiet satisfaction expressed by his companions regarding his spirit and writings, we may without loss of emotional proportion repeat the names of *Indicator* essays honoured with illustrious praise. "Hazlitt's favourite paper (for they liked it enough to have favourite papers) was the one on *Sleep*; perhaps because there is a picture in it of a sleeping despot; though he repeated, with more enthusiasm than he was accustomed to do, the conclusion about the parent and the bride. Lamb preferred the paper on *Coaches and their Horses*, that on the *Deaths of Little Children*, and (I think) the one entitled *Thoughts and Guesses on Human Nature*. Shelley took to the story of the *Fair Revenge*; and the paper that was most liked by Keats, if I remember, was the one on a hot summer's day, entitled *A Now*. He was with me while I was writing and reading it to him, and contributed one or two of the passages." It would have pleased Hunt to see the pious particularity with which a former owner of the biographer's copy of *The Indicator* has written in these distinctions. Selectors of prose have agreed, and many reprints have made us familiar with those and other *Indicator* essays, as, the paper against "Angling," in which Hunt with one of his momentary flashes of indignant genius says of our beloved Walton, "He looks like a pike, dressed in broad cloth instead of butter"; the "Old Gentleman," and "Old Lady"; "Shaking Hands," with the allusion to Hazlitt's incompetence in that courtesy, and the plot to "meet his hand with a fish-slice"; the "Maidservant," beginning "Must be considered as young, or else she has married the butcher"; and several more examples of decent valour, courtesy, learning, wit and faith co-ordinated.

Among the contributors who assisted this slight but permanent work, Lamb, Shelley and Keats were the masters, and it was here that Keats as "Caviare" sent out *La Belle Dame sans Merci*. Shelley's *Love's Philosophy* filled in a blank corner, and was at once accompanied with a phrase of pictorial criticism such as characterises Hunt but not many others: "We may fancy Mercury playing, and Love singing." Lamb, ever finding time to do a kindness, and mask it with whimsicality, lightens the editor's burden of writing with his jokes and occasional pieces. The character of the work as a whole leaves the impression that Lamb's conversation had enlightened and emboldened Hunt both for manner and for matter; and, as the later numbers appear, Hunt's pleasure with all that Lamb was is marked by his numerous borrowings and recommendations of his friend. *The Indicator* was one of the various campaigns conducted by Hunt as critic for the wider glory and transmission of his great contemporaries, Shelley, Keats, Lamb, and Coleridge in his hours of poetry without snuffling. It also enabled him to cultivate the international conception of art and letters, to direct his readers to the romance and charm in the mind, mythology, and exotic perfume of Egypt or Japan equally with Athens, Rome and Covent Garden—partly, by retelling their human narratives; and partly by his spontaneous lyrical translations, which read as though there were no barriers between us all. It was Dryden's *Ovid*, perhaps, that had matured this quality in Hunt.

The death of Benjamin West in 1820 was an event which caused Hunt to pause gravely in his too busy life, and wonder whether his age had arrived. In two numbers of *The Indicator* he paced round the haunts of his childhood, "those long carpeted aisles of pictures" in West's house. "We have walked down them with him at night to his painting room, as he went in his white flannel gown with a lamp in his hand, which shot a lustrous twilight upon the pictured walls in passing: and every thing looked so quiet and graceful, that we should have thought it sacrilege to hear a sound beyond the light tread of his footsteps. But it was the statues that impressed us, still more than the pictures. It seemed as if Venus and Apollo waited our turning at the corners; and there they were,—always the same, placid and intuitive, more human and bodily than the paintings, yet too divine to be over-real." The sale of the artist's treasures seemed "a villainous necessity." "We entered the gallery, which we had entered hundreds of times in childhood, by the side of a mother, who used to speak of the great persons and transactions in the pictures on each side of her with a hushing reverence as if they were really present. But the pictures were not there—neither Cupid with his doves, nor Agrippina with the ashes of Germanicus, nor the Angel slaying the army of Sennacherib, nor Death on the Pale Horse, nor Jesus healing the Sick, nor the Deluge, nor Moses on the Mount, nor King Richard pardoning his brother John, nor the Installation of the old Knights of the Garter, nor Greek and Italian stories, nor the landscapes of Windsor Forest, nor Sir Philip Sidney, mortally wounded, giving up the water to the dying Soldier. They used to cover the wall; but now there were only a few engravings. The busts and statues also were gone. But there was the graceful little piece of garden as usual, with its grass plat and its clumps of lilac. They could not move the grass plat, even to sell it. Turning to the left, there was the privileged study, which we used to enter between the Venus de Medicis and the Apollo of the Vatican. They were gone, like their mythology. Beauty and intellect were no longer waiting on each side of the door."

By this sad-lighted reflection Hunt shows us how much of his courageous *Examiner* experience and customary rule and reference of life were due to his old kinsman's home, and he dwells on that obligation. "Into the parlour, which opens out of the hall and into the garden, we did not look. We scarcely know why; but we did not. In that parlour, we used to hear of our maternal ancestors, stout yet kind-hearted Englishmen, who set up their tents with Penn in the wilderness. And there we learnt to unite the love of freedom with that of the graces of life; for our host, though born a Quaker, and appointed a royal painter, and not so warm in his feelings as those about him, had all the natural amenity belonging to those graces, and never truly lost sight of that love of freedom. There we grew up acquainted with the divine humanities of Raphael. There we remember a large coloured print of the old lion-hunt of Rubens, in which the boldness of the action and the glow of the colouring overcome the horror of the struggle. And there, long before we knew anything of Ariosto, we were as familiar as young playmates with the beautiful Angelica and Medoro, who helped to fill our life with love."

Hunt now published, and dedicated to John Keats, his choice translation of Tasso's *Amyntas* into a mode of verse and diction learned from *The Faithful Shepherdess*, *Comus* and *Samson Agonistes*. He did not rank the Italian pastoral under his hand very near those English achievements. "It wants," he wrote in his preface, making me run the risk of quoting him too often, "the crust of the old barks, the heaps of leaves, the tangled richness of exuberance, the squirrels, glades and brooks, the ancient twilight, the reposing yet vital solitudes, the quaint and earthy population, the mid-way world between men and gods; the old overgrowth and beardiness of nature. . . ." The words have a sensuousness as though they arose from conversation with Keats, who during the summer of 1820 manifested his victorious acceptance of Leigh Hunt with all his faults, and all his female relations, by coming to them to be nursed at 13, Mortimer Terrace. To this we now proceed, merely noting that *Amyntas* was the last of the series of poetical pocket-books comprising Hunt's first real adventures in search of a laureateship—a set of volumes glimmering with a fine chance of perfection, ruined by the fluidity of his taste and an exaggerated consciousness of the technique of verse.

When Charles Brown left Wentworth Place, Hampstead, for a second tour in Scotland, his housemate Keats decided to seek refuge from his loneliness in the house of the Hunts, and there from May 1820 until the close of August he was either a guest or a frequent caller, entirely at liberty yet always able to command such vivacity, philosophy, and nursing as the Hunts had to offer. Deep-struck by love and consumption, he was nevertheless the Keats whose sturdy humour would not be outfaced by orders to march against a battery. He joined Hunt in his *Indicator* preparations, and lent him the manuscript of his "comic faery poem"; took part in social meetings, and though "under sentence of death" engaged punsters and raised laughs. The former satirist of Scott had now filled some shelves with Scott's works, before which Keats "spoke with admiring delight of Scott's creations, and touched especially on the character of Balfour of Burley and the scene in the cave." "Mr Hunt," he wrote to his sister about July 22nd, "does every thing in his power to make the time pass as agreeably with me as possible. I read the greatest part of the day, and generally take two half hour walks a day up and down the terrace which is very much pester'd with cries, ballad singers and street music." Hunt hardly discerned either the fury of Keats's illness or the exhausting revolutions of his mind over Fanny's meaning. Hunt knew that there was a secret: "Seeing him once change countenance in a manner more alarming than usual, as he stood silently eyeing the country out of the window, I pressed him to let me know how he felt, in order that he might enable me to do what I could for him; upon which he said, that his feelings were almost more than he could bear, and that he feared for his senses. I proposed that we should take a coach,

KEATS, BY MARIANNE HUNT

FROM A SILHOUETTE IN THE POSSESSION OF THE RT. HON. SIR WILLIAM BULL, BART.

and ride about the country together, to vary, if possible, the immediate impression, which was sometimes all that was formidable, and would come to nothing. He acquiesced, and was restored to himself." As they sat afterwards on the melancholy bench in Well Walk, Hampstead, fronting the formerly all-gracious heath, Hunt was astonished to see that Keats "suddenly turned upon me, his eyes swimming with tears, and told me he was dying of a broken heart." Hunt subsequently maintained without hesitation that Fanny returned his friend's love. As for the consumption, Hunt was not the man to believe in death before it came. In March 1821 he was writing of Keats in Italy, "I hope to the last, especially as I have seen remarkable recoveries in consumptive cases." The calm and brave renewal of affection between these two men was only interrupted, not injured, when one day in August 1820 a servant who was under notice played a trick, as she thought, on Mrs Hunt, and delayed the delivery of a letter from Fanny to Keats. It was not only delayed; it was found open in the hands of Thornton, who gave it to his mother with the explanation that he had done as the servant told him. Keats, already in agonies, mistook the matter, broke down, and despite Hunt's scarcely less pained appeals left the house. Almost immediately Keats "saw better," and the affair was over. "Hunt has behaved very kindly to me," says Keats about August 20th, and Hunt writes very kindly to "Giovanni Mio" almost at the same date, soon after which he is writing cheerfully to Shelley, "Keats, who is better, is sensible of your kindness, and has sent you a letter and a fine piece of poetry by the Gisbornes. He is advised to go to Rome, but will call on you in the spring."

Throughout this season, Keats was the object of discerning public praise, such as the splendid essay by John Scott in his *London Magazine*, and one by Lamb, but the fact did not make Hunt's repeated assertions of his genius less welcome or ultimately less beneficial, and two numbers of *The Indicator* that August were devoted to Hunt's early and late task of making England read Keats. "The author's versification is now perfected, the exuberances of his imagination restrained, and a calm power, the surest and loftiest of all power, takes the place of the impatient workings of the younger god within him." Too soon the poet, with this mountain-height of artistic tranquillity at his feet, had to bid farewell to the unavailing loyalty and foredoomed expectancy of his friends; the "Maria Crowther" dropped down the Thames with Keats aboard, "the rains began to fall heavily," and Hunt deserted an attempt to write a jocular *Indicator*, ending instead with a troubled farewell to the voyager. It does not appear that Keats in the short time he had to live wrote to Hunt again, nor is it surprising if he did not; the last expression of the friendship was made by Hunt in the well-known letter to Severn, and made (such is the way of life and death) when Keats was already dead and gone.

Vale of Health, Hampstead: March 8, 1821.

Dear Severn,—You have concluded, of course, that I have sent no letters to Rome, because I was aware of the effect they would have on Keats's mind; and this is the principal cause; for, besides what I have been told of his emotions about letters in Italy, I remember his telling me upon one occasion that, in his sick moments, he never wished to receive another letter, or even see another face, however friendly. But still I should have written to *you*, had I not been almost at death's door myself. You will imagine how ill I have been, when you hear that I have just begun writing again for the "Examiner" and "Indicator," after an interval of several months, during which my flesh wasted from me with sickness and melancholy. Judge how often I thought of Keats, and with what feelings. Mr Brown tells me he is comparatively calm now, or rather quite so. If he can bear to hear of us, pray tell him,—but he knows it already, and can put it into better language than any man. I hear that he does not like to be told that he may get better; nor is it to be wondered at, considering his firm persuasion that he shall not recover. He can only regard it as a puerile thing, and an insinuation that he cannot bear to think he shall die. But if his persuasion should happen to be no longer so strong upon him, or if he can now put up with such attempts to console him, tell him of what I have said a thousand times, and what I still (upon my honour, Severn) think always, that I have seen too many instances of recovery from apparently desperate cases of consumption not to be in hope to the very last. If he cannot bear this, tell him— tell that great poet and noble-hearted man—that we shall all bear his memory in the most precious part of our hearts, and that the world shall bow their heads to it, as our loves do. Or if this, again, will trouble his spirit, tell him that we shall never cease to remember and love him; and that the most sceptical of us has faith enough in the high things that nature puts into our heads to think all who are of one accord in mind or heart are journeying to one and the same place, and shall unite somewhere or other again, face to face, mutually conscious, mutually delighted. Tell him he is only before us on the road, as he was in everything else; or whether you tell him the latter or no, tell him the former, and add that we shall never forget that he was so, and that we are coming after him. The tears are again in my eyes, and I must not afford to shed them. The next letter I write shall be more to yourself and more refreshing to your spirits, which we are very sensible must have been greatly taxed. But whether our friend dies or not, it will not be among the least lofty of your recollections by-and-by that you helped to soothe the sick-bed of so fine a being. God bless you, dear Severn.

Your sincere Friend,
Leigh Hunt.

During this period Hunt's wit had been stimulated, and something of his first political strength and liveliness recalled,

by public affairs, and while Keats was with him the trial of
Queen Caroline particularly moved his disgust. He wrote a set
of ironical verses on the "evidence" against her which might
escape fame in those days of satirical abundance, but would now
be a welcome surprise: as,

> You swear—you swear—"Oh Signor, si"—
> That through a double floor, eh,
> You've seen her *think* adulterously?
> "Ver' true, Sir—Si, Signore."

There is nothing unintelligible to our day when Hunt reports
to Shelley, "You may look upon the British public, at present,
as constantly occupied in reading trials for adultery." From
this great vision of John Bull's innocent pastime, he turns to his
own minor concerns; he is going (August 1820) to read at the
British Museum, and to drink tea with the Gisbornes according
to Shelley's plan; has heard that Byron "came to town on
Saturday, with a packet for the Queen," and wonders if this
revenant will send for him; sings out his welcome to *Prometheus*,
"What noble things in it! What grand lines and affectionate
thoughts! But it is liable to some of the objections against the
Revolt of Islam." Shelley in his next letter justly speaks of
Hunt's "incredible exertions" in his journals, and those exertions duly take their toll. At the time when Keats was finally
sinking in Italy, his friend was struggling through a serious
illness at the Vale of Health; he "almost died over the later
numbers of the 'Indicator,'" which had to be given up. This illness is the background of Hunt's letter to Shelley of March 1st,
1821, in which the new conviction of John Hunt for political
libel is noticed, and his imprisonment foretold. It was not
Leigh Hunt's fault that he did not this time have the honour
of sharing his brother's sentence: "I had," he remarks, "for
some time withdrawn from the paper by his particular wish,

in order that Government might not be able to imprison both of us at once."

Probably these pages have failed to repeat as often as they ought to have done the name of William Hazlitt, a name that to Hunt was very little less agreeable and glorious than those of Shelley, Keats and Lamb. In 1821 Hazlitt must enter our gallery with his famous frown. The occasion was the publication of his *Table Talk*, in which he disported himself in his grim fashion with a veiled description of Hunt's Hampstead vanities, and took a tremendous swipe at "the author of the Prometheus Unbound." The results are given at full length by Mr Howe in his *Life of Hazlitt*. Hunt wrote instantly to the table-talker, on behalf of Shelley and of himself; to this strong counter-attack Hazlitt replied instantly and inimitably. "My dear Hunt, I have no quarrel with you, nor can I have. You are one of those people that I like, do what they will; there are others that I do not like, do what they may. . . . I was in a cursed ill humour with you for two or three things when I wrote the article you find fault with (I grant not without reason). If I complained to you, you would only have laughed; you would have played me the very same tricks the very next time; you would not have cared one farthing about annoying me; and yet you complain that I draw a logical conclusion from all this, and publish it to the world without your name." The candour of Hunt's answer is equal to Hazlitt's—"I have often said, I have a sort of irrepressible love for Hazlitt, on account of his sympathy for mankind, his unmercenary disinterestedness, and his suffering; and I should have a still greater and more personal affection for him if he would let one; but I declare to God I never seem to know whether he is pleased or displeased, cordial or uncordial—indeed, his manners are never cordial. . . ." This letter concluded with an earnest request to Hazlitt to publish something in

Shelley's favour as amends, which Hazlitt did incidentally (I think) in *The Examiner*; and in the meantime Shelley was given an account of the interlude and Hunt's last word on it—"If he attacks you again, I have told him in so many words that he must expect me to be his public antagonist."

The unbalanced hostility of Haydon, rashly brought to its fullness by Hunt's loquacious criticism of formal Christianity, had for some time past created a silence between the two. It was a silence fated to go on for twenty years, with only one or two moments of conciliatory promise. Some time in 1821, Haydon writes on the subject of distance and its hard sentence on "our readings, and quotings, and Shakespearings, Miltonings, and Spenserings and Ariostoings," and in his effusive way assures Hunt, "I look back on the two or three first years of our attachment like a thing that's never to be again—however I hope it will be again." In spite of this pensive impromptu, Haydon disappears from Hunt's path for years, and only now and then is heard behind the hedge, laughing like a satyr at the whims and oddities of his former friend.

Shelley and his wife never failed the Hunts, and this in spite of some actions and inactions on Hunt's part which might have been "by distance made less sweet." Such was the refusal of Hunt to publish *The Masque of Anarchy* in *The Examiner*, his judgment being "that the public at large had not become sufficiently discerning to do justice to the sincerity and kindheartedness of the spirit that walked in this flaming robe of verse." Another point of possible trouble is shown by Shelley's complaints, "*Why* don't you write to us?" or (to Ollier), "I hear nothing either from Hunt, or you, or any one." But there was a spirit of union between the Vale of Health and Pisa which was not to be mistaken, or worn out. *The Examiner* might fall off lamentably, as Hunt had to admit in 1821; John Hunt might be ill and in prison; little Mary Florimel and the other young children might have a terrifying visitation of measles and of fever; Hunt himself might feel that his best powers had been expended, and his brain resisted his will and his contracts; yet one certainty glowed in the meridian—Shelley. And Shelley was calling him to Italy. In August 1821 Hunt began to accept this call as destiny.

"My dearest Shelley . . . It was what I should have longed to do, and have often spoken of as a beautiful impossibility; but your friendship has put it in my power; and, mind, if I do not get rid of my deadly symptoms, if they come upon me again and threaten to do away the only use of my remaining, I shall come to you and your fine climate as 'my friend and my physician.'. . . But you talk of the *Examiner*. Alas! my dear friend, the whole difficulty lies there. It had got to so low a pitch, and my absence reduced it so much lower, that we feared for its very existence, and upon this depends not only my family, but my brother's. Judge what I felt, seeing him, too, at the same time suffering in his health from anxiety, and cast into a prison for his honest indignation. Judge, also, what I must feel on the other side, when my return, joined with the late interesting public circumstances, appears to have brought back some *hundreds* of our readers. . . . I need not say what I have suffered in money matters. Your kindness guesses it but too well. But I have lived with such economy, voluntary as well as involuntary, that as soon as I have paid off what I am every week paying off, I shall be much easier again, and my friends need be under no concern for any more extra embarrassment, *provided* we can keep up the paper. Now, at *present*, it seems necessary for that purpose that I should be on the spot. . . . There are subjects starting up every day, which the public are interested in seeing handled in a piquant manner; and though my brother would be the first to say to me 'Go,' if he thought it necessary for my health, I know he is extremely anxious that I should notice as many of these instantaneous matters as possible; and, remember, I should leave him in prison. He has been there now three months, and has got nine more. . . ." Hunt mentions the Sketches of the Living Poets which he is, somehow or other, striking off for *The Examiner*, and asks, "Will you oblige me by sending me a few dates and mechanical matters, such as birth, parentage, and education? *You* know how I can do justice to all the rest." But the series ended suddenly without Shelley. Hunt concludes, "I saw Horace Smith before he left us for Italy, but he slipped from me without letting me know when I could see him again, which he promised. Tell him, *in revenge*, that we caught the scarlet fever of him, and that, perhaps, we shall bring it him back again in Tuscany. All good things bless and preserve you."

At almost the same time Shelley was insisting on the migration. What he wrote is important, for Hunt regarded him as wise in both worlds, and in this crisis Shelley was definite and powerful, and supported by the magic name of Byron. "My dearest Friend, Since I last wrote to you I have been on a visit to Lord Byron at Ravenna. The result of this visit was a determination on his part to come and live at Pisa. . . . He proposes" (this should be noted by those who think Byron had no responsibility for Hunt in Italy) "that you should come and go shares with him and me in a periodical Work, to be conducted here, in which each of the contracting parties should publish all their original compositions, and share the profits. He proposed it to Moore, but for some reason or other it was never brought to bear. There can be no doubt that the profits of any scheme in which you and Lord Byron engage, must, from various, yet coöperating reasons, be very great. As to myself,

I am for the present only a sort of link between you and him until you can know each other, and effectuate the arrangements; since (to entrust you with a secret which for your sake I withhold from Lord Byron), nothing would induce me to share in the profits, and still less in the borrowed splendour of such a partnership. . . . I am, and I desire to be, nothing. I did not ask Lord Byron to assist me in sending a remittance for your journey; because there are men, however excellent, from whom one would never receive an obligation in the worldly sense of the word. And I am as jealous for my friend as myself. I, as you know, have not it; but I suppose that at last I shall make up an impudent face and ask Horace Smith to add to the many obligations he has conferred on me—I know I only need ask."

By September 21st, 1821, Hunt had summed up the problem, his health, the weather, the "cheapness of living and education at Pisa," Byron's proposal, John Hunt's approval, Shelley's affection, "Italy, Italy, Italy." He wrote, "We are coming." The only trouble projecting above the seas between seemed to be "the money, Shelley?" and he had a notion that by the help of John and the security of his friend he would raise enough to carry his little clan to Italy. Much had to be left behind, including a most promising attempt to throw open Novello's "cave of harmony" to the public by means of a volume, the collaboration of the tuneful man of letters and the versatile musician, called *Musical Evenings*. It remains in manuscript, with a hymn-tune or two that Hunt composed. But Shelley had the art of simplifying all the minutiae of action. His movement order ran, "Put your music and your books on board a vessel, and you will have no more trouble." Hunt arranged to leave England in September, but on October 6th Shelley was writing to him again with directions for the conveyance of family and furniture, and Hunt had time to act upon these. On November 15th Novello, Lamb and other friends came down the staircase of the brig *Jane* at Blackwall to cheer the travellers on. There seemed nothing now at hand to interrupt the adventure. The *Jane* was not large—120 tons her burden; all the Leigh Hunts were aboard, even the rascally young John. Equipment had been studied with great zeal; and a friend, probably the rural Cowden Clarke, anxious that the breakfast milk should not be missing on the way South, had embarked a goat. Next morning Hunt was awakened by the pulse of the brig as she made her way out of the river, and Shelley appeared the next prospect.

XII

Won and Lost

Bᴜᴛ Hunt was one of those erratic figures whose fate it is to be the only one on parade, or a day after the fair, or a millionaire in cancelled notes, or otherwise innocently nonplussed. Even the goat so strategically supplied proved a failure, for the storms through which the *Jane* was flung and beaten drove away her milk. Then there was the affair of the gunpowder. The *Jane* was ordinarily laden with sugar, but somehow Hunt observed that fifty barrels of another sort came aboard at the last moment without marked publicity—they were going to promote independence in Greece. In theory, Hellas and heroism were warmly welcome; but this literal form of revolutionary sentiment produced a colder sensation. Marianne especially thought it improper. The weather obliged the *Jane* to put in at Ramsgate, and wait—nearly three weeks. Here Hunt read Condorcet, and met Cowden Clarke and his parents. On December 11th, the ailing Marianne was carried back to the boat in a sedan, and the *Jane* proceeded with the expectation of good weather among a hundred other ships, "the white sails of which as they shifted and presented themselves in different quarters, made an agreeable spectacle, exhibiting a kind of noble minuet." The dance was transformed into something less graceful by the return of foul weather next day. "The pump was constantly going," and Captain Whitney, who powdered his hair to disguise the fact that it had turned grey in a shipwreck, let fall the consoling remark that they were "in the hands of God." The *Jane* was beaten up and down on the extremity of the Atlantic; on December 19th the captain tried to bring her into Falmouth, but could not; on the 22nd he succeeded in putting in at Dartmouth.

During this ordeal Hunt did what he could for his family, his theories, and the captain. It was indeed nerve-racking when the drunken cook with the goblin face was prowling round the gunpowder barrels towards his larder, a naked candle flaring in his hand; or when an Indiaman in the blackness and the great commotion suddenly bore down as though the *Jane* must be trampled under without hope. Hunt, deputising, lit and handed up the lanterns, and the Indiaman avoided a collision. Through these and other trying experiences, the romantic bookman enjoyed a dizzy glory, in which illness and imagination rode the tempest. "The white clothes that hung up on pegs in the cabin took, in the gloomy light from above, an aspect like things of meaning; and the wind and rain together, as they ran blind and howling along by the vessel's side, when I was on deck, appeared like frantic spirits of the air, chasing and shrieking after one another, and tearing each other by the hair of their heads. 'The grandeur of the glooms' on the Atlantic was majestic indeed: the healthiest eye would have seen them with awe. The sun rose in the morning, at once fiery and sicklied over; a livid gleam played on the water, like the reflection of lead; then the storms would recommence; and during partial clearings off, the clouds and fogs appeared standing in the sky, moulded into gigantic shapes, like antediluvian wonders, or visitants from the zodiac; mammoths, vaster than have yet been thought of; the first ungainly and stupendous ideas of bodies and legs, looking out upon an unfinished world."

So, at Christmas 1821, the Hunts were at Dartmouth, which gave Leigh as the lover of Chaucer a pleasant chance to think of the "Schipman," but otherwise was found rather depressed and depressing. The *Jane* was in no hurry. Hunt resolved, no matter how expensive the change was, to abandon the winter voyage, and to await the sweet season at Plymouth; yet he thought again, and would have sailed in February, had not Marianne been "obliged to lose forty-six ounces of blood in twenty-four hours, to prevent inflammatory fever on the lungs," and subsequently to remain in bed, still losing blood. The emigrants lodged in Stonehouse, and as the year 1822 advanced might console themselves for the temporary frustration of their Italian dreams in the deep green calm of wooded Mount Edgcumbe. Hunt was pleased to be able to give his friends the address: Mrs L'Amoureux, Devil's Point, Stonehouse. Moreover, *The Examiner* was read in Plymouth, and in those days of solid tastes and opinions it only needed a rumour that *The Examiner's* editor was in the town to bring a number of gentlemen with compliments and invitations to the door. They also brought a silver cup, inscribed to their hero. The best known of Hunt's Plymouth friends were Rogers, one of the many good provincial landscape-painters of the age of Crome, and Hine, the energetic schoolmaster who was the first man to make an edition of Wordsworth for schools.

The Italian manœuvre gave fresh opportunity to Mr Blackwood's young men, who now brought forth the neatest and most amusing of their anti-Cockney poems, with correct "local colour":

> Signor Le Hunto, gloria di Cocagna,
> Chi scrive il poema della Rimini,
> Che tutta apparenza ha, per Gemini,
> D' esser cantato sopra la montagna
> Di bel Ludgato, o nella campagna
> D' Amsted, o sulla margi Serpentini,
> Com' esta Don Giovanni d' Endymini,
> Il gran poeta d' Ipecacuanha!
> Tu sei il Re del Cocknio Parnasso,
> Ed egli il herede apponente,
> Tu sei un gran Giacaso ciertamente,

> Ed egli ciertamente gran Giacaso!
> Tu sei il Signor del Examinero;
> Ed egli soave Signor del Glystero.

But, like Hunt, we must keep our eyes on Shelley, to whom the news of the storms and the postponements were promptly sent. On January 25th, 1822, Shelley wrote, "I send you by return of post £150," hinting that this was not done without embarrassment. "Lord Byron has assigned you a portion of his palace, and Mary and I had occupied ourselves in furnishing it. . . . We had hired a woman cook of the country for you, who is still with us. Lord B. had kindly insisted upon paying the upholsterer's bill, with that sort of unsuspecting goodness which makes it infinitely difficult to ask him for more. . . . The evils of your remaining in England are inconceivably great if you ultimately determine upon Italy; and in the latter case, the best thing you can do is, without waiting for the spring, to set sail with the very first ship you can. . . . There is no serious danger in a cargo of gunpowder, hundreds of ships navigate these electrical seas with that freight without risk. . . . Pray tell me in answer to this letter, unless you answer it in person, what arrangement you have made about the receipt of a regular income from the profits of the *Examiner*. You ought not to leave England without having the assurance of an independence in this particular; as many difficulties have presented themselves to the plan imagined by Lord Byron, which I depend upon you for getting rid of." A further appeal from Hunt caused Shelley to approach Byron, and obtain from him a loan of £220: "I do not think poor Hunt's promise to pay you in a given time is worth very much; but mine is less subject to uncertainty, and I should be happy to be responsible for any engagement he may have proposed to you."

The doubt whether Byron was whole-hearted in his

"imagination" of a periodical publication was flung aside when Shelley wrote on March 2nd, "He expresses again the greatest eagerness to undertake it, and proceed with it, as well as the greatest confidence in you as his associate. He is for ever dilating upon his impatience of your delay, and his disappointment at your not having already arrived. He renews his expressions of disregard for the opinion of those who advised him against this alliance with you, and I imagine it will be no very difficult task to execute that which you have assigned me— to keep him in heart with the project until your arrival. . . . No feelings of my own shall injure or interfere with what is now nearest to them—your interest, and I will take care to preserve the little influence I may have over this Proteus in whom such strange extremes are reconciled, until we meet—which we now must, at all events, soon do." The wavering of Byron, of course, had been principally due to the excitable jealousy of Thomas Moore, but that is best displayed in its full agility later on under the criticism of Hazlitt. Shelley again wrote to Hunt, reporting Byron's reiterated desire to carry out the great plan, and explaining more freely his own sense of injury and dishonour at Byron's hands. While Shelley thus essayed to control, equip and energise the Hunt expedition, his wife allured as best she could the harassed Marianne southwards. "How I wish you were with us in our rambles. Our good cavaliers flock together, and as they do not like *fetching a walk with the absurd womankind*, Jane (*i.e.* Mrs Williams) and I are off together, and talk morality and pluck violets by the way. I look forward to many duets with this lady and Hunt. She has a very pretty voice, and a taste and ear for music which is almost miraculous. The harp is her favourite instrument; but we have none, and a very bad piano; however, as it is, we pass very pleasant evenings, though I can hardly bear to hear her sing

Donne l'amore; it transports me so entirely back to your little parlour at Hampstead—and I see the piano, the bookcase, the prints, the casts—and hear Mary's *far ha-ha-a*! ... Perhaps, as it was with me, Italy will not strike you as so divine at first; but each day it becomes dearer and more delightful; the sun, the flowers, the air, all is more sweet and more balmy than in the Ultima Thule that you inhabit."

Having spent some of his time in reviewing *Adonais*—"the most Delphic poetry I have seen a long while"—and interpreting Shelley in Plymouth—an art which might be harder nowadays—with gladness at the liberal intelligence found blooming there, Hunt shepherded his family into the *David Walter* on May 13th, 1822. The only alteration in the party was the inclusion of "a jolly Plymouth damsel" as maid, her predecessor having had enough marine romance on the way from London. The passage was favoured with fine winds and sea-scenery, and Hunt had plenty of inspiration for filling his prose sketch-book, and time for discovering the full tones of his beloved poets, particularly Spenser. Probably he was never happier, or more completely beyond the "rigid griffs" of society. This may be seen in the proud dramatic turn of his annotations: "The first sight of Africa is an achievement." "It is something to sail by the very names of Granada and Andalusia." Of vessels hailing, "The captain applies his mouth with a pomp of preparation, and you are startled with the following primitive shouts, all uttered in a high formal tone, with due intervals between, as if a Calvinistic Stentor were questioning a man from the land of Goshen.

"'What is your name?'

"'Whence come you?'

"'Whither are you bound?'

"After the question 'What is your name?' all ears are bent

to listen. The answer comes, high and remote, nothing perhaps being distinguished of it but the vowels. The 'Sall-of-Hym' you must translate into the *Sally* of Plymouth. 'Whence come you?' All ears bent again. 'Myr' of 'Mau' is Smyrna of Malta. 'Whither are you bound?' All ears again. No answer. 'D—d if he'll tell,' cries the captain, laying down at once his trumpet and his scripture." What an autobiographer we might have had, if the gods had sent Leigh Hunt round the world before he became a sensitive plant in his own opinion!

In that spirit of ease which rewards the voyager sometimes for his apprehensions, when he discovers that the ship is gliding into harbour as in a day-dream and even apprehension is gone astern, the Hunts drew near to Genoa, "queen-like city, crowned with white palaces," the sky a perfect blue, the sea of amber, and beyond, the mountains. It was June 15th. There was only one shadow on the day; Hunt had not wished to go to Genoa, but to Leghorn; yet that could be only a few blissful expectant days farther on. "We felt as if the country Shelley was in embraced us for him." He at once wrote to the Shelleys, with playfulness: "I forgot to notice what Shelley says about his downfall from the angelic state. Does he mean his taking to veal-cutlets, or that he has fallen in love with somebody who does not deserve it?" He also wrote descriptively to the Novellos and others. By an odd stroke, Captain Whitney of the *Jane* was here at Genoa; the worthy man accompanied Hunt ashore, and invited him to dinner. Daily Hunt went into the churches for "their quiet, their coolness, and their richness." A reply from Shelley came late on June 21st, while the *David Walter* was still unloading. It spoke of Shelley's intention to set off for Leghorn as soon as he knew Hunt had sailed again; of Edward Williams, "one of the best fellows in the world," of Jane, "a most delightful person," of

Mary Shelley's being ill, of "a Mr Trelawny, a wild but kind-hearted seaman." It told Hunt to look out for "a white house with arches" near Lerici. "We shall look out," replied the new-comer, and on June 28th the *David Walter* continued her voyage south, only one immeasurably glorious thunderstorm breaking the calm. Hunt witnessed this at about the place which shortly became painfully well known to his imagination.

At the beginning of July the amateur emigrants landed in Leghorn, where they immediately recognised the Mr Trelawny described by Shelley, aboard a boat called the *Bolivar*, which was soon known to them as Lord Byron's. Trelawny had heard all about them from Shelley, who wrote to him on June 18th asking for news of them, and Byron had said—in view of the Cockney School reputation—"You will find Leigh Hunt a gentleman in dress and address." Trelawny was not disappointed: "I found him that, and something more; and with a quaint fancy and cultivated mind. He was in high spirits, and disposed to be pleased with others. His anticipated literary projects in conjunction with Byron and Shelley were a source of great pleasure to him—so was the land of beauty and song. He had come to it as to a new home, in which, as the immortal Robins would have said: 'You will find no nuisance but the litter of the rose-leaves and the noise of the nightingales.' The pleasure that surpassed all the rest, was the anticipation of seeing speedily his friend Shelley." Before Hunt saw Shelley, he paid a visit to Lord Byron at his country house, on Monte Nero. After toiling unphilosophically through the heat and dust, he found a flaring red house, and was admitted. "Upon seeing Lord Byron, I hardly knew him, he was grown so fat; and he was longer in recognizing me, I had grown so thin. He was dressed in a loose nankin jacket and white trowzers, his neck-cloth open, and his hair in thin ringlets about his throat:

altogether presenting a very different aspect from the compact, energetic, and curly-headed person, whom I had known in England." But this was not the only novelty in the situation. Hunt observed the Countess Guiccioli in great agitation, and her brother with his arm in a sling; he had just intervened as peace-maker in a servants' brawl, had been stabbed, and looked like being stabbed again; for the man with the knife and the picturesque red cap was waiting outside, "glancing upwards like a tiger." Assassin or no assassin, Byron was for his evening ride, and the prayers of his Countess could not dissuade him; so all went out, "squeezing to have the honour of being the boldest," when—Leigh Hunt was learning—the villain collapsed, wept, wailed, asked pardon, and "requested Lord Byron to kiss him." This was not the kind of kissing in which Byron excelled, and he contented himself with pardoning the man; Guiccioli pardoned him; Pietro pardoned him; and, though to avoid police questions the man departed, he crowned his exploit by calling on Shelley, "who was shocked at his appearance, and gave him some money out of his very disgust, for he thought nobody would help such a fellow if he did not."

The Hunts were at an inn in Leghorn when Shelley came into the harbour with his yacht, and then Thornton Hunt, who had last seen Shelley "packing up his pistols—which he allowed me to examine"—four years earlier, was moved "by the shrill sound of his voice, as he rushed into my father's arms, which he did with an impetuousness and a fervour scarcely to be imagined by any who did not know the intensity of his feelings and the deep nature of his affection for that friend. I remember his crying out that he was 'so *inexpressibly* delighted!—you cannot think how *inexpressibly* happy it makes me!'" Thornton surveyed his old companion. "It was easy to see that a grand change had come over his appearance and condition. The southern climate had suited him, and the boat which caused his death had in the meanwhile been instrumental in developing his life. . . . He had *grown* since he left England. For instance, in the interval since I had seen him his chest had manifestly become of a larger girth. . . . His voice was stronger, his manner more confident and downright, and, although not less emphatic, yet decidedly less impulsively changeful. I can recall his reading from an ancient author [Plato], translating as he went, a passage about the making of the first man; and I remember it from the subject and from the easy flow of his translation, but chiefly from the air of strength and cheerfulness which I noticed in his voice and manner."

What the small boy had detachment and curiosity to see, the father's emotion perhaps obscured, for he says, "I will not dwell upon the moment. We talked of a thousand things, past, present, and to come. He was the same as ever, with the exception of less hope. He could not be otherwise. But he prepared me to find others not exactly what I had taken them for." This preparation did not illuminate Hunt's thought very deeply, as, with the prospect bright before his eyes and his expectancy, with his friend regained, he and Shelley and Williams, with the women and children, took their way to Pisa. There Shelley ("assisting us," Mrs Hunt wrote, "in any, and every way, almost anticipating our wishes before we had formed them, with an instinct that nothing but an entire abandonment of self, and deep regard for others can give") tried to make his friends at home in the ground floor of Byron's house, Casa Lanfranchi, and called in a noted physician, Vaccà, for Marianne. Vaccà gave his opinion; Marianne was "in a decline"; and as others said she would scarcely last a year, Hunt was faced with a darker side of his Italy. Now, another fear forced itself upon him. We read of it in a letter from Williams to Trelawny:

"Lord B.'s reception of Mrs H. was—as S. tells me—most shameful. She came into his house sick and exhausted, and he scarcely deigned to notice her; was silent, and scarcely bowed. This conduct cut H. to the soul; but the way in which he received our friend Roberts, at Dunn's door, shall be described when we meet:—it must be acted." The soul of Shelley, at this hour at the mercy of various enigmas, was also cut by the many-sided failure indicated by this Byronic gesture, but he kept up his outward cheerfulness. On July 4th he wrote to Mary of Vaccà's adverse report on Marianne ("her case is hopeless"), of Byron's whims, of Hunt's penniless state. "Lord Byron must of course furnish the requisite funds at present, as I cannot; but he seems inclined to depart without the necessary explanations and arrangements due to such a situation as Hunt's. These, in spite of delicacy, I must procure; he offers him the copyright of the *Vision of Judgment* for the first number. This offer, if sincere, is *more* than enough to set up the journal, and, if sincere, will set everything right." Mary meanwhile was strangely aware of something wrong, and intensely wrong, but what it was she could not decipher.

Byron, in Hunt's rosy view, appeared ardent for the new partnership. "He has given directions to put a variety of MS. into the hands of my brother John for it, and Shelley has some excellent MS. ready also. The title, I believe, will be the *Hesperides*.... It is Lord Byron's own. Lord B. made me a present the other day of a satire on Southey, called the *Vision of Judgment*, which my brother has accordingly to get from the hands of Murray, and print for our mutual benefit...."

The Sunday afternoon of July 7th was passed in Utopian delight by Hunt and Shelley among the towers of Pisa (the Leaning Tower not being neglected), before the paintings of Cimabue and Giotto, and in the cathedral. Like Pepys, they looked round them during the service: Hunt "saw finer faces than in Genoa," and Shelley said, "these are surpassed by those in Rome." Perhaps that day Hunt's memory chiefly received the picture of Shelley gazing at the fire-flies. "The last fragment he wrote, which was a welcome to me on my arrival from England, began with a simile taken from their dusk look and the fire underneath it, in which he found a likeness to his friend." That day certainly Shelley remarked to Marianne, "If I die tomorrow, I have lived to be older than my father; I am ninety years of age." Anyone who contemplates the mass of his biography and works accepts the figure. And that night Shelley borrowed Hunt's copy of Keats's last volume, with the *Hyperion* in it that he had so frequently praised. It was the only one procurable in Italy, and Hunt made him promise to keep it till he could return it with his own hands. Many years later he made Browning smile to himself by the mild delusion that Shelley would still in the wonderful future do as he had said. Then Shelley and Williams got into the postchaise, "meaning to come back to us shortly," and had disappeared into the dark along the Leghorn road.

What happened next day is the most vividly familiar passage, as it is the most lamented, in all the lives of the poets. Shelley was drowned on his course from Leghorn to his seaside house, and Williams with him. The Hunts saw the night opening and shutting with "horrid lightning," and heard the madness of the wind and rain, in appalled anxiety; yet, as the morning had been fine, it was possible that the *Don Juan* had got clear. Byron came down to Hunt's study, ran his eye over the books, borrowed two or three, theorised in his fine rapid style. On Wednesday Trelawny came to Pisa, and revealed to Byron and Hunt his fears of a disaster; Hunt had written to Shelley asking for a reassuring note. This appeal, arriving at Shelley's house on Friday, brought Mary and Jane Williams in haste to Pisa.

On the way Mary resolved to "ask the fearful question of Hunt, 'Do you know anything of Shelley?'"—a fantastic first necessity after four years of friendship in absence. But, as Byron was still at Pisa, Mary was spared this shock, which she had so dreadfully conjectured. At last the truth was known to all.

Hunt now found his Hesperides in total eclipse. It was for him a tragedy arranged by some hostile presence such as hitherto existed only in Webster. Attempting to break through the pause of all wishes and futurities, he wrote to Mary Shelley on July 20th, speaking of his complete devotion to "those whom Shelley loves," and the next day he called at her lodgings, sending up a note: "Will you let the bearer know whether you can see me now, or whether I shall wait longer? I have persuaded Marianne to let me come alone first." He communicated the catastrophe to Bessy Kent in London and Horace Smith in Paris. The first letter was to be shown to Hogg: "I had already begun to enliven Shelley's hours with accounts of his pleasant sayings, and hoped to—but, good God! how are one's most confident expectations cut short! I embrace him, as my friend and Shelley's." Even here, that ironical contradictory spirit which made such a kaleidoscope of Hunt's career might have been espied reading with a burning eye.

Trelawny, who also seems to have emanated from the brain of Webster, perfected the final adieu to Shelley's mortal shape. His funeral pyre on the Italian shore lacked nothing in mournful apparatus; the frankincense and wine were there. Italian soldiers, officials, sightseers came to the cremation, to which Byron and Hunt were driven in a carriage. Hunt found in the very temper of nature some Shelleian portent, the autumn day being now serene. "The Mediterranean, now soft and lucid, kissed the shore as if to make peace with it. The yellow sand and blue sky intensely contrasted with one another: marble mountains touched the air with coolness, and the flame of the fire bore away toward heaven in vigorous amplitude, waving and quivering with a brightness of inconceivable beauty. It seemed as though it contained the glassy essence of vitality. You might have expected a seraphic countenance to look out of it, turning once more, before it departed, to thank the friends that had done their duty." Into the flame Hunt threw the *Lamia*, found in Shelley's bosom. For the forced equipoise with which he witnessed this daemonically beautiful burning, he paid by getting half-drunk with Byron, and driving through the forests of Pisa with shouts and scraps of songs and moody laughter.

In Hunt there was an element not merely of the unconventional but of the abnormal. Trelawny took the heart of Shelley from the flames. Hunt begged to have it, and Trelawny gave it to him; the words which one habitually uses do not convey this transaction. Mary Shelley that night demanded the heart, Hunt claimed it; she immediately called on Byron to support her demand, and Hunt still asserted his right in as singular a letter, if it is read without the context of Hunt's life, as was ever written. "It is not that my self-love is hurt, for that I could have given up, as I have long learnt to do, but it is my love,—my love for my friend; and for this to make way for the claims of any other love, man's or woman's, I must have great reasons indeed brought me. I do not say it is impossible for such reasons to be brought, but I say that they must be great, unequivocal, and undeniable. In *his* case above all other human beings, no ordinary appearance of rights, even yours, can affect me. With regard to Ld B. he has no right to bestow the heart, and I am sure pretends to none. If he told you that you should have it, it could only have been from his thinking I could more easily part with it than I can." Presently, however, he gave up the heart, *cor cordium* as it was to him; that was relinquished, but he never gave up his instinct that Shelley was his.

XIII

Byron stands in Shelley's Place

"LORD Byron requested me to look upon him as standing in Mr Shelley's place, and said that I should find him the same friend that the other had been." Hunt, with whose aspect we are concerned, was unconvinced of the identical quality; he was more deeply dependent upon what had been urged upon him as a "proposition"—the periodical "Hesperides." As he saw the situation, Byron had been responsible for the plan and for his arrival in Italy. It was one of those instances of our imperfect human nature in which a legal contract is more to the point than the most promising personal respect, admiration and asseveration. Making no contract, Hunt (called from England to Italy, from an established post to an experiment) was obliged to live in the presence of two sphinxes. First, would the purpose of Byron stand firm? Second, would the projected review succeed? The first question, if it could not be wholly answered by Hunt's own ability to win Byron's sociable collaboration, would be considerably affected by that. The answer to the second, though largely controlled by the first, remained to be seen. It is seldom that a journal travels successfully from an editorial office in one country to a public in another, but the power of Byron was European, and literary taste was friendly to quarterly miscellanies.

While the first number of what Lord Byron now, with better judgment, called *The Liberal*, was being prepared between Leigh Hunt and John, familiar and often gay conversation went on between the exiles in Casa Lanfranchi. "Leontius!" Byron would call at the window of Hunt's study, across the ivy and orange leaves, opening the way to a talk. The yellow-haired Countess would sometimes join in. Hunt joined Byron in the cooler hours for a ride or a drive, and Trelawny with his cigar sometimes made a third. But the easy current of amiability was not undarkened by some turbid impulses. Byron was disinclined to transfer much of his money to the man whom his proposal had brought as an editor to Italy, and what he did part with on this score was "doled out" to Hunt by his steward. Moreover, Byron and Marianne Hunt were not friends. Probably this fact, which a more sophisticated man than Hunt might have viewed as saving trouble, irritated Marianne's husband, with his desire to see all his intimates admired. Mrs Hunt had nothing to thank Byron for, not even a *billet-doux*; she made retorts (such as that on his remarking, "Trelawny has been speaking against my morals! What do you think of that?"—"It is the first time I ever heard of them"), and even cut out with her scissors an unflattering portrait of the milord with his sneer, at the end of his daily ride. "What a pity it is," she wrote in her diary, "the good actions of *noblemen* are not done in a *noble manner*! Aye princely I would have them be."

As for *The Liberal*, the mere announcements of a junto so undignified and malevolent were causing the usual tub-thumpers to hold special meetings—*Blackwood's* and *John Bull*. For the effect on others of different political livery, call Hazlitt as historian: "Who would have supposed that Mr Thomas Moore and Mr Hobhouse, those staunch friends and partisans of the people, should also be thrown into almost hysterical agonies of well-bred horror at the coalition between their noble and ignoble acquaintance—between the patrician and 'the newspaper-man'? Mr Moore darted backwards and forwards from Cold-Bath-Fields Prison to the *Examiner* office, from Mr Longman's to Mr Murray's shop in a state of ridiculous trepidation, to see what was to be done to prevent this de-

gradation of the aristocracy of letters, this indecent encroachment of plebeian pretensions, this undue extension of patronage
and compromise of privilege. The Tories were shocked that
Lord Byron should grace the popular side by his direct
countenance and assistance; the Whigs were shocked that he
should share his confidence and counsels with any one who did
not unite the double recommendations of birth and genius—
but themselves! Mr Moore had lived so long among the great,
that he fancied himself one of them, and regarded the indignity
as done to himself. Mr Hobhouse had lately been black-balled
by the Clubs, and must feel particularly sore and tenacious on
the score of public opinion. Mr Shelley's father, however, was
an elder baronet than Mr Hobhouse's; Mr Leigh Hunt was
'to the full as genteel a man' as Mr Moore, in birth, appearance,
and education; the pursuits of all four were the same—the
Muse, the public favour, and the public good." The friends of
Byron, absurd as they are made to look in Hazlitt's chronicle,
had the power to unsettle him. Moore darting through London,
Hobhouse rushing over the Alps with "horrid warning,"
gained the victory after a short resistance. The only thing which
might have saved *The Liberal* after all was immediate and sustained success.

About September 1822 the first number was issued, and
received with automatic insults. "This so much puffed and so
long promised work, has just appeared. Those who know anything of literary gossip, are aware that *The Liberal* is the joint
production of Lord Byron, the late Mr Shelley, and Mr Leigh
Hunt, and some other translated cockneys; they are, therefore,
prepared for blasphemy and impurity of every kind to a certain
extent, but we doubt that they can anticipate all the atrocity of
The Liberal." This was one of the whisperings of the storm,
the first chord of an agony which ends with Byron's supreme

offence: "Once the admirer of Milton, Dryden, Pope, he has become the associate of the Cockney Bluestockings, and the panegyrist of Lady Morgan; or to give one which comprehends all other degrees of metamorphosis and degradation, he has sunk from the station of an English nobleman, and the highest place in English literature, to be the colleague of Mr Leigh Hunt, the author of *Don Juan*, and a contributor to *The Liberal*." But in 1822 people were accustomed to this temperature in critical coquetry, and the first number of the abominable magazine was considerably though not overwhelmingly popular.

No first lines in the first article of a first number could have been more likely to secure attention, than Byron's opening to the *Vision of Judgment*:

> Saint Peter sat by the celestial gate,
> His keys were rusty, and the lock was dull.

This perfect example of the satirical panorama was enough to make *The Liberal* sell, without the support of Hunt's essays and fables, his account of Pisa, his beautiful translations, and Shelley's glorious specimen of Goethe in English. In the second number of *The Liberal*, Byron's *Heaven and Earth* opened the innings; presently came Hunt with a satire, *The Dogs*, directed against the abusers of the southern quarterly, and written with the Byronic fling which Hunt began to imitate. Byron's friends regarded this journalistic adroitness (intended to give *The Liberal* a distinctive unity) as a sin against their leader's immortal soul. Charles Brown, Hazlitt, Hogg, Mary Shelley contributed, and Shelley's *Song Written for an Indian Air* appeared. In the third number, *The Blues* by Byron was not highly distinguished, Hazlitt outdistancing the rest with his enlargement of an *Examiner* note into the great essay *My First Acquaintance with Poets*. Hunt, throwing in his usual variety of prose and verse, exhibited a growing delicacy

of poetic tint in the *Book of Beginnings*, a piece from which we
may take in due course the picture of himself in his Utopia.
Horace Smith supplied a brilliant traveller's sketch, *A Sunday's Fête at St Cloud*. The fourth and final *Liberal* contained
Byron's translation of *Morgante Maggiore*, Hunt's thoughtful
and ingenious poem *The Choice*, and two essays by Hazlitt. In
brief, *The Liberal* was a miscellany of disconnected writings
without the momentum of a controlling mind, or the course
of the most recent intellectual and artistic considerations (as,
the reviews of new books), to give it the air of an immediate or
permanent aid to reflection. And the articles were anonymous.

I am inclined to sum up the internal difficulties of this ex-
perimental periodical, the decline and fall of Byron's interest in
it, the machinations of his friends to detach him from it, in few
words, and to present the tendency of the first instigator as it
appeared to Hunt. "Byron's plan of a periodical publication
was no sudden business; he had proposed it more than once,
and to different persons; and his reasons for it were, that he
thought he should get both money and fame.... The failure
of the large profits—the non-appearance of the golden visions
he had looked for—of the Edinburgh and Quarterly returns—
of the solid and splendid proofs of this new country which he
should conquer in the regions of notoriety, to the dazzling of
all men's eyes and his own,—this it was, this was the bitter
disappointment which made him determine to give way....
From the moment he saw the moderate profits of *The Liberal*,
he resolved to have nothing farther to do with it in the way of
real assistance. He made use of it only for the publication of
some things which his Tory bookseller was afraid to put
forth." Some modification might be made in this general
verdict, and Hunt himself made it, without shaking the foundation of the censure. Besides Byron's clever and melancholic

evasiveness, Hunt had to fear the simple precipitancy of his brother, the publisher, who regarded the work as a gun to shoot Tories. Then there was the awkwardness of the distance between Old Bond Street and Italy. The sensational but disastrous *Vision of Judgment*, from which Leigh Hunt would have recommended that some passages should be withheld, went from Murray to John Hunt, and as Byron had retained no copy in Italy, Leigh Hunt saw the fateful first article of his first *Liberal* only when copies of the magazine arrived in Italy.

A note of the financial results of *The Liberal*, nos. I and II, is extant at the British Museum, with a letter from John Hunt to his brother dated February 25th, 1823: "The sale has certainly not answered my expectations. Of the 1st. No. 7000 were printed, after I had obtained the best information I could of the probable sale of Lord B.'s performances. Of that No. 4050 have been sold. Of the 2d. 6000 were printed, but of that only 2700 have yet come off." In view of Lord Byron's advice that the attempt should be abandoned, he adds, "I would suggest to you the employment of your pen in a publication which might be made a companion to *The Examiner*, under the title 'The Literary Examiner.' You might resume *The Indicator* in it." By the cash account, the first *Liberal* had made a profit of £377 odd, the second had lost £41; payments of £28 to Hazlitt, £36 to Mrs Shelley, 18 guineas to Brown, the same to Hogg, and six guineas to the oppressed Suliotes are entered.

By the end of 1822 Hunt had received from England versions or perversions of Byron's "idle phrases" on the *Liberal* situation[1], which did not improve his hopes. Soon after the pro-

[1] They were not hidden from the public. Reviewing the first number of *The Liberal*, Theodore Hook in his *John Bull* remarks: "[Lord Byron] is weary and sick to death of the Hunts; he repents that he ever went into partnership with them in the money-making speculation of the magazine. He writes word that 'Hunt is a bore: he is,' says his

duction of the accounts of sales just noticed, Byron's discontent became so sharp and contrived such justifications for a withdrawal that Hunt wrote in this style:

Dear Lord Byron   Albaro, 7 April 1823

Among a variety of letters which Shelley wrote me from Italy, in several of which to the best of my recollection the proposal was mentioned, there is at all events one in my possession, in which he directly makes it to me as by your special request; and it was this letter which induced me to come over.

I do not wish to comment upon the manner in which the next sentence is worded. I must merely be allowed to say that I did *not* (at least not in the spirit which those strange words seem to imply) "produce the very next day after my arrival at Pisa my brother's letter with a request for money to the amount of two hundred and fifty pounds." Shelley saw me change countenance at a letter which I received by the post when he was with me; and learning the contents, he immediately with his usual kindness set about helping me the best way he could in a matter which he saw gave me great anguish. I do not mean to say I should not have applied to you, had he been absent. I should. I should have overcome the pain of that abruptness by a greater. But I should have had no notion, at that time, that the application would ever have appeared to you in the light which I fear it seems to have done. When I arrived in Italy, it was with great surprise that I found there were some doubts of the proposed work taking place; and if I did not say any more upon that subject, it was certainly out of no want of delicacy to [   ]; and I will only remark for the present, that the failure of *The Liberal*, if it has failed, is no doubt partly owing to its having contained, from your pen, *none* but articles of a certain character, however meritorious in themselves, and to a certain want of superinduced cordiality towards it on your part, which

lordship, 'a proser; Mrs Hunt is no great things; and the six children perfectly untractable.'" Hook adds pleasantly, "We should think the children must have done the greatest part of the first number of *The Liberal*."

you unfortunately allowed to escape to the public. Unquestionably, there was in other respects also a battle to fight; but in this, as in all other respects, fighting cordially and inflexibly is, I conceive, every thing. . . .

Ever yours truly

Leigh Hunt.

P.S. I agree with you that there *appear* no reasons why *The Liberal* should be dropped. However injured, I do not know that it has failed altogether, though my brother seems to think your secession must be followed by its abandonment. . . .

The next day Hunt addressed Byron on the subject of Byron's darker misconceptions of John Hunt's character: "As your own impression with regard to my brother has been done away, and as my brother has the greatest esteem for dear S.'s memory, I think it would only be putting him to a great and surprising pain to let him know that such a mistake ever existed, especially as he felt very sensibly your kindness respecting the *Vision of Judgment*; and as to his habit of reserve and mystery, which brought those suspicions upon him, you see what he himself acknowledges in his last letter. I will press however the danger of it upon him still more, and tell him in general terms that Shelley liked it as little as others; which I am sure will have a great effect.

"With regard to my connection with my brother, it is no longer inextricable. I might dissolve it tomorrow, if I pleased. But unless his fortunes were changed, I should never think of doing so, because I plagued him a long time with my bad habits of business, and conceive I am bound to make up for them in every way I can. When that letter came to me at Pisa I was not only in debt to him myself, but he was bound for me to several petty creditors, whose claims altogether made up a large sum, for *us*; and when to these claims upon me, is added his own illness at the time, just emerging from a second imprisonment, and the dangerous illness of his dearest and most useful son, who was all but given over, I am sure you will think not only that it was impossible for him to help writing, but that the subject of his letter was, after all, really an affair of my own." By such representations, and through the amenities of occasional talks in pleasant mood, Hunt succeeded in obtaining from Byron some occasional productions to maintain his collaboration with *The Liberal*, until it had to stop.

Leaving these tedious sparrings and appeals for a time, we resume the other Italian experience of the Hunts, who were at Pisa when *The Liberal* was launched in such stormy atmosphere. Hunt's *Letters from Abroad* in that publication tell us something of his impressions, and the imaginative discoveries which tempered his almost desperate drudgery. "It is curious to feel oneself sitting quietly in one of the old Italian houses, and think of all the interests and passions that have agitated the hearts of so many generations of its tenants; all the revels and the quarrels that have echoed along its walls; all the guitars that have tinkled under its windows; all the scuffles that have disputed its doors. Along the great halls, how many feet have hurried in alarm! how many stately beauties have drawn their quiet trains! how many huge torches have ushered magnificence up the staircases! how much blood perhaps been shed!" This reverie was counterchanged with the lively joy of the pastoral all round, the festoons of vines, the cornfields, the Titianesque colours, the general fruitfulness. It was Hunt's home, if only Shelley had remained. Needy, incapable of making a shilling do even the work of sixpence, confronted with a "distrest poet's" future, Hunt had his treasure: "You learn for the first time in this climate, what colours really are. . . . A red cap in Italy goes by you, not like a mere cap, much less anything vulgar or butcher-like, but like what it is, an intense specimen of the colour of red. It is like a scarlet bud in the blue atmosphere." The Chaucerian procession of paintings on the cloister walls of Pisa brought him deep delight: "I have enriched my day-dreams and my stock of the admirable, and am thankful that I have names by heart, to which I owe homage and gratitude. Tender and noble Orcagna, be thou blessed beyond the happiness of thine own heaven! Giotto, be thou a name to me hereafter, of a kindred brevity, solidity and stateliness, with that of thy friend Dante!" The woods of olives like "huge hazy bushes" pleased him well, and when his wife had said that they looked as if they only grew by moonlight, better still; the fireflies' diamonded dance in the velvet dark held him watching in an elemental calm, which ended with recollections of the old poets and one young poet now starrily fixed in their firmament: "S. used to watch them for hours. I look at them, and wonder whether any of the particles he left upon earth help to animate their loving and lovely light. Do you recollect coming down to Buckinghamshire one summer?"

That September Byron decided to leave Pisa for Genoa, "restless, as he had always been"; at the northern town he could "hover on the borders of his inclination for Greece." He went with his own "caravan" by land, and Hunt with his "kraal" by sea, independently; but at Lerici they met, and, Byron falling ill, all remained several days. Trelawny brought the *Bolivar* along, and it was he who led Hunt into the depressing Villa Magni. Hunt wrote to Bessy Kent, "I have a few myrtle leaves for you, which I took from the garden of Shelley's house near Lerici; and there I saw those melancholy rooms, to which he was returning, and did not return. The house is on the very edge of the sea, and had been a convent of Jesuits. I saw the waves foaming and roaring at the foot, and with an impatience which has seldom gone so far with me, could almost have blasphemously trampled at them, and cried out." He was disposed to identify all that the region could disclose with the cruel calamity of his friend, and again he wrote: "The place is wild and retired, with a bay and rocky eminences; the people suited to it, something between inhabitants of sea and land. In the summer-time they will be up all night dabbling in the water, and making wild noises. We paced over the empty rooms, and neglected garden. The sea fawned upon the shore, as though it could do no harm." Then away again, Byron's boat, and Trelawny's, and Hunt's felucca gaily twinkling over the blue waves towards Sestri—a passage of the true classical vitality, to which the final stage of the transit was an anticlimax, for it passed over dull mountain-slopes, "great doughy billows, like so much enormous pudding, or petrified mud." Mrs Shelley had gone ahead, and the Hunts arrived at Genoa to find that she had chosen them a house at Albaro, a village on a hill near by. It was the Casa Negroto, containing "about forty rooms" at a rent of £20 a year—space enough for Mrs Shelley and the numerous Hunts to live together yet alone.

Relations between Mary Shelley and Leigh Hunt were candid, and well graced, but there were moments of discord. Hunt was under the impression that she had been difficult towards Shelley, and he could not mask his feeling. At the same time, Byron was making her the recipient of some of his malice against Marianne and her children: "I have a particular dislike to anything of Shelley's being within the same walls with Mrs Hunt's children. They are dirtier and more mischievous than Yahoos. What they can't destroy with their filth they will with their fingers... six little blackguards." Mary at the close of 1822 was eloquent of her dismal change of condition: "What can I say of my present life? The weather is bitterly cold with a sharp wind, very unlike dear, *carissima* Pisa; but soft airs and balmy gales are not the attributes of Genoa, which place I daily and duly join Marianne in detesting. There is but one fireplace in the house, and although people have been for a month putting up a stove in my room, it smokes too much to permit of its being lighted. So I am obliged to pass the greater part of my time in Hunt's sitting-room, which is, as you may guess, the annihilation of study, and even of pleasure to a great degree. For, after all, Hunt does not like me: it is both our faults, and I do not blame him, but so it is. I rise at 9, breakfast, work, read, and if I can at all endure the cold, copy my Shelley's MSS. in my own room, and if possible walk before dinner. After that I work, read Greek, etc., till 10, when Hunt and Marianne go to bed. Then I am alone."

An enormous letter from Jane Williams to Hunt, of later date, may be introduced here in order that we may see what the degree and point of the disputatiousness between Hunt and Mary were, and then hurry on to better understanding. Jane went to London instead of remaining with the others; she there met Bessy Kent, and presently received word that Hunt was strangely regarding her as a "cause." She at once poured forth her mingled retaliation and reconciliation.

"I write to you my dear friend without awaiting the arrival of your long promised letter: the truth is your message through Miss Kent has perplexed me so much that I felt it necessary to discuss the subject with you; in the hope that I shall convince you I am not so culpable as you imagine on one point, tho' I cannot entirely acquiesce in your opinions on another. In the first place you say, 'The truth is she perplexed me very much in my intercourse with Mrs S. by giving me accounts which exceedingly embittered it and made me cold and almost in-hospitable, and yet at the same time never hinting a word on the subject to Mrs S. unless indeed she did say something in her letters now and then which I suspected from the effect which her correspondence used occasionally to have.' The inference to be drawn from the above paragraph is this—that my representation of Mary's conduct was the cause of your coldness to her. Now pardon me if I say this is somewhat unjust. If I recollect rightly our discussion concerning Mary arose from her conduct on a certain occasion (which I need not mention) to which you were a witness as well as myself: and if that sad circumstance had not called it forth, I imagine the discussion would never have been entered into, at all events I did not conceive I was speaking to a stranger who would receive an evil impression from what *I* said: on the contrary I had always heard you spoken of by Mary as her most intimate friend: as one who had known her long, and had lived for some time under her roof. Now it is utterly impossible to do this, and not know whether a person's temper be bad or good: you I imagine as well as myself had seen that the intercourse between Shelley and Mary was not as happy as it should have been; and I remember your telling me that our Shelley mentioned several circumstances on that subject that distressed you during the short time that you were together, and that you witnessed the pain he suffered on receiving a letter from Mary at that period. Now had you been an entire stranger to Mary I should have been inexcusable in having entered into any conversation that would tend to give you an unfortunate impression of her; and you would have been equally so, in having acted towards her upon such an impression; so that I must still hope and believe your own observation alone guided you in your conduct to her and not anything I might have said to you in the discussion to which I allude.

"With regard to the effect my correspondence produced on Mary sometimes I am unable to give any explanation: it must have proceeded from subjects entirely different to the one in question, which has never occupied either my thoughts or my pen since that time. I do not recollect having named you in my letters otherwise than in the way of remembrance, and I naturally concluded you would see them. You then say, 'What was my awkward situation when I discovered that Mary was bitterly repenting of the trouble she had occasioned Shelley. I felt as if I could not sufficiently make her amends for my former treatment' &c. Now I do not see why Mary's repentance should cause you to feel remorse. You acted coldly because you thought her conduct merited that coldness, as you I am sure are incapable of showing it. Mary repents: there is then no reason for coldness and with her returning good feeling your kindness to her returns. This is as it should be: but I think you tax yourself with injustice to her improperly when you talk of feeling remorse: and I think you will agree with me when you have reconsidered the subject. You say 'Tell Jane, if I suspect her of a fault it is of allowing herself to say too much, (not untruly God knows), about a person to others while she says *nothing* of the matter to the person herself.' I differ from you *entirely*, as to the necessity of my telling Mary her faults: for I feel convinced I should only make her unhappy while I should fail in producing the desired effect. That task I leave to you, my dear friend, who are so well able to correct human follies and to drop a tear of pity on human weaknesses— in me it would be arrogance and presumption. Nobody can better appreciate Mary's many noble qualities than myself. The feeling of repentance shows a kindly disposed heart and the avowal of it a God-like mind. The tear-drop of repentance was the gift that gained a paradise for the Peri: let us hope that the one shed by *our* Peri will gain for her that Paradise she has so well earned, the love of her friends."

The winter of 1822 and spring of 1823 passed without much radiance of prospect for Hunt, although Byron showed himself more pleased with the third *Liberal* than the others. Byron, perhaps merely for recreation and variety, perhaps from a genuine value he had for the invigorating "moments" characteristic of Leigh Hunt's opinion and utterance, walked, talked, and dined with the man who, in spite of all his retrospective dismay and anticipative melancholy, essentially desired to have Byron's esteem. But it is not necessary to follow all that Hunt himself wrote of his conversations with Byron in order to feel that, in this part of Byron's career, even the most delightful aspects of the great wanderer would usually be rendered painful by some intervening caprice or prejudice. That may be seen in Mary Shelley's letters announcing her departure from Genoa in the summer of 1823, and Lord Byron's; these also are happy in respect of the misunderstanding with Hunt, which had been removed. Mary remained until Mrs Hunt's confinement was safely over, a crisis peculiarly feared because of Vaccà's grave opinion against Mrs Hunt's chance of surviving even an ordinary twelvemonth.

"The day after Marianne's confinement, the 9th June,"— we quote from Mary's letter to Jane Williams—"seeing all went on so prosperously, I told Lord Byron that I was ready to go, and he promised to provide means. When I talked of going post, it was because he said that I should go so, at the same time declaring he would regulate all himself. I waited in vain for these arrangements. But ... he chose to transact our negotiation through Hunt, and gave such an air of unwillingness and sense of the obligation he conferred, as at last provoked Hunt to say that there was no obligation, since he owed me £1000.

"Glad of a quarrel, straight I clap the door! Still keeping

up an appearance of amity with Hunt, he has written notes and letters so full of contempt against me and my lost Shelley that I could stand it no longer, and have refused to receive his still proffered aid for my journey. . . . In the meantime Hunt is all kindness, consideration and friendship—all feeling of alienation towards me has disappeared down to its last dregs. He perfectly approves of what I have done." Hunt attempted to negotiate another claim of journey-money with Byron—his own, and though it was no monstrous figure that he asked, he did not succeed in getting Byron to do for him what, had the positions of patron and petitioner been reversed, he would have done for Byron. The thrifty saviour of Greece, annoyed, ashamed, and bored, even avoided a farewell meeting with Hunt before he went off on his crusade, as is reported by Mary Shelley in sharp terms: "Lord Byron, Trelawny and Pierino Gamba sailed for Greece on the 17th July. I did not see the former. His unconquerable avarice prevented his supplying me with money, and a remnant of shame caused him to avoid me. But I have a world of things to tell you on that score when I see you. If he were mean, Trelawny more than balanced the moral account . . . Hunt's kindness is now as active and warm as it was dormant before; but just as I find a companion in him I leave him. I leave him in all his difficulties, with his head throbbing with overwrought thoughts, and his frame sometimes sinking under his anxieties. Poor Marianne has found good medicine, *facendo un bimbo*, and then nursing it, but she, with her female providence, is more bent by care than Hunt."

And in this way what had threatened to be another of Hunt's disenchantments in friendship was redeemed. When Mary left Genoa, on July 25th, he and "dear Thorney" went the first twenty miles with her; she wrote to Jane Williams in complete acceptance: "This was much, you will say, for Hunt. But, thank heaven, we are now the best friends in the world. He set his heart on my quitting Italy with as comfortable feelings as possible. . . . You know somewhat of what I suffered during the winter, during his alienation from me. He was displeased with me for many just reasons, but he found me willing to expiate, as far as I could, the evil I had done, so his heart was again warmed; and if, my dear friend, when I return, you find me more amiable, and more willing to suffer with patience than I was, it is to him that I owe this benefit, and you may judge if I ought not to be grateful to him. I am even so to Lord Byron, who was the cause that I stayed at Genoa, and thus secured one who, I am sure, can never change."

On her way Mary found her thoughts ever returning with love to the household doomed to linger on at Albaro, and she wrote several letters from which we may conjure up some more intimate notions of that home than even the domesticated but abstracted Hunt allows us. We see him—"You rose early, wrote, walked, dined, whistled, sang and punned most outrageously, the worst puns in the world,"—and Marianne with her "new darling," repeating her lectures on dress, yet still bidding her husband to lift his eyes to the hills in a beautiful strangeness of light. We see the patient boy Thornton, and the impatient John. At Susa Mary proposed a new and limited pantisocracy: "Absolutely, my dear Hunt, I will pass some three summer months in this divine spot—you shall all be with me. There are no gentlemen's seats or palazzi, so we will take a cottage, which we will paint and refit, just as this country inn is in which I now write—clean and plain. We will have no servants, only we will give out all the needlework. Marianne shall make puddings and pies, to make up for the vegetables and meat which I shall boil and spoil. Thorny shall sweep the rooms, Mary make the beds, Johnny clean the kettles and pans, and then we will pop him into one of the many streams hereabouts, and so clean him. Swinny being so quick shall be our Mercury, Percy our gardener, Sylvan and Percy Florence our weeders, and Vincent our plaything; and then to raise us above the vulgar, we will do all our work keeping time to Hunt's symphonies; we will perform our sweepings and dustings to the March in *Alceste*, we will prepare our meals to the tune of the *Laughing Trio*, and when we are tired we will lie on our turf sofas, while all our voices shall join in chorus in *Notte e giorno faticar*."

XIV

North and South

DISTURBED as he was by so many forms of uncertainty and want, Hunt during 1823 seems naturally to have published less than usual; much in *The Liberal*, occasional pieces in *The Examiner* and *Literary Examiner*, but otherwise only a pamphlet. This was the too ingenious yet stinging satire, *Ultra-Crepidarius*, which ends, "Men called the thing Gifford," Hunt's final answer to that impersonation of irritability who had so many times darted venom at Shelley, Keats, Lamb and himself. Another publication of 1823 might be fairly reckoned as part of the bibliography of Hunt. Elizabeth Kent's *Flora Domestica* owed much to him; he had sent various poetical translations for it, and conceivably had instructed the dear authoress where to look among the English poets for beauties congenial to her design. The book was that of a clever botanist, who was so zealous in her study as to enter into a long correspondence with the poet Clare about the orchids and the birds of his countryside. Besides many vignettes borrowed from Clare's ever accurate and freshly springing verses, she frequently decorates her treatise with the flowers of Shelley, Keats, Horace Smith, Hunt; she gives us indeed not only the Flora of the Vale of Health lyrists, but also that of the older writers with whom they all revealed a fond affinity. Her work was a practical embodiment of the general Huntian principles of making dark days and close streets shine and be glad; and in its small way it prospered, a third edition appearing in 1831. Whoever loves Shelley should love it, for it contains Bessy Kent's pledge of friendship to him, and admiring reminiscence of him "returning home with his hat wreathed with briony or wild convolvulus; his hand filled with bunches of wild-flowers plucked from the hedges as he passed, and his eyes, indeed every feature, beaming with the benevolence of his heart."

It was not long after Mary Shelley's landing in England (she had finished her journey by the surprising steamboat) that she called on Bessy Kent, and from this time the correspondence of these ladies with Leigh Hunt is a copious supply of information about him, both in his own action and in the news of English life which refreshed his banishment. With these, a number of long letters between him and other friends survive. The problem is to find the passages which meant most to him, and have a value besides. One thing is clear: having lost Shelley and Keats, Hunt now found the effect of Lamb's genius and personality a great comfort, and the news from England became for a time particularly concerned with that friend. What was life to Hunt is worth renewing from the originals, being partly unpublished, and touching Charles Lamb.

Mrs Novello writes: "How I wish you could see the new house these kind souls have purchased at Shacklewell—there is such a garden to it!—and Mr Lamb has taken one at Islington, also with a Garden—and a pear tree in it, with pears on it! and for the first time in his life, he says, he is master of a fruit tree, and accordingly behaves like a schoolboy at the prospect of a sudden windfall, or an indigent heir at another, and unlooked-for, windfall. . . . Shall I horrify you by the news that that saturated blackguard Theodore Hook lives in the Vale of Health?" July 27th, 1823.

Mary Shelley: "On Saturday, August the 30th, I went with Jane to the Gisbornes'. I know not why, but seeing them seemed more than anything else to remind me of Italy. Evening came on drearily. The rain splashed on the pavement, nor star nor moon deigned to appear. I looked upward, to seek an image of Italy, but a blotted sky told me only of my change. I tried to collect my thoughts, and then again dared not think, for I am a ruin where owls and bats live only, and I lost my last *singing bird* when I left Albaro. It was my birthday, and it pleased me to tell the people so—to recollect and feel that time flies; and what is to arrive is nearer, and my home not so far off as it was a year ago. This same evening, on my return to the Strand, I saw Lamb, who was very entertaining and amiable, though a little deaf. One of the first questions he asked me was, whether they made puns in Italy. I said, 'Yes, now Hunt is there.' He said that Burney made a pun in Otaheite, the first that was ever made in that country; at first the natives could not make out what he meant, but all at once they discovered the pun, and danced round him in transports of joy. L. said one thing, which I am sure will give you pleasure. He corrected for Hazlitt a new edition of *Elegant Extracts*, in which living poets are included. He said he was much pleased with many of your things, with a little of Montgomery and a little of Crabbe. Scott he found tiresome. Byron had many fine things, but was tiresome; but yours appeared to him the freshest and best of all. These *Extracts* have never been published; they have been offered to Mr Hunter; and seeing the book at his house, I had the curiosity to look at what the extracts were that pleased L. There was the canto of the Fatal Passion from *Rimini*, several things from *Foliage*, and from the *Amyntas*. L. mentioned also your 'Conversation with Coleridge,' and was much pleased with it. He was very gracious to me, and invited me to see him when Miss L. should be well. . . .

"On Tuesday, Sept. 2nd, I dined with Mr Hunter and Bessy, and she afterwards drank tea with me at the Strand. One thing at Mr Hunter's amused me very much. Your piping Faun and kneeling Venus are on the piano; but from a feeling of delicacy they are turned with their backs to the company." September 9th, 1823.

Cowden Clarke: "I have lately been introduced to one of

Keats's latter friends; Woodhouse, who (for a Lawyer) is an enthusiast in poetry; and—for a Lawyer—a rather good fellow—he made me a present of the *Endymion*; and I should have had no fault to find with him, had he not told me that he desired Keats, when he took leave of him at Gravesend, to draw upon him for what money he might want!!—I fear he panted to impress me with his spirit of munificence. However he appears to have a high reverence for that fine young mind— and that of itself is very redeeming. . . .

"Lamb has talked very much of the letter he has received from you and promises an answer quickly—his spirits have lately been sadly clouded by a return of his sister's mysterious malady; you are no doubt acquainted with its nature. I called upon Mr Dyer the other day and he and I are to dine with Lamb as soon as he can receive us. That choice specimen of 'white simplicity,' Dyer, is very well, and I think looks just the same as when I was a little Boy, and when he came to see my Father at Enfield. I remember quelling the rude quizzings of some of the little mercantile spirits in the School, when he once entered there, by telling them that 'he was a great Greek scholar, and a Poet.'" September 20th, 1823.

Charles Lamb (to Robert Southey and mankind at large in the *London Magazine*): "Accident introduced me to the acquaintance of Mr L. H— and the experience of his many friendly qualities confirmed a friendship between us. You, who have been misrepresented yourself, I should hope have not lent an idle ear to the calumnies which have been spread abroad respecting this gentleman. I was admitted to his household for some years, and do most solemnly aver that I believe him to be in his domestic relations as correct as any man. He chose an ill-judged subject for a poem; the peccant humours of which have been visited on him tenfold by the artful use, which his adversaries have made, of an *equivocal term*. The subject itself was started by Dante, but better because brieflier treated of. But the crime of the Lovers, in the Italian and the English poet, with its aggravated enormity of circumstance, is not of a kind (as the critics of the latter well knew) with those conjunctions, for which Nature herself has provided no excuse, because no temptation.—It has nothing in common with the black horrors, sung by Ford and Massinger. The familiarising of it in tale or fable may be for that reason incidentally more contagious. In spite of *Rimini*, I must look upon its author as a man of taste, and a poet. He is better than so, he is one of the most cordial-minded men I ever knew, and matchless as a fire-side companion. I mean not to affront or wound your feelings when I say that, in his more genial moods, he has often reminded me of you. There is the same air of mild dogmatism—the same condescending to a boyish sportiveness—in both your conversations. His hand-writing is so much the same with your own, that I have opened more than one letter of his, hoping, nay, not doubting, but it was from you, and have been disappointed (he will bear with my saying so) at the discovery of my error. L. H. is unfortunate in holding some loose and not very definite speculations (for at times I think he hardly knows whither his premises would carry him) on marriage—the tenets, I conceive, of the Political Justice, carried a little further. For any thing I could discover in his practice, they have reference, like those, to some future possible condition of society, and not to the present times. But neither for these obliquities of thinking (upon which my own conclusions are as distant as the poles asunder)—nor for his political asperities and petulancies, which are wearing out with the heats and vanities of youth—did I select him for a friend; but for qualities which fitted him for that relation. I do not know whether I flatter myself with being the occasion, but certain it is, that, touched with some misgivings for sundry harsh things which he had written aforetime against our friend C[oleridge],—before he left this country he sought a reconciliation with that gentleman (himself being his own introducer), and found it.

"L. H. is now in Italy; on his departure to which land with much regret I took my leave of him and of his little family— seven of them, Sir, with their mother—and as kind a set of little people (T[hornton] H. and all), as affectionate children, as ever blessed a parent. Had you seen them, Sir, I think you could not have looked upon them as so many little Jonases— but rather as pledges of the vessel's safety, that was to bear such a freight of love.

"I wish you would read Mr H.'s lines to that same T. H. 'six years old, during a sickness':—

> Sleep breaks at last from out thee,
> My little patient boy—

(they are to be found in the 47th page of *Foliage*)—and ask yourself how far they are out of the spirit of Christianity. I have a letter from Italy, received but the other day, into which L. H. has put as much heart, and as many friendly yearnings after old associates, and native country, as, I think, paper can well hold. It would do you no hurt to give that the perusal also." October 1823.

Mary Novello: "Now, while the atmosphere of pleasure and music is circulating nimbly round, let me endeavour to give you some idea of the commemoration that has taken place this day. It is just two minutes after one, and you are snug in bed, unless thoughts of England and the friends there celebrating your birth should keep you waking. Ah! you may be assured your idea has not been from them this day. We have had Mrs Shelley and Mrs Williams, the Gliddons, with George, &c. last come from you, C. C. C., E. Holmes, H. Robertson, Mr Nyren [the cricketer], C. Evans, Francesco Novello, Vincenzo,

nd Wilful Woman. Miss Kent, unfortunately, was not in
own. . . . We had bay in honour of our poet, laurustinus, Cuba
aponica, &c. Our friends were with us at one in the day,
xcepting those who were at Smith Street, and who joined us
etween five and six. Then our day fairly began; your name
an through the room like a charm, and your spirit seemed to
nimate them all; as though they could not better manifest their
levotion, an universal spirit of enjoyment broke loose; puns—
ood and bad—badinage, raillery, compliments; but, above
ll, music was triumphant. We began with some of the most
lelightful motets—Mozart, Haydn, Handel, Beethoven; then
he March in *Alceste*, with a part of the same arranged to Latin
words by Vincenzo, and which he hopes shortly to forward to
Italy. Then came *Figaro*, *Così fan Tutte*, *Don Giovanni*, *La
Clemenza*, finishing with *Connoscete*, until nearly midnight.
You may imagine the merry supper that succeeded, further
aided by a dozen of champagne (British), which C. C. and E. H.
sent in to assist the gaiety and to drink your health worthily.
Your health *was* drunk *con amore*; and by this time, being pretty
well elated with so many excitements, they sang round the
table *Beviamo*, *How sweet is the Pleasure*, and many other
musical merriments; in short, they were in 'excellent fooling,'
and declared unanimously that such an evening had never been
spent before. Indeed, it only rates second to the Twelfth-night,
and much reminded us of that meeting; yet so closely allied,
as you well know, are pleasure and pain, that several times, and
particularly during the singing of *Ah, Perdona*, many tears
were shed by friendly eyes." October 19th, 1823.

Edward Holmes: "I was much delighted with the Letter to
Mr Novello in the last number of the *Liberal* and particularly
with your description of the no-state of music in Italy and
thought how happy you would feel if you could even get a

fugue to hear; notwithstanding all the Jokes that you and Keats made the last evening I saw him, about their being like two Dogs running after one another through the Dust, &c., &c." 1823.

Mary Shelley (to Marianne Hunt): "After all, I spend a great deal of my time in solitude. I have been hitherto too fully occupied in preparing Shelley's MSS. It is now complete, and the poetry alone will make a large volume. Will you tell Hunt that he need not send any of the MSS. that he has, (except the *Essay on Devils*, and some lines addressed to himself on his arrival in Italy, if he should choose them to be inserted), as I have recopied all the rest? We should be very glad, however, of his notice as quickly as possible, as we wish the book to be out in a month at furthest, and that will not be possible unless he sends it immediately. It would break my heart if the book should appear without it. . . . I have another favour to ask of you. Miss Curran has a portrait of Shelley, in many things very like, and she has so much talent that I entertain great hopes that she will be able to make a good one; for this purpose I wish her to have all the aids possible, and among the rest a profile from you. If you could not cut another, perhaps you would send her one already cut. . . .

"I heard from Bessy that Hunt is writing something for *The Examiner* for me. I *conjecture* that this may be concerning *Valperga*. I shall be glad, indeed, when that comes, or in lieu of it, anything else. John Hunt begins to despair." November 27th, 1823.

The last words quoted bring us in view of a new chasm in Hunt's life. The picture of England in 1823 which, by some of the elements in it, we may presume the exile to have formed as a whole, was generally a smiling prospect; it is doubly melancholy, then, to observe that it was traversed by a gloom arising out of a fraternal alliance, that had once seemed beyond

the troubler of mankind. Even love, set among business affairs,
is liable to changes, and inferior to law. The proprietorship of
The Examiner was obscurely determined, its sales were none
too splendid, John Hunt was doing the work, Leigh was contributing occasionally and relying on John for remittances.
During 1823, John pointed out to his brother, with the quiet
honesty natural to him, that he could not easily involve himself
further, Leigh then owing him some £800; by the new year,
the debt was the ominous one, even according to our modern
ideas of pounds sterling, of £1790. 19s. 10d. Yet Leigh did not
hesitate to declare that his *Examiner* rights were sound, and
separate from private finances; so that a difference between
these two brothers began, and widened into a coldness, by
means of a ponderous correspondence, and in spite of the
mediation of Vincent Novello, Charles Brown and others. Our
reflection of Hunt's visions of England must have its rosiness
dimmed by this growing cloud.

John Hunt: "I have seen Mrs Shelley twice (who appears
to be a very unaffected and agreeable woman) and she has
intimated to me, that if I could state to you what your receipt
would be likely to be in future, it would be a useful piece o
information. Now this is a matter wholly out of my power.
The *Liberal* volumes may or may not turn to some account.
The Literary Examiner does not at present quite pay its way,
though it rises gradually—and you will see on the other side
the sums I have paid to you and for you for 1822-23. *The
Examiner* after nearly a year (owing to the change of price)
yielding absolutely nothing, is now getting up again, and producing profits; and, under all the circumstances of the last two
years,—as well as the present state of the paper and your entire
secession from it,—I should like to hear your opinion as to the
extent of the claim on your part which Mrs Shelley hints about.

I stated to her, that I should not think myself a proper judge, on a question of this nature, and that possibly it would be well if a friend of yours (Mr Novello for instance, or Mr Procter, or both of them) should decide upon it—for any such decision would be a law to me. Think of this at once.

"You will perceive from the accounts, that you have drawn a considerable sum for your own use in Italy—that is, considerable, considering the source from which it comes, and the value of money in Italy, which is, I find, *at least double* what it is in England. . . .

"Mrs S. will have consulted you on writing some account of her late husband, to accompany an edition of his works she is going to publish. Have you not got something of the sort by you?

"Do you not think the Fables from Chaucer would make a good publication? I mean, that you should take those already done well by Dryden, Pope, &c., and make a selection of the best of the sort, with others by yourself. Mr Hazlitt thinks such a work should sell. Pope wrote a rhapsody called the *Messiah*— What do you say to a philosophical poem called 'Jesus'? in which the divine doctrine of 'loving one another' would be done justice to and all his benevolent actions displayed and contrasted with modern Christianity? There would be ample food for *satire* on the Christian Pharisees, and the picture therefore not wanting in contrast. My belief is, that *you* could make a fine thing of this, as well as a novel and useful one." September 19th, 1823.

Leigh Hunt did not much attend to the need for new fables, nor did the proposed Christiad take shape in his study; but he called Vincent Novello in as an envoy, and on December 15th that musician was able to report, "John says he is willing to secure you an Annuity of One Hundred Pounds from *The*

Examiner as long as it continues in existence under his controul, in consideration of your former exertions in raising the reputation of the Paper. He will also pay a certain sum for whatever articles you may in future contribute towards it." Novello had asked that the annuity should be increased if the sales rose above a certain number. "To this proposition your brother also assented with the utmost readiness, and indeed manifested the most unequivocal disposition to conciliate matters and to meet all your wishes if possible." But matters dragged on. At least, Leigh seems to have temporarily accepted the annuity, and *The Examiner* through 1824 and most of 1825 entertained his series of "Wishing-Cap Papers," for each of which he received two guineas. "I never wrote better prose in my life," he thought, when the impulse and the device were fresh; but presently his regularity failed, while in June 1824 his brother reported that the irregular inclusion of the essays sent was due to "the press of temporary matter." John Hunt mentioned his own financial anxieties: "solitary as my nature is, I have been obliged to admit a widower and his three children to board and lodge in my house. Lord B.'s remains," he proceeds, "have just reached England. He is to be buried in Poets' Corner, but privately." A few days later John Hunt writes of his punishment for publishing *The Vision of Judgment*: "This affair was settled this morning—and in some respects more happily than I expected. The sentence of the court is, a fine of £100, and to give sureties (for five years) to the amount of £2000. . . . The fine I expect (but am not sure) will be part returned to me by Lord B.'s Executors. . . . Of course the death of Lord B. is a heavy blow to me, as I had only just begun to obtain some advantage from the connexion. In a short time, you will receive a statement of accounts from the beginning of this year. . . . A volume of Mr Shelley's Posthumous Poems has just been published.

Mrs Shelley waited as long as possible for a notice from your pen—and not getting it, made a brief one herself; in which she alludes to the want of yours, and hopes it may yet be supplied. The volume promises to repay something—at least the expenses. So another, of prose, will be prepared—and for this I hope you will be able to furnish some Account of Mr Shelley's Life &c. A Review of the Poems by Mr Hazlitt will appear in the next No. of the *Edinburgh Review*. I have put your *Bacchus in Tuscany* into the hands of a Printer."

The "Wishing-Caps" becoming more and more at the mercy of "temporary matter," John wrote on July 20th recommending his brother to profit by a request from Henry Colburn, and to contribute to that publisher's *New Monthly*; at the same time he desired Leigh to cease drawing bills "on us," and reminded him that Shelley's prose works would "shortly go to press, as the sale of his poems will justify the risk." This tribute to the commercial competency of Shelley's verse must have been almost the earliest. In October Colburn called on John Hunt again and desired him to obtain from Leigh £150 worth of prose and verse *per annum* for the *New Monthly*, and John, passing on the renewed opportunity, told Leigh that one "Wishing-Cap" a fortnight would be welcome for *The Examiner*; he noted that, although Charles Brown advised him to cancel what Leigh owed him, he "could say nothing about it till the arrangement between us is completed." Voluminous expositions of the issue in Charles Brown's writing are extant, dated November 17th, 1824, and later. He told John Hunt's son that he had examined the accounts independently. "They were the most perplexing papers ever laid before me." (Brown had been a merchant in St Petersburg.) The trouble was partly the result of John Hunt's calling in a third party to finance *The Examiner*—an independent step by which he defined himself the proprietor, and Leigh the editor. Leigh, genially taking wing to Italy, had ceased to be editor. And John at last had reduced the problem to that simple, if unfraternal, view. Brown, who before considering the affair closely expected to find Leigh in the wrong, very vigorously declared him in the right. Apart from the more technical reasonings, Brown has a striking thing to say of John Hunt's errors: "He will recollect my telling him how wrongly, in my opinion, he had acted in having assisted his brother when his income was more than sufficient; that such assistance had fostered his imprudence. . . . I am aware how bitter a thing it is, to hear that our best actions have been real injuries. . . . It would have been better had [Leigh Hunt] endured an ounce of suffering at first than thus be crushed with a ton at last. . . ."

The year 1825 came in, and the brothers were sharply divided. The efforts of Brown for bringing them together had now been simplified into plain iterations of his claim that Leigh Hunt was still a partner in the newspaper, and his blame of John for making Leigh's descent into a debtor's Avernus so easy. Hazlitt, and Seymour Kirkup, also bent their brows over the mass of papers; they rose convinced that Leigh Hunt was justified. Kirkup drew up a paper of proofs of this. John Hunt issued a paper of "Proofs that L. H. has forfeited (not *given away*) his Proprietorship." It was perfectly arranged by the ironical angel of Leigh Hunt's life that, amid this tumult, his brother should be the publisher and the dedicatee of his glorious *Bacchus in Tuscany*; the inscription, dated January 1st, 1825, ends, "May it give you a hundredth part of the elevation which you have often caused to the heart of your affectionate Brother, Leigh Hunt." In his preface to "Strafford," Robert Browning salutes this *Bacchus*.

We may now take a liberty with time, and turn back to the

Italian experiences of our wildly confused but still shining hero
since Byron left him positively to find his way for himself, beginning with the autumn of 1823. On August 22nd the family
had left Genoa, in blazing sunshine, for Florence, where the
first two words he distinguished in the talk of bystanders,
"Fiori" and "Donne," seemed to him to light up the future
again. After a short pause in the city, he established himself at
Maiano, on the neighbouring hillside—a coign of vantage before which "Florence lay clear and cathedralled," and round
which the souls of immortal poets and painters lingered. Of
these it was Boccaccio's spirit that Hunt thought he realised
most intimately: he afterwards wrote, "I lived with the divine
human being, with his friends of the Falcon and the Basil, and
my own not unworthy melancholy; and went about the flower-
ing lanes and the hills, solitary indeed, and sick to the heart, but
not unsustained. In looking back to such periods of one's
existence, one is surprised to find how much they surpass many
occasions of mirth, and what a rich tone of colour their very
darkness assumes, as in some fine old painting. My almost daily
walk was to Fiesole, through a path skirted with wild myrtle
and cyclamen; and I stopped at the cloister of the Doccia, and
sat on the pretty melancholy platform behind it, reading, or
looking through the pines down to Florence. In the Valley of
Ladies, I found some English trees (trees not vine and olive) and
even a meadow; and these, while I made them furnish me with
a bit of my old home in the north, did no injury to the memory
of Boccaccio, who is of all countries, and finds his home wherever we do ourselves, in love, in the grave, in a desert island."

Soon after the arrival in Florence, Fanny Burney's niece
passed that way, and gratified the Hunts with talk of Charles
and Mary Lamb. A less transient means of revisiting the
glimpses was the near residence of Charles Brown, who, as his

friend Keats would have sparkled to see, had managed to take over as his lively headquarters what had been a convent. "We discoursed of love and wine in the apartments of the Lady Abbess," and Brown's beloved Hogarth surely made himself at home on the mystic walls. Presently Brown moved from this "pleasant lair" into Florence, and he appears to have taken with him, in an optimistic firmness, one of Leigh Hunt's troubles, as yet not come to full size but quite active—the urchin John Hunt Junr. Of this boy's psychological abnormality—a collocation of brilliance, good-nature, savage temper and criminal subtlety—Thornton Hunt gives some account. In childhood "he attacked his brothers with knives" more than once, and "in order to extort some indulgence from his mother, whose state of health has already been mentioned, he held the carving-knife over the soft part of the head of an infant brother." The cordial and knowing Brown attempted to educate John's best and eradicate his worst, but by January 21st, 1824, he was convinced that the task was beyond him[1], and he returned the precocious rogue, who had the knack of catching what his seniors said and making use of these pieces of information, to his father. "You had earnestly hoped, as I had confidently expected, to receive him, at the end of six months, from my own hand, a good affectionate boy, and I cannot bear to think of your disappointment. Yet, as I have told you before, he is better in respect to truth, honesty and cleanliness, and for that amendment he merits your praise." The subsequent caprices of

---

[1] R. Westmacott to J. Severn, May 10th, 1824: "I feel I should have liked Mr Hunt more and more every time I met him. . . . I thought our old plague, Johnny Hunt, looked very ill. I think he must be improved, for altho' he tried to bolt up to me with his *taking, innocent*-sounding 'Ah! how d'ye do, Sir?' I saw he made himself scarce as soon as possible— poor child! or rather, poor parents! I suspect a bad child is a curse of which we single gentlemen can't even *imagine* the bitterness."

John became one of the forces in Hunt's life which did most mischief but were least revealed.

At this period Brown was the closest confidant of W. S. Landor, who then lived at Florence, and Hunt now felt a veneration for that great heretic much more profound than his gay critical disrespect of years before. "He is like a stormy mountain pine, that should produce lilies. After indulging the partialities of his friendships and enmities, and trampling on kings and ministers, he shall cool himself, like a Spartan worshipping a moonbeam, in the patient meekness of Lady Jane Grey." Acquaintance began over a strand of Lucretia Borgia's hair, which had been given to Hunt. Landor wrote on it:

> Borgia, thou once wert almost too august,
> And high for adoration;—now thou'rt dust!
> All that remains of thee these plaits infold—
> Calm hair meand'ring with pellucid gold!

Hunt nicknamed Landor "Wat Sylvan," and was especially impressed with one part of Landor's autobiography, "He had shot at a pheasant, and *many hours afterwards* found it where it had fallen, not dead, and in manifest torment. Since then he has never drawn a trigger." Landor liked Hunt, and consulted him on the question of his publisher John Taylor and his "villany" over *Imaginary Conversations*, receiving satisfactory support from one who already entertained no excess of gratitude towards Taylor. To have manuscript annotations by Landor in one or two books was not Hunt's only reward; later on he received some of the furious abundance of poems and articles which Landor lavished on favourite newspapers. Florence gave Hunt, as well as this new alliance, the acquaintance of the leisurely artist Kirkup and the spirited patriot Lord Dillon.

And yet the Londoner languished for want of several old friends. His letters to the Novellos and to his sister-in-law developed into jesting, yet inwardly serious petitions: "Tell me when are you coming," "*When*, WHEN, WHEN do you come?" What would have been the setting and circumstances of their friend if they had arrived? Had it been six in the morning (we rely on Hunt's veracity), they would have found him interchanging English and Italian with "a young man of the name of Giannetti, who made a very kind and attentive master to his children, and promised to be an excellent instructor." Or, at more familiar hours, he would "have been writing a long set of prayers and meditations for the use of those who are not of the Established Religious Opinion, which he felt it his duty to do, and which half killed him." Or, the servant problem being as usual, he would be nursing the baby. Or he might be reappearing with a few books and prints under his arm, captured on the stalls in Florence. One thing is certain; his study was precisely what Keats and Shelley would have desired in walking out of the vines and fig-trees into their Indicator's modest mansion. The portrait of Keats hung there now. Locks of his and of Shelley's hair lay carefully ordered beside that one of Milton which they had liked to gaze upon; Napoleon and Lucretia Borgia were now their neighbours in this queer eternity. Paintings from *Il Penseroso* by Havell recalled the flourishing season when Hunt had played his little part in encouraging British artists, by buying their works, and visiting their exhibitions. Extensively alluring, the fifty-two volumes of that wonderful anthology the *Parnaso Italiano* occupied their accustomed place, among the accustomed rivals, from the *Arabian Nights* to the *Faerie Queene*, from Anacreon to La Fontaine, from the Greek Mythology to the Greek Lexicon. Beside the *Republic* of Plato stood Diogenes Laërtius's *Lives of the Philosophers*. "These two works belonged to dear S.," and had the double appeal of being concerned in the writing of

Adonais. Among these distressing consolations Hunt wrote his literary and personal articles with a beating brain and a shaking hand, while Marianne "at the very least fright and surprise" continued to alarm him almost daily by bringing up quantities of blood.

However, Marianne did not die; she went on with her needlework and her protest that the local tradesmen were a rabble of thieves, and she became more and more a domestic fixture. She threatened her sister Bessy, if she came to Italy, with a share of the needlework; but Bessy was not coming, partly because of that prospect, chiefly because of previous discords excited by her presence in Marianne's household—the same that had once made her throw herself into a pond at Hampstead, while Keats was waiting for his breakfast. So Marianne and Leigh went on playing chess in the intervals of business: "Marianne and I are fairly equal players."

The thoughts of home became more dominant, and were freshened by news of and from Charles Lamb. Mrs Novello wrote at the close of 1824: "Miss Lamb is as kind and delightful as ever, Mr Lamb has not improved his peevishness by having taken lately to theological subjects; he sometimes swears at the folly of infidels and calls us cursed hereticks, and the next moment relates some blasphemous anecdote he told when in company with Mr Irving the Scotch preacher." To Hunt, now author of a manuscript manual of intimate devotions, there must have appeared some sly motive in Lamb's letter to him, written at about the same time: "I was with the Novellos last week. They have a large, cheap house and garden, with a dainty library (magnificent) without books. But what will make you bless yourself (I am too old for wonder), something has touched the right organ in Vincentio at last. He attends a Wesleyan chapel on Kingsland Green. He at first tried to laugh it off—

he only went for the singing; but the cloven foot—I retract—
the Lamb's trotters—are at length apparent. Mary Isabella
attributes it to a lightness induced by his headaches. But I
think I see in it a less accidental influence. Mister Clark is at
perfect staggers! the whole fabric of his infidelity is shaken.
He has no one to join him in his coarse insults and indecent
obstreperousnesses against Christianity, for Holmes (the bonny
Holmes) is gone to Salisbury to be organist, and Isabella and
the Clark make but a feeble quorum. The children have all nice,
neat little clasped pray-books, and I have laid out 7s. 8d. in
Watts's Hymns for Christmas presents for them. The eldest girl
alone holds out; she has been at Boulogne, skirting upon the
vast focus of Atheism, and imported bad principles in patois
French. But the strongholds are crumbling. N. appears as yet
to have but a confused notion of the Atonement. It makes him
giddy, he says, to think much about it. But such giddiness is
spiritual sobriety." Lamb presently changes his note as he
seriously commends Edward Irving, "this Boanerges in the
Temple," to his now distant correspondent.

One immortalised distant correspondent of Elia, Barron
Field, had returned to England during 1824. By way of
welcome to this old friend Hunt sent the *New Monthly*, among
his first literary supplies to Colburn's order, a paper of verses,
which, having been overlooked and forgotten, I shall introduce
here with several intentions; first, to show how vividly Hunt
could picture what lay beyond the horizon; second, to illustrate
that zeal for the public benefit which rose clear from private
perplexities; then, to exemplify the ability he had in subjects
not commonly connected with him; next, to give his matured
power over metre and vocabulary and the Dryden manner its
due; but, as much as anything, to offer a diversion to those who
have marched through so much thirsty prose. We are still in

sad confusion over metropolitan improvements. It will be amusing to hear the complaints that earlier improvements, which were their superiors, drew from a mind that is too often associated with promiscuous enjoyment.

Epistle to B. F. Esq.

But just returned from Australasian shores,
Rich in rare plants, and scientific stores,
Gazing around you with bewildered eye,
"What's this? Stands London where it did?" you cry.
Alas, dear F., no wonder that the clown
Exclaimed "Gadzooks! why, Lunnun's out of town."
Ask you by what disease 'tis bloated thus?
A giant wen, a Titan Polypus!
Bursting with brick and mortar every vein,
Spreads the huge carcase o'er the circling plain.
Where fields, parks, groves but lately soothed thine eyes,
Squares, places, quadrants endlessly arise;
While streets that intersect a thousand ways
Make the whole scene a labyrinthine maze,
No more a city, but a province, thick
With houses sown—a wilderness of brick.

This is Improvement's age: we grant as much,
If pulling down and building up be such;
If architecture's rules we may neglect,
And most enrich the poorest architect,
That which was wisely hidden give to view,
Remove old eyesores, and establish new.

If here and there some purer pile be placed,
Free from the blunders of distorted taste,
How many still offend the classic eye,
With wild caprice, or dull deformity,
And from their barbarous fronts defiance throw
To all the rescripts of Palladio,
An order of disorder, true to none,
Or formed of all confounded into one.

See the grand street! each paltry tenement,
Mean in materials, meaner in extent,
Whose lath and brickwork through thin stucco gleams,
Soaked by a shower, or cracked by solar beams,
Their poverty more inconsistent made,
(Like beggars dressed in tatters of brocade,)
By porticoes that half the building hide,
Rams-horn pilasters propped on either side,
Each tottering pillar an inverted cone,
Made to support all weights, except its own,
And balustrades at top, whose ponderous row
Squeezes the shallow pediment below;
Parts disproportioned to the end designed,
Tasteless when separate, and worse combined,
Flimsily executed, proudly planned,
Pompously mean, and pitifully grand.

Nor do our private buildings show alone
These wild anomalies of brick and stone;
Blindly to Christian churches we transfer
The types and emblems of the Idolater:
The skull and garlands of the victim ox,—
Why not the knives and sacrificial blocks?
The tripod's base, whose use no soul can guess,—
Why not the tripod and the Pythoness?
The lantern of Diogenes resigns
Its Pagan purpose, and a belfry shines:
Such the dull freaks of plagiarists in stone,
Who know not others' meanings, nor their own.

If among heathen temples they must search
Emblems to deck the exterior of the church,
For its internal structure they prefer
The model of some gaudy theatre,
Fitted for souls polite, who cannot pray
Unless the place remind them of the play,
And deem all sermons doubly orthodox
At which they slumber in a private box.

Here is the loggia and the colonnade,
Wisely invented in the South for shade,
Formed but to chill and darken where the sun
We seldom see, and never wish to shun.
There, is the modern Gothic, where we seek
In vain the genuine features of the antique.
A motley pile where every age has thrown
Some heterogeneous fragments of its own,
To all false taste impertinently true,
As old unreverenced, and scorned as new.

At least, you cry, our higher ranks ensure
Patrons more wise, and models less impure;
Some classic structure will their zeal provide,
To grace the present, and the future guide.
Turn to our teachers, and that hope withdraw;
Behold a cottage-palace thatched with straw,
Or view that gew-gaw bauble by the sea,
Each barbarism's dread epitome.
Kremlin, Alhambra, and Pagoda join
Their own, and every Vandal fault purloin,
To show at once whatever can displease
In Tartar, Russ, Moor, Savage, or Chinese;
Without, a nondescript that all deride;
A mere bazaar and baby-house inside,
Poor in effect, though mighty in pretence,
And only truly royal in expense.

Strange that our artists should new names devise
In works like these their share to signalise,
And from posterity desire the shame
Of having built what every age must blame.
Lucky! their works, too crumbling to abide,
With rapid ruin will defeat their pride,
And both shall lie in joint oblivion wrecked,
The flimsy pile, and nameless architect.

But the influence of Hunt's ancient goblin the Regent had
not, after all, reduced all London to architectural polygamy,

and, though he made terms with misfortune by professing to make Italy his study and source of future literary productions, it was only his want of money that kept him from hurrying back even into the vicinity of Mrs Fitzherbert's Villa. His Wishing-Cap might take his soul, almost with the five senses, into Covent Garden; "spiritual eyes might have seen it shot over from Tuscany into York-street, like a rocket"; but even Leigh Hunt possessed a solid body, which at the end of his day-dream reminded him that he was in a far country, with its mountains determined to petrify him too, its voices louder than any London cries, its summer sun dustily overdoing the part of Apollo. At the close of 1824, there he was waiting at Maiano for Bessy Kent's box of books, and wondering why Nature should make a jest so often of his life. Surely she could not be guilty of so heartless a practical joke as to inurn him there. He brooded over the guilt, as far as his isolated penury was concerned, of a more readily imaginable though now departed humorist—the author of *Don Juan*, and the originator of *The Liberal: Verse and Prose from the South*.

A story was put about which at any rate satisfied the spiritualistic Mary Howitt, and I am not prepared to deny what that good woman believed. One day Richard Westmacott, Leigh Hunt and others were taking the air and conversing. A black butterfly of remarkable size and beauty settled near them. They watched it with fascination. Hunt commented on the Psyche of the Greeks. The butterfly remained for an unusual length of time. The day was April 19th, 1824,—the day of Byron's death at Missolonghi.

The Refugee

HAZLITT arrived in Florence early in 1825, and all the rich poetry in him was up to greet the picture, real and ideal, which Leigh Hunt's windows commanded. It was the end of February, but "like April weather in England." Hazlitt was moved: "Might I once more see the coming on of Spring as erst in the spring-time of my life, it would be here!" It is unlikely that Hunt agreed with him in this, though usually their renewed conversation accorded vigorously in contempt for Gifford, and the *Quarterly*, and those who had apparently seduced Byron's courage away from *The Liberal*—Tom Moore and Hobhouse. Hazlitt did not think that Hunt appreciated his Italian opportunities sufficiently, and later on reported him (if we may take Haydon's authority!) as being "dull as a hen under a penthouse on a rainy day." Hazlitt proposed a visit to Venice, Hunt would not stir; to Rimini—the author of *Rimini* could live without it. On the other hand, Hunt had seen the Venus de' Medici, and was disappointed; Hazlitt thoroughly agreed with him. The friendship between these two men was of that sinew and growth which could endure agreement or disagreement, and one evening at Maiano the new Mrs Hazlitt was amused by Hunt's handing her husband a paper, in which he had reproved Hazlitt for his splenetic irregularities. Dinner waited while the admirable reprobate read through the case against himself, and when he had done, his comment was, "By God, sir, there's a good deal of truth in it."

Busy as he was with writing essays, as gay and sociable as he could make them, for his brother and for Colburn—the "Wishing-Cap" for *The Examiner*, and "The Family Journal" in the character of Harry Honeycomb for the *New Monthly*—

Hunt now endeavoured to adapt himself to his local possibilities and to set up a journal for the English residents in Italy. In Florence at that time there were two hundred English families, and elsewhere it seemed probable that such a journal would find support. The prosperity of the Galignanis with their English publications in France also encouraged the projector, who now in his most flowing calligraphy prepared the

Prospectus of a New Monthly Publication
to be entitled
Molini's English Magazine.

The hope was "to supply English people in Italy, whether travellers or residents, with the best portions of the current literature of their own country"; the safeguard was that religious and political matters would be avoided; the allurement, that "there are periodical writers now flourishing in England, who need not fear comparison with some of the most honoured names of our literature." He pointed to Elia and the author of *Table Talk* as examples. Mr Molini the bookseller had at first hailed this idea as one of the best schemes for hitting up an income which could have been made; but then "the Tuscan authorities" took a hand, and presented the insuperable difficulties of ensuring that religion and politics did not creep in past their censorship. So nothing was done, and Mr Molini was left groping for comfort over his charcoal brazier, and inappropriately assuring the distressed Hunt, "Ah, you are veree happee in England; you can get so much money as you please."

Whatever Hunt had to say of religion, for the time, had been said in a manuscript sent to John Hunt, who acknowledged it: "The Meditations &c. have been received. It is not in my power to offer any sum for them. If you please, I will print and publish them at my own risk, and share with you whatever profit may arise. It is a question, I think, whether persons who belong to no religious sect will feel an interest in such productions; but they may; and there is a novelty in them which may strike." For several years these attempts at creating a new sect remained unpublished, and they may be suitably considered later on.

An advance of money from, and a mortgaging of literary services to, Henry Colburn, seem to have been the means of releasing the Hunts from Italy. By June 1825 the northern hope was crowned with certainty. "I shall set him down as the most *engaging* of publishers. What I mean to do for him is infinite. . . ." The bliss of Leigh Hunt in every fresh appearance of good luck is too rare a thing to be gravely questioned; who, that might have known, would have warned him that even here his roses were to turn to poison-berries? Colburn's rescue was to be paid for in a sensational work which Hunt could neither refuse to supply, nor write without injustice and danger to himself. But naturally the prisoner of Maiano was not going to consider a large cheque as a sibylline leaf; it meant England. "Mud—mud is our object." Hunt lived too soon for the real mud era of 1914 to 1918, but even that would not have deterred him from hiring the famous *vettura* in which that September of 1825, at six in the morning, his flock of ten left the haunt of Boccaccio, on their road to Calais. The anglicising eye of Hunt saw in their driver's appearance a resemblance to Charles Lamb, now so soon to be repossessed. It was a month before the party could embark on the steamboat at Calais, and in that time they felt all the odd pleasure of hurrying by unusual and beautiful places, and the vitality of rapid impressions. Hunt was by no means unenterprising in the capture of "associations," the touch of Tassoni, or Ariosto, or Alfieri, and at Turin he witnessed with rapture "the finest dancer I ever saw"—de' Martini.

At Chambéry he hurried to the white house of Rousseau, and in Paris he stood in the place where the guillotine had done its work. The bookstalls with the profusion of Voltaire pleased him well. He had a vision of himself as a bachelor, lodging over a bookseller's shop on the Quai de Voltaire, and airing himself of an evening towards the Champs Elysées. But shortly his large household was being jolted along once more, to Calais, where all went aboard the steamboat for London, on October 12th, 1825. The Novellos had been entrusted with the choice of lodgings for them in London. For a time after their arrival they had to be content with living in Bloomsbury, but the northern heights of London still called Leigh Hunt, and he haunted Highgate until in 1826 he found a house there.

Enraptured with his return, he put most of his work aside, and gave himself up to the pleasure of calling on his old friends, even reviving his most ancient companionships with Tommy Hill and Dubois, the wits of Sydenham twenty years before; while he now saw another of that set, Thomas Campbell, in his capacity as editor of the *New Monthly*. One need not emphasise his cheerful return to his heartiest intimacies and recreations, unless to quote Mary Cowden Clarke: "Pleasant were the walks and talks taken arm-in-arm with such a host and entertainer as Leigh Hunt. . . . He also shone brilliantly in his after-breakfast pacings up and down his room. Clad in the flowered wrapping-gown he was so fond of wearing when at home, he would continue the lively subject broached during breakfast, or launch forth into some fresh one, gladly prolonging that bright and pleasant morning hour. . . . At the time of which I am speaking, Leigh Hunt was full of some translations he was making from Clement Marot and other of the French epigrammatists; and as he walked to and fro he would fashion a line or two, and hit off some felicitous turn of phrase, between whiles whistling with a melodious soft little birdy tone in a mode peculiar to himself of drawing the breath inwardly instead of sending it forth outwardly through his lips. . . . He was also cogitating the material for a book which he purposed naming 'Fabulous Zoology'; and while this idea was in the ascendant his talk would be rife of dragons, griffins, hippogriffs, minotaurs, basilisks. . . ." This notion, caught up from the appendix of a work published in 1826, resulted only in a few gracefully erudite essays.

There was one friend to whose door Leigh Hunt refrained from going, nor, had he stirred, would it have opened to let him in. It was his brother John's. John refused to meet him, or to go to places where he might appear. It is probable that some private complications interfered with the originally answerable problem of *Examiner* property, and provoked the tolerant John into his extreme irrecognition of his brother. The gulf between the two old brother Reformists, as it could not be concealed—an unlucky dinner invitation would reveal it in a moment—obviously threatened to weaken Leigh Hunt's more public position, and to give his enemies a new rumour of his discredit. Leigh attempted to meet the danger by writing explanations here and there, and at least he could say that, when the main point at issue was finally submitted to arbitration, the award was in his favour. But even such an admirer as Cyrus Redding of the *New Monthly* could not feel the excellence of the explanations: "Mr John Hunt had told me the cause, and a man of greater probity I never knew."

Hazlitt's must have been one of the warmest welcomes home that Hunt met with, for it was in 1825 that he brought out his *Spirit of the Age*, with a sketch of his friend's merits in it. "[Hunt] improves upon acquaintance. The author translates admirably into the man. Indeed, the very faults of his style are virtues in the individual. His natural gaiety and sprightliness of manner, his high animal spirits, and the *vinous* quality of his mind, produce an immediate fascination and intoxication in those who come in contact with him, and carry off in society whatever in his writings may to some seem flat and impertinent. From great sanguineness of temper, from great quickness and unsuspecting simplicity, he runs on to the public as he does at his own fireside, and talks about himself, forgetting that he is not always among friends. His look, his tone are required to point many things that he says: his frank, cordial manner reconciles you instantly to a little overbearing, overweening self-complacency. 'To be admired, he needs but to be seen': but perhaps he ought to be seen to be fully appreciated." In thus lauding Leigh Hunt as a man, Hazlitt might be taken as discommending his literary powers, but he presently attends to those also: "He is the only poet or literary man we ever knew who puts us in mind of Sir John Suckling, or Killigrew, or Carew; or who united rare intellectual acquirements with outward grace and natural gentility. Mr Hunt ought to have been a gentleman born, and to have patronised men of letters. He might then have played, and sung, and laughed, and talked his life away; have written manly prose, elegant verse: and his 'Story of Rimini' would have been praised by Mr Blackwood. As it is, there is no man now living who at the same time writes prose and verse so well, with the exception of Mr Southey (an exception, we fear, that will be little palatable to either of these gentlemen)." Hazlitt goes on to specify the third canto of *Rimini* and the *Epistle to Byron* as masterly; but he might have given Hunt still more pleasure if he had said a word for some more recent effusion.

The *New Monthly* now had the services of the three best essayists in England—Lamb, Hazlitt and Hunt. The unities

of this triumvirate have been described by their friend B. W.
Procter (Barry Cornwall), and while he perceives their varying
originality, he settles the secret of their natural alliance: "Each
of them understood the others, and placed just value on their
objections when any difference of opinion (not infrequent)
arose between them." The delicate, unalterable Procter was one
of those who delighted in Hunt's homecoming, and offered
him choice refection for body and mind. Among Procter's
letters of 1826 we find one to Hunt dated July 27th at once
amusing and touching: "Have you seen the Caricature of
Charles Lamb? I went into the shop of a Printseller (whom I
know) and remonstrated with him on the heinousness of selling
such a libel—but he attempted to justify himself by saying that
it was not intended as a piece of scandal or libel—that it was
done by an acquaintance of C. L. who did not *intend* to libel
him—and finally that he had sold all the copies he had of this
eminent Critic and Essayist!"

Among the publications which came to Hunt's notice about
the time of his return from Italy, two or three, besides what
have been mentioned, contained something relating to himself.
I need not reckon up the usual horrified outcries of *Blackwood's* against his writings and his morals; these were now
mere routine; I pause rather over kindlier testimonies of wit
to his influence. His verse was parodied in a little known
collection called "Warreniana; by the Editor of a Quarterly
Review"—in which the literati were represented as uniting in
apostrophes to Warren and his blacking. Here, Hunt's poetic
idiom was obliged to produce little felicities like "Apollo
followed arter"—but then Coleridge's mastiff in *Christabel* also
had to

> Bark her chorus of bow, wow, wow,
> *Bow* for the quarters, and *wow* for the hour.

Hunt's prose was imitated by P. G. Patmore in a strangely savourless but amiable successor to the *Rejected Addresses*, entitled *Imitations of Celebrated Authors*. A stranger with a right taste inscribed to Hunt his *Day in Stowe Gardens*[1]; and now Bessy Kent put forth her companion volume to the *Flora Domestica*, called *Sylvan Sketches*, in which the naturalists and poets are assembled to admire trees, and Keats and Shelley and Hunt are of the commission. The familiar love between British botany and verse at that period would occupy enquiry agreeably for many a winter's evening, and it is singular to see how widely the words and names of the Romantic poets travelled by the indirect means of works like *Sylvan Sketches*.

Meanwhile Henry Colburn was sending out numerous and ostentatious biographical works, and I find it stated that one of these, the theatrical memoirs of Michael Kelly, was arranged by Hunt; but the true editor was Theodore Hook. Hunt brought out no volume during 1826 and 1827.

> Had time and change not blotted out
> The love of former days,

it may be pictured how merrily busy he would have been with transforming old predilections into new books; for it was now that his nephew Henry and his old friend Clarke were colleagues in a publishing campaign, which ended in a dismal financial breakdown, but not before the unlucky firm had done well by literature. Hunt and Clarke have left us a cleverly chosen and convenient series of the best Autobiographies, which atones for the trouble they caused Hazlitt.

And Hazlitt once again gave trouble to Leigh Hunt, in 1826, by publishing a new outcry against Shelley. Was peace never to be obtained, even though the exile in Florence had now be-

---

[1] Lamb was asked what he thought of the book. He answered, "A day ill bestowed."

come the neighbour of the sage of Highgate? Chilled with the injury to a beloved memory, Hunt yet had the unassailable refuge of Shelley's faithful love; and it was not long after Hazlitt's outbreak that Mary Shelley gave him fresh evidence of that. "I told you, long ago, that our beloved lost Shelley intended, on rewriting his will, to have left you a legacy; I think the sum he mentioned was 2,000 *l.* I trust that hereafter you will not refuse to consider me your debtor for this sum, merely because I shall be bound to pay you by the laws of honour instead of a legal obligation. . . . I have as yet made no will, but if in the meantime I should chance to die, this paper may serve as a legal document to prove that I give and bequeath to you, dear Leigh Hunt, the sum of two thousand pounds sterling. But I hope we shall both live—I to accomplish our Shelley's intentions, you to honour me so far as to permit me to be the executor." This blessed hope was silently accompanied with a meditation on the imminent death of Shelley's father, who nevertheless deferred that incident for eighteen years longer. The £2000 at a blow, like the tower at Penshurst[1] promised to Hunt by Shelley, to whom the estate of Philip Sidney might have come, never happened.

---

[1] Leigh Hunt had mentioned this imaginatively in the *New Monthly* for March 1825. "That house was to have become the property of a beloved friend, now no more. He promised me a turret of it, which was to be called by my name; 'and here,' said he, 'if there is such a thing as heaven upon earth, will you and I realise it.' We were to have had books infinite, horses, a boat. The manor-house supplied us with excellent neighbours. 'If I happen,' said my friend, 'to die in the midst of our enjoyments, I will stay and live with you still in spirit, for a diviner corner than this I cannot imagine.' Alas! he died before he entered into possession, and I am not rich enough to inherit it for him. But if I am rich in any thing, it is in memory and affection. I live near the place; the property of the house is contested, and likely to be so; it is now uninhabited. I sit looking at it, as I used to do at Claude's picture of the Enchanted Castle; and fancy my departed friend still living with me according to his promise.

One regrets to turn aside once again to a private dispute, but it is the depressing fact that Leigh Hunt, essentially a man of peace, was always in the wars. This time the enemy was his mother-in-law. "Amongst his female relatives," runs the cautious record of his eldest son, "there was one for whom he had, at a boyish age, conceived a very high and a just esteem." This lady, whom we saw first as Mrs Kent and then as Mrs Hunter (not Leo Hunter), seems to have agreed with him entirely, and when presently he defended Bessy Kent from her indignation she smelt treason. Another door was closed, "with force and eloquence," on the dilapidated mediator. But when in September 1827 little Swinburne Hunt was lying dead, the calmness of that pale child-countenance woke in the father an irresistible sense of the wasteful stupidity of vendetta among the living; and he wrote nobly to persuade the Hunters into a new beginning and the way of peace. "There is nothing worth contesting here below, except who shall be kindest to one another." The appeal was heard, the spell broken.

But another and a more extensive upheaval was already being prepared by and for Leigh Hunt. It appears (for documents are not to be found) that he had promised Colburn, in return for his timely advances of money, a volume or two on Italy, and a selection from his writings with a memoir of himself; and he found himself drifting downstream without completing what he had undertaken. In an honourable anxiety to be fair to his publisher, he hurried into a modification of the original plans, and one which Colburn naturally encouraged and

He will not do so the less, because my enjoyments are disappointed. I delight to sit here on warm sunny days, and build all sorts of imaginations. I fancy my friend with me. Sometimes we live in the castles of Ariosto; sometimes in the East amidst enchanted gardens; sometimes with Theocritus in Sicily, with Plato in Greece. We often visit Lemnos, to comfort Philoctetes."

influenced—an autobiography with a heavy proportion of Byroniana. Colburn would not lose by this "literary event." The theme, being a painful one, also commanded a peculiar energy in Hunt; there is no greater source of prolix phraseology than a bitter confidence that one has been wronged; frustration must be retrospective. So Colburn's *New Monthly* began to contain preliminary examples of Hunt *versus* Byron's Immortal Memory, and watchers like Haydon began to realise new opportunities for disgust. "Have you read Leigh Hunt's last bit on Byron in 'Campbell's Magazine'? If not, read it without further fatal procrastination. 'The noble lord,' says Leigh Hunt, 'complains in *Don Juan* that he could never make a lady tell her age!' 'But,' says the amiable and chivalrous Leigh, '*we* have been more fortunate with our fair informants than the noble lord.' Oh! Heavens! *His* fair informants! Who be they? Mrs Gliddon, the tobacconist's wife, or the lady of 'Hampstead ponds,' who, in trying to be pathetic, and hoping she might *not* be drowned, threw herself off a wooden footpath into a Hampstead puddle where it was six inches deep. . . . Poor Leigh! Why does he write such twaddle? He is now writing his life, which will be a monkish mixture of petticoat twaddling and Grandison cant." Haydon was here largely satisfying his envy, but there were many others who were similarly prepared to howl Hunt down on the subject of Byron.

To those who were not, there must have been recreation in Hunt's prelusive notes. Let one of them be gleaned from the *New Monthly*; it concerns Hunt's copy of Cotton's *Montaigne*, lent by him in Italy to Byron. "Lord B. had a particular way of marking the pages that pleased him. He usually made a double dog's-ear, of a very tight, and, as it were, irritable description; folding the corner twice, and drawing his nail with a sort of violence over it, as if to hinder 'the dog's' escape from

him. I will begin the extract with one that he has marked with
a *triple* dog's-ear. The reader will observe in it a very obvious
application to himself. I must premise that these dog's-ears
are the only marks: so that the reader must notice for himself
such passages as he thinks the noble poet may have had more
particularly in view. There is another dog's-ear two pages
further on. . . ." The passage in question expounds literary
egotism.

Men of dawning ability in literature seem to have entered
into Leigh Hunt's circle at any time, and soon after his return
from Italy he attracted the friendship of a young novelist afterwards known to everybody as Harrison Ainsworth. One early
effect of this was Hunt's only appearance (so far as I know)[1]
among the contributors to the early Annuals—those pretty
though capitalistic combinations of steel engravings, watered silk
bindings and well-groomed prose and rhyme. Hunt appeared,
if anonymous articles constitute appearance, in Ainsworth's
Keepsake for 1828 (issued in 1827), and it happened that he was at
his best in his " Dreams on the Borders of the Land of Poetry."
These are aphorisms and something more, and in them Hunt's
style is what it should have been, could life have let him write
when and how he desired; yet perhaps I err; perhaps without
the surge and speed of common demands he could not have
achieved the tenderness, the fullness of these care-charming
dreams. "Sometimes music poured in, as from a hundred
fountains; and sometimes a goddess called. Not a leaf then
stirred; but the silence trembled. I heard Venus speak; which
was as if there should never be sorrow more."

[1] In 1826 Charles Ollier had tried to obtain Hunt's assistance for
A. A. Watts's *Literary Souvenir*. Everyone, apparently, had been enlisted
except Scott, Lamb, whom Watts found "sulky and coy," and L. H.

XVI

The Book about Byron

THE hybrid work on Hunt's life and Byron's characteristics was huddled together, old articles being gathered up with new into the mass; but before it was published Colburn had excited the general anticipation with "puffs preliminary" and with specimen passages in the journals. Besides, Hunt had given his main feeling on the subject of Byron in his conversation, and the relations of the two in Italy were being discussed. Hazlitt met Mrs Shelley and asked her whether Byron was as poor a talker as Hunt said. She at first misunderstood and "said, nothing could be meaner than he was, and gave some instances of it." On Hazlitt's explaining his question, she said that Byron was *not* commonplace, adding, "Hunt was hardly a fair judge. The other had not behaved well to him, and whenever they met, Hunt always began some kind of argument, and as Lord Byron could not argue (nor indeed Hunt either, for that matter) they made but a bad business of it, and it ended unsatisfactorily for all parties." Hazlitt reported on this to the painter Northcote, who did not know Hunt, and Northcote, sure that Hunt was a foolish egoist, at once dismissed his claims to a hearing. This would be a typical occurrence.

The situation was as perilous for Hunt as it was profitable for Colburn; and the fun which had been mingled with his adversaries' satire turned into malice impatient for results. Tom Moore, self-established patentee of the truth about Byron, resolved to strike in good time, and he forestalled the arrival of the book with a malodorous fable, printed in *The Times*, called "The Living Dog and the Dead Lion." It will be found in the current collected edition of Moore's poems, and one reading will be enough, while we proceed to

LORD BYRON

AND

SOME OF HIS CONTEMPORARIES

WITH

RECOLLECTIONS OF

THE AUTHOR'S LIFE

AND OF HIS

VISIT TO ITALY.

BY LEIGH HUNT.

"It is for slaves to lie, and for freemen to speak truth.

"In the examples, which I here bring in, of what I have heard, read, done or said, I have forbid myself to dare to alter even the most light and indifferent circumstances. My conscience does not falsify one tittle. What my ignorance may do, I cannot say."   MONTAIGNE.

LONDON:

HENRY COLBURN, NEW BURLINGTON STREET.

1828.

So stood the title-page of Leigh Hunt's book, an expensive quarto. Opposite the title sat Byron's ghost[1], or what looked like it; a white figure on a black ground, cut by Mrs Hunt—a fat Byron with a finely sneering nose and mouth, and a riding-crop lackadaisically tilted over his shoulder. Of the more than 500 pages following, the first half-dozen contained a preface, uneasily apologising for the work, and for the fact that the Byroniana came unnaturally in front of the rest, and the auto-

---

[1] This engraving was originally issued by itself, with a descriptive paragraph, in October 1826. In spite of the dislike which it expresses, it was considered a very accurate "effigy" of Byron, and a valuable antidote to the romantic and theoretical pictures of him which then multiplied.

biography was split up into "detached portraits." "But my publisher thought it best." Lord Byron occupied about one-third of the volume, and was followed in the doubtful precedency by Moore; then came Shelley, "with a criticism on his genius, and Mr Trelawney's Narrative of his Loss at Sea"; Shelley received above seventy pages. Keats next found a greater advertisement, though in these surroundings none too sure of success, than had ever before been attempted for him; Lamb and Coleridge among others of less note were in this gallery, the whole being concluded with Hunt's recollections of his own life and travels. We may be sure that at least the Byroniana were read with rapidity; for a second and cheaper edition was out the same year, and there was another in Paris, so prolific in print about Byron, with additional matter.

What was it that Leigh Hunt was doing, apart from the obscured question of his obligations to Byron, and of the gentility and propriety of his speaking out or holding his tongue? It is clear enough. Byron was not, to the imagination of most of England, a man; he was a miracle. He was lightning and thunder, he was love and beauty, he was a dynast; and of course he was only following the Olympian traditions when in his glorious way he made female loveliness bow at his feet, or exercised his caprice at the cost of petty men. Anyone who doubted this must be the poor, mean victim of some intellectual squint, or defective upbringing; but the man who affected to divest Byron of his mythological mystery and reveal a soured and slightly tipsy actor brooding over the playbill on which his own huge name was followed by others was surely a *person*. Such a creature could clearly possess neither the instincts of recognisable decency nor the faculty of literary expression. A shameless and poisonous book. "Lend me your copy."

'It's lent already. Shouldn't advise you to read it." "No, but 'd just like to glance—."

They did read it. The two copies before the present bio-grapher are both beautified with marginalia, which preserve he spirit in which those eyes pursued the horrid details of Hunt's profane ingratitude from page to page. Hunt writes of Genoa: "There are no fences there—there are only walls." The public retorts: "Cockney dog! did he never hear of a stone ence," and as usual forgets the question-mark. Hunt, thinking of Moore's former pleasantness: "the advantage of personal intercourse would have been on my side." The public: "d—n our egotism!" Hunt: "What I can lay before the public, I do"; public: "and what I can't, I don't." Shelley, quoted, mentions Hunt's "kind and earnest face"; the female public adds: "Like a *white Negro* making a point! Vide Engraving." (That engraving indeed was lamentable[1], and unlike Hunt, and yet it is to this day the usual selection for reproduction.) Hunt: "greater ones." Britannia: "vile solecism, never used by any *classical* writer; how can there be two ones!!!" Hunt, of a crew being packed in: "like so many herrings." Public: "low." Hunt: "the vessel, tumbling about, looked like a wash-house in a fit." Public: "very low." Hunt, describing his inner chaos after Shelley's death: "Good God!" Orthodoxy: "It is truly shocking to find the name of the Almighty so wantonly sported with." Hunt quotes the *Ode to the Nightin-gale* at full length. Magnanimity: "This poem has some merit." Hunt specifies his birthplace, and this at last meets with the true British cheer: "Probably the house now called Southgate

---

[1] Hunt thought it made him look as if he had just stolen a tankard, and went to Colburn to have it changed. Colburn, clasping his hands together, "declared that it must stand, 'For,' said he pathetically, *I have paid for it!*'"

House in the occupancy of Mr Walker the brewer. Brilliant double Ale!!" But this anthology must end. We believe Byron would have refused to let the "non tali auxilio, nec defensoribus istis" hinder him from laughing over it.

Since Byron's edited correspondence copiously displays the mood in which he thought of Hunt and his family as neighbours in Italy, and the inclination which he had to follow private and public advice and "cut the Cockney"—tempered with some respect for Hunt's powers—it is unlikely that Hunt's rendering of their relations was seriously inexact. The narrative was garrulous, petty, perplexed, but Hunt was not a liar. In the tumult of his troubles, the feeling that Byron was the cause of most of them disordered his judgment, and deformed his style, but it was not the substance of his statement that could justly be condemned. Even those who defend Byron in his indifference to Hunt's marooned state in Italy do not go so far as to call it a proof of magnanimity; they assume that Hunt, by ceasing to have a hold on *The Examiner*, had broken some moral obligation to Byron in respect of *The Liberal*. Hunt himself did not realise that *The Examiner* was no longer his province and part-property; and John, even if he thought Leigh had "seceded," used and was determined to use the paper for Byron's benefit at any time. In short, Byron's conduct to Hunt, whatever its apparent reasons might be, exhibited little but commonplace calculation; the noble imagination was wholly wanting. This fact needed no such irritable compilation of minor casualties as Hunt produced for Colburn; a short and striking chronicle of the main promise, risk, undertaking, and disappointment would have done good. Anecdotes might have been added, and Hunt had many to tell, some laughable, some pathetic; but he made them the texts for rambling sermons, if indeed in his fevered tenacity he did not mismanage them altogether. Byron, for instance, had said one day to the mischievous John, "You must take care how you get notions in your head about Truth and Sincerity, for they will hinder your getting on in the world." This was at once artful and well meant, but Leigh Hunt took it solemnly as an attempt to corrupt a poor child.

It may be discerned through Hunt's long recriminations and contentions that he would have gloried in Byron, had not certain characteristics on both sides clashed, and obscured the view. Hunt was effusive, and probably that spoiled all; a vocal idealist—and Byron was not built that way. Hunt hoped to see Byron at his best—and the virtuous anticipatory smile made Byron, still a mischievous boy, play at showing off his worst. Byron suspected Hunt of offering invisible tracts, and "began to curse and to swear" at the new gospeller. Hunt became aware of this: "Lord Byron was always acting, even when he capriciously spoke the truth"; but, even after the banter of Lamb, Hunt had not the wit in intercourse to bring the performance out unspoiled by the emphasis of chagrin and graver deductions. In spite of these handicaps, he was fascinated by Byron, his memory recorded impressions of Byron when everything else drifted hazily by, and such moments of unblemished kindness as Byron happened to offer him were to him almost the finest thing in the world. The passage in which Hunt has acknowledged this is an example of candour and philanthropy, not to be easily or casually comprehended, but when fully thought on nobly worthy of one of Lamb's friends; it may have missed fire in 1828: "It is a credit to my noble acquaintance, that he was by far the pleasantest when he had got wine in his head. The only time I invited myself to dine with him, I told him I did it on that account, and that I meant to push the bottle so, that he should intoxicate me with his good company. He said he would have a set-to; but he never did it. I believe he was afraid. It was a little before he left Italy; and there was a point in contest between us (not regarding myself) which he thought perhaps I should persuade him to give up. When in his cups, which was not often, nor immoderately, he was inclined to be tender; but not weakly so, nor lachrymose. I know not how it might have been with every body, but he paid me the compliment of being excited to his very best feelings; and when I rose late to go away, he would hold me down, and say with a look of intreaty, 'Not yet.' Then it was that I seemed to talk with the proper natural Byron as he ought to have been; and there was not a sacrifice I could not have made to keep him in that temper; and see his friends love him, as much as the world admired. Next morning it was all gone. His intimacy with the worst part of mankind had got him again in its chilling crust; and nothing remained but to despair and joke."

When Hunt withdrew from his confusions and apologies into simple studies of those whom he accepted without shadows, his style grew bright, his sense of proportion serene; and so his unlucky quarto was redeemed by the beautiful utterances on Shelley, Keats, Coleridge and Lamb. For Shelley and Keats he was still the chief spokesman, although in 1828 George Croly included Keats in a small volume of *Beauties of the British Poets* and praised him in the preface. It was probably due to Hunt's laudations in the book on Byron that the works of Coleridge, Shelley and Keats were brought out in one cover by Galignani in 1829. He took the opportunity of adding to his memoirs of his dead friends several of their most perfect passages of verse, with his exclamations of pleasure and discernment, and in this faculty of choosing and inviting us to the feast he can never be surpassed. Nor can he be justly charged with promiscuity of rapture, though he temperamentally liked to enjoy. A page is devoted to the "fault" of Shelley's poetry, and he dares to hold that "for ordinary or immediate purposes" a great deal of it "ought to have been written in prose." But how marvellous the sureness of his prophetic finger is! The Indicator was magnetic. Remembering Gibbon's exhortation to the family of the Spensers, that they should consider the *Faerie Queene* the "brightest jewel in their coronet"; remembering Shelley's kinship with Sir Philip Sidney, and that "he would have allowed no claim for superiority to be put in there," Hunt nevertheless summons up the blood: "If I had a right to speak like Gibbon, and if affection might be allowed to anticipate the voice of posterity, I would 'exhort' in like manner the race of the Shelleys to pierce through the din of existing prejudices, and consider no sound so fair as the name of their aspiring kinsman."

The same divination characterised the tribute to Keats. Giving precise localities to the occasions of certain poems by that writer, Hunt remarks, "I mention these things, which now look trivial, because his readers will not think them so twenty years hence." That would be 1848; the actual year of Monckton Milnes's wonderfully influential biography of Keats. But Leigh Hunt was prepared to guarantee Keats for longer than that; discussing the apathetic incuriosity of the critics at large towards Keats's first book—a book which most of us had we been contemporaries would have thought mere Georgian Poetry—he placidly observes, "To admire and comment upon the genius that two or three hundred years have applauded, and to discover what will partake of the applause two or three hundred years hence, are processes of a very different description." Again and again Hunt repeats his message, to and from the ages to come, that Keats is glorious; "I venture to prophesy, as I have done elsewhere, that Mr Keats will be known here-

after in English literature, emphatically, as *the Young Poet*";
and Hunt's biographer should not hesitate to give room enough
to this prospective instancy among the episodes of Hunt's life.
It is unchronological, but here was a dunned and bullied
optimist in 1828 with 1928 in his possession. While Hunt was
writing in his study, gowned and slippered, he was living no
less dramatically than if he had been flying to America; he was
helping to make the future; and he saw, "all clear, as it was
bright," a result that at that minute probably only three or four
could guessingly conjecture.

Meanwhile the unsound parts of *Lord Byron and Some of
His Contemporaries*, and the exasperated maledictions of many
public writers, entangled Leigh Hunt into writing long letters,
paraphrases or extensions of things in his book, to *The
Examiner* and *Morning Chronicle*. When the second edition
appeared, it was his intention to include those letters, but "my
advisers" rejected this, as threatening to do more harm than
good, nor would they agree to his offering "an attempt to
estimate my own character," although it was printed in readiness for issue. Mr Brimley Johnson in his short biography of
Hunt has given us the opportunity to read it after all; it is easy
to see why Hunt's friends feared the reverberations it might
have, in an arena of *Quarterly* and *John Bull* construction.
"I am at once the sickliest and most sanguine of my race, the
liveliest and most thoughtful, the most social and the most
solitary, the most indolent and the most laborious." "I am not
naturally a teller of truth." "In a family of men remarkable for
their bravery, I am the only timid person." These detached
candours would have been free beer for the executioners.
Restrained from this misplaced psychological generosity, Hunt
in his second edition added a new preface and an appendix, in
which at any rate timidity is not the prevailing temper. He calls

his *Blackwood* barrackers "unprincipled cowards," he dismisses
his *Quarterly* opponent with "I am noticing this born slave
more than I intended," and Tom Moore is a "turn-spit." He
offers a short analysis of *The Liberal* complication—but even
as he does it he lends his tormentors a hand by saying, "The
commonest rules of arithmetic were, by a singular chance,
omitted in my education." He darkly suggests, "I have told
nothing but the truth, but I am far from having told all the
truth—and I never will tell it all. Common humanity would
not let me"; he thinks on the other hand that Byron's little
ways "perhaps really made me undervalue his genius. . . . My
spleen came across me, I own, as I called him to mind." But
what must have pained Hunt most was the necessity of clearing
Horace Smith from what he would not have imagined to be
unwelcome to that now vacillating friend, and of stating in
italics that "Mr Horace Smith differed altogether from Mr
Shelley upon points of religion"; or it may have been the letter
of his old schoolfellow Charles Le Grice, defending the memory
of his brother Sam—Lamb's early intimate—from Hunt's un-
wary epitaph, "He died a rake." Hunt very properly printed
the letter in full and pleaded "a school report" as his only
extenuation. He should have known better than to have
accepted this report; but the whole affair of "Lord Byron and
his Contemporaries" was weakened by hasty composition, and
a fevered judgment. Misery like his might overwhelm the
detachment of most men.

While the noise aroused by his book was at its height and
his least offensive adversaries were proposing that his likeness
might adorn the new instalment of his friend Landseer's
Monkeyana, Hunt appears to have been subdued. He attempted
to establish *The Companion*, a successor to *The Indicator*, and it
struggled on for half a year. Hazlitt: "I like *The Companion*

very well." In 1830 the *Beauties of Shelley* was published, and the compiler acknowledged her indebtedness to Hunt's biographical information. Removing his household to Epsom, he went on with his work for Colburn, who required him to write a novel; Hunt took the opportunity to bring together his remarkable quantity of notes on the period of Charles II in the animated scenes of *Sir Ralph Esher*. It was a sort of *Pelham*, and appeared anonymously in January 1832; but the authorship was not very rigidly concealed by Colburn. *Sir Ralph Esher* was rewarded with a little more than the usual select audience of the graceful writer. That epithet does not cover all the value of Leigh Hunt. Once more settling in London, he collected his courage and his abilities for an enterprise which would have daunted an ordinary man. He began to produce a daily journal of books, plays, and humanities, called *The Tatler*, four pages folio. The mere scribbling of enough matter to make this up would have seemed almost impossible, but Leigh Hunt wrote almost all *The Tatler* himself, and his standard of writing in it was high. In the course of two years, illness caused him to obtain assistance, and he resorted to devices of reprinting his own articles or selections from others. Yet *The Tatler* needs only to be seen—its thick and tall volumes have grown rare—in order to illustrate the energy which Hunt had, and which his feminine mannerisms have helped to overcast.

Before *The Tatler* there had been the *Chat of the Week*. The first sentence of *The Tatler* explains: "The Stamp Office having contested with us the legality of the new shape which we gave to our *Chat of the Week*, we have thought it better to undergo an entire metamorphosis, than vary our efforts to no purpose." The title was due to the recent revival of *The Spectator*, which Hunt in the asphodel may be watching as it goes on past its hundredth year. Hunt immediately resumed his dramatic criticisms; and in the first number he slashed John Galt's biography of Byron. With Galt he put Jerdan, editor of *The Literary Gazette*, in the corner. Jerdan was a minor Gifford.

It is impossible to do more here than describe several outstanding passages in *The Tatler*; first, the Byroniana. In December 1830 Macready's adaptation of "Werner" was put on at Drury Lane. Hunt was there. He felt that the plot was unstable, an "attempt to make a comet of a scarecrow." He declared, "Lord Byron's real genius is to be found in *Don Juan*. He is fine in passages only of his graver writings, chiefly those in which sarcasm is to be found, and a reference to his personal experience. His spirit was self-revolving and satirical: he could not go out of himself sufficiently to sympathize with varieties of men, and therefore he wanted the very stuff of which the drama is made." Early in 1831 the 823 quarto pages of Moore's *Life of Byron* appeared. It was expected that Moore would in some sort handle Hunt; he did, in the baser sort, and he knew that he had a large public echoing every imputation and accepting every suppression or manipulation of details. *The Tatler* replied by printing a series of letters from Moore to Hunt and by seasoning these with reminiscences of those confidential moments when Byron had shown a feeling of the ridiculous and smug in Tom Moore. "Our great object is to shew that the author is an insincere man of the world," and that Byron was well aware of it. It was a pity—Moore is a poet worthy of many praises; but it was not difficult to demonstrate it. John Hunt had a letter, for instance, from Byron. In it was the sentence, "I leave it to others to circumcize their Angels with their 'bonnes fortunes' to the drawing-room and clerical standard." "Others" had been substituted for "Mr Moore."

One of the anecdotes may also reappear, as explaining some

of the excessive fury which has raged against Hunt's book on
Byron: the talk had been, between Hunt and Byron, on Moore's
weakness for good eating, and Byron said, "Do but give Tom
a good dinner, and a Lord, and he is at the top of his happiness.
Oh!" he added, bringing his fist down joyfully at the word
"loves," "TOMMY *loves* a Lord."

The Tatler contained frequent, though brief, laudations of
Shelley and Keats; for two sonnets to their memory it was indebted to one of the poets of that period who looked like being
great, and are still faintly luminous—Thomas Wade. In
noticing the lack of Greek tragedies in English verse, Hunt
wrote, "Mr Shelley should have given us an Aeschylus. The
living writer most capable of rendering him we take to be
Mr Wordsworth." Successors of the old masters now came
into sight. On February 24th, 1831, Hunt began a eulogy,
which ran through four numbers, of two new books: *Poems
Chiefly Lyrical*, by Alfred Tennyson, and *Sonnets* by Charles
Tennyson. He began without beating about the bush: an
apology for delay, and then, "We have great pleasure in stating,
that we have seen no such poetical writing since the last volume
of Mr Keats; and that the authors, who are both young men,
may take their stand at once among the first poets of the day.
We mean, that Mr Wordsworth and Mr Coleridge may give
them the right hand of fellowship; and that all who love genuine
poetry, will read them, and quote them, and feel personally interested about them, and like to live in the world of their
thoughts." Hunt thought the moment fortunate for them. "It
is not now as in the days of Mr Shelley and Mr Keats though
the period is so little distant. The Tennysons have come at a
happier time." Of the incidental criticisms, here is one: "The
lines entitled *The Burial of Love*, especially the one containing
a classical superlative, 'With languor of most hateful smiles,'

remind us of Mr Shelley; except that there is talk in it of Love having his 'revenge.' Mr Shelley, for what may be called the material creation of a poem, had not so severe and discriminating a taste of nature as Mr Keats; but no man surpassed, perhaps ever equalled him,...in the rejection of all incompatible moral assumptions, and figments not to be granted." The scenery of *Mariana* elicited from Hunt a phrase which still suits Tennyson well: "nothing can be better painted." The critic was puzzled for a time by the question, which would be *the* Tennyson; in his last instalment he gave a decisive answer. "We are bound to state, that the more closely we have become acquainted with Alfred Tennyson's poems, the more the author has risen upon our admiration. Perhaps we feel ourselves the more inclined to prefer him to Charles, because—."

The musical and dramatic criticisms of Hunt were extensive, yet often preserving a minute animation. He gloried in Kean, in Pasta, in Paganini; Paganini especially aroused his finest verbal impressionism, until like the player the enthusiast seemed "to throw handfuls, as it were, of staccatoed notes, in distinct and repeated showers, over his violin, small and pungent as the tips of pins." But some time afterwards Hunt wrote still more blissfully, and with yet brighter play of unexpected images, of Paganini, in a poem which Tennyson admired. With Hunt, one may visit the theatres and concert-rooms of a century ago almost as though in the body; and even the way through the streets of his London, the weather, the movement, is ours. November 6th, 1830, and a rough night for going to see *Popping the Question*; but, no mistake about it, we are going. "The wind roared, the rain came down in torrents; pattens clacked; the lamps were like beacons in the tempest; old gentlemen were seen, by their light, pulled along by their inverted umbrellas; the hackney coaches plunged about like

Dutch luggers; the carriages were the skiffs; the 'mudshine' was seen in all its horror, gleaming through the dark, in gutter and on pavement; in short, all the world was roar, clatter and deluge. The coach lands at the step of a mansion inviting as an enchanted house in the Black Sea: we enter, and find hundreds of faces all bent upon the dry and comfortable platform called a stage, and laughing at the pleasant woman yclept ORGER."

In May 1831 the weather had improved, and Hunt's health too. He arose, and took a walk from St John's Wood to Finchley. The district was changing. Gigs and barouches and port-complexioned horsemen had invaded the rurality. New houses "built in an old style," or otherwise, were spreading. The inn at Finchley was not what it was; much joy-riding had spoiled its character. There would be no footpads hereabouts in these degenerate days, where one of the Hunts had formerly broken the arm of a would-be robber. Old memories, even before the time of Keats and Shelley, returned to Hunt. At Finchley, to be sure, forty years earlier, his mother had been told that he was suffering from an incurable disease. She consulted "a speculative physician, who by a singular chance was also a doctor in divinity, and was thought eccentric"— William Trinder of Mill Hill. Trinder (his notion was the Application of Oils to the Human Body) said he would cure the child—and he did. And "what a number of illnesses did he enable us to see! content if we have not suffered in vain, nor failed in making the reader partake of our pleasures."

In spite of his conscientious labours, Hunt now experienced worse poverty than ever. Some creditors prosecuted him. John Forster, his friend and Lamb's, went to great trouble in another scheme, that of publishing his collected poems by subscription. There should have been also a companion volume of essays, but the copyright could not be obtained from "a bookseller."

The subscription list nevertheless seemed to prosper. "It is the anxious wish of those who differ or agree with Mr Hunt in opinion, that minor circumstances should on this occasion be forgotten, and that all should unite as in a common cause to testify respect for genius; and whatever may be the issue of this appeal, it must ever be to Mr Hunt a pleasant and consolatory recollection, that the honoured of all parties have given to it the sanction of their name." Besides most of the famous writers (Thomas Moore among them, who, setting aside the question of proprietorship in Lord Byron's biography, took five copies), one notices in the list the reminders of past circles. J. H. Reynolds, Charles Dilke, and Miss Brawne represented the companionship with John Keats. Another former associate reappeared with the following letter, which a sounder man than Haydon might have been proud to write:

Dear Hunt,

I am sorry my own necessities prevent the possibility of my aiding you effectually as you would have aided any Friend at any time, if possessed of the Power. I will take two copies of your Poems and wish I could send you a check for a good Sum. But I can't my dear old Friend—and feel bitterly for you, in your yellow leaf. I have not forgotten, nor ever shall, the many delightful hours we once spent together—I have no wish to recommence because we should not agree one half hour. . . . The Public have yet a debt to pay you. They are not sufficiently aware of what they owe you. If I live to publish my own life, they shall be told, for no man knows better than I do. . . .

March 12, 1832.   B. R. Haydon.

Moxon, whose high taste as a publisher had been commended in *The Tatler*, brought out Hunt's *Poetical Works*, 1832, in a nobly printed book. As a representation of Hunt's verse, it was inadequate; his nervousness was now too keen to allow him a mature freedom of feeling towards his own productions. But, if this over-chastened modesty excluded much verse worthy of preservation, Hunt felt better when he sat down to write the fine and copious preface, in which he speaks with touching reverence of the mysteries of poetry, and with a radiant face of the Romantic period through which he had travelled, and on which he could now gaze in retrospect. "With the growth of this formidable mechanical epoch, that was to take all *dulce* out of the *utile*, we have had the wonderful works of Sir Walter Scott, the criticism of Hazlitt, the imagination of Keats, the tragedy and winged philosophy of Shelley, the passion of Byron, the wit and festivity of Moore, tales and novels endless, and Mr Wordsworth has become a classic, and the Germans have poured forth every species of romance, and the very French have thought fit to Germanise, and our American brethren have written little but novels and verses, and Sir Humphry Davy has been dividing his time between coal-mines and fairy-land (no very remote regions); and the shop itself and the *Corn Laws* have given us a poet, and Mr Crabbe has been versifying the very Parish Registers; and last, not least, the Utilitarians themselves are poetical."

Such exclamations, though genuine in their delighted quickness, were the escape from puzzles which the subscription list of his book was insufficient to solve. He had been aware of "frightful knocks at the door" in his early childhood. They came again. "Last Friday I was sitting down to dinner, having just finished a most agitating morning, when I was called away by a man who brought an execution into my house for forty shillings. It is under circumstances like these that I always write." He even thought of selling what was to him almost as the sun in heaven—his *Parnaso Italiano*. The trouble was such that of his numerous children only one could be kept in respectable clothes—"the one that I must send out" on such errands as rescuing the family linen from the unpaid and untrusting washerwoman. In spite of all his torment, Hunt continued to write with a measure of his best gift in verse and in prose; and, while he himself was in want, he had not lost the power of perceiving others in want as well. There remains from the dreary period after the fall of *The Tatler* a scrap of paper, on which he arranges a subscription in sixpences to procure a bed for Elizabeth Jerrold, charwoman, aged 69. T. Carlyle and Mrs Carlyle were brought in, and the list also includes L. E. L. and Hunt's literary enemy Mr Jerdan. (The day was coming which, in the general beam of the Great Exhibition, would discover Hunt on the committee for the Jerdan testimonial!)

XVII

Hunt at Fifty

THE infelicity of some of Hunt's friendships has been seen; some momentary discord between him and Hazlitt has been noticed. But only the death of Hazlitt in September 1830 brought that friendship to a close. What the loss meant to Hunt may be seen, in a broad way, in the gradual diminution of the fighting spirit in his writings after 1830; the immediate sense of it is represented in the allusions and tributes to Hazlitt which were printed in *The Tatler*, beginning with a paragraph upon his death: "Mr Hazlitt was one of the profoundest writers of the day, an admirable reasoner (no one got better or sooner at the heart of a writer than he did), the best general critic, the greatest critic on art that ever appeared (his writings on that subject cast a light like a painted window), exquisite in his relish of poetry, an untameable lover of liberty, and with all his humour and irritability (of which no man had more) a sincere friend, and a generous enemy." Soon afterwards, a longer account appeared: "Passing the other night through Wardour-street, by the church of St Anne, Soho, in the burial-ground of which the mortal remains of this admirable writer had been deposited, we thought how different the edifice and the whole scene looked to us in consequence."

That Hazlitt should die, was a thing that Hunt had not thought of. "The first time we heard of his illness was but a fortnight before, and the news was accompanied with the intelligence that he was getting well. We had often seen him in fits of illness, such as at last carried him off, and had been used to his getting over them. We therefore went on, toiling, among other hopes, in the daily one of resuming our old evenings with him, of filling them cram full of the late glorious events and all

that were to come, and of enjoying his company at the entertainment he loved best in the world—the theatre. It is all gone
—a series of delightful hours cut short, unexpectedly, and in a
moment—the interchange of hopes and fears—the talk of
books—the more than Johnsonian cups of tea—the little
quarrels, soon appeased (the quarrels of the lovers of truth are
like those of other lovers)—the pleasure of welcoming and
regretting on his side, and of forgiving and being instructed on
ours." Hazlitt's sayings came back to Hunt as he sat, impoverished, with his slave and master the pen. Now it was that time
when Hunt had lamented a great writer's faith that evil pre-
dominates—"an awful fact." "He had just lost his money,"
said W. H. Now it was the comment on a phrase in Moore's
book—"I never can put on the proper pathetic face in reading
Hunt"—"Damn his face! What has that to do with it? Does
he always *put on* a face when he goes to read anything serious?"
And now Hunt thought of Hazlitt's first diffidence on meeting
a stranger, and how, when he had gone to consult Abernethy,
that physician had misconstrued it, and lectured Hazlitt scorn-
fully, only to receive from him a "burst of admonition and
dissection" of terrible force in return.

Occasionally the bitter jests of Hazlitt had Hunt for their
object. The repetition of theories concerning the reform of
marriage upset him, and he would say, "Damn it, it's always
coming out like a rash! Why doesn't he write a book and have
done with it?" But Hazlitt was Hunt's friend, not to be
estranged. He has written on him in many places, most
conspicuously in *The Spirit of the Age*, 1825, where he slily,
and with the support of certain similarities, places his portraits
of Moore and Leigh Hunt in one article. He shows the differences also. Having compared Moore's vision of Chimborazo
to a strawberry ice, and his wild harp of Erin to a musical snuff-

box, he explains the sincerity and the natural elegance of
Hunt. But this passage has already been noticed. The place
of Leigh Hunt in Hazlitt's range of friendship and intellectual
respect may be seen in the part that Hunt plays in the
colloquy "Of Persons one would Wish to have Seen." The
pleasure which Hazlitt had in reading Hunt's verse was shown
in the extracts which appeared in Hazlitt's *Select Poets*—until
the book was suppressed on account of infringed copyrights.

Of those to whom Hunt had given his heart on account of
genius, personality, and aim, Shelley, Keats, Hazlitt were now
gone. Lamb survived, but had passed, in his setting sun, to
some distance from most of his old company. The sorrowfully
experienced Hunt had over a quarter of a century still to live,
but the circles in which he was to pass his middle age lack
the glory of his "Libertas" galaxies. It has been observed, by
whom I forget, that if Hunt had died at about the same time
as Keats or Shelley, his memory would have gained in tragic
romance and intellectual wonder. His innovating spirit, indeed,
never ceased to be doing something. After 1830 he produced a
quantity of good literature, principally reflective and commendatory; he conversed with most of the eminent Victorians in
the world of books; he saluted and helped many young poets
of distinct endowments. But we are now faced with the long
postscript, or at least the afternoon, to his truly active period.

His acquaintances, though no longer attracting the most
eager attention of literary history, became more and more
numerous. Watching his course after Hazlitt's departure, "you
will see other friends of ancient and merry times—Novello,
Clarke, Harry Robertson, Ollier"; and many with better
remembered names. Tennyson, who had been originally commended to him by Hallam in 1827, appeared at one moment
likely to become one of his intimates, but only a slight record

of suppers at Moxon's has come before me. Bulwer Lytton, from whom a kindness towards Hunt and his peculiarities would be nothing surprising, had more occasion, in connection with his *New Monthly* editorship, to meet and correspond.

> Bulwer, genius in the thick of fame,
> With smiles of thrones, and echoes from the Rhine,
> He too extends his grounds to Fairy-land.

Lytton was exemplary in his sympathy with Hunt, helping him with opportunities, plans and rewards. In July 1832 he is found asking him for more essays, such as "Recollections of Keats," and poems—"Your poem on June is *most exquisite*. I am learning it by heart." During 1833 Macready, once the hopeful candidate for Hunt's favourable stage criticism ("Leigh Hunt, as the editor of *The Examiner*, seemed to hold my destinies in his grasp"), met the man. In *The Tatler*, Hunt had spoken of Macready's merits—and Kean's genius. It was ominous. Macready was to meet Hunt occasionally for many years, but what at first seemed mutual regard dropped away, and the final estimate of Hunt in Macready's superhuman diary is, "*Particularly disagreeable*."

Strangely enough, it was with Carlyle that Hunt made one of the completest of his later friendships. Carlyle too had grown up with a strong sense of expectancy and admiration for the editor of *The Examiner*. The two reformers met in 1832, and in 1834 became neighbours at Chelsea, where they talked at considerable length of the improvable state of human systems, especially under the heading of holy matrimony. Mrs Carlyle called Hunt the "Talking Nightingale"; she called Mrs Hunt other names, which may be guessed when the following observations on all the Hunts by the two Carlyles have been read afresh.

Thomas Carlyle, May 24th, 1834: "Hunt's household in

Cheyne Row, Chelsea. Nondescript! Unutterable! Mrs Hunt asleep on cushions; four or five beautiful, strange, gipsy-looking children running about in undress, whom the lady ordered to get us tea. The eldest boy, Percy, a sallow, black-haired youth of sixteen, with a kind of dark cotton nightgown on, went whirling about like a familiar, providing everything: an indescribable dream-like household." The eldest boy was actually the Italianate Thornton, of whom Carlyle had written in 1833, "There looks thro' him that fair openness of soul which, besides its intrinsic price and pricelessness, I have ever found the sweet presage of all other gifts"; and of whom Carlyle many years later repeatedly expressed admiration. He was absent, uncertain whether to become a painter or a journalist. Such slight pen-and-ink sketches of his as survive display an artist's instinct; but he was liable to illness from the effluvia of pigments, and soon apprenticed himself earnestly to the profession of political and miscellaneous leader-writing, relieved with short stories and articles on painting and pictures.

Thomas Carlyle, June 27th, 1834: "Hunt is always ready to go and walk with me, or sit and talk with me to all lengths if I want him to. He comes in once a week (when invited, for he is very modest), takes a cup of tea, and sits discoursing in his brisk, fanciful way till supper time, and then cheerfully eats a cup of porridge (to sugar only), which he praises to the skies, and vows he will make his supper of at home. He is a man of thoroughly London make, such as you would not find else-where, and I think about the *best* possible to be made of his sort: an airy, crotchety, most copious clever talker, with an honest undercurrent of reason too, but unfortunately not the deepest, not the most practical—or rather it is the most *un*-practical ever man dealt in. His hair is grizzled, eyes black-hazel, complexion of the clearest dusky brown; a thin glimmer of a smile plays over a face of cast-iron gravity. He never laughs—can only titter, which I think indicates his worst deficiency. His house excels all you have ever read of—a *poetical Tinkerdom*, without parallel even in literature. In his family room, where are a sickly large wife and a whole shoal of well-conditioned wild children, you will find half a dozen old rickety chairs gathered from half a dozen different hucksters, and all seemingly engaged, and just pausing, in a violent *hornpipe*. On these and around them and over the dusty table and ragged carpet lie all kinds of litter—books, papers, egg-shells, scissors, and last night when I was there the torn heart of a half-quartern loaf. His own room above stairs, into which alone I strive to enter, he keeps cleaner. It has only two chairs, a bookcase, and a writing-table; yet the noble Hunt receives you in his Tinkerdom in the spirit of a king, apologises for nothing, places you in the best seat, takes a window-sill himself if there is no other, and there folding closer his loose-flowing 'muslin cloud' of a printed nightgown in which he always writes, commences the liveliest dialogue on philosophy and the prospects of man (who is to be beyond measure 'happy' yet); which again he will courteously terminate the moment you are bound to go: a most interesting, pitiable, lovable man, to be used kindly but with discretion."

It was necessary that Carlyle should go through a time of harsher notions about Hunt before arriving at a settled tolerance for his Utopiana and recognition of his merits. The temporary irritation found expression in July 1834: "Hunt is limited, even bigoted, and seeing that I utterly dissent from him, fears that I despise him; a kindly clever man, fantastic, brilliant, shallow, of one topic, loquacious, unproductive." This mood, however, did not last; friendship continued, in spite of other ruffling breezes which Mrs Carlyle describes.

September 1st, 1834: "I told Mrs Hunt, one day, I had been very busy painting. 'What?' she asked, 'is it a portrait?' 'Oh, no,' I told her; 'something of more importance—a large wardrobe.' She could not imagine, she said, 'how I could have patience for such things.' And so, having no patience for them herself[1], what is the result? She is every other day reduced to borrow my tumblers, my teacups; even a cupful of porridge, a few spoonfuls of tea, are begged of me, because 'Missus has got company, and happens to be out of the article.'" Matters went from bad to worse. The ideal housewife from the North complains, on November 21st, 1834, "Mrs Hunt I shall soon be quite terminated with, I foresee. She torments my life out with borrowing. She actually borrowed one of the brass fenders the other day, and I had difficulty in getting it out of her hands; irons, glasses, teacups, silver spoons are in constant requisition; and when one sends for them the whole number can never be found."

The fact that Mrs Carlyle was the heroine of Leigh Hunt's successful trifle, "Jenny kissed me," adds a zest to the pleasant malice of the story she tells, I suppose of Harriet Martineau's visit in October 1835. Tea at Leigh Hunt's. "He sang, talked like a pen-gun, even to —, who drank it all in like nectar, while my mother looked cross enough, and I had to listen to the whispered confidences of Mrs Hunt. But for me, who was declared to be grown 'quite prim and elderly,' I believe they would have communicated their mutual experiences in a re-tired window-seat till morning. 'God bless you, Miss —,' was repeated by Hunt three several times in tones of ever-increasing

---

[1] However, the Carlyles did not refuse a present of the bust of Shelley made by Marianne, which was reproduced about 1830 for the friends of the Hunts. Browning had a cast from it. Hunt used to say that the likeness of the bust to Shelley was such as sometimes to startle him. Why is it not more commonly reproduced, as an alternative to Miss Curran's pretty picture? But opinions of it differ.

pathos and tenderness, as he handed her downstairs behind me. —, for once in her life, seemed past speech. At the bottom of the stairs a demur took place. I saw nothing; but I heard, with my wonted glegness—what think you?—a couple of handsome smacks! and then an almost inaudibly soft, 'God bless you, Miss —!' Now just remember what sort of looking woman is — —; and figure their transaction! If he had kissed me, it would have been intelligible, but — —, of all people!"

In 1839 when John Hunter of Craigcrook ("friend of Leigh Hunt's verse"—and purse—"and lover of all duty") was on a visit to London, he found Hunt and Carlyle still neighbours, friends, and determined disputants. Nor was Mrs Carlyle a hostile presence. Hunter's notes of one evening may be taken as a representation of what passed many evenings with Carlyle and Hunt together. The two "were in great force, and came out in their full strength. They form decided contrasts to each other in almost every respect, and the occasional collisions that took place between them drew out the salient points and characteristic powers of each in the most striking manner possible. I never saw Carlyle in such vigour, and was delighted, even when I most differed from him, with the surging floods of his sonorous eloquence which he poured forth from time to time, illuminated, as they always were, by the coruscations of a splendid fancy, sometimes lurid enough, to be sure, and heated to boiling fervour by the inextinguishable fire of deep emotion that is for ever gnawing his heart and brain. Hunt again was all light and air, glancing gracefully over all topics, and casting the hues of his own temperament on every subject that arose. I do not mean to make any attempt at giving an account of the conversation. . . . We had the Scottish Kirk, Wordsworth, Petrarch, Burns, Knox and Hume, the Church of England, Dante, heaven and hell." Carlyle made short work of Wordsworth's pretensions to a thousandth part of Burns's poetic quality, and proceeded to expunge Petrarch's "weak, washy twaddle about another man's wife." Hunter retaliated, and was in appalling danger when "Hunt interposed to the rescue with, 'Well, that's very good. Carlyle knocks down all our idols with two or three sweeps of his arm, and having so far cleared his way to us, he winds up by knocking down ourselves; and when we cry out against his rough work, he begins to talk of —politeness!' This was followed by a peal of laughter, in which Carlyle joined with all his heart; and then addressed me cordially and kindly—'I believe, after all, you are quite right. ...I honour and love you for the lesson you have taught me.' This was felt to be noble. 'There is Carlyle all over,' said Hunt; 'that's what makes us all love him. His darkest speculations always come out to the light by reason of the human heart which he carries along with him. He will at last end in glory and gladness.' Towards the conclusion of the evening we had a regular discussion between Carlyle and Hunt, involving the whole merits of their several systems, if I may so call Hunt's fantastic framework of *agreeabilities*, which Carlyle certainly shattered to pieces with great ease (though without disconcerting Hunt in the slightest degree) in order to substitute his eternal principles of right and wrong, responsibility, awe of the Unseen....Hunt told us a good story of Lamb. Someone had been talking about eternal punishments and the like, when Lamb turned round on him with 'No; that won't do for me. I can't give up my hell.'"

Perhaps the final view of Hunt and Carlyle in action is symbolised in R. H. Horne's story of the starry night, through which they and other friends were making for their homes. Hunt began, and grew very eloquent, with his meditations on the sweet influences of which the heavens were telling, of the music of the spheres, and destined Shelleian transcendencies of consciousness. He paused, and Carlyle (the "comic Ezekiel," perhaps) spoke—only just. "Man, it's a sad sight." Hunt, defeated for the moment, and lacking words for once, "sat down on a stone step."

Too many friends of humanity are restricted in their knowledge of Hunt to a few anecdotes of his shortage of money, among which that known as "Carlyle's Sovereigns" has had a vogue. I do not claim to have traced that one to its first form, but here it is as Augustus Hare gave it in *The Story of My Life*: "Mr Hannay knew Carlyle very well, and often went to see him, but it was in his poorer days. One day when Mr Hannay went to the house, he saw two gold sovereigns lying exposed in a little vase on the chimney-piece. He asked Carlyle what they were for. Carlyle looked—for him—embarrassed, but gave no definite answer. 'Well, now, my dear fellow,' said Mr Hannay, 'neither you nor I are quite in a position to play ducks and drakes with sovereigns: what *are* these for?'— 'Well,' said Carlyle, 'the fact is, Leigh Hunt likes better to find them there than that I should give them to him." Surely this tale is spurious. It implies that Hunt would steal money, or at least cause it to vanish from a friend's room; he would not. It also implies that Carlyle, in such a matter, would give currency to a most damaging accusation by an ambiguous speech; he would not. It does not present Hannay in a creditable light with his inquisitive persistency. It we turn to Hannay's *Characters and Criticisms*, we find an outspoken review by him of Hunt's *Correspondence*, 1862, which clears the air at once; for in it occur these sentences: "[Hunt] outlived his early faults. He developed successfully all the nobler parts of his nature.... Leigh Hunt, then, was no parasite....Among men of letters who stuck by him, was our own illustrious Carlyle, for a considerable time his near neighbour, among the red-brick terraces and quiet trees of Chelsea.... Mr Dickens caricatured him as Harold Skimpole, in 'Bleak House.' *The Athenaeum* gave him several sly stabs. Yet, having lived down so much, he also lived down these things."

Augustus Hare yields an anecdote or two of better quality. A Mr Bourton said: "[Hunt] is the only person, I believe, who, if he saw something yellow in the distance, and was told it was a buttercup, would be disappointed if he found it was only a guinea." Lady Airlie had known him in her childhood; "he had taken her into the garden, and talked to her, and asked her what she thought heaven would be like, and then he said, 'I will tell you what I think it will be like: I think it will be like a most beautiful arbour all hung with creepers and flowers, and that one will be able to sit in it all day, and read a most interesting novel.'"

Hard times for Hunt, at any rate, prevailed in 1834, when he was fifty. There were reasons which he could not see perfectly, nor if seen would they have been within his power to cancel. Absorbed in his work—and he worked with fantastic resolution—he did not notice that Marianne had deteriorated. Friends helped him, but she made further demands on them in secret. Bitter language is used by one observer of "his mismanaging, unthrifty wife, the most barefaced, persevering, pertinacious of mendicants. Whenever she made a good collection she was sure to be seen the next day, with her daughters and a son or two, driving about London in what the French call a *voiture de remise*, and what we used to designate a 'glass coach.'" My purpose in transcribing such strictures (no doubt excessive) is not to invoke curses on Marianne, but to take away the reproach of common chatter from Leigh Hunt. Another of that bookman's attendant evils was his son John, who had followed a course such as Hogarth might have painted.

Thornton Hunt, who had written too many leading articles to spend long in giving particulars, admits that "[John] used his father's means, and sometimes his father's name; and it is almost certain that this abuse was extended to cases which have never been traced. The consequences visited Leigh Hunt, sometimes in money lost, sometimes in still more painful forms." Hunt, as Thornton says, had two skeletons in his house. He kept their secret.

After several sporadic employments as essayist or reviewer, Hunt was engaged by Charles Knight in the cause of popular literature, which Knight and the brothers Chambers (who sent their congratulations from Edinburgh) were then so usefully and decently spreading. *Leigh Hunt's London Journal* (from the Steam-Press of C. and W. Reynell) first appeared on April 2nd, 1834, price three-halfpence. It resembled *The Tatler* in form and in matter, but was more miscellaneous, and drew more upon other works. The editorial note, too, sounded more "improving." In this *London Journal* Carlyle printed a poem, and Landor several, including an "Ode to a Friend," with an invitation to Hunt:

> And live, too, thou for happier days
> Whom Dryden's force and Spenser's fays
>   Have heart and soul possessed:
> Growl in grim London, he who will;
> Revisit thou Maiano's hill,
>   And swell with pride his sunburnt breast.
>
> Old Redi in his easy chair,
> With varied chant awaits thee here,
>   And here are voices in the grove,
> Aside my house, that make me think
> Bacchus is coming down to drink[1]
>   To Ariadne's love.

[1] The allusions are to Hunt's poem *Bacchus and Ariadne*, and his translation of Redi.

17-2

Hunt's best-known article here is that, published on the proper day, on the "St Agnes' Eve" of Keats. It was, indeed, a reprint of the whole poem, with frequent pauses for interpretation; and the interpretation was intended for those who probably knew little of the ways and resources of poetry, but wished to learn. The phrases and lines which Hunt revelled in most were printed in italics, his notion being that this was akin to reading with his reader. He has often "indicated" poetry in this manner. At that date, English criticism was almost mute concerning Keats's poetry. Hunt felt an honest pride in his early discoveries of genius, and shortly after his fresh panegyric on "the young, and divine Poet" he expressed it. "The Editor of this Journal believes he may say, that in the various periodicals which he has conducted, it has been his good fortune to introduce more talent and genius to the public than any other.... Not only are the splendid names of Shelley and Keats in his list....It has ever been his boast that he has been a sort of literary Robin Hood, and got companions to act under him who have beaten him at his own weapons." The occasion of this was the introduction of a young scholar, musician and wit named Egerton Webbe to the reader. Webbe was fated to die young, and no permanent confirmation of Leigh Hunt's prophetic word was left by him.

Leigh Hunt's London Journal lived single until May 27th, 1835, and was then united to Knight's *Printing Machine*. In spite of editorial capers and beautifications on the occasion, the union was far from comfortable, and at the end of 1835 it came to a stop. Its two folio volumes, which are not uncommon, were for a time considered worth taking to solace long sea-voyages; and any of Hunt's periodicals might still be used for that purpose. On one occasion a few volumes of his *Examiner* afforded the present writer much pleasure in the intervals of declining to play deck tennis or to dispute about several popular writers; and a masterly poet of our time, making the same voyage, dipped into them with hearty enjoyment.

In 1834 some stupid misstatements of Allan Cunningham, hastily reviewing the literature of half a century, induced Hunt to write new letters on the topic of Byron and the cash account to the press; and, as ill luck would have it, the death of Charles Lamb indirectly produced a passing difference between Hunt and Procter. On hearing the news, Hunt wrote a rather brief character of his friend, and published it in his journal on January 7th, 1835. It was not deficient in truth and loyalty: "[Lamb] was only at his ease in the old arms of humanity; and she loved and comforted him like one of her wisest, though weakest children." But Hunt insisted too much on the melancholy of Lamb: "now and then, as if he would cram into one moment the spleen of years, he would throw out a startling and morbid subject for reflection, perhaps in no better shape than a pun; for he was a great punster." The notice ended with a metaphor of Death looking kindly at Lamb and claiming his kind word. Procter wrote to tell Hunt he had treated Lamb's memory coldly, and that the notice was condemned by everyone. "What man," Hunt commented to Forster, "has praised him more frequently and warmly than myself in his lifetime?" Lest any doubt should linger, Hunt gathered into his *London Journal* while it lasted all the prose elegies on Lamb he met with, and many times made his own comment, with the result that the second volume of the work provides a Nenia Eliana, an anthology of the grief for Elia.

A few months before Lamb's death, Cowden Clarke had told Hunt of a project which was judiciously abandoned when Lamb was beyond consultation for ever: "Lamb wants me to take up the *Old Dramatists* after the fashion of his Shakspeare tales, and has even been so kind as to start me with an adaptation of his own from the 'Cupid's Revenge.' What do you think of that for a compliment!! I confess that the thought of following such a man almost paralyses me."

News came from a sonnetteering worthy in Calcutta that subscriptions to Hunt's Poems were increasing there. Hunt looked up from his *Bibliothèque Orientale*, and blessed the day. "It gives me a peculiar species of gratification"—his letters fell into this style too often now—"to think the *native* editors of the *Reformer* and the *Inquirer* have interested themselves on my behalf. You know I delight in associations of old books and romances; India to me is an Arabian Night country; all the modern commonplaces of it which I have ever seen are accustomed to give way in my mind before its old exclusively Oriental aspect; and in finding that I have friends there, time and space seem to roll apart like a cloud, and I fancy myself a new kind of living, yet ancient Sindbad, taken by the hand after a shipwreck by strangers with dusk faces and white drapery, under a glowing sun." And yet Hunt would have been as deeply stirred as anyone, had *Mother India* been a book of his day and brought forward to extinguish his vision.

Nearer home, there were signs that his worst troubles were passing. His powerful ally, Hazlitt, was unable to help him fight his battles now; but the fighting was surely dying down. Just before Hunt's fiftieth birthday John Wilson ("Christopher North") in *Blackwood's* made an end of all that had been said of Hunt there in other times:

"*Shepherd*. Leigh Hunt loved Shelley.

"*North*. And Shelley truly loved Leigh Hunt. Their friendship was honourable to both, for it was as disinterested as sincere; and I hope Gurney will let a certain person in the City understand that I treat his offer of a reviewal of Mr Hunt's

London Journal with disdain. If he has anything to say against Us or against that gentleman, either conjunctly or severally, let him out with it in some other channel, and I promise him a touch and a taste of the Crutch. He talks to me of Maga's desertion of principle; but if he were a Christian—nay, a man —his heart and head too would tell him that the Animosities are mortal, but the Humanities live for ever—and that Leigh Hunt has more talent in his little finger than the puling prig, who has taken upon himself to lecture Christopher North in a scrawl teeming with forgotten falsehoods. Mr Hunt's *London Journal*, my dear James, is not only beyond all comparison, but out of all sight, the most entertaining and instructive of all the cheap periodicals; and when laid, as it duly is once a-week, on my breakfast-table, it lies there—but is not permitted to lie long—like a spot of sunshine dazzling the snow."

Among the harsher sounds of his poverty, this came over Hunt like the sweet South; and he made his own best bow in the *London Journal*. The tribute to Shelley gave him a chance which he took with characteristic anxiety: "[Christopher North] will not take it amiss, if we add, that we had another friend, with whom he would have shared a mutual admiration had he known him, and with whose writings should we ever find him getting better acquainted (for we can only think he has hitherto but impatiently glanced, not steadily looked at them), we shall love him. He will know whom we mean; one, who was idly said to be killed by the criticism of the *Quarterly Review*; but whose end, though assuredly none the happier for want of success, was long visible in a frame of extreme sensibility, and delicacy of organization, and was hastened by affectionate vigils at the bed of a dying brother....And Mr Keats's life was neither so short nor so unhappy as many might suppose it. He lived ten years to another's one. His thoughts,

for the most part, were steeped in the riches of a generous heart
and a luxuriant imagination."

In the same year, *Fraser's Magazine* honoured Hunt with a
place in the "Gallery of Literary Characters," a character-
sketch accompanying the engraving by Maclise. *Fraser's* was
still swashbuckling and uproarious. The character-sketch was
not complete without comic cuts of Jack Straw's Castle and
"theatrical orange-suckery," and "bits" from *Rimini*. But the
last paragraph was so much the more valuable: "He is now
coming somewhat beyond that *mezzo cammin* of which Dante
sings, and fortune has not smiled upon him. The party to
which he formerly attached himself is in power, but all his old
labours in the libel line on their behalf are forgotten. Those
who abused the Prince Regent with far greater virulence than
Hunt ever did are high in office, and glorying in their elevation.
They have of course left him to struggle as he can. We hope
that his struggling is successful—we understand, indeed, that
his *Journal* has, as it deserves to have, a prosperous sale. It is
as refreshing as his former productions, and of a pleasanter
spirit. He has been an excessively ill-used man in many respects,
and by none more than by Lord Byron, and those who pane-
gyrise his lordship

With the twaddle of Allan, the meanness of Moore.
And so fare thee well, and prosper, 'Signor le Hunto, gran
gloria di Cocagna.'" On the opposite page was the drawing
by Maclise; if Hunt knew himself at all, he might see there that
his fears and his valour, his tribulations and his dreams had
been perceived by *this* artist.

After ten years of almost unrelieved London, Hunt took a
holiday in August 1835. Egerton Webbe went with him
through Oxford and Stratford-on-Avon ("inscribed our
names") into Wales. He was the guest of Anna Maria Dash-

Yours &c. Leigh Hunt.

AUTHOR OF "BYRON & HIS CONTEMPORARIES".

wood at Bodryddan, and, to judge from the verses that he
wrote in his happiness, the visit was one of his triumphs of life:

> There, walls were books; and the sweet witch,
> Painting, had there the rooms made rich
> With knights, and dames, and loving eyes
> Of heav'n-gone kindred, sweet and wise;
> Of bishops, gentle as their lawn,
> And sires, whose talk was one May-dawn.
> Last, on the roof, a clock's old grace
> Looked forth, like some enchanted face
> That never slept, but in the night
> Dinted the air with thoughtful might
> Of sudden tongue which seemed to say,
> "The stars are firm, and hold their way."

The whole poem may be discovered, in its pathetic grace, in
Mr Milford's edition. I am sorry to turn from it to a new instance of Hunt and the tantalising fates. Mrs Dashwood, it is
stated somewhere, assured to him an annuity; but presently,
wishing to marry again, she asked him to give it up.

XVIII

Ghosts of Chelsea

In his study at 4, Upper Cheyne Row, Chelsea, Hunt heard with pleasure, distinct in the quietness of the place, the street cries and the other sounds of ancient peace. They mingled in his mind with rumours of war then current, or rather they made those rumours seem infinitely terrible. With an unusual passion, he determined to speak out on the side of peace, and found himself writing one of his most remarkable poems, "Captain Sword and Captain Pen." This condemnation of armaments and battle-fields is the more honourable to its author because he had not himself been exposed to the miseries which he had in his mind. He took great trouble to know from authorities, with scarcely tolerable pain of thought, what *can* happen to flesh and blood in war; he was aware how little the narratives of soldiers and the detached reminiscences of other witnesses would be consulted before a new war was made unavoidable, and he wished in his long and well designed ballad to strike home. Moreover, he had a sense of the secondary havoc of war, "how many maimed and blood-saddened men are still suffering in hospitals and private houses; and how much off-spring, in all probability, is rendered sickly and melancholy. The author of the present poem believes that he owes the worst part of his constitution to the illness and anxiety caused, to one of the best of mothers, by the American war."

In the cinematography of verse, Hunt was no unskilful performer, and, having swung into a rhythm well agreeing with the subject of war's false romance, he now produced what may be compared to a very good moving-picture drama. First, he put on Captain Sword marching away:

> And ever and anon the kettle-drums beat
> Hasty power midst order meet;

And ever and anon the drums and fifes
Came like motion's voice, and life's;
Or into the golden grandeurs fell
Of deeper instruments, mingling well,
Burdens of beauty for winds to bear;
And the cymbals kissed in the shining air,
And the trumpets their visible voices reared,
Each looking forth with its tapestried beard,
Bidding the heavens and earth make way
For Captain Sword and his battle-array.

*   *   *

And Captain Sword went whistling gay,
"Over the hills and far away."

The scene changes to a scene of sun and harvest, and "thousands of faces"—and "bloody argument," and the "dark breath" of explosions, and "red mud," and "the horse-tempest," and—a victory. The scene changes. A ball to Captain Sword—the country-dance, waltz, galopade, minuet; the table loaded with "gold, and flowers, and sweets."

Well content was Captain Sword;
At his feet all wealth was poured;
On his head all glory set;
For his ease all comfort met;
And around him seemed entwined
All the arms of womankind.

The scene changes. Night, and storm; women by their fireside, with letters from the front, good news in them of "him." "Behold him!" The picture moves to the battle-field. One after another, in brief but intense light, the dying and dead are shown in many forms of agony. And on marches Captain Sword. He becomes overproud. He is

King of kings and lord of lords.

At last (Hunt means the American War),

> Three thousand miles across the waves
> Did Captain Sword cry, bidding souls be slaves;
> Three thousand miles did the echo return
> With a laugh and a blow made his old cheeks burn.

And Captain Pen arose. With the vision of this new power calling the spirits and souls of the righteous together and gaining a bloodless victory over Sword by means of the diffusion of new understanding, the last scene reaches its ending in "a world of swordless men." This poem found a welcome. The age of Richard Cobden, however, might have demanded more than three editions. In the third (1849), Hunt was able to reinforce his notes with an appeal to the arguments against war, humane and economic, of the invincible Cobden.

From this high-serious remonstrance, Hunt the poet turned in 1836 to a lighter theme—the ladies, God bless them. Never were there more literary ladies in England. The thought suggested to Hunt a variation on his former notion of a Feast of the Poets; and duly he exhibited his *Blue-Stocking Revels*[1], *or, the Feast of the Violets*. This jaunty and often trivial adventure in verse criticism, with all its floral decorations, is useful chiefly for the light it sheds on a literary chapter as yet imperfectly written. The Violets by the mossy stones deserved a historian, though Hunt was not too easy with his compliments. His Apollo said some unlucky things. For instance, praising Margaret Cullen's novels,

> "You make me sleep sometimes," quoth Phoebus, "'tis true;
> But I do even that, let me tell you, with few."

Margaret might have misunderstood that. Lady Blessington also might have wondered when Hunt wrote, addressing the reader,

---

[1] Re-named by a friend, "Blue Devils' Rivals."

Perhaps you have known what it is to feel longings
To pat silken shoulders at routs, and such throngings;
Well, think what it was at a vision like that!
A Grace after dinner! A Venus grown fat!

Yet, the early Victorians indulged this vein. Hunt was only in
the fashion. His virtue was the extent and cordiality of his
blue-stocking reading, and the readiness of his recognition. Of
Elizabeth Barrett he wrote,

> I took her at first for a sister of Tennyson.

He did not forget lonely Mary Lamb, "the fine brain."—There
was one Violet, who, had Phoebus omitted her, would not
have been quite satisfied;

> But, what pleased me hugely, he called to my wife,
> And said, "You have done Shelley's mood to the life."

Blue-Stocking Revels, intended for *The New Monthly*,
which in 1836 passed under the editorship of Hunt's former
scourge Theodore Hook, did not appear in it. Another opportunity arose. W. J. Fox, M.P. for Oldham, and others who
had an interest in *The Monthly Repository*, not succeeding very
well with it as a journal for progressive minds, made a present
of it to Hunt. Jointly with Reynell, who had printed such a
quantity of his writings, he undertook to make something of
it. Nor were able pens wanting to assist him: Landor, Carlyle,
Robert Browning, R. H. Horne and several others did what
they could. But an old connection with the Dissenters haunted
the title of the magazine, or the memory of those who heard it
mentioned; its dissent was not of the lucrative kind; and in
1838 the last number was published.

It was Hunt's hope that he might enlarge the still small
audience of Keats's poetry through his new journal. He asked
Charles Brown, then editing a journal of his own at Plymouth,

for some specimens of the unpublished verse. Brown replied, "I have all Keats's unpublished poems, to which you are most welcome, piecemeal or at one fell swoop, but I send none to you at present, for the following reason.—Geo. Keats has empowered Mr Dilke to lay an injunction against the publication of any of his deceased brother's works." The fact accounts for the incompleteness of the editions of Keats which appeared so obscurely in 1840 and 1841. Brown also questioned whether Keats was yet a name to the public; he reported that the Life which he had written as a lecture for the Plymouth Institution had given him an impression that "his fame does not yet stand high enough," and that the publishers whom he had approached with the work had sent him "rather a cool reply." However, in 1838, a chance came for Hunt to speak once more of Keats and his genius. This was the request of S. C. Hall that he should provide biographical information for the third volume of a large and embellished anthology, the *Book of Gems*.

It was a congenial request. Hunt produced a memoir of Keats, in which, after beginning "John Keats, one of the most poetical of Poets, and therefore by nature one of the most refined of men," and referring to his "most generous" use of his small independence, and correcting the legend that Keats died of his coarse critics, he sketched the man and his quality. "Mr Keats was under the middle size, and somewhat large above, in proportion to his lower limbs,—which, however, were neatly formed; and he had any thing in his dress and general demeanour but that appearance of 'laxity,' which has been strangely attributed to him in a late publication [Coleridge's *Table-Talk*]. In fact, he had so much of the reverse, though in no unbecoming degree, that he might be supposed to maintain a certain jealous care of the appearance and bearing of a gentleman, in the consciousness of his genius, and perhaps not without some sense of his origin. His face was handsome and sensitive, with a look in the eyes at once earnest and tender; and his hair grew in delicate brown ringlets, of remarkable beauty.

"Mr Keats may truly be pronounced a Poet of the most poetical order, for he gave himself up entirely to the beautiful, and had powers of expression equal to an excess of sensibility. His earlier poems, especially the 'Endymion,' are like a luxuriant wilderness of flowers and weeds ('weeds of glorious feature'); his latest, the 'Hyperion,' was a growing wood of oaks, from which the deepest oracles of the art might have been looked for. Indeed, there they were, as far as he gave his thoughts utterance. It has been justly said, that he is 'the greatest YOUNG Poet that ever appeared in the language'; that is to say, the greatest who did not live to be old, and whose whole memory will be identified with something both young and great. His lyrics (the Odes to the Nightingale and the Grecian Vase) are equal to the very finest we possess, both for subtle feeling and music. His 'Eve of St Agnes' is as full of beauty as the famous painted windows he describes in it; and there was such a profusion in him of fancies and imaginations, analogous to the beautiful forms of the ancient Poets, that a university-man expressed his astonishment at hearing he was not a Greek scholar. Of our lately deceased Poets, if you want imaginative satire, or bitter wailing, you must go to the writings of Lord Byron; if a thoughtful, dulcet, and wild dreaminess, you must go to Coleridge; if a startling appeal to the first elements of your nature and sympathies (most musical also), to Shelley; if a thorough enjoyment of the beautiful—for beauty's sake—like a walk on a summer's noon in a land of woods and meadows, you must embower yourself in the luxuries of Keats."

The companion memoir of Shelley contained the most concise biographical notice, and then these paragraphs, not less eminent for their humanity and perception than those on Keats: "Mr Shelley was tall, and slight of figure, with a singular union of general delicacy of organization and muscular strength. His hair was brown, prematurely touched with grey; his complexion fair and glowing; his eyes grey and extremely vivid; his face small and delicately featured, especially about the lower part; and he had an expression of countenance, when he was talking in his usual earnest fashion, which has been described elsewhere, as giving you the idea of something 'seraphical.'

"Mr Shelley's poetry resembles that creation, for the moral harmony of which he was so anxious. It is wonderfully flowing and energetic, round and harmonious as the orb,—no less conversant with seas and mountains, than with flowers and the minutest beauty,—and it hungers and thirsts after a certain beauty of perfection, as the orb rolls in loving attraction round the sun. He is remarkable for mixing a scholarly grandiosity of style with the most unaffected feeling and the most impulsive expression, and for being alike supernatural and human in his enthusiasm,—that is to say, he is equally fond of soaring away into the most ethereal abstractions, as if he were spirit; and of sympathizing with every-day flesh and blood, as though he had done nothing but suffer and enjoy with the most earth-bound of his fellow-creatures. Whether interrogating Nature in the icy solitudes of Chamouny, or thrilling with the lark in the sunshine, or shedding indignant tears with sorrow and poverty, or pulling flowers like a child in a field, or pitching himself back into the depths of time and space, and discoursing with the first forms and gigantic shadows of creation; he is alike in earnest, and AT HOME. His faults arise from the very excess of his sympathies with all things. He is sometimes obscure in the remoteness of his abstractions, and sometimes so impatient

with the forms of error, as to seem contradictory to his own
tolerant doctrine. He not only

> 'Relishes all things sharply,
> Passioned as we'—

he is far more passioned, and relishes them with a sharpness
that makes him cry out like one constituted almost too delicately for existence."

Besides these two critical melodies, the *Book of Gems*
preserves some notes by Hunt on Tennyson ("he is of the
school of Keats; much, however, as he reminds us of Keats,
his genius is his own: he would have written poetry had his
precursor written none; and he has, also, a vein of metaphysical subtlety, in which the other did not indulge"). Here,
too, out of Mrs Hall's album, first appears one of those lucky
poems which are instantly household words—"Abou Ben
Adhem." It was one of the many apologues which Hunt's
passion for the literature of the Near East, so far as he could
get at it in translation, bade him renovate in English verse; and
indeed it is not one of the most sensuously poetic. But its touch
of glory, like a sacred flame on a clear and graceful altar, has
captured the succeeding generations; "Ben Adhem's name led
all the rest." At a later date Miss Adelaide Procter, the poetess
of *Legends and Lyrics*, gave the author a copy of his poem
illuminated in the mid-Victorian taste, which he hung above
his writing-table; and he was not unknown to transcribe the
piece in fresh albums.

Of all the kit-cats of the late Sir Edmund Gosse, whose
attitude to Hunt as man and as poet was, as I remember from
his conversation, just and affectionate, none has a stronger air
of anecdotal enjoyment than the sketch of R. H. Horne. This
strange specimen of Victorian paradox, whom Sir Edmund
quoted to me during the last visit I paid to him, was frequently

at Hunt's house about the year 1838. Alike on account of his
independent way of thinking and acting, his adventurous youth
with its background of the Gulf of Florida and snowy Orizaba
and Jamaica's orange-groves, his talent for historical tragedies
and ballad romances, Horne was a valued companion. Besides,
he had known Hazlitt, and did not forget Hazlitt's idea that
Hunt should have been a gentleman of fortune, who patronised
men of letters. "And so you shall," declared the not very
cautious Horne, who at least put Hunt on a footing with the
old-fashioned patron by dedicating to him his "Death of
Marlowe"; Hunt wished that it might have been transmitted
to "the old Globe, or Blackfriars Theatre" and spectators
"who just remembered the days of Marlowe." This was in
1838. In 1870 Horne dedicated the fourth edition to Hunt's
"dear Memory—deservedly dear to all who knew him, and to
a world of others who know his books."

When he was intimate with Hunt's daily life, even Horne,
who was an eccentric, was amused by his friend's eccentricities.
"I once heard him discourse while standing in front of a bed
of winter cabbages covered with a sparkling hoar-frost, as
though it were Nature's jewellery of emeralds and diamonds
set in frosted silver." Horne had another tale of Hunt in all
seriousness entreating a poor man who perhaps could not find
the price of a few flowers to take his wife home a handful of
grass, and contemplate Nature. But Horne's most celebrated
story, which Sir Edmund Gosse handed on, was of a winter's
day, and Hunt discovered playing and warbling at a grand
piano, dragged close against a lively fire. "But, Hunt, you'll
ruin the piano!" "I know.... I know.... But it's delicious."

Horne remembered more pathetic points of innocence. "I
have heard Hunt quite apologise to his wife and daughters for
having expended eighteenpence at an old book stall, explaining

how useful and valuable the work would be to him,—and this at a time when the improvidence of others had brought him into trouble." The observer knew more about that than he said. He was one of the friends who raised and administered a private fund for Hunt. The following letter, dated Gray's Inn, June 6th, 1840, illustrates their frustration, and Hunt's:

My dear Mrs Hunt,

...I am still in debt £10 to Mr Kirkman for the old "Private List" account, Mr Blanchard not having yet paid me, —and of course I cannot ask one who has been so kind and true in his feelings to you all. He is himself in great difficulties just now. I received a letter from a subscriber to the "Private List" *some weeks ago* who asked if it was true that you had received nothing from the "Private List" fund for these *last eight months?* As you received the weekly payments up to the week when Mr Hunt's play came out, this report is rather vexatious. Can you at all conceive who could have set it afloat?...

R. H. Horne.

As the Lity. Fund gave £50 last year, it would be of no use to apply again so soon—indeed it would be injurious, as they would perhaps make troublesome enquiries, with regard to the Queen's donation, &c. In short, as I said, the affair is altogether most confusing.

The other trustee of the private list was T. N. Talfourd. He was obliged to return many, and more abrupt refusals to Mrs Hunt.

These unsatisfying circumstances were not allowed to escape to the public, and Hunt was sought out as a distinguished man of letters and the friend and fellow-worker of so many great writers. His ever cheerful messages to the age attracted to him a poet now seldom read in spite of his qualities—William Bell Scott. Scott, a choice artist as well as poet, had written long poems in 1832 to the memory of Shelley and of Keats. In "the season of primroses," 1837, he came to Chelsea to see their friend, who was always in his room with his "venerable" piano and his "Parnaso Italiano." ("Mrs Hunt I never saw but once by chance on the staircase.") Primroses in a jar, a "Petrarchan" inkstand caught the visitor's glance. On the hob a small iron pot simmered, with a kind of bread pudding in it. A cup of tea was the only refreshment. Hunt did not gloss his poverty. He said he should like to spend a few shillings on old books; "but I can deny myself even that." He spoke of Shelley, perfect, without a flaw; of Keats, if Scott read him right in his reticences, not so confidently. Scott thought he had "misgivings about Keats's general poetic workmanship." In the essence of poetry, Hunt then ranked "Coleridge above all others," and mentioned an Italian day among wild tulips when he was haunted by *Kubla Khan*; "the place, the climate and the poem were homogeneous." Bentham, "the only undemonstrative atheist," and Godwin, were subjects of the talk. Hunt wished that Scott would call on Tennyson in Mornington Crescent. On one occasion at least, Scott saw Hunt in another setting. It was in Church Street, Kensington, where Thornton Hunt, Smith Williams (later known as reader to Messrs Smith, Elder), someone else, and their wives and children "united in the same household." G. H. Lewes was there, singing and playing fluently.

Lewes had originally made Hunt's acquaintance in youth as a would-be contributor to his periodicals. He was still only twenty-two. It was a long time before he was to be disciplined by one who was heard to declare, "I should not think of allowing George to stay away a night from me." In his freedom he felt no difficulty in addressing Hunt like an old friend. In 1840 he praises *Sir Ralph Esher* which Hunt disparages, and observes that the book's fault is "not so much the absence

LEIGH HUNT, G.H.LEWES, VINCENT HUNT AND W.B.SCOTT

ETCHED BY W.B.S.

of a regular and exciting story" but "the want of intellectual ventriloquism—all the characters speak L. H. more or less, and they are all subtle and refining."

It may not be unnecessary to say that Leigh Hunt had an always faithful friend in his eldest son, Thornton, and Thornton was by 1839 a journalist of great promise. He had begun writing under his father, particularly as an art critic; in 1837 he had assisted Laman Blanchard in *The Constitutional*. There he attracted the attention of Edward Gibbon Wakefield by a paper on the disposal of colonial lands, and became Wakefield's coadjutor. After editing for short periods the *North Cheshire Reformer* and *Glasgow Argus*, he came back to London and joined *The Spectator*, for which he was to write until 1860. His steadiness consoled Leigh Hunt for the mischief of John, who was also a journalist, but, in his brother's metaphor, had only a fruit-stall in the market. John, it came out one day, was married. The elder, and very different, John Hunt, who had retired into the West of England, in 1837 made up the old *Examiner* quarrel with Leigh. He sent him reminiscences, and presents of books. The other *Examiner* Hunt, whose chief feat in this world was his unkind review of Blake—see Blake's *Poetical Works!*—was growing old and solitary. He had once exhibited his own pictures at the Royal Academy. That was past; and Robert Hunt was only a threadbare, nameless reporter of exhibitions. Stephen Hunt, once Leigh's employer, was dead.

It would be fortunate to discover plain traces of the early acquaintance of Thackeray, Dickens and Robert Browning with Leigh Hunt; but I do not find them. These three writers were "of the commission" by 1837. Hunt may have met Dickens, whom Forster introduced to him, in the office of *The True Sun*; he was at one moment in danger of depriving the world of the *Pickwick Papers*, for the publishers, casting about for an author to ballast their comic artist, thought of Leigh Hunt. He could report vulgar conversations well, and described the ridiculous with gusto[1].... But one cannot think of a world without Mr Pickwick himself, immortal and unchanged. It was Maclise's Dickens of the silky hair and all-seeing eye who first met Hunt, and moved him to say, "What a face is his to meet in a drawing-room! It has the life and soul in it of fifty human beings."

From his earliest literary years Hunt had had the ambition to write plays, and he had written some without finding anyone to take them. In the sublime endeavour of the early Victorians to rival the dramatists of the Elizabethan theatre he was naturally concerned; in 1835 he had told Forster, "The more I think of Henry the Second, the more I am sure he would make a glorious drama, crammed full of interest." His outlined plot was crammed full of Becket, and Becket was being overworked by the five-act men. Hunt, however, had another subject. It seemed to give Macready something like what he asked. Hunt wrote the play. Then came hopes, disappointments, advice, alteration; but at length, in October 1838, Sheridan Knowles "proposed to come and hear me read it, and the honour thus done me made me crave for more, emboldened by the opinions expressed by those who had already done so; I therefore invited Procter, Dickens, and others, who will all come; and I expect Carlyle, who is looked for every day from Scotland."

George Craik, the literary historian, and John Hunter of Craigcrook, visited Carlyle some months later. Hunt came, and read his play. At the close, Hunter records, "Carlyle,

---

[1] So good a novelist as Harrison Ainsworth wrote to Hunt some years after this, "I firmly believe you paved the way to Dickens's great popularity. He has derived some of his best notions from you, and is, so to speak, reaping your harvest." Here is an opportunity for someone seeking matter for a graduation thesis. Compare, for instance, Hunt's writings on Christmas with those of Dickens.

Craik and I arose; on which Hunt said, 'I am satisfied with my verdict, and care not now what any person may say of my play. I know it has life in it, since it has touched all of you.' Carlyle spoke earnestly and candidly of it; told him it was a piece of right good stuff, solid and real, with a pulse of life and play of passion in every scene and line, and capitally dramatised. The only thing like objection was, that we all thought the conclusion might be better brought out in *action*, so as to have more of dramatic interest than it has at present, by a long, but most admirable and indeed Shakespearean speech from a Cardinal giving judgment as to the divorce. Hunt at once acquiesced, and said he would endeavour to alter it agreeably to our suggestions."

> One step to the death-bed,
> And one to the bier,
> And one to the charnel,
> And one—oh where?

These slightly misquoted lines from the *Ginevra* of Shelley were prefixed to, and hint at the original germ of, Hunt's play *A Legend of Florence*. It was again read by the author before the management of Covent Garden, "received with acclamation, and all sorts of the kindest expressions, by Mr and Mrs Charles Mathews, Mrs Orger, Mr Robertson (treasurer, an old friend), Bartley, stage manager, and Planché (I believe reader), and the performance is to follow Knowles's, in the thick of the season." Covent Garden Theatre was that season, 1839–1840, under control of Madame Vestris. She gave Hunt a suggestion: "Now, Hunt, if you will change the movement and close of the last act, it will be far more popular and profitable." Give Agolanti his wife back, and "your play will run for a hundred nights." Leigh Hunt at once demurred, "Impossible—I can't give him back Ginevra." Planché was astonished by the beauty of Hunt's reading, and said, "Hunt had the wildest ideas of dramatic effect, and calculated in the most Utopian spirit upon the intelligence of the British public. As I often told him, if he read his scenes himself, the magic of his voice, the marvellous intonation and variety of expression in his delivery, would probably enchain and enchant a general audience as it did us; but the hope of being so interpreted was not to be entertained for a moment." Mr and Mrs Mathews, equally impressed, directed Robertson to pay Hunt £100 and secure whatever dramatic production should follow *A Legend of Florence*.

On November 1st, 1839, Horne wrote to Hunt, "Wordsworth the other day (after sitting silent an hour) suddenly said, 'I wish I could be in London in January.' Margaret Gillies asked, 'Why?' 'To make my hands burn,' said he, 'in welcoming Leigh Hunt's play.'" This was a pleasant surprise, but a humanity nearly as pleasant and even more surprising happened to Hunt before his *Legend* was produced. The following is from Benjamin Haydon's journal for February 5th, 1840:

"Met Leigh Hunt after an interval of many years, looking hearty, gray, and a veteran. We hailed each other. 'Haydon,' said Hunt, 'when I see you hosts of household remembrances crowd my fancy.' 'Hunt,' said I, 'I am going to write my life, and I'll do *you* justice. You would have been burnt at the stake for a principle, and would have feared to put your foot in the mud.' Hunt was affected.

Hunt. 'Will you come and see my play?'
Haydon. 'I will; when?'
Hunt. 'Friday.'
Haydon. 'I'll applaud you to the skies.'
Hunt. 'Bring your wife; I'll put your names down.'
Haydon. 'I will.'
'God bless ye.' 'Goodbye.' We parted."

XIX

The Poetical Horizon

HAYDON was one of the audience at Covent Garden on February 7th, 1840. Hunt's friends, a goodly company, were eager for the occasion. For two of his scenes Vincent Novello and Egerton Webbe[1] had composed "solemn and affecting strains of vocal music." *A Legend of Florence* promised well in every way. Ellen Tree as Ginevra had already fascinated Hunt as the heroine, and the stage-manager (Bartley), indeed everyone concerned, had kindled his mind with their "freshness of imagination" in the production. What followed may be best enjoyed in the words of Hunt's friends. Laman Blanchard wrote, "Do tell me how you felt when you heard your name ringing through the walls of the great theatre. Are you aware that when you came on, you stood on your head instead of your heels? What did you think of Mrs Hunt and your small family when you were making that considerable bow? And when you saw all those people didn't you say to yourself, 'Lord, what a few children I've got at home to what there are here'? Had you any notion in what part of the House the 1s. gallery was situate? Did you feel at all like a man who stands silent upon a peak in Darien?—Seeing as from a tower the end of all? Eh? What did you think of the fiddlers—and of that man with the bassoon who, I understand, stood in the same attitude gazing on the spot where you stood till 2 in the morning—hours after all the

---

1 Webbe composed a dirge. He himself died that August. Hunt wrote a biographical memorial of him for *The Morning Chronicle*, which Mr Ingpen discovered to have reappeared as a pamphlet. "Alas! that such a man, so good and affectionate a son, so loving a friend and brother, so admirable a wit, so promising a writer, philosopher, musician, should have looked forward in despondency to the early fate that prevented him from being a father himself, and a man of great renown."

audience had left—when he was removed by three policemen? Some say that Bartley came on with you, but others are doubtful, there was such a lustre all about you."

In the *Modern British Dramatists* of G. H. Lewes, 1867, a retrospect is found: "It was really an exciting scene, that first night! So many of us were intensely anxious for the success of the poet; so many were delighted to see the poetical drama once more triumphing; and the tears and the plaudits of that night, genuine though they were, had something feverish and exaggerated in them. Had it not been so, the play would have continued to excite this enthusiasm; instead of which, it was only performed some fifteen or twenty nights, and is now only at rare intervals revived for a night or two in the provinces." Hunt himself, in the preface to the second edition of his play, thanked alike his "old readers," who seemed to him to make up half the audience, the press "of all parties," and the actors. We may glance at the printed play. Agolanti is jealous of his wife Ginevra, whom Antonio Rondinelli still loves. Agolanti's provocations and misunderstandings torment her. Rondinelli, struck by her misery, contrives to meet Agolanti. High words ensue, and are interrupted by the news that Ginevra is dead. Her funeral takes place; but in the night, Ginevra comes and calls at the window. Agolanti takes her for a ghost and "closes the shutters." She visits Rondinelli.

> I am Ginevra—buried, but not dead,
> And have got forth and none will let me in.

Rondinelli receives her. Agolanti comes and demands her. She escapes to a convent. Agolanti is killed. Such is the tale, and Hunt has enlarged it with minor characters; his main persons are thoughtfully and originally studied; his eloquence, though lacking in the sharpness and hardness of the great dramas, is various and beautiful. Sir John Hanmer, one of the neglected poets, wrote to Moxon the publisher, "If Bulwer sets up for *the* dramatist of this day, he must hide his diminished head"; and I am inclined to think that, among the many semi-Elizabethan attempts of Victorian dramatic poets, *A Legend of Florence* is eminent for emotion, movement and unpretentious dignity of style.

The dedication "To Armorer Donkin, Esq., of Newcastle," reveals to us the name and benevolence of a man not otherwise recorded in the literary world.

Happy and wooing as were the first fortunes of *A Legend of Florence* (Queen Victoria[1] herself had come to see it more than once, and had spoken most graciously of it), the subsequent story is pathetic. Lewes summarises it: "Such as it was, the success sufficed to inspire Leigh Hunt with the hope that he had at last found his real vocation, and a profitable mine. For some years he devoted himself to the composition of plays, and had to endure the tortures of an unacted dramatist, for not one of these plays could he get produced." Lewes forgot one exception, to which this book of rainbows and shadows will duly come. Three of the unlucky ones in manuscript rest in the libraries of American collectors. Fragments elsewhere confirm the general lucklessness of the hard-working Hunt, lured on[2] by that enchanting first night at Covent Garden, and baffled again and again.

---

[1] An unimprovable note appears at the end of Act II: "I trust that the 'touch of nature which makes the whole world kin,' and the delight which nations experience at all evidences of graceful feeling in their princes, particularly when accompanied by actual beneficence, will save me from a charge of indecorum in stating, that on the second night of her Majesty's presence at the performance of this play, when the lovely organ strain, composed by my friend Vincent Novello, began to double the tears of the audience, a fair hand was observed to come from behind the royal curtain, and press the congenial arm next to it, as if in affecting remembrance." (1844.)

[2] "The author of one successful piece is easily persuaded to write another." L. H., Introduction to *Wycherley*, etc., 1840.

During 1840 his theatrical passion found a byway of expression in editorship. The indignation that he had formerly felt against Sheridan as the friend of the Regent did not impede him from supplying an introduction to Moxon's reprint of Sheridan's comedies. But he was, and in print he said he was, "conscious of a want of enthusiasm for the genius of Sheridan." A larger and better work was the editing of Wycherley, Congreve, Vanbrugh and Farquhar in one thick volume for Moxon's "Dramatic Library." Hunt here showed more of the scholarly interest than usual, unearthing facts and documents, but was duly taught a few points (by Peter Cunningham) in *The Athenaeum*. In spirit, his acquaintance with personalities of the Queen Anne era was peculiarly fine; he moved among them, in his library, with a smiling ease. The closing part of his essay was a quotation and discussion of the opinions of Lamb and Hazlitt on the artificial comedy; Hunt agreed generally with Lamb's vindication of its writers from Mrs Grundy's charges, but preferred Hazlitt's for being itself less artificial in argument. "At all events," he wrote, the reader must have "the opinions of two out of the three great critics whom we not long ago had among us," and he went on to lament that neither Hazlitt nor Lamb was "again coming down the street to his door." Had they been able to do so, they must have thanked him for so capable and useful an edition of their dear comic writers.

Moxon, it happened, dedicated *Wycherley, Congreve, Vanbrugh and Farquhar* to Thomas Moore, dating his inscription October 1840. Moore, now issuing a collected edition of his poems, did not leave out the verses which he had flung off in a fury against the writer of *Lord Byron and Some of His Contemporaries*. Their perpetuation drew from Hunt, on June 8th, 1841, the following letter: "The remembrance of other days makes me dislike to call you 'Sir,' and for obvious reasons it might not be proper to say 'Dear Sir,' yet this letter comes to own to Mr Moore how sorry I was, this morning, to find that he had reprinted the verses from *The Times*. I confess I should almost as soon have expected their republication in your collected works (a packet for posterity) as I should have thought of repeating the letters from *The Tatler* in the selection of papers lately published under the title of *The Seer*.... If, indeed, any imaginary circumstance should have induced you to misconstrue these evidences of goodwill, all I can say is, that I have never written a syllable, during these late years, with the intention of wounding you, and that I never utter a syllable in private at variance with that I write. How could I renew hostilities, after consenting (permit me to use that word on the present occasion) to receive a favour from you—the subscription to my *Poems?* and allow me to ask, how could you, after I had received the favour, suffer the attack on me to be reprinted?..." I do not find a reply from Moore, who lost an opportunity of producing an Irish melody which would have done him credit.

But if Moore's doggerel epigram has been perpetuated, something on the other side, arising from the volume in Moxon's "Dramatic Library," has been so too. I mean, of course, Macaulay's essay in the *Edinburgh Review* for January 1841, entitled "Leigh Hunt." Macaulay's business was to assail, once and for all, the "obscenity" of Wycherley, Congreve, Vanbrugh and Farquhar. In doing that he contradicted Lamb and Hunt, but he paid them both tributes which will not be forgotten. At that date, what a noble thing it was in him to begin his essay with a manifesto, that may still be tributary to the fair name of Leigh Hunt! "We have a kindness for Mr Leigh Hunt. We form our judgment of him, indeed, only from events of universal notoriety, from his own works, and from the works of other writers, who have generally abused him in the most rancorous manner. But, unless we are greatly mistaken, he is a very clever, a very honest, and a very good-natured man. We can clearly discern, together with many merits, many faults both in his writings and in his conduct. But we really think that there is hardly a man living whose merits have been so grudgingly allowed, and whose faults have been so cruelly expiated."

The assistance of Hunt was sought in 1840 by Vincent Novello, who was preparing a "green book" of songs to be sung in the open air, or, as he called it, remembering *Rimini*, *Parties in the Greenwood Shade*. And Haydon wrote, "My dear Hunt, Will you detail to an old Friend any habits of walking, standing on his feet, sitting, thinking, looking, or musing, which Byron had—the cut of his frock coat—his boots—had he a stick and what sort of one—can Mrs Hunt enclose a pen sketch, or will she cut him out as he used to stand on his feet—did he have a hat—or cap—&c.?" In 1840, too, the Hunt family moved to 32, Edwardes Square, Kensington; here they had a garden to refresh them, and at no. 45 Thornton Hunt who had married Kate Gliddon, and John Gliddon who had married Mary Florimel Leigh Hunt, were sharing house. Here also came young poets, seeking counsel and finding besides a household that they would remember. One of these was W. J. Linton, the wood-engraver. He called first with a protest against capital punishment, to which he desired, and instantly received, Hunt's signature. Afterwards he became almost one of the family, and even liked Marianne ("genial, motherly woman"), as Hunt talked, and she peeled walnuts for the visitor. One night, after an exhausting dinner-party elsewhere, Hunt sat to the piano to play, among other things, the "Halcyon Days" from Purcell's *King Arthur*. Linton was not able to give the same praise to the children of Hunt, whom he called "a Bayard," as to the "delightful old man." He noted some of John's adventures: "after breakfasting with a friend, he would borrow a book, and pledge it at the nearest pawnbroker's; he would try to borrow money in his father's name from his father's friends, on one awkward occasion the father being in the house at which he called."

A name less shadowy now than Linton, William Allingham, comes into the life of Leigh Hunt at Kensington. Correspondence on poetical topics preceded the meeting, when the young Irish lyrist, having once seen a cab with a white horse driving off from no. 32, and heard that Hunt was in it on his way to a rehearsal, arrived at a good moment. ("If I had been one minute sooner [last time] he might have taken me with him —perhaps even into the theatre! Wild thought!") The meeting at last was in Hunt's study. Allingham had been encouraged by Hunt so eagerly, at distance, as "a youth manifestly of very extraordinary promise and no mean performance" that the first nearer view was a great occasion. Leigh Hunt told him to visit Browning, and was pleased with Allingham's term for that writer—"the Turner of poetry." He referred with zest to his recent adventure of meeting Hans Andersen, "a large child, a sort of half-angel." This was in 1847, when, too, Allingham made a note that Hunt "looks wonderfully different in the street from in the house. There, a spare old man in a frock coat and black stock, with weak eyes and rather careworn look; here, a young man (though of sixty), with luxuriant if gray locks, open shirt collar and flowing dressing-gown, bright face, and the easiest way of talking in the world." Meeting Hunt in Piccadilly once, Allingham soliloquised, "If I ever have any doubts about him, they vanish at one glance from his eye."

In his *London Journal*, Hunt had printed a little poem, one of his own, entitled "An Angel in the House." An early contributor to *The Examiner*, and friendly parodist and acquaintance,

P. G. Patmore, had a son, who was destined before many years
to be illustrious for another, longer poem, called *The Angel
in the House*. Patmore sent the youth with an introduction
to Edwardes Square, in 1840 or so. The letter of Coventry
Patmore to Sir Edmund Gosse, long afterwards, in memory
of that incident, has not escaped the observation of Mr Max
Beerbohm: "...I was informed that the poet was at home, and
asked to sit down until he came to me. This he did after I had
waited in the little parlour at least two hours, when the door
was opened and a most picturesque gentleman, with hair flowing
nearly or quite to his shoulders, a beautiful velvet coat and a
Vandyck collar of lace about a foot deep, appeared, rubbing
his hands and smiling ethereally, and saying, without a word
of preface or notice of my having waited so long, 'This is a
beautiful world, Mr Patmore!' I was so struck by this remark
that it has eclipsed all memory of what occurred during the
remainder of my visit." As Mr Beerbohm says, "there was
nothing wrong about the words themselves"; they were "exactly,
exquisitely, inevitably the right words. But they should have
been said sooner." In *Ainsworth's Magazine*, after a still longer
delay, Hunt warned "youngest England" not to be too youth-
fully dashing, to regard health and regularity. "Hear this,
Coventry Patmore! you who want nothing but experience, and
the study of the mechanism of verse, to become equal to the
finest poets existing." At the same time Hunt "hailed some
other names, just now emerging in the poetical horizon"—
Lowell, Ebenezer Jones (why is *Studies of Sensation and Event*
such a secret?) and Aubrey de Vere.

But Hunt's aspirations were not all for the poetry of others.
He himself was writing verse, and had decidedly purified his
poetical style. His individuality still kindled his words in verse
as in prose. His sense of the Royal Family was now all that it

should have been; for, as Hazlitt and others had perceived, his life might have been passed with charming fitness in the courtly days among poetic cavaliers. Macaulay wrote to him in 1841, "I heard the other day, from one of poor Southey's nephews, that he cannot live many weeks: I really do not see why you might not succeed him. The title of Poet Laureate is indeed ridiculous. But the salary ought to be left for the benefit of some man of letters. Should the present government be in office when a vacancy takes place, I really think that the matter might be managed." With these and other observations to encourage him, Hunt was nevertheless fated to remain merely a volunteer laureate. In 1842 he wrote an "Envoy" for his light and generous love-story *The Palfrey*, inscribing it

> To HER, who loves all peaceful glory,
> Therefore laurelled song and story;

confessing that he had not begged leave,

> And yet how beg it for one flower
> Cast in the path of Sovereign Power?

The spirit of the Old Court Suburb appears to have aided his literary methods, and he sent forth from Kensington a series of books and periodical writings to prove that he did not boast in vain of his green and invincible old age. Moxon, whom he called a secreter rather than publisher of books (and also "a bookseller among poets, and a poet among booksellers"), printed in 1844 two thousand copies of his *Poetical Works*. It was a pocket volume, of a companionable size which is generally denied to the poets of the present date, but concise as it was Hunt was not sure that he had reduced the collection drastically enough. He wrote to Allingham, "Should you ever meet with it, I hope you will tear it to pieces. But indeed I always long to make my editions just half or a fourth part of what they are, to give myself a better chance of life. I should like to be a thin, very thin little book, which people would carry in their pockets, like Gray and Collins. The most flattering of my dreams is, that by and by perhaps somebody may pare me down to this." One half-looked to see the signature "Ralph Hodgson" appended to this stern and sensible dream. The Moxon edition was popular, as such things go. A remark in the preface deserves emphasis. Hunt has been commonly condemned for imposing the errors of his own poetics upon the verse of Keats. In reconsidering his own early poems, he incidentally makes it clear that he did not think of himself as Keats's poetical trainer, and probably would not have understood the charge against him: "He had not the luck to possess such a guide in poetry as Keats had in excellent Charles Cowden Clarke."

A friend of Leigh Hunt, having lent him £40, had received as a security a manuscript work entitled "True Poetry." He suspected, as he looked at it, that the £40 would have been a better sight on his study table. But the senior member of Messrs Smith, Elder, came to dinner, took up the work, paid the £40, and with an additional sum of £60 had soon secured Hunt's consent to the publication of what was named afresh as *Imagination and Fancy*. It appeared in 1844, was reprinted in 1845, 1846, and many times since, and, in my judgment, will always be an illuminating work. Its object, fairly achieved, was "threefold;—to present the public with some of the finest passages in English poetry, *marked and commented*;—to furnish such an account, in an Essay, of the nature and requirements of poetry, *as may enable readers in general to give an answer on those points to themselves and others*;—and to show, throughout the greater part of the volume, what sort of poetry is to be considered *as poetry of the most poetical kind*...in its element, like an essence distilled." The authors chosen by Hunt, for his aim of making Coleridgean principles of criticism a little nearer the mental flights of the general reader, show how decisively he was now minded to distinguish genius; they were Spenser, Marlowe, Shakespeare, Jonson, Beaumont and Fletcher, Middleton, Decker and Webster, Milton, Coleridge, Shelley and Keats. Much as he had written in praise of the two last, he again voiced sweet anthems to their honour. Besides, his particular comments were of a cordiality greatly contrasting with the customary dry and taskmaster style of expositors in English literature. At Keats's "magic casements" he pauses, haunted with the possibilities: "This beats Claude's Enchanted Castle, and the story of King Beder in the *Arabian Nights*. You do not know what the house is, or where, nor who the bird. Perhaps a king himself. But you see the window, open on the perilous sea, and hear the voice from out the trees in which it is nested, sending its warble over the foam. The whole is at once vague and particular, full of mysterious life. You see nobody, though something is heard; and you know not what of beauty or wickedness is to come over that sea. Perhaps it was suggested by some fairy tale. I remember nothing of it in the dreamlike wildness of things in *Palmerin of England*, a book which is full of colour and home landscapes, ending with a noble and affecting scene of war; and of which Keats was very fond."

The anthologist intended, if the volume met with success enough, to go on with his work, and to add similar annotated selections of the poetry of *Action and Passion*, *Contemplation*, *Wit and Humour*, and *Song*. The word was, "*none but genuine poetry*," and on that head Hunt's judgment was as good as any man's. The success of *Imagination and Fancy* was sufficient. But ill health obliged him to be content with only one volume more of the excellent series projected, *Wit and Humour*, although *Action and Passion* (narrative and dramatic poetry) was announced for publication in 1847. *Wit and Humour*, not quite on the level of its predecessor, was nevertheless spirited and original, and new editions were called for. Although he had stated that its range would be from Chaucer to Byron, the author of *Don Juan* was only introduced, certainly with cheerful eulogy, in the essay prefixed; and Byron's name must be sought in the corresponding part of *Imagination and Fancy* also.

In the same year as *Wit and Humour*, the two volumes of *Stories from the Italian Poets*, embodying what had been in and out of his thoughts for most of his life, were brought out by Messrs Chapman and Hall. I shall notice a few details, leaving the merits of Hunt as a translator in the warm light of praise from several eminent judges. The volumes were dedicated to Sir Percy Shelley, Bart., by "your Father's Friend." The London Library received the thanks of one who has probably enriched some of its volumes with notes and marks of exclamation. Hunt on Dante was here, as elsewhere, extremely independent, and summed him up as "this great semi-barbarian." He indulged a dream of the English Church perfected into a "flower of Christian charity." And he asserted (as his favourite William Collins had done a century before) that Edward Fairfax "upon the whole, and with regard to a work of any length, is the best metrical translator our language has seen."

Hunt collaborated, during his earlier years at Kensington, in one or two unimportant works with which R. H. Horne was associated. In 1740 a modernised Chaucer had been published, since when it had slept sound; in 1841 Horne hoped to do better, and he called together Wordsworth, Miss Barrett, Hunt and one or two unfamiliar poets to dash to Dan Chaucer's assistance. In his introduction he wrote of the recent lyrical modulations of rhythm and ascribed the greatest advances in versification to

Coleridge, Shelley, Leigh Hunt and Tennyson; he pointed out *A Legend of Florence* as Hunt's latest triumph in metrical effects. Hunt "translated" *The Squire's Tale* and *The Friar's Tale*, and did so with that vitality which might be expected of so mellow a Chaucerian. The whole subject, however, is one of the unlucky ones which "refuse to start"; the nature of the case is dealt with by Skeat, and Horne's modernised Chaucer sleeps as sound as Ogle's.

For *Heads of the People*, 1840, a set of character-drawings by Kenny Meadows, Horne obtained papers not only from Leigh Hunt but from Thornton too; and father and son appeared together in another performance—Thornton's novel *The Foster-Brother*, 1845, to which Leigh Hunt supplied an introduction. The year after, a less co-operative son, John, died. He had been in low water for some time. I have seen a tragic letter from him to his mother, apparently of the year 1843, bitterly blaming her for instilling the worst opinions of him into the mind of Leigh Hunt, and for refusing him help. "Does he know that I write for *Cleave's Gazette* at one shilling per column? *No.* But he *is* told I write petitioning letters—and therefore thinks I won't work....I am dreadfully ill. I see only something worse at hand than this starving." Carlyle had thought that "ranting Johnny" would at length rise above his misdeeds and his perplexities. His epitaph is written by Thornton, who assisted his destitute family until they departed to Australia: "It must be said that, from the very earliest to the very latest, he never lost a sense of deference and affection for Leigh Hunt."

The worst part of Leigh Hunt's private difficulties, though many still beset him, were now at an end. The series of considerable works which he had produced for the stage and the library had brought him money enough to stave off the evil day with some confidence. Shelley, who had rescued him before, was his benefactor now; on April 20th, 1844, Mary wrote that Sir Timothy's condition was not what it had been; "ere long there will be a change." (Sir Timothy had had his money's worth in regard of Mary's expectations!) The £2000, volunteered by Mary in continuance of Shelley's wishes twenty years before, would not now be possible; she explained; but she and her son Percy were eager to relieve Hunt of care and necessity. Accordingly, "From the time of Sir Timothy's death I shall give directions to my banker to honour your quarterly cheques for £30 a quarter; and I shall take steps to secure this to you and to Marianne if she should survive you. Percy has read this letter, and approves. I know your *real* delicacy about money matters, and that you will at once be ready to enter into my views; and feel assured that if any present debt should press, if we have any command of money, we will take care to free you from it." Sir Timothy departed, and the £120 a year began.

In spite of it, the position was insecure, and two years later a voluminous correspondence grew between the friendly Forster —Thornton Hunt, greatly daring, called him the Beadle of the Universe—and the veteran, on the subject of his troubles, and the chances of a pension. Forster obtained from Hunt a retrospect of old events, with some reflection of their financial aspect, even to the cerulean paintings on the ceiling of the prison cell of "Libertas." While Hunt was writing out these memoranda, and lamenting that he had been compelled to apply to Sir Percy Shelley "for leave to draw a year's advance on the annuity" (the very thing Sir Percy wished to protect him from), a newspaper was brought in. He presently glanced at it. It contained the news that B. R. Haydon, historical painter, had committed suicide.

"*Twelve o'clock.* I have just read of poor Haydon! how dreadful! how *astonishing*! for he is one of the last men of whom

I should have expected such a thing. I looked upon him as one who turned disappointment itself to a kind of self-glory—but see how we may be mistaken. Poor fellow! but then, poor *family*! That is the worst."

Almost twenty years after Hazlitt's *Spirit of the Age*, R. H. Horne, who erratically appears in and vanishes from so many Victorian biographies, edited *A New Spirit of the Age*, with the assistance of Miss Barrett and others. "Of those [writers] selected by Hazlitt, three are introduced in the present publication"; and Hunt was one of the three. This time he shared an article with William Wordsworth—an article dressed with a fancifulness instructed by his own. "In religious feeling he has been misrepresented. It is certain that no man was ever more capable of the spirit of reverence; for God gifted him with a loving genius—with a genius to love and bless. He looks full tenderly into the face of every man, and woman, and child, and living creature; and the beautiful exterior world, even when it is in angry mood, he smoothes down softly, as in recognition of its sentiency, with a gentle caressing of the fancy—Chaucer's irrepressible 'Ah, benedicite,' falling for ever from his lips!" There are not lacking comparisons, "excess of light," invocations of Beaumont and Fletcher, of Addison, and, in the name of Reform, even Melanchthon. However, I shall do no harm by abbreviating the purple draughts, and growing, with Horne, to a point thus: "The work that Leigh Hunt has done, may be expressed in the few words of a dedication made to him some years since. 'You have long assisted,' says the dedication, 'largely and most successfully, to educate the hearts and heads of both old and young; and *the extent of the service is scarcely perceptible, because the free and familiar spirit in which it has been rendered gives it the semblance of an involuntary emanation. The spontaneous diffusion of intelligence and good feeling is not calculated, however, to force its attention upon general perception, etc.' The meaning of all this is, that Leigh Hunt has no 'system,' and no sustained gravity of countenance, and therefore the fineness of his intellect and the great value of his unprofessor-like teaching have been extremely underrated. The dedication also marks this disgrace to the age—which shall be as distinctly stated as such a disgrace deserves—that while the public generally takes it for granted that Mr Leigh Hunt is on the Pension List, he most certainly is *not*, and never has been!"

XX

The Youngest Son

"SIR,—I have much pleasure in informing you that the Queen has been pleased to direct that, in consideration of your distinguished literary talents, a pension of Two Hundred Pounds yearly should be settled upon you from the funds of the Civil List. Allow me to add, that the severe treatment you formerly received, in times of unjust persecution of liberal writers, enhances the satisfaction with which I make this announcement." The letter is dated Downing Street, June 22nd, 1847, and the writer was Lord John Russell. There was naturally an outburst of rejoicing at 32, Edwardes Square, and in applauding the good fortune Hunt did not fail to appreciate the Minister's second sentence. "I am proud, indeed, of being thus sympathised with by a Russell, and feel as if history itself were deigning to speak to me as a friend."

Among those patient defenders of Leigh Hunt who had urged the question of the pension, Carlyle will be conspicuously recalled, since he drew up a paper of "Memoranda concerning Mr Leigh Hunt" in no half-hearted way. It was of a date much earlier than the accomplishment of its purpose, but it did its work. I quote its sixth clause: "That such a man is rare in a Nation, and of high value there; not to be *procured* for a whole Nation's revenue, or recovered when taken from us, and some £200 a year is the price which this one, whom we now have, is valued at; with that sum he were lifted above his perplexities, perhaps saved from nameless wretchedness. It is believed that, in hardly any other way could £200 abolish as much suffering, create as much benefit, to one man, and through him to many and all."

Had the pension been withheld, the year 1847 would not have been without its solace to Hunt, for his friends had laudably worked upon two plans of subvention; and both were crowned with success. The second was the provincial performance of Ben Jonson's *Every Man in His Humour* by that amateur company including Charles Dickens (as Bobadil), Forster (as Kitely), Lewes, Cruikshank, Leech, and Douglas Jerrold. July 26th, 1847, saw them at Liverpool, July 28th at Manchester. After the overture at Liverpool Forster recited an address or rather prologue by Lytton:

> The base may mock, the household asp may sting,
> The bard, like Lear, is "every inch a king."
> Want but anoints his head with holier balms—
> He claims your tribute, not implores your alms!
> Mild amidst foes, amidst a prison free,
> He comes—our grey-hair'd bard of *Rimini*!
> Comes with the pomp of memories in his train,
> Pathos and wit, sweet pleasure and sweet pain!

As I transcribe these lines, I cannot but recall the graceful candour and brilliant sympathies of a later Lytton whose subaltern I was; and the unfailing regard for Hunt on the part of the novelist to whom Mr Michael Sadleir is devoting his labours becomes exceedingly clear to the imagination. The prologue at Manchester was from the pen of Talfourd. The amateur comedians found favour, as on many other occasions, and the sum of four hundred guineas was presented to Hunt. On September 15th, the Museum Club, of which he was a greatly prized member, gave a dinner in his honour. His public speeches were rare. Macready heard one and disapproved of it. But this at the Museum Club "made a profound impression on his audience"; and well it might, for it was a reminiscence of some outstanding matters in his literary life. And if we could go this evening to hear Hunt speak of Shelley, and Keats, and Lamb, and Hazlitt, we would. And of Byron?

Better circumstances did not beguile Hunt from his steady production of books. *Men, Women and Books* appeared in 1847, its contents being gathered from essays in remote and recent periodicals. *A Jar of Honey from Mount Hybla*, 1848, was the slightly revised form of essays on pastoral poetry and kindred pleasures first written for *Ainsworth's Magazine* in 1844. "The pencil of Doyle" adorned their reappearance. Hunt quietly dedicated the book to Horace Smith, who was at Brighton, and had lately sent Hunt his collected poems. The renewal of friendship filled Hunt with the epicurean-spiritual mood, but Smith was destined to read no more Christmas books, dying in 1849. In *The Town*, 1848, a contemporary declared that Hunt "had illumined the fog and smoke of London with a halo of glory, and peopled the streets and buildings with the life of past generations." He might have added, besides the streets and buildings, the trees. Such notes as the old Londoner made for subsequent improvements were given to Peter Cunningham for his systematic and richly minute *Handbook of London*. *Readings for Railways* shows Hunt's notion of what literature a civilised race might take on a journey; *A Book for a Corner*, also issued in 1849, was one of his unions of "the sweet fields" and the study; "antiquity hung with ivy-blossoms and rose-buds; old friends with the ever-new faces of wit, thought and affection." Its contents were almost entirely—apart from his own remarks—of the eighteenth century.

He continued to write plays. His friends continued to encourage him to write plays. As he enjoyed that, or any other form of fancy's exercise, the non-reception of the finished works by the theatres should not appear in too dark a colouring.

In 1848 a packet arrived, with a letter in it, and some poems and translations by one D. G. Rossetti, who asked Hunt to read and advise. Hunt treated all such correspondents alike. He read and advised, and in replying he observed, with reference to some roughness of metre in the translations, "I guess indeed that you are altogether not so musical as pictorial." He discerned in the poems "an unquestionable poet, thoughtful, imaginative, and with rare powers of expression. I hailed you as such at once, without any misgiving." But he gave Rossetti a warning, "Poetry... is not a thing for a man to live upon while he is in the flesh, however immortal it may render him in spirit." Rossetti was twenty years old, and the Prae-Raphaelite Brotherhood was just taking shape.

One by one Hunt saw the survivors of earlier brotherhoods depart. Talfourd had had some dispute with him latterly, and that friendship closed obscurely before the lawyer-dramatist's death. John Hunt, his brother, died on September 7th, 1848. He had the advantage of Leigh in many points ("*My* Mr Hunt," his wife would say significantly!), both of personality and circumstance; and although not much is known of him, every witness speaks with wonderful directness of his excellence as a man. What he was like in his prime is suggested by P. G. Patmore's recollection: "I have never seen in any one else so perfect an outward symbol or visible setting forth of the English character, in its most peculiar and distinguishing features, but also in its best and brightest aspect, as in Mr John Hunt. A figure tall, robust, and perfectly well-formed; a carriage commanding and even dignified, without the slightest apparent effort or consciousness of being so; a head and a set of features on a large scale, but cast in a perfectly regular mould; handsome, open, and full of intelligence, but somewhat hard and severe; an expression of bland benevolence, singularly blended with a marble coldness of demeanour almost repulsive, because almost seeming to be so intended:—such were the impressions produced on me by the first *abord* of John Hunt, as I saw him within his prison walls." There, with a table, two chairs, and a painting by Hazlitt, John Hunt waited the triumph of Reform. "There was one man, and one only, towards whom Hazlitt seemed to cherish a feeling of unmingled personal affection and regard," and this was the man. Horace Smith noted him too as a patriot and a philanthropist. "Calm, firm, upright, he reminded you of Horace's 'justum et tenacem propositi virum,' though perhaps his character might have found a better prototype in the republican, than in the imperial days of Rome."

In *The Examiner*, then arrived at a great pitch of perfection, Albany Fonblanque assessed the moral nobility and political work of John Hunt. "His devotion to truth and justice had no bounds; there was no peril, no suffering, that he was not ready to encounter for either. With resolution and fortitude not to be surpassed, he was one of the gentlest and kindest of beings. His own sufferings were the only sufferings to which he could be indifferent.... We never heard him repine; seldom, on the other hand, had he occasion to rejoice, and never for long. He took whatever befell him, calmly, as his portion, and with a manly yet sweet resignation.... Unconscious prejudice might enter into his views occasionally: but they were honest, according to his lights; and in the days of martyrdom a martyr he would cheerfully have been for what he deemed the truth. John Hunt never put forth a claim of any kind on the world. He had fought the battle in the front ranks when the battle was the hottest: but he passed into retirement in the very hour of victory as if he had done nothing, and deserved nothing of the triumphant cause. The ever-kind Lord Holland, however, did not forget him. He procured an appointment in the West Indies for one of his sons, an excellent young man, who was doing well and promising to be a stay for his father's old age, when he was suddenly cut off by one of the diseases of the climate."

John Hunt has another title to remembrance. As a publisher of books, he was not vastly enriched; but his authors were such as Byron, Shelley, Hazlitt, Jeremy Bentham, and his brother. There is a house in Maida Vale which ought to have a small tablet affixed, and a grave, I cannot discover where, that the young Liberals of an easier England would appropriately restore.

Of the children of Isaac Hunt, Stephen, solicitor in Bedford Row, had died years before. Besides Leigh, there remained the art critic, Robert, and he was not prosperous. An application by Leigh in 1848 was rewarded in May 1850, when the Queen offered a vacancy in the Charterhouse to Robert Hunt. He did not live many months in that safe retreat. One other ageing member of the family, Elizabeth Kent, was in distress during 1848. Thornton Hunt promised to be her rescuer with money and a home.

The "nondescript" nature of Leigh Hunt's household had not changed at all with the change from Chelsea to Kensington. It is worth revisiting, so far as we are able to picture its inmates and details, in the evening. Hunt, with his "singing robes" about him, is striding up and down his study, dictating to his helper Vincent, who looks haggard, and coughs now and then. But Vincent will not be excused duty. "Let's go on." Or else, Leigh Hunt is having his supper, and recommending it to his visitor—dried fruit, bread, and water; or three boiled eggs. Perhaps some of his children have come in. The pure-hearted Vincent is almost certainly there, talking to his sister Julia, the girl with the sparkling black eyes and the fine soprano. Henry, when he sings, has as fine a tenor; and the two have a trick of going out dressed as street singers and giving favourite passages from operas in West End squares. They have often been asked in, and sometimes recognised. Julia, a coquette, did not grow old. There is also Jacintha. Captain Thomas of the Bengal Lancers thinks of writing a poem on her; but Leigh Hunt observes, "Jacintha is herself a verse." Captain Thomas punningly hopes not. We do not expect to see Thornton. He is a busy man, both at the newspaper offices and at his large house at Hammersmith, where he keeps open house on Sunday nights—bread and cheese and beer for revolutionary refugees, emancipated novelists, clergymen with Socialist views, painters. We do not see Mrs Hunt; it is hinted that she dislikes any exertion, and she remains in her room. You never know, however, what celebrity may walk in. Procter, Mr and Mrs Browning, Allingham, Lewes—it is an unusual parlour in this as in other respects.

Towards 1850, Hunt combined old and new passages of his recollections for the book which has generally been esteemed his best—his *Autobiography*. Even so, he was not wholly eager to produce it. In the preface to the first edition, in three volumes, he says so with force: "The work...was commenced under circumstances which committed me to its execution, and would have been abandoned at almost every step, had those circumstances allowed." Some of the pages had been written under most painful feelings, nor is that surprising, seeing that even the present volume omits numerous instances of Hunt's troubles and contentions; but the dignity and poetry of the autobiographer transform the pain into the reader's easy and beautiful travel. The most familiar eulogy of this *Autobiography* is Carlyle's: he says, for example, "Well, I call this an excellent good book, by far the best of the autobiographic kind I remember to have seen in the English language." But I cannot help liking still more the letter of that most courteous and natural of patrons, the Duke of Devonshire (June 15th, 1850).

"My dear Sir,—I do not like to have received so much pleasure and amusement from the perusal of a book, as your *Autobiography* has given me, without making my acknowledgements to you. And though you tell in it, it was a task unwillingly performed, the success of its execution calls for the sincere congratulation of your friends.

"Your recollections of music and old songs are the same as mine: one of the latter named by you transplants me back into the nursery. The whole story of Christ's Hospital is admirable, and your actors on the stage are my actors, all reproduced to a not bad memory.

"How interesting the account is of your imprisonment, and your crime! I had wanted much to know the extent of it: and what feelings of regret are mine, seeing its *excessive* punishment, that one whom I loved should have denied himself the happiness of forgiving, and preventing its fulfilment!

"How graphic the history of your first suffering voyage, and what a relief its contrast the second and prosperous one is to your readers—what it must be in reality!

"Let me thank you for other-worldliness, and the Lamb-punned lampooner; also for Munden's pronunciation; but I will not inflict hundreds of similar thanks.

"Lord Byron never interested me; but I know and love Genoa....Believe me, my dear sir, most truly and faithfully yours, DEVONSHIRE."

But how often Leigh Hunt was forced to confirm the wisdom of Shakespeare's wounded Sergeant:

> From that spring whence comfort seem'd to come
> Discomfort swells!

Friends, especially Forster, were annoyed at the insufficient or altogether missing allusion to themselves in the *Autobiography*. Douglas Jerrold was particularly annoyed at finding one there.

Only three years had passed since the dinner at the Museum Club, when Jerrold had proposed Hunt's health—"Even in his hottest warfare his natural sense of beauty and gentleness is so great that, like David of old, he arms his sling with shining pebbles of the brook, and never pelts even his fiercest enemy with mud"; and Hunt had replied, "If my friend Jerrold has the sting of the bee, he has also his honey." Jerrold was not much pleased with Hunt's new work at large; he resented the unfairness, as he thought it, of the old man towards his young audacious self; but what especially incensed him was a trifling note in the index. Hunt said, in effect, that Jerrold would have found theatre-managers less kind had he not been "a journalist and one of the leaders in *Punch.*" Jerrold vindicated his dramatic powers and his journalistic principles in a long letter, welcomed by *The Athenaeum.* He became very agitated indeed. He had idolised —the writer of that awful note in the index. He set his teeth, and threw away all the books by Leigh Hunt in his library.

The Athenaeum watched Hunt with the avidity of a drill-sergeant, and was particularly concerned that at the death of Wordsworth nothing disgraceful should occur to the butt of sack. "Mr Leigh Hunt ought not to have a double benefice." Opinions differed. Mrs Browning thought that Hunt might be the new Laureate and no harm done. Thackeray, after the appointment, wrote, "I hope dear old Leigh Hunt won't take the loss of the laurels to heart after bidding for them so naïvely as he did in those pleasant memoirs." But Hunt himself, before the appointment, had made his public statement; editing a new periodical, he says on December 7th, 1850, that he "has particular reasons for wishing to give his opinion on the subject in his own person, and his opinion is that if the Office in future is really to be bestowed on the highest degree of poetical merit, and on that only, then Mr Alfred Tennyson is entitled to it above any other man in the kingdom; since of all living poets he is the most gifted with the sovereign poetical faculty, Imagination."

The selection of a new Laureate was, and will again be, good opportunity for the comic writers. Bon Gaultier made play with the presumed competitors, in *The Laureates' Tourney*:

"The lists of Love are mine," said Moore, "and not the lists of Mars";
Said Hunt, "I seek the jars of wine, but shun the combat's jars!"
"I'm old," quoth Samuel Rogers.—"Faith," says Campbell, "so am I!"
"And I'm in holy orders, sir!" quoth Tom of Ingoldsby.

"Specimens" of these starters were also produced, the parody on Hunt being one of the wittiest of all that his early poetry ever provoked.

FRANCESCA DA RIMINI

To BON GAULTIER

[ARGUMENT.—*An impassioned pupil of Leigh Hunt, having met Bon Gaultier at a Fancy Ball, declares the destructive consequences thus.*]

Didst thou not praise me, Gaultier, at the ball,
Ripe lips, trim boddice, and a waist so small,
With clipsome lightness, dwindling ever less,
Beneath the robe of pea-y greeniness?
Dost thou remember, when, with stately prance,
Our heads went crosswise in the country-dance;
How soft, warm fingers, tipped like buds of balm,
Trembled within the squeezing of thy palm;
And how a cheek grew flushed and peachy-wise
At the frank lifting of thy cordial eyes?
Ah, me! that night there was one gentle thing,
Who, like a dove, with its scarce feathered wing,
Fluttered at the approach of thy quaint swaggering!

There's wont to be, at conscious times like these,
An affectation of a bright-eyed ease,—
A crispy cheekiness, if so I dare
Describe the swaling of a jaunty air;
And thus, when swirling from the waltz's wheel,
You craved my hand to grace the next quadrille,
That smiling voice, although it made me start,
Boiled in the meek o'erlifting of my heart;
And, picking at my flowers, I said, with free
And usual tone, "O yes, sir, certainly!"

* * *

But when the dance was o'er, and arm in arm
(The full heart beating 'gainst the elbow warm)
We passed into the great refreshment-hall,
Where the heaped cheese-cakes and the comfits small
Lay, like a hive of sunbeams, brought to burn
Around the margin of the negus urn;
When my poor quivering hand you fingered twice,
And, with inquiring accents, whispered "Ice,
Water, or cream?" I could no more dissemble,
But dropped upon the couch all in a tremble.
A swimming faintness misted o'er my brain,
The corks seemed starting from the brisk champagne,
The custards fell untouched upon the floor,
Thine eyes met mine. That night we danced no more.

It is now time to speak of the victim's new, and last, periodical.
A young Manchester man, engaged in the cotton trade, had
written "in the purest Carlylese" a life of Mirabeau; he still
remained hopeful, and, selling some property, came to London,
and published a denunciation of "Social Aspects." Some of his
capital survived this, and he sought out Leigh Hunt with the
view of establishing a new journal. Hunt was willing—"Leigh
Hunt's Journal." The capital was set flowing, and Hunt applied
to Landor, and Allingham, and Carlyle, and Tennyson for contributions. The first three contributed, and Hunt was under the

impression that he would be able to pay such writers hand-somely. At first this "Miscellany for the Cultivation of the Memorable, the Progressive, and the Beautiful" looked like justifying him. Poor Smith, however, soon felt the pinch, and objected to the scale of payments, especially those to Landor for the benefit of "the patriots of Germany." Four months saw the end of this *Journal*. Then "Turpentine" Smith took the train to Manchester. He satisfied his feelings by printing some savage remarks on Leigh Hunt and Mrs Leigh Hunt, not very accurate ones either; and then he gave up literature as a pro-fession and became rich.

Meanwhile Thornton Hunt and G. H. Lewes had started *their* new periodical, *The Leader*. With them were associated other reconstructors of the social plan, and some of the money was put up by the Rev. E. R. Larken—the first clergyman, it is famed, to wear a beard in the pulpit. They were all "shocking" people, patronised by Mrs Milner Gibson, and instructed by Robert Owen. Mrs Lynn Linton has portrayed them very carefully and amusingly as they assembled in their Philanstery. Her admiration for Thornton Hunt lasted long after the affectations and iconoclasms of *The Leader* had died out. But her account of the group is seldom studied by those who glibly repeat the only "fact" that they know of Thornton Hunt, *viz.* that he ran off with Mrs Lewes. Sir Edmund Gosse even, with his championship of Leigh Hunt, was completely bigoted against that good man's eldest son. My best comment is, again, Consult Eliza Lynn Linton. I did not dare to tell Sir Edmund to do this!

The worst of Leigh Hunt in later life from the biographer's point of view is that he allowed himself to be so often "ratherish unwell." He occasionally mounted an omnibus to visit some exhibition, or called a cab and drove off to a dinner, but he grew more and more sedentary. The glittering, sounding Great Exhibition (how excellently Mr Osbert Sitwell has appealed for the restoration[1] of the Crystal Palace to Hyde Park!) ought to have drawn him forth, but he was in the hands of the doctor, and there was another cause, which may be explained a little further on. In 1851, at any rate, he moved to another address at Kensington, and we see some of his daily airings in the grateful book *The Old Court Suburb*, published in 1855. He is ever an observant metropolitan. "When we quit Piccadilly for Hyde Park Corner, we always fancy that the air, somehow, feels not only fresher, but *whiter*." He must have gazed at almost every window and shrub in Kensington, soon losing the present actuality in his zeal for those bygone inhabitants who to him were so vividly present. He discovered the one lady who, when Coleridge walked in Edwardes Square, had been honoured with a kiss. He endeavoured to identify his outlook with that of the Frenchman who, as it was reported, in the time of Napoleon's threatened invasion, built the square; he imagined him musing, "Here shall be cheap lodging and *fête champêtre* combined; here, economy in-doors, and Watteau without; here, repose after victory; promenades; *la belle passion*; perusal of newspapers on benches; an ordinary at the Holland Arms— a French Arcadia in short, or a little Palais Royal, in an English suburb."

The cause mentioned above as intervening between him and so wonderful a materialising of his own "fairyland of science" as

---

[1] Hunt disagrees. He had noticed "a *dust* and *kick-up* about the once quiet approach to Kensington, a turmoil of crowds and omnibuses, and cabs, of hot faces, loud voices, of stalls, dogs, penny trumpets, policemen, and extempore public-houses." He was glad at length "to have the old trees and turf back again, undisturbed." His anecdote of the two foreigners squabbling in the vicinity of the temple of European brotherhood is capital: a pot-boy stopped to bawl out, "Go it, *all nations!*"

the Great Exhibition was the illness of Vincent, his youngest
son. He had long relied on this willing and sweet-tempered
young man for collaboration in almost every matter. He had
seldom been without Vincent for nearly thirty years, all Vincent's life. Besides the virtues, the talents of the youngest son
delighted the parent. Vincent wrote on flowers, and even
succeeded in publishing a sonnet or two in *The Athenaeum*. He
played the piano with something like his father's rapture.
Instead of quoting here such verse of Vincent's as might give
colour to the view that he would have been a remembered poet,
I give a sonnet disclosing, in his own words, the anxious devotion that he trembled with as he watched his father asleep.

> The fire-light flickers on the wall of books,
>   While my dear father slumbers in its shade,
>   And leaning as he sits, his head he's laid
> 'Gainst his beloved Spenser; and he looks,
> As though his mind through those delicious nooks
>   Of Fairy-land with perfect Una stray'd,—
>   List'ning to all the lovely things she said
> In voice far sweeter than Spenserian brooks.

> Alas! that that so loved fine face should be
>   Scor'd by life's sufferings more than by its years,
> So that in calmest sleep it is not free
>   From sorrow-marks that dim mine eyes with tears:
>   And yet (thank God!) that patient kind face wears
> A youthful vigour still, divine to see.

Vincent became ill. In a better interval he visited a friend,
and on the way home he obliged a washerwoman with his place
inside the omnibus, riding instead through the night's winter
rain on top. He arrived in a bad state, and through the summer
of 1851 was in danger. He rallied. That September his father,
following medical advice, found him rooms with a Birket
Foster view at Ewell—"one of the prettiest villages in all the

county of Surrey." Here father and son remained, and Vincent would have his father with him. "Adieu therefore, wonders and organs, and concourse of all nations, which I must never behold except in fancy." In December 1851, Vincent was better for a time, and both returned to Hammersmith. But there was no hope, despite attempts to read into hours of apparent stimulation and appetite a chance of real recovery. In July 1852 Leigh Hunt was writing to Dr George Bird, because he had read a paragraph in *The Times* concerning the miracles of electricity, to enquire whether an electrical treatment might rescue Vincent. Southwood Smith also was consulted much, and now as ever was Hunt's unselfish friend. Poor Hunt, so often bereaved and disenchanted, was now in an incessant agony. Vincent faded with the leaves; "It was a colder break of dawn than usual, but equally beautiful, as if, in both respects, it came to take him away, when my son died. His last words were poetry itself. A glass of water had been given him at his request; and on feeling the refreshment of it, he said 'I drink the morning.'"

From this time Hunt became more mysterious in his thought, more reserved. His belief in the spiritual world became more speculative; he seems to have thought of mystical communication with the souls of Shelley and of Vincent. He formed a habit of keeping miniature private notebooks, in which he wrote lamentations, and hopes and apprehensions of the immortals in the universe—perhaps in his room. "The vortex of living multitudes" in the new heaven would soon be seen and known. But meanwhile—

> Waking at morn, with the accustom'd sigh
> For what no morn could ever bring me more,
> And again sighing, while collecting strength
> To meet the pangs that waited me, like one

Whose sleep the rack hath watched, I tried to feel
How good for me had been strange griefs of old,
That for long days, months, years, inured my wits
To bear the dreadful burden of one thought.

One; the monotony; the isolation; for Leigh Hunt the ticking
minutes in the homelessness of his study; for Vincent—

His mornings, noons, evenings, and nights, all one.

XXI

The Great Beneficence

With his longing eyes on the mansions of the freed spirits, Hunt nevertheless was not able to avoid the affairs of this nether world; the first considerable occurrence in his life after the death of Vincent was one of the most unfortunate that even he had experienced. So far as he knew, he had preserved the unimpaired friendship of Charles Dickens. He had welcomed in an occasional poem of obvious sincerity the coming of *Household Words*, 1850. In that journal Dickens published two of his ballads in 1852. In 1852, however, Dickens was issuing *Bleak House* in numbers, with two characters in the story who were identified in some mannerisms with two eminent authors. "Boythorn" would be Landor. "Harold Skimpole"—who but Leigh Hunt? Now Skimpole, at first harmless with his impecunious foppery, ends by being a plain knave. It is clear that, once the idea got abroad that Hunt was intended in the airs and graces and philosophic nonsense and domestic incompetence of the first stage, the public would take it that Dickens meant Hunt in the last stage of ruthlessness. (Mr Chesterton has observed with fine judgment that Dickens, apart from the subject of Leigh Hunt, was unjust to Skimpole.)

The public had every reason to believe that Skimpole was a study of Hunt. Money talks, the want of it talks far louder. Skimpole had no money, no arithmetic. "Every man's not obliged to be solvent. I am not. I never was. I have not the power of counting. Call it four and ninepence—call it four pound nine. They tell me I owe more than that. I dare say I do. I dare say I owe as much as good-natured people will let me owe. If they don't stop, why should I?" Skimpole had a wife —"who had once been a beauty, but was now a delicate high-

nosed invalid suffering under a complication of disorders"—
and daughters—"Here," he says, "is my Beauty daughter,
married these three years. Now I dare say her marrying another
child, and having two more, was all wrong in point of political
economy; but it was very agreeable.... She brought her young
husband home one day, and they and their young fledglings
have their nest upstairs. I dare say, at some time or other,
Sentiment and Comedy will bring *their* husbands home, and
have *their* nests upstairs too. So we get on; we don't know how,
but somehow." Skimpole was a nature-worshipper; a tasteful
pianist, a dabbler in musical composition; wished to emulate a
flower or butterfly; took peaches and light wine; tattled of
social harmony, ever "fresh and green-hearted."

The day came when Hunt became aware that this figure of a
trickster was *of course* cut for gentle Leigh. He was an old man
now, nearly seventy, with hardly a fair chance. The confusions of
his life, though not all were to be ascribed to anything but his own
inability to grow up, could be explained very powerfully if he
would open his mouth, and speak of secrets. His loyalty, however, was of the kind which never studies the worthiness of its
object. He had his wife for his trustee, and the burdens of the
trustee's faults were to be borne by him. All his free thoughts
on matrimony could not make him "modern" in regard of a
bond that he had undertaken. So he published no comment on
the published rumour that Dickens had exhibited him as
Harold Skimpole.

It is convenient to collect here some other effects of Dickens's
thoughtless descriptiveness (for he, on the occasion, acted with
a simplicity rivalling that of Hunt). In 1855 he (anonymously)
reviewed Hunt's "Stories in Verse" very ably in *Household
Words*, under the title "By Rail to Parnassus[1]." The review is

---

[1] Or did Henry Morley write the review? Edmund Ollier, who should
have known, ascribes it to Dickens. Morley, in a letter to Thornton Hunt,

an imaginary conversation in a railway carriage. The gentleman who interrupts the poor clerk with the book is told, "I have nothing just now in my mind except this book of stories—which is just a book of stories, all of them good ones, written in such verse as may be read by rich and poor with almost equal pleasure. They are only told in verse in order that the music may give force and beauty to the sense; read them or print them how you will, you cannot destroy their music or convict them of being by a syllable too wordy; they discharge their burden in plain sentences, without even going out of their way to avoid expressions common in the mouths of the people. Every picture in them is poetical in its conception, and in its expression musical. There is nothing far-fetched—there is no mystification; these are just stories in verse which may be enjoyed by the entire mass of the people. There is even as little as possible of simple meditation in them, though that would have been welcome from the mind of a pure-hearted man, beloved of poets in his youth and in his prime, now worthy to be loved of all mankind. Of him there are fewer to speak ill than even of Robin Hood, when not a soul in Locksley town would speak him an ill-word; the friars raged; but no man's tongue nor even feature stirred; except among a very few, who dined in the abbey halls; and then with a sigh bold Robin knew his true friends from his false." The imaginary reader proceeds, "I was

recollected that Dickens had asked him to contribute an article on a collection of poems by Leigh Hunt, and that the request was expressed with true regard for their author. In either case, my main narrative remains the same. When the article had appeared, Dickens wrote to Hunt (June 28th, 1855): "...But I hope you will not think it necessary to renew that painful subject with me. There is nothing to remove from my mind—I hope nothing to remove from yours. I thought of the little notice that has given you (I rejoice most heartily to find) so much pleasure—as the best means that could possibly present themselves of enabling me to express myself publicly about you as you would desire. In that letter and unmistakable association with you by name, let all end."

not talking or reading to my neighbour with the pipe. I do not know at what stage of my discourse or meditation I had left my hold upon his ear. I had been thinking about Leigh Hunt to myself, and went on reading to myself of those unfaithful comrades, Roger the monk, and Midge, on whom Robin had never turned his face but tenderly; with one or two, they say, besides—Lord! that in this life's dream men should abandon one true thing, that would abide with them."

Leigh Hunt intended as his hour drew near to allude to the Skimpole mystery in the revised edition of his *Autobiography*, and I have a note of the passage which Thornton Hunt or Forster rejected. "While the worst part of this affliction [Vincent's death] was subsiding, an American paper was sent me for my astonishment and indignation, a writer in which, availing himself of some matters of taste in music and singing, with which the character of a scoundrel in a work of fiction had been embellished, and in which I had the reputation of partaking with no very numerous class of persons in England, was pleased to inform his readers, that the scoundrel himself was intended for me, and this too by a friend of mine. I was not aware at that time of the astounding lengths to which personalities against men of the very greatest excellence in all respects were carried on in some of the papers in the United States.... As to the friend, who was thus supposed to have become an astounding enemy, all I need say is that he was deeply grieved at an enormity so afflictingly as well as ridiculously unfounded, and that I never possessed, I believe, a warmer esteem on his part, than I do at the present moment[1]."

---

[1] "June 11, 1858. Your letter has moved me very much. I heartily thank you for it. It is worth suffering something, to be so remembered. God bless you. Ever affectionately yours, C. D." (Communicated by Mr Luther A. Brewer.)

The principals, therefore, had had no difficulty in disposing of the hobgoblin. Dickens had reviewed Hunt with the warm liking and reverence that we have seen, and Hunt had gone on contributing to *Household Words* and received "the highest rate of payment" for his articles. Review and articles, however, were anonymous. The old Adam, male or female, delights to "know for a fact" any awful scandal that may or may not be a fact. If it is not, a direct authoritative denial has sometimes seemed to be of use; that axe laid at the root of the tree is better than nothing. The friends of Hunt, being under that impression, desired to see in print a statement by Charles Dickens, disentangling Hunt from the Skimpoliad. Hunt's death, stirring up the minds of the malicious, made them more importunate for this. Several letters exist by which this episode may be pieced out. Thornton Hunt wrote to Dickens announcing the death of his father. Dickens without delay replied (August 31st, 1859): "...I had the kindest of letters from him not many weeks ago, and I was looking forward to giving him the book I am now writing, and little thought I should never see his bright face again. Let me once more cordially assure you that I am truly sensible of your remembrance of me in the midst of your own occupations and boding uneasiness. I hope I shall never forget, or be un-deserving of, his gentle and affectionate consideration." Thornton was now advised by old friends of his father, such as J. W. Dalby, that there was a "necessity of something being done." Dalby (October 19th, 1859): "When your father so feelingly complained of 'the great blow' which came so un-expectedly and so staggeringly upon him, ought not Mr Dickens to have told the world that it was never aimed? To me his silence, then and now, appears unaccountable, unexplainable, inexcusable.—And we see what rascally inferences are drawn from it." Dalby referred to some cuttings from the *Illustrated*

London News and elsewhere. Thornton approached Forster, who gave Dickens his opinion, and Dickens replied *via* Forster: he would see Thornton, if it were convenient, at the *All the Year Round* office on October 28th; "Will you also let him know, from me, that I hold my course to be plain in this matter. What I said to his poor father in your presence, I will say in any way Thornton Hunt likes;—that there are many remembrances of Hunt in that character and especially in all the pleasantest parts of it, but that is all." And again, in reference to press paragraphs, "I must not judge of the fitness or unfitness of noticing such contemptible trash. What I told Hunt, and what I promised Hunt, when you were by, to tell to anybody, I will not reserve, qualify, or in any way with-hold. I am quite sure Thornton Hunt will be manful and open with me, and he may rely on my being so with him." The interview resulted in an article by Dickens on the new edition of Hunt's *Autobiography*, and on December 4th he wrote to Thornton: "I hope to be able to send you a proof on Thursday morning; of course you shall see it and approve of it before I send it to the press." On the 7th, he invited Thornton to call and look over the article with him the following noon—the final inspection. "I hope it is clear, explicit and beyond mistake. But whatever you desire it to be, it shall be—if it be not already."

The article appeared on December 24th, 1859, entitled "Leigh Hunt. A Remonstrance." It opens with connected extracts from Thornton's introduction to the *Autobiography*, and the rest must be repeated in Dickens's precise words. "These quotations are made here, with a special object. It is not, that the personal testimony of one who knew Leigh Hunt well, may be borne to their truthfulness. It is not, that it may be recorded in these pages, as in his son's introductory chapter, that his life was of the most amiable and domestic kind, that his wants were few, that his way of life was frugal, that he was a man of small expenses, no ostentations, a diligent labourer, and a secluded man of letters. It is not, that the inconsiderate and forgetful may be reminded of his wrongs and sufferings in the days of the Regency, and of the national disgrace of his imprisonment. It is not, that their forbearance may be entreated for his grave, in right of his graceful fancy or his political labours and endurances, though

> Not only we, the latest seed of Time,
> New men, that in the flying of a wheel
> Cry down the past, not only we, that prate
> Of rights and wrongs, have loved the people well.

It is, that a duty may be done in the most direct way possible. An act of plain, clear duty.

"Four or five years ago, the writer of these lines was much pained by accidentally encountering a printed statement, 'that Mr Leigh Hunt was the original of Harold Skimpole in *Bleak House.*' The writer of these lines, is the author of that book. The statement came from America. It is no disrespect to that country, in which the writer has, perhaps, as many friends and as true an interest as any man that lives, good-humouredly to state the fact, that he has, now and then, been the subject of paragraphs in Transatlantic newspapers, more surprisingly destitute of all foundation in truth than the wildest delusions of the wildest lunatics. For reasons born of this experience, he let the thing go by.

"But, since Mr Leigh Hunt's death, the statement has been revived in England. The delicacy and generosity evinced in its revival, are for the rather late consideration of its revivers. The fact, is this:

"Exactly those graces and charms of manner which are remembered in the words we have quoted, were remembered by the author of the work of fiction in question. Above all other things, that 'sort of gay and ostentatious wilfulness' in the humouring of a subject, which had many a time delighted him, and impressed him as being unspeakably whimsical and attractive, was the airy quality he wanted for the man he invented. Partly for this reason, and partly (he has since often grieved to think) for the pleasure it afforded him to find that delightful manner reproducing itself under his hand[1], he yielded to the temptation of too often making the character *speak* like his old friend. He no more thought, God forgive him! that the admired original would ever be charged with the imaginary vices of the fictitious creature, than he has himself ever thought of charging the blood of Desdemona and Othello, on the innocent Academy model who sat for Iago's leg in the picture. Even as to the mere occasional manner, he meant to be so cautious and conscientious, that he privately referred the proof sheets of the first number of that book to two intimate literary friends of Leigh Hunt (both still living), and altered the whole of that part of the text on their discovering too strong a resemblance to his 'way.'

"He cannot see the son lay this wreath on the father's tomb, and leave him to the possibility of ever thinking that the present words might have righted the father's memory and were left undone. He cannot know that his own son may have to explain

---

[1] Writing from Boulogne, on September 25th, 1853, to Mrs Richard Watson, of Rockingham Castle, Dickens had said: "Skimpole—I must not forget Skimpole—of whom I will proceed to speak as if I had only read him and not written him. I suppose he is the most exact portrait that was ever painted in words! I have very seldom, if ever, done such a thing. But the likeness is astonishing. I don't think it could possibly be more like himself. It is so awfully true that I make a bargain with myself 'never to do so any more.' There is not an atom of exaggeration or suppression. It is an absolute reproduction of a real man. Of course, I have been careful to keep the outward figure away from the fact; but in all else it is the life itself." (Published in *Harper's Magazine*, April 1906.)

his father when folly or malice can wound his heart no more, and leave this task undone."

Let us now turn our eyes from the "fatal error[1]" and the impassioned correction, from the anticipated wreath and tomb, to Leigh Hunt, a little bowed, a little disheartened, saying goodbye to Kensington. It is the spring of 1853. He has had many homes in London; he goes to the last and perhaps the smallest of them, at Hammersmith. He takes with him his work —not so much his dramatic attempts, though recently the Queen ordered *A Legend of Florence* to be played at Windsor Castle, as his meditations on the nature of things, and the future of human beings. One book in particular calls for speedy publication; Vincent and he have toiled at it perhaps too strenuously, and indeed it seems to him to enfold and preserve all the best of his meaning, in life and literature, for the past thirty years. Charles Lamb seems to have referred to it in *Grace Before Meat*—with a slightly quizzical side-glance: "I own that I am disposed to say grace upon twenty other occasions in the course of the day besides my dinner. . . . ; commending my new scheme for extension to a niche in the grand philosophical, poetical and perchance in part heretical liturgy, now compiling by my friend Homo Humanus, for the use of a certain snug congregation of Utopian Rabelaesian Christians, no matter where assembled." And that was in 1823.

In 1832 John Forster, filled with admiration for his first

[1] "The simple and final reply," says Swinburne, "should have been that indolence was the essential quality of the character and philosophy of Skimpole, and that Leigh Hunt was one of the hardest and steadiest workers on record, throughout a long and chequered life, at the toilsome trade of letters: and therefore to represent him as a heartless and shameless idler would have been as rational an enterprise, as lifelike a design after the life, as it would be to represent Shelley as a gluttonous, canting hypocrite, or Byron as a loyal and unselfish friend." (*Quarterly Review,* July 1902.)

"distinguished literary man," had paid for the printing of *Christianism*, which was privately circulated; and that little book had now been extended to four or five times its original size. It was published under the title *The Religion of the Heart* in 1853. Hunt was persuaded to put his name to it, though he feared that it might "mar the influence of the book, by causing it to be considered as one of an author's numerous productions, not worse perhaps than the rest, but no better." It was not a book, he thought; it was a "little heaven below"—not because it was his own. "It is not mine, except as the framer of its words; the school is not my own, except inasmuch as I am a teacher under its masters." Something of the sort had been tried by John Toland long before. *The Religion of the Heart*, which *The Athenaeum* reviewed like an old lady removing a dead rat with a pair of tongs, would not seem peculiar or godless to many modern readers. It is in full accordance with the spirit and meetings of an adult Sunday School in 1930. It begins with a creed of the Great Beneficence. Then come forms of service, resembling free verse, the "organ or seraphine" not being discommended. Here is an "Aspiration to be Repeated at Dusk":

"1. Blessed be God: blessed be his Beneficence, working towards its purposes in the evening.

2. The portion of the globe on which I live is rolling into darkness from the face of the sun.

3. Softly and silently it goes, with whatever swiftness.

4. Soft and silent are the habitual movements of nature;

5. Loudly and violently as its beneficence may work, within small limits and in rare instances.

6. Let me imitate the serene habit;

7. And not take on my limited foresight the privilege of the stormy exception.

8. May I contribute what I can, this evening, to the peace and happiness of the house in which I live;

9. Or of the fellow-creatures, anywhere, among whom I may find myself."

Next, Hunt advances a number of "exercises of the heart in its duties and aspirations," short homilies, in fact. One of them is of spiritualist sympathy, and prays for an enlarged consciousness. Another is a prose hymn to the great benefactors of the world, particularly Confucius. But it is in the last half of the book, which is a definition and selection of *The Only Final Scriptures*, that Confucius comes most prominently before us. Here Hunt is the librarian of his little church, and he is eager to set on high those religious interpreters who do not threaten even Dives with pangs of fire. He is himself a half-Oriental with his sense of the wonderful, his ability to live on "a little oil and root," or to admire without envy the sublime invention of rich monarchs. He regards the Oriental fabulists, of whom he counts Jesus one, as writers of "final scriptures." Socrates, Epictetus, Marcus Aurelius, St Francis de Sales, Whichcote, Shaftesbury, Emerson, Carlyle, the poets (as Thomson, Wordsworth and Coleridge, Keats, Shelley, Horne, Tennyson)—all these he recommends; "nor shall a false modesty hinder us from saying, that passages for Discourses might be found in the volumes entitled *The Indicator* and *The Seer*." In conclusion, he asks some questions touching the next phase of the soul's experience; he asks them with a curious hypnotic rhythm: "What is it we shall first look at? which way turn? what life lead, and how long? and after that life whither go, ever hand in hand, to another? on what electrical wings? from what planet to planet and sun to sun, each sun being a heaven (for does not the sun look like a heaven, with all that beauty and goodness?) and then, when we seem to have got to our final heaven, or to one in which we can feel but one mightiest desire to go further, whither shall we find ourselves once more, and once for all, travelling? whither still going? where arriving? what unspeakable vision at last circuiting, closer and closer; yearning towards it more and more; drawn irresistibly towards it, but with perfect love and transport, and no fear, and all still together;—towards what?—towards WHOM?"

Such flights did Hunt etherealise in his room at 7, Cornwall Road, Hammersmith. Here came many persons, perhaps not suspecting him of a mystical enthusiasm, but well aware of his sublunary beams and influences, and desirous of pleasing his old age with their homage. A series of visitors from America honoured him—Colonel Fuller (author of *Sparks from a Locomotive*), James T. Fields the publisher, the poet Bayard Taylor, and Nathaniel Hawthorne among them. Hawthorne, who came with a letter of introduction from Procter, wrote an account of his first visit to Hunt "occupying a very plain and shabby little house, in a contiguous range of others like it.... A slatternly maidservant opened the door for us, and he himself stood in the entry, a beautiful and venerable old man, buttoned to the chin in a black dress-coat, tall and slender, with a countenance quietly alive all over, and the gentlest and most naturally courteous manner[1]. He ushered us into his little study, or parlour, or both—a very forlorn room, with poor paper-hangings and carpet, few books, no pictures that I remember, and an awful lack of upholstery.... I have said that he was a beautiful

[1] Hawthorne says much more in praise of this "courteous manner," agreeing with Emerson, who had called on Hunt in 1848. "Hunt charmed him," says Alexander Ireland, who brought Emerson. "His courteous and winning manner was on this occasion tempered by a certain delicate reverence, indicating how deeply he felt the honour of being thus sought out by his distinguished visitor." Emerson retained the opinion that de Quincey and Leigh Hunt had the finest manners of any literary men he had ever met.

old man. In truth I never saw a finer countenance, either as to the mould of features or the expression, nor any that showed the play of expression so perfectly without the slightest theatrical emphasis. It was like a child's face in this respect. At my first glimpse of him, I discerned that he was old, his long hair being white and his wrinkles many.... But when he began to speak, and as he grew more earnest in conversation, I ceased to be sensible of his age; sometimes, indeed, its dusky shadow darkened through the gleam which his sprightly thoughts diffused about his face, but then another flash of youth came out of his eyes and made an illumination again. I never witnessed such a wonderfully illusive transformation, before or since....

"Leigh Hunt loved dearly to be praised. That is to say, he desired sympathy as a flower seeks sunshine, and perhaps profited by it as much in the richer depth of colouring that it imparted to his ideas. In response to all that we ventured to express about his writings (and for my part, I went quite to the extent of my conscience, which was a long way, and there left the matter to a lady and a young girl, who happily were with me), his face shone, and he manifested great delight, with a perfect, and yet delicate, frankness for which I loved him. He could not tell us, he said, the happiness that such appreciation gave him; it always took him by surprise, he remarked, for—perhaps because he cleaned his own boots, and performed other little ordinary offices for himself—he never had been conscious of anything wonderful in his own person. And then he smiled, making himself and all the little parlour about him beautiful thereby.... Nevertheless, it was not to my voice that he most favourably inclined his ear, but to those of my companions. Women are the fit ministers at such a shrine.... I rejoiced to hear him say that he was favoured with most confident and cheering anticipations in respect to a future life; and there were abundant proofs, throughout our interview, of an unrepining spirit, resignation, quiet relinquishment of the worldly benefits that were denied him, thankful enjoyment of whatever he had to enjoy, and piety and hope shining onward into the dusk—all of which gave a reverential cast to the feeling with which we parted from him...."

Hawthorne's visit occurred in 1855, a year which increased Hunt's bibliography with *The Old Court Suburb, Stories in Verse*, and his bowdlerised *Beaumont and Fletcher*. The *Stories in Verse*, already glanced at, includes a stately renewal of the art of writing a dedication (to the Duke of Devonshire), and another of Hunt's long prefaces, which even so are not too long. Hunt wrote to Allingham, as on previous occasions, commenting on his work. He felt now that *Rimini*, apart from a fine line here and there, was "conventional, not rich and aromatic, and tending to prose." He was "not unwilling to be judged, as to final amount of capacity, by the *Mahmoud*, the *Ben Adhem*, *Inevitable*, *Wallace and Fawdon*, and one or two others of the smallest pieces." In truth, he had during his later life become a poet, not remarkably strong and glowing, but clear, various and following his own course. For the select *Beaumont and Fletcher*, Bohn had paid him partly in books chosen from the ever-charming Bohn Libraries; he excitedly saw before him the whole works of Plato, many early English Chronicle histories, and a heap of scientific books. With these at his elbow, he could write many more of his half-sheets of information and starting-point for Thornton, that harassed dictator of leading articles. The *Beaumont and Fletcher* was dedicated to Procter, but Bohn did not print dedications in his series; he consented to the inclusion of Hunt's tribute in "a certain number of copies." I must also mention that the preface does not omit some words in praise of that sometimes glorious poet George Darley; otherwise, it would have seemed that Hunt had for once failed to recognise a man of genius, as he did in the instance of John Clare and, I believe, de Quincey. But the vast amount of his reviews still interred in old newspapers might yet reveal his "Indicator" faculty more richly.

Languid and ailing often, Hunt busied himself throughout 1856 with an edition of his prose and verse, suggested by an American devotee, and new papers of Londiniana. He also sunned his weariness in the Indian summer of friendships now almost half a century established—with Novello, Ollier, Charles Reynell, Sir Frederick Pollock, and others of not unworthy maturity, as Procter's and Forster's. The condition of his wife, more than half a century his partner, was worse than his own. Southwood Smith had advised, in 1855, that "she should guard the hands, arms, chest and indeed every part of the body from contact with cold air. She should therefore never sit up in bed without having on a sleeved jacket or some other efficient covering and endeavour never to sleep except when properly covered with the bed-clothes." Hunt had never rested, and, if away at night, the terror of a fire and the vision of Marianne's helplessness tortured him. Southwood Smith behaved magnificently then, as for years and years before;

Ages will honour, in their hearts enshrined,
Thee, Southwood Smith, physician of mankind;

but he could not prolong Marianne's existence indefinitely, and she died towards the close of January 1857.

The decline of Marianne Hunt physically and morally, which Hunt did his utmost to conceal, and which he would probably forbid even a recorder seventy years afterwards to dwell upon, has from time to time made its mark upon this biography. About thirty years ago, there were living the grandson of Leigh Hunt, and the doctor who, with Southwood Smith, attended

Marianne. (That doctor could have written a curious book on many well-known Victorians.) The following letter wants no more preamble:

To Mr Walter Leigh Hunt.   June 27th, 1899.

My Dear Walter,

I sympathise with you, as you know, in your keen desire to remove the adverse impression created by the reiterated attacks on your grandfather. I sympathise because I have always felt the deepest respect and admiration for the man as well as the writer. I never think of him or hear his name without an emotion of, I may say, veneration for his nobility of character. I have often longed to put in print my own personal recollections touching the persistent calumnies and misconceptions that pursue his reputation. I have withheld any public expression because of giving pain to his descendants, but I have felt pain and grief whenever I heard him calumniated. I have done my utmost by word of mouth, especially with literary men of the day, to put things in their proper light.

To speak plainly, the source of most of this misrepresentation was no other than his wife, Mrs Leigh Hunt. In my opinion, she was mendacious, self-indulgent, and incapable of controlling her household. When I first knew her, about 1851, she was an intemperate woman and sodden from drink. How much Leigh Hunt knew of this infirmity I do not know. One day he said to me, "Isn't a bottle of brandy a day, which I hear you have ordered my wife, too much?" As her doctor I had ordered abstention from spirituous drinks. Going one day into her room, Leigh Hunt kicked over a bottle of foaming beer, partly hidden under the bed. "It's milk, my dear," said Mrs Leigh Hunt, and he accepted the explanation, with what reservations of his own I cannot tell.

Naturally this state of things led to acute domestic disorganisation and embarrassment with tradesmen, and to giving ceaseless notes of hand. On one occasion I intervened to pacify a pressing tradesman. The embarrassment led to Mrs Hunt's

LEIGH HUNT, BY HIS WIFE

FROM A SILHOUETTE IN THE POSSESSION OF THE RT. HON. SIR WILLIAM BULL, BART.

borrowing and begging from friends. There is a painful reference to the daily troubles in the *Correspondence*, Vol. ii, p. 164 ff. The veiled influence is there alluded to by the editor, his eldest son, Thornton. A letter is given (by Macaulay, I believe) remonstrating with Mrs Leigh Hunt on her applications for money and for keeping her husband in the dark.

I believe I am the only contemporary of Leigh Hunt who could testify to these facts concerning his wife, and for the sake of Leigh Hunt I put them on record before I pass away. I attended professionally Leigh Hunt, Mrs Hunt, his beloved son Vincent, and others of the family. Vincent died in 1852.

As to the lamentable Dickens caricature which arose out of the borrowings, I don't see how that is to be remedied. No doubt Dickens did put Leigh Hunt in the pillory. He afterwards repented and made a sort of retraction, but the injury he inflicted remains, alas! to this date. I am glad to write these few words to you, Leigh Hunt's eldest grandson, as I know you take adverse criticism to heart.

I am, dear Walter Hunt, faithfully yours,

George Bird, M.D.
(now in my 82nd year).

It is not easy to be graceful in bringing forward evidences against a woman living or dead, but the more that Hunt's inner life is investigated, the plainer appears the justice due to him and the reproach to be taken away. After Marianne's death, he began to wonder whether she had not sometimes borrowed money without informing him. He addressed Procter, for example, on the question. He received a deeply affectionate but unnerving reply (May 16th, 1858):

"In reference to your Letter, I declare to you I know not what to say—I have *no* scrap whatever. I keep—and I kept no accounts. As far as I can *recollect* there were, in the first Instance, 3 or 4 Sums sent to poor Mrs Hunt, amounting altogether to

£140—afterwards a trifle or two—I do not know what— something—almost nothing. The last time I had any communication, I grieve to say that I got angry and wrote angrily to her—Forgive me—I did not know then—as I know now— what a host of faults I myself had—what a host of faults everybody has—and what *trouble*—but I will say nothing, lest I should say something to give you pain, and God knows that is not my intention."

Fifty pounds sent from the Queen's private purse in January 1857 lightened Hunt's latest difficulties. On the other hand, his American friend, S. Adams Lee, who succeeded in bringing out a six-volume edition of Hunt that year, caused him to drudge with his usual gay studiousness over an anthology of sonnets. Lee was unlucky, for, entrusting to a stranger on his way to Europe £30 in gold to be paid to Hunt, he heard no further from the stranger; nor was that gentleman seen at Hammersmith. Long after Hunt's death the ordinary edition of *The Book of the Sonnet* was published; the large-paper copies did not come out until 1885—a record which at one time it was feared might be broken by the present performance. Hunt's share of *The Book of the Sonnet*, if I may say so at a moment when the composition of fourteen lines with a special shape and cadence is regarded as work for an undertaker, is most entertaining and instructive. The authors from whom he made his selections form an illuminating catalogue too; good minor poets in England have been legion. A very considerable number both of the great and small writers in his book had been recognised by him, and had entered the wide circle or fireside group of his friends.

A serio-comic play of Hunt's, called *Lover's Amazements*, was to his surprise put on at last at the Lyceum Theatre in January 1858. What surprised him more (for he went to see it acted) was that it threatened to be popular. He appeared once again, to

bow his thanks to the audience. The press all round spoke
handsomely of the play. The manager, however, Charles
Dillon, added one more amazement—he became bankrupt, and
the "theatre and the play were thus stopped together." Hunt
had, besides the honour, "just forty pounds." But what had
"Mr H." produced for Charles Lamb?

In this period Hunt chanced to receive aids, if he needed any
aids, to the recollection of two young poets. Procter, sending
a brace of partridges in September 1858, wrote, "I made the
acquaintance, at Brighton, of a bookseller of the name of
'Keats.' I said 'Mr Keats, you bear the name of a very fine
poet'—'Yes, sir'; (he answered) 'I was a second cousin of Mr
Keats. I have more than once talked about him, with Mr Leigh
Hunt.'—'Well, I know Mr Leigh Hunt very well and I knew
Mr Keats the poet also.' 'Ah!—I am related also to Mr Sheriff
Keats—' 'I don't know him' (I replied) 'but you may depend
upon it that the poet was the greatest man. I advise you to
stick to him.'—Our friend proceeded—'I was in business in
London—and Mr Carlyle and a great many literary gentlemen
used to come to my shop—' He mentioned several—and was
thoroughly surprised to learn that I knew them all. At last,
I said, that I had once ventured within that charmed circle myself and had printed a book. I saw clearly that I had gained some
additional respect from this disclosure."

The name of Shelley became frequent in his letters again for
more serious reasons. Sir Percy Shelley wrote on the appearance of Hogg's biography of his father in great anger and
anxiety. He thought it "right to inform you of the history of
it, because without some explanation you may consider me and
my wife (whose name figures in a dedication) responsible for
the bad taste and contemptuous tone of scurrility with which
the book is filled—to say nothing of the reckless publication of

letters, which ought to have been considered confidential."
There were many other troublesome aspects of Hogg's wild
book, and other letters followed, asking Hunt to assist in the
business of "saving Shelley's beloved memory from such handling as Hogg" would give it if he published more. On July
2nd, 1858, Hunt wrote a letter of many pages in judgment on
Hogg and his book. He thought the "enormities and vagaries"
in it unaccountable unless Hogg was out of his wits; he defended the honesty of Shelley in such points as "the attempted
assassination in Wales." "More will be required to settle these
points, than the judgments of the garbler. During the whole
time that I knew your father, I never knew him violate the truth
in the slightest degree, either in letter or in spirit. My faith in
his veracity was so great, that a single shadow of incompatibility
with it in a letter respecting myself, which was republished the
other day by one of his premature biographers (to say nothing
of other reasons), instantly renewed my opinion of its being a
forgery.... This foolish book of an imbecile pretender, whose
misdirected absurdities have made me in my own old age speak
of a fellow-creature in a manner to which I thought I had bidden
a long adieu, and for whom those three poor human words, *old
age* and *imbecile*, may after all furnish an excuse, which I have
not sufficiently borne in mind...."

The reply from Boscombe was that Hunt's letter "was very
acceptable," and his counsel against any advertisement of Hogg
was considered and approved. "The little volume which we
intend publishing" would not be a good place for the letter,
which nevertheless, Sir Percy felt, might do good "as a sort of
notion of Hogg's *Life*" if published in a magazine. Hunt was
still preparing his mind on the question of vindicating Shelley
when (in 1859) a curious, though minor incident occurred.

A stranger named C. H. Taylor wrote to inform him that he,

as a postal clerk, had rescued "a remarkable letter written by poor Shelley to the late Mrs S. 42 years ago, and which in some unaccountable manner had been but now reposted, and returned to the office as 'unknown at the address.'" It was the letter to Mary at Bath dated December 15th, 1816, with the sentence near the beginning in praise of Hunt's kindness, and the history of Harriet's catastrophe further on. Hunt saw the copy, if not the original.

Had he lived in the days of Dr Robert Bridges, he might have been in America on that occasion, for, in April 1859, his cousin Mrs Swift beckoned him: "My object in writing now is to persuade you to visit America. A cordial welcome would await you wherever you might go. The name and fame of Leigh Hunt is known and appreciated by every reading American. It is the land of your forefathers—your dear mother's natal home. What shall I write more to induce you to come? You know what a golden harvest Thackeray has gathered here by his lectures; think if you were to give us—."

One day in 1859 Joseph Severn came to see Hunt, and he brought with him Frederick Locker, perhaps the last of all Hunt's "young poets." (He was rather an old young poet, I admit.) "Jacintha, give Mr Locker another cup of tea." Locker deserved it. His pages on Hunt in *My Confidences* are among the most spirited in that quick-witted work. Noticing Hunt's passion, he records, "When I got home I sent Mr Hunt some curious and rare tea, which Elgin had lately despatched from China, and he thanked me in a delightful letter. His handwriting was as beautiful as Tennyson's."

Among Leigh Hunt's latest writings for periodicals, "The Occasional" in *The Spectator* stands out. Under that general title he wrote the memoir of Charles Ollier, and two papers on Shelley. He looked forward to better health for several reasons,

but greatly because he was invited that August to Boscombe.
An essay that he wrote for *Fraser's* in counterblast to Cardinal
Wiseman's attack on the "wantonness, voluptuousness and de-
bauchery" of some of his favourite poets never met his eye in
print[1]. It was the last chance he had to speak for Keats, and
since his words on this occasion are as vigorous as they are
unfamiliar, I will revive them here. "And Keats, an enthusiast
for the beauty of nature, the Cardinal mentions only to dis-
parage for the very enthusiasm, saying it amounted to something 'almost frenzied,' and accusing him at the same time of
its being 'icy cold,' and exhibiting nothing but 'cheerless,
earthly affections,' things void of all 'moral glow,' and of
every 'virtuous emotion'! Such are actually his words! I must
own that, desirous as I am to observe conventional proprieties,
and to treat with due courtesy a personage who is said to be so
distinguished for urbanity of manners in private as this great
church dignitary, I find it difficult to express myself as I could
wish in regard to a passage like that. For I knew Keats himself
as well as his poetry; knew him both in his weakness and his
strength; knew how far removed both of them were from want
of impressibility by his fellow-creatures; knew in particular
how he felt for those connected with him by ties of natural
affection, and with what 'glow' and 'emotion' he has written
of the best moral principles, public and private. But he shall
speak for himself presently. My own feelings I shall endeavour
to content with observing, that a robust, prosperous, and
satisfied elderly gentleman might have spared, if he could not
pity or do justice to, the inspired and impassioned youth whose
death was embittered by the agonies of a love which he was
never to enjoy, and the like of which, in reverence to the
maiden sincerity of the Catholic priesthood, his Eminence is

[1] "English Poetry *versus* Cardinal Wiseman," *Fraser's*, Dec. 1859.

to be supposed never to have felt—certainly never gave way to."

After pointing out the pomp and glory which the Cardinal liked to dwell on, Hunt continued, "Yet fond as he thus is of noise and show, he finds the 'bright' poetry of Keats 'icy cold,' with 'no moral glow' in it, 'no virtuous affection,' 'no sight of that real Sun, the "intellectual Light" of Dante, without whom nature is dull' to 'observe the most dainty landscape.' His 'affections' are 'cheerless'; and it is no wonder that 'Endymion, the enamoured of the cold moon,' should be their type. It is to be regretted perhaps that Keats, under the combined impulse of a sense of his lofty aims as a youth and of his admiration for some fair object of his affections whose beauty may have been thought to have a look of coldness, took Endymion for the hero of his first considerable effort in poetry; and it is not to be denied that the poem, with all its genius, is as sensuous of its kind and as full of external glitter as the Cardinal's favourite descriptions are in their own way. But Dante's 'intellectual sun' had a side to it, the heat of which was more calculated to wither up the best affections, human and divine, than all the coldest earthly materialities conceivable. Modern emissaries of his creed take care never to mention it. Keats was sorry afterwards that he wrote *Endymion*; but it is only one of his poems, and a most false impression is left upon the minds of his critic's believers by constituting it the representative of all which his poetry contains. Even *Endymion* is not without strong evidences of an affectionate and warm-hearted nature to those who are not unwilling to find them; and there is a passage in it which, offensive as it was to the then ruling powers (those of the Regent), and severely visited as it was by the literary portion of their servants, hurt perhaps other readers not so desirous, till they came to it, of finding fault.

It is at the beginning of Book the Third, where the poet speaks of personages

> Who lord it o'er their fellow-men
> With most prevailing tinsel;

and who, without one redemption

> Of sanctuary splendour, are still dight
> By the blear-eyed nations in empurpled vests.

"But what does the Cardinal say to the bold personal denouncement of the Regent himself, as the 'minion of grandeur,' with his 'wretched crew'? is there no 'moral glow' there?—or to the poet's prayer for his 'country's honour,' in the *Ode to Hope*?—to his enthusiastic praises, more than once, of Alfred the Great and Kosciusko?—or to the numerous affectionate little poems addressed to his brothers and friends, the former in particular, evincing a loving domestic nature, willing to be content with the gentlest household pleasures? Is there 'no virtuous emotion' in all these effusions? Even in the Paganism of his last and greatest production, the noble fragment of *Hyperion*, a sentiment is put into the mouth of one of the gods, the loving and truly divine beauty of which might have shamed many a theological opinion not so consistent with it, as all Keats's religious opinions were. 'I am smother'd up,' says decaying Saturn,

> And buried from all god-like exercise
> Of influence benign on planets pale,
> Of admonitions to the winds and seas,
> Of peaceful sway above man's harvesting,
> And all those acts *which Deity supreme*
> *Doth ease its heart of love in.* . . ."

Charles Reynell, who had been Hunt's printer and benefactor almost 50 years, decided to carry him off to Putney and restore him to the world which he thought of leaving. (Hunt had just lost his teeth, and said that he exulted in this advance towards immortality!) His friend and Dickens's, Charles Kent, was a witness of his last evening at home. Hunt seemed to feel premonitions, and his talk showed him often looking far back and farther ahead. He spoke of his imprisonment, and the humorous side of it. There was rain on the window, darkness came on, and—we will believe Charles Kent—a barrel-organ down the street struck up *Home, Sweet Home*. A few minutes more, and daughters, and grandchildren, and friend were at the gate, and the wheels of Hunt's cab made their own music as they rolled away.

He took with him a bundle of books, including the copy of his *Autobiography* which he was still correcting and modelling. It was August 9th, 1859. From Reynell's house he wrote several letters, one to Lady Shelley promising the two "little articles which I have written in *The Spectator*, on occasion of the notice of the *Memorials* in that paper." She visited him, amid smiles and tears; for which he thanked her on August 24th. The visit to Boscombe was not now in his hopes. He complained mildly of uneasiness, for he found his breath failing; he sent his last blessings to absent friends, and told those who were with him how deeply he felt their kindness. One of his sons "gave him music" from the next room; another answered his "minute, eager and searching questions" on the progress of liberalism in the country of his friend Mazzini. Death was not unkind to this lover of life, although his eldest son's note "August 28, 1859. Work unfinished" was correct. He rested from his labours.

Kensal Green and beyond

THORNTON HUNT duly took charge of his father's affairs, personal and literary. John Forster acknowledged the news on August 29th: "He was the first distinguished man of letters I ever knew; and the charm of his conversation was such as I have never known in any other man. I seem never to have seen anything since in the wonderfully sunny light he threw upon everything then. 'The beautiful is vanished and returns not.'" Other friends expressed their emotion in sonnets:

> I heard; and sudden clouds came o'er the day....
> The world grows empty....

Survivors from the heroic past, Trelawny and Joseph Severn, desired to be present at the funeral, which took place at Kensal Green Cemetery (where many of Hunt's literary friends are buried). Leigh Hunt left no will, and his property was sworn at under £250. In order to assist his daughter Julia, Forster endeavoured to sell the celebrated collection of locks of hair; he succeeded better in the effort to secure part of Hunt's pension for this young woman. Thornton Hunt took up the work, or some of it, which his father had not finished—a complete edition of the poems, and the revised *Autobiography*. Forster read the proofs of the latter, with some disapproval at not seeing himself chronicled by Leigh Hunt. "His silence, when a word would have been so grateful, is strange and unlike him." Thornton tactfully offered to discuss and explain the omission in his introduction, and Forster accepted this. The book appeared in 1860, with an introduction of remarkable psychological skill, and general excellence of writing; but it was not the son's only revaluation of his difficult subject.

Bringing out the first number of *The Cornhill Magazine* for January 1860, Thackeray invited Thornton Hunt to write a study of the essayist who would have been a contributor, and that study ("A Man of Letters of the Last Generation") supplements the other both with personal traits and comments.

The recurrence of the Skimpole problem, and the solution arrived at by Thornton Hunt and Dickens, were noticed in an earlier passage. With the article published in *All the Year Round*, the eldest son could claim to have achieved one part of what was due to his father's memory. He next produced the *Poetical Works*, which came to his hand almost ready, in their author's judgment, for the press. It is a comfortable book, but the words "Now Finally Collected" on the title-page drew from John Hunter a remonstrance, deploring the absence of *Talari Innamorati*, *Abraham and the Fire-worshipper*, *The Fancy Concert*, and other important poems. Hunter was right. Those are poems of a decisive character, and such as cannot be imitated, however they may be surpassed in force of genius; for the spiritual and mental combination in them was peculiar to their author. However, sixty years after, Mr Milford made what probably will be the final collection of the poems— one, which could have turned Hunter's anger into smiling gratitude.

Next, Thornton, overworked as he was, prepared an edition of his father's *Correspondence*. It was not easy. Mountains of paper had accumulated, varying in point and worth from old laundry bills to the manuscript of *Hyperion*. Besides, he sent out requests to as many acquaintances of Leigh Hunt as he thought would have letters, and duly received a fresh accumulation. He resolved on a method of displaying the correspondence which did not work very well; he wrote a kind of biography, with the letters grouped under the names of the

22-2

friends concerned in each chapter. The later letters are garrulous, but Thornton knew how much they meant to the recipients, and was not severe on them; at the same time, he was not as careful as a Buxton Forman with the earlier documents, touching the lives of several immortals. Or perhaps he could not obtain the letters he sought, especially those from his father to Keats and Byron. We miss equally those to Lamb, John Hunt the elder, Hazlitt, Carlyle and Dickens[1]. Now and then, it was discovered that there had been little correspondence in spite of acquaintanceship. T. L. Peacock had had hardly a note from Leigh Hunt, though he had often met him "at his houses in Hampstead and the New Road, at Shelley's house in Marlow, and at my house in London." The two volumes that Smith, Elder published in 1862 were to have been followed by a third, but it never appeared; and the whole performance, where success would have been surprising, is unsuccessful.

Forster supervised the work so far as he could, read the proofs, and recommended the suppression of passages in Leigh Hunt's letters to Elizabeth Kent. They could not have offended her, for she died on March 25th, 1861. It is our loss that she had not occupied her later years in writing her recollections of the poets of the Regency. Among the mild distinctions of her long life, besides those which have been mentioned, I may name her encouragement of John Clare. J. C. Loudon admired her as a botanist. She prepared a book on *British Birds*, but I cannot identify it; and in 1831 she

---

[1] Dickens to Thornton Hunt, August 5th, 1861: "I have no sufficiently strong objection to the publication of the letter whereof you send me a copy, since you desire to use it. Perhaps Forster explained to you that I had many letters from your late father by me, but they were all destroyed a year or so ago in a general sacrifice of letters that I resolved to make." (From Mr Luther A. Brewer.)

published a collection of *New Tales* for children. Thornton
Hunt himself did not survive her many years, yet long enough
for T. P. O'Connor to experience his kindness and prudence
on the staff of *The Daily Telegraph*. He visited America at the
critical time when "anything might have happened," and was
well received, especially by Lowell and Holmes. He spent
much labour on at least two massive works which were never
published, one an examination of the progress of society, and
the other an edition of William Maginn—that strange figure.
Gladstone, Ruskin, Lytton, Kingsley, Sir Arthur Helps,
A. H. Layard—these are a few of the men who knew the
extent of Thornton Hunt's self-sacrificing labours. The proprietors of *The Daily Telegraph* recognised them generously.
His services for them closed, greatly to his distress, in 1872,
when his industry had clearly reduced his powers; and in
1873 he died, long before he need have done.

The quality and influence of Leigh Hunt, if they have not
reflected themselves in the course of this book, will not be
effectively disclosed in a few last words; but I cannot leave
him without some lingering looks, and further illustrations of
the essential man. What is most conspicuous in all his decades
is his idealising faculty, applied alike to social and intellectual
situations. From it he derived intense pleasure, and to it he
might have learned to attribute much misery. He decorated
his prison and forgot the painter's bill and the long strain of
catching up again. He chose friends and intimates under the
impression that they embodied a special capacity or virtue,
which in fact was not their distinction or direction. He satirised
those whom he judged to be asking for such treatment, because
in his library there was abundance of eighteenth-century satire,
and it was amusing and brilliant; then he found that there are
no unbreakable restrictions in warfare. He talked of himself

and his own with his pen, spontaneously as a singing-bird hails a bright day, and was amazed, though never lastingly instructed, to be ridiculed and struck at by those who had reasons to silence him, either as unnecessary or as monotonous.

When we contemplate the frequency with which a bright beginning in Hunt's relations with life was followed by a failure or disenchantment, and how even his fine and beneficial characteristics seemed to sow the seeds of future hardship, misunderstanding, and calumny, it is natural to recall a story of his own. He once took up, in a shop of plaster casts, the model of a hand, beautifully turned, "though" (to give his own words) "I thought it somewhat too plump and well-fed. The fingers, however, were delicately tapered; the outline flowing and graceful. I fancied it to have belonged to some jovial beauty, a little too fat and festive, but laughing withal, and as full of good nature. I was told it was the hand of Madame Brinvilliers, the famous poisoner." Something of this picture was simulated when circumstance seemed to stretch a graceful and welcoming hand towards him. The hand was perilous. It changed, and became deadly. In spite of all his disasters, Hunt never grew really old. He was sure of the millennium, when every invitation, every conversation would lead only to newer beatitudes and mutual illuminings. No new occasion dismayed him because he had so often found himself in deep waters; no hatred of life curved his lip, as he reached precarious safety and began his Progress once more.

His eldest son, discussing his delusive habit of judgment, ascribes the error of his expectations to his passion for reading. "He saw everything through books, or saw it dimly." He lived, largely, in the world of the novelist, "and hence endowed his friends, all around, with fictitious characters founded on fact." One of his chief suppositions, with its serious consequences, was that of "the thrifty housewife." One may suppose, too, with probability enough, that his ordeals in the disputes with and over Byron arose from his projecting a romance of real life in which the two were to exist with perfect grace—the young aristocratic poet and the young reformist chanting canticles of concord, the barriers that might conventionally or temperamentally occur vanishing in the light of gay compliment and noble utterance and national applause. "And so, adieu, dear Byron."

Seeing the importance of his books as a factor in his emotional life, we must take a closer view of Hunt as a reader. Although the library that he gathered has long been broken up, information concerning it is not uncommon. The American publisher, J. T. Fields, purchased from his son 450 volumes, most of which have subsequently been dispersed; but Mrs Fields took the opportunity to compose one of those friendly, unambitious works which are not so fashionable lately, *A Shelf of Old Books*, with copious descriptions and numerous facsimiles of what Hunt read. The most fascinating item, possibly, was his Galignani edition of Coleridge, Shelley and Keats, the beautiful triumvirate of *Imagination and Fancy*; he had underlined the print with almost ubiquitous pleasure. Other books that he fed upon like a bee were the *Arabian Nights*, Plato's *Republic*, Sterne, Allan Ramsay's *Gentle Shepherd*, Sadi, Boswell, and the precursor of the *Origin of Species—Vestiges of Creation*. His Milton was made the receptacle for comments recalled from the talk of Keats and others. His *Decameron* was the present of the editor of *Blackwood's Magazine*; how Keats would have laughed over that symbol of victory! His Ben Jonson was "full of new suggestions," and a multitude of close comments crowded his Chaucer ("Finished my third regular reading of this great poet and good-hearted man, whom I admire more than ever, September the first, 1857").

I have before me a volume of Pope's letters, which testifies to the almost tranced condition into which Hunt passed when he had a favourite book in his hand. The world became a duodecimo, and he had no bad dreams in it, or very few, at such times. He is unbodied, except for the hand that holds the pen, and in the fullest significance enters into the spirit of the intellectual universe. His private marks and monologues in the margin prove his happiness. Yet it was in Spenser that his Arcadian adventurousness found its greatest liberty and reward. His copy—or the chief of his copies—was given to Forster by Thornton Hunt a week or so after his death, and may be seen at South Kensington. The following notes, transcribed from the end of Canto VIII, epitomise the friendship for life between this reader and *The Faerie Queene*:

"Finished reluctantly, and with gratitude for many hours which it has almost abstracted from disease, my second regular reading of this divine poem. May 23rd, 1814."

"Finished with greater reluctance, far greater—for the more I read Spenser, the more I see in him—and get out of him, as out of an ever growing, and superabounding forest of orchards—my third regular reading of the divine poem—wondering after all that that it is only the third, for I read him always,—this January 23rd, 1858.

"(58!! strange indeed: nearly forty four years' distance!) But what a consolation has my perpetual wandering in his enchanted ground been to me! I seem to possess it like a property, to which I have recourse whenever I wish to shut myself away (as much as it is possible for me to do so) from care and sorrow. Here, if anywhere, I have attained the end of the 'wings of the dove,' and 'been at rest.' LEIGH HUNT. No disparagement

the above effusion to those whom I love and have loved, and
without whose companionship my being can never be but
wanting, here or hereafter. But love itself is often full of
anxiety (what so full?) and the remote enchantment must be
flown to, to tranquillize perseverance.

"Same day and moment. *Absentes lugens, omnia post mortem
sperans.*"

Occasionally a paragraph on those for whom he mourned
arises from his reading. In the *Sketches* of Hazlitt, 1839,
he re-reads the statement that Lord Byron "seemed desirous,
in imitation of Mr Shelley, to run the gauntlet of public
opinion," and he exclaims, "What an imitation! Of excessive
sympathy by unfeeling vanity! It is a pity Mr Hazlitt could
not leave his greater brother-reformer alone. I had a great
quarrel with him when alive on that score, and therefore may
express the regret now." Beside the words "*bores* (mostly
German ones)," he remarks "Hazlitt punning!" At the end of
one of his volumes of Shakespeare (which he read with
immense enthusiasm, even if it was rather in the direction of
the "Romeo and Juliet" Shakespeare), he records: "In three
instances during my life have I known what it is to undergo
the anguish of an impatience with the ordinations of Providence,—a feeling, the absurdity of which was speedily
subjected to the consideration that Providence itself gave me
the very humanities which resented its apparent cruelty. One
only of the occasions was a real one. It was when I stood
on the sea-coast at Lerici, during the search for the body
of my drowned friend. The two others were the catastrophe (the sepulchre-scene) of 'Romeo and Juliet,' and
the scene in 'Lear' when he comes in with the body of
his daughter."

In prose and verse, Hunt has given remarkable pictures of

himself in the paradise of books, none more spirited than the
stanzas in *The Liberal*, which remain intimately true of his
latest years:

> So when my turn comes to repose, I read
> My magic books, and then with a bird's eye
> Dart me far off, as he does to his bed,
> Now to some piping vale of Arcady,
> Now to some mountain-top, which I've heard said,
> Holds the most ghastly breath in Tartary;
> And then I'm cradled 'twixt my Apennines,
> Spying the blue sky through the yellow vines.
>
> And then I'm all with Ovid and his changes,
> Or all with Spenser and his woods, or all
> With Ariosto and his endless ranges,
> Riding his Hippogriff, till I grow too small
> For eye to see:—then lo! I'm by the Ganges,
> Quick as that fatal wight[1], who gave a call
> To Solomon to send him out o' the way
> Of Death, and met him there that very day.
>
> And then again I'm playing fast and loose
> With girls, in isles that stud the Grecian sea:
> And then I'm in old Greece, and Œdipus
> Holding his blind eyes up, creeps quietly
> By his dear daughter's side, whom I would chuse,
> Were I a god, my worshipp'd wife to be:
> And then I'm in the valley, 'wonder deep,'
> Where the cold waters lull old Sleep to sleep[2].
>
> And then I'm all for Araby, my first love;
> I'm Giafar, I'm a 'genie,' I'm a jar;
> I'm Sindbad in some very horrid grove,—
> Which is delicious: I'm the Calendar

[1] He found the story in Voltaire.
[2] See the poem which Leigh Hunt and his contemporaries accepted as
"Chaucer's Dream."

Who with the lady was *one* hand and glove;
I am the prince[1], who shot his bow so far,
And found that cellar, with a stock divine
Of lips to kiss, still redder than the wine.

Such were his fantasies; and in the story of his conduct
when the actual thrust its Coavinsian body into his dream
one topic has always been popular—his incompetence, which
some have called a grosser name, with money. There is no
doubting his incompetence, in details and in general effect. The
story of his bewilderment when endeavouring to find 3s. 6d.
from some half-crowns and shillings—he could not find the
odd sixpence—is from trustworthy sources. He put a strain
on Shelley's means,—but with the name of Shelley we arrive
at the entire point: Neither Shelley nor Hunt had the conventional feelings about money. They worked in other values.
It will be urged, perhaps, that it was convenient for Hunt to
set no great store by money, since he was usually receiving it,
not giving it. Yet no man was more generous in act so far as
he had the means of serving another man. Shelley and Keats
made his home theirs when they wished, and Haydon acknowledged the assistance that both John and Leigh Hunt gave him;
any brother (or sister) author who desired him to give his
time, trouble and rich information for a literary undertaking
was sure to receive. I have mentioned S. C. Hall with his
Book of Gems and Peter Cunningham with his *Handbook of
London*; other instances are J. I. Wilson's *History of Christ's
Hospital*, 1821, and Jesse's *Beau Brummell*. R. H. Horne
describes the minute critical labour which Hunt was willing
to lavish on manuscripts or proofs submitted to him (as Lamb
was). It is Horne who points out, without eulogising Hunt for

1 "'The Story of Prince Ahmed and the Fairy Pari Banou.' The reader
knows it of course." L. H.

his improvidence, that Hunt did not feel "grateful" in the common meaning. He was incapable of feeling that he had himself conferred obligation, and he thought that at any rate the spirits of finer tone whom he met also avoided that idea. It was delightful to do well, and that virtue was its own reward. Horne maintains that Hunt, having received a benefit, was apt to be irritated when the doer asked for a service in return. But, metaphysically, the words "in return" or the implication of them were non-existent. Metaphysicians are a trying kind of men.

Any charge of calculation and dishonesty against Leigh Hunt will fail to survive an investigation of the evidence; this will be more readily admitted at the close of a biography in which more attention has been paid than previously to the obliquity of Marianne Hunt and her son John. But a few more statements will not be grudged, where such a harmful tradition has clouded a good name. In 1823 Trelawny volunteered to lend Hunt money. Hunt's reply was: "No, I *will* take the money when I feel it in justice due to me, and I will *not* take it from a generous man who has already but too little to spare. You will therefore not think of sending it from Leghorn, as it will only put me to the trouble of sending it you back again to Greece." In 1843 there was quite a comedy between Hunt and Macaulay. Hunt repaid a loan. Macaulay sent back the cheque. Hunt returned it. Macaulay sent it back again. Hunt returned it. In 1847 G. J. de Wilde, the editor of *The Northampton Mercury*, reading that Hunt was ill and noticing weariness in his articles, proposed a fund, and sent £5 towards it. Hunt sent it to him again: "You must not think ill of me for returning the five-pound note. Should occasion render its re-appearance advisable, I promise you I will let you know; and I esteem and regard you so much, that were you a man of princely fortune I would not hesitate to accept a hundred times as much from you; but poets and humanists like my friends de Wilde and Dalby...must have thousands of things to do with the fruits of their industry, which, short of the most loving necessity, must not be interfered with; and therefore you must be content with resuming the money, and leaving the obligation on my heart. *That* it shall never part with." This does not read like Horne's metaphysician.

I might linger over J. R. Lowell's intended large gift to Hunt, and Hunt's declining it; or over the Duke of Devonshire's admiration for Hunt on his repaying a considerable loan on the day when he said he would. (That repayment and the Duke's further liberality are recorded by John Forster and by J. P. Collier.) But a more immediate tribute to Hunt has been communicated to me very obligingly by Mr G. Reynell, nephew of Charles Reynell, who lived until 1892. Shortly before the old printer of *The Examiner* died, he called for Mr Reynell, and with strong emotion desired him to protect the memory of Leigh Hunt as a man. He had, he said, during a friendship of such length, frequently lent Hunt money; and it had been invariably repaid. He handed on his certainty that in money matters Leigh Hunt was himself, apart from some of his household, scrupulously honest. It is a kindly thing to see the name "Reynell" still in Chancery Lane, almost where Hunt was accustomed to see it, and to reflect on its remarkable and generous associations.

The question, at what point a biographer should close his book, is not answered by the statute-book yet. In the instance of Leigh Hunt, death would have been an uncongenial terminus, neither recommended by his own sense of the survival of his friends, nor by the vibrations which his personality and his writings created. "Vivid dreams of Leigh Hunt" caused his friend

Dalby to write a poem years after the disappearance of the bright face from daily paths. It would be in tune with Hunt's own feelings towards literature to descant on the editors of his essays and verses, who have been numerous, though we still lack any comprehensive edition of his prose. The last few years have seen a fresh succession of volumes by and about him, even though the current of his earlier productions has slackened, and the best of them are chiefly out of print.

Almost ten years after his death, S. C. Hall went to work to distinguish his grave in Kensal Green Cemetery. A committee was formed, which met several times, once under the chairmanship of Robert Browning. The names of Carlyle, Dickens, Procter, and Sir P. F. Shelley were on the list. A fund was soon raised, the subscribers including many persons who had, one way or another, felt Hunt's influence. Thus, old Jerdan, whom he had attacked for attacking Lamb in 1830, and Cowden Clarke, who had brought Keats to him in 1816, and Fonblanque, who had so well followed him as editor of *The Examiner*, and Charles Knight, who had financed his *London Journal*, and Forster, who had printed the first sketch of his manual of faith and duty, and Tennyson, whom he had seen as everybody's Tennyson from almost the first, were assembled with a number of other supporters, "persons of all shades of opinion, and of various ranks of life." While it was undecided what words should be inscribed under the bust that Joseph Durham had designed, William Allingham published, in *The Athenaeum*, the following lines, which had reference to a passage in one of Hunt's letters to him, "You will live to write my epitaph":

EPITAPH

Our dear Leigh Hunt, whose earth here lies in earth,
Thyself, we trust, enjoying peace and mirth;

If thou from Heav'n behold, by leave Divine,
This tombstone (England's honour more than thine),
What wouldst thou we had carved thereon to praise
The Patriot's honest voice, the Poet's lays,
The subtle Critic, Essayist refined,
In all, brave, sympathetic, pungent, kind?—
These words methinks, Leigh Hunt, from thine own pen
"Write me as one that loves his fellow-men."
That *loves*, we say, not *loved*; a man like thee
Is proof enough of immortality.

Allingham's selection was that of the committee, and in 1869 Lord Houghton unveiled the Kensal Green monument bearing the words which every schoolboy knows. Hunt no doubt would have admired the application, gazing at it with the large lustrous eyes; and he deserves it. But he had been accustomed to recite, as the kind of epitaph most eloquent of human life, an ancient one which might almost have fallen from the pen of Thomas Hardy:

> Here lieth Martin Eltenbrod:
> Have mercy on his soul, O God!
> As he would have, if he were God,
> And Thou wert Martin Eltenbrod.

Appendix 1

BOOKS BY LEIGH HUNT

1. JUVENILIA; or, a Collection of Poems.   1801
  3rd ed. 1802. 4th ed. 1803.
2. CLASSIC TALES, Serious and Lively: with Critical Essays
  on the Merits and Reputation of the Authors. 5 vols. 1806–7
3. CRITICAL ESSAYS ON THE PERFORMERS OF THE LONDON
  THEATRES.   1807
4. AN ATTEMPT TO SHEW THE FOLLY AND DANGER OF
  METHODISM.   1809
5. THE FEAST OF THE POETS, with Notes, and Other Pieces in
  Verse.   1814
   2nd ed. "amended and enlarged," 1815
6. THE DESCENT OF LIBERTY, a Mask.   1815
  2nd ed. 1816.
7. THE STORY OF RIMINI, a Poem.   1816
  3rd ed. 1819.
[8. THE ROUND TABLE: a Collection of Essays. 2 vols. 1817
   Hazlitt's; but Hunt contributed 10 of the 52 papers.]
9. FOLIAGE; or Poems Original and Translated.   1818
10. HERO AND LEANDER; AND BACCHUS AND ARIADNE, two
  original Poems.   1819
11. THE POETICAL WORKS OF LEIGH HUNT. 3 vols.   1819
   His previous volumes bound together with general
   title-pages.
12. AMYNTAS, a Tale of the Woods; from the Italian of
  Torquato Tasso.   1820
13. THE MONTHS descriptive of the Successive Beauties of the
  Year.   1821
   Repr. 1893, 1929.
14. ULTRA-CREPIDARIUS; a Satire on William Gifford. 1823
15. BACCHUS IN TUSCANY, a Dithyrambic Poem, from the
  Latin of Francesco Redi.   1825
16. LORD BYRON AND SOME OF HIS CONTEMPORARIES; with
  Recollections of the Author's Life, and of his Visit
  to Italy.   1828

   2nd ed., 2 vols. 1828, with an added Preface;
   3rd ed., Paris, 3 vols. 1828, with letters from *The
   Morning Chronicle.*

17. Sir Ralph Esher; or, Memoirs of a Gentleman of the Court of Charles II. 3 vols.   1830
      See Dr Alexander Mitchell's Bibliography, on this edition. The 2nd was dated 1832. 4th ed. 1850.

[18. The Masque of Anarchy, a Poem by Percy Bysshe Shelley. Now first published, with a preface by Leigh Hunt.]   1832

19. Christianism; or Belief and Unbelief Reconciled. 75 printed.   1832

20. The Poetical Works of Leigh Hunt.   1832

21. The Indicator, and the Companion; a Miscellany for the Fields and the Fireside. 2 vols.   1834
      See "Periodicals" below. Rep. 1840.

22. Captain Sword and Captain Pen, a Poem.   1835
      2nd ed. 1839. 3rd ed. 1849. Both vary from the first and from each other.

[23. Literary Hours; by Various Friends. Poems by L. H.]   1837

[24. The Book of Gems. The Modern Poets and Artists of Great Britain. Ed. S. C. Hall.   1838
      L. H.'s memoirs of Keats and Shelley, and the first appearance of "Abou ben Adhem."]

[25. Heads of the People...with Original Essays by Distinguished Writers.   1840
      Thackeray, Jerrold, L. H. and others.]

26. The Seer; or, Common-Places Refreshed.   1840–41

27. A Legend of Florence. A Play. In Five Acts.   1840
      2nd ed., with a preface added, 1840.

28. The Dramatic Works of Richard Brinsley Sheridan. With a Biographical and Critical Sketch by L. H.   1840

29. The Dramatic Works of Wycherley, Congreve, Vanbrugh, and Farquhar. With Biographical and Critical Notices by L. H.   1840

30. Notice of the late Mr Egerton Webbe.   1840
      A pamphlet, pointed out by Mr Ingpen.

[31. The Poems of Geoffrey Chaucer, Modernized. By R. H. Horne, E. B. Barrett, Wordsworth, L. H. and others.]   1841

32. The Palfrey; a Love-Story of Old Times.   1842

33. One Hundred Romances of Real Life.   1843

48. BEAUMONT AND FLETCHER; or, the Finest Scenes, Lyrics, and Other Beauties of those Two Poets, now first selected....   1855
49. STORIES IN VERSE. Now first collected.   1855
50. THE POETICAL WORKS OF LEIGH HUNT. Now first entirely collected, revised by himself, and edited with an introduction by S. Adams Lee. 2 vols. Boston.   1857
51. THE PROSE WORKS OF LEIGH HUNT. 4 vols. American ed.   1857
52. THE POETICAL WORKS OF LEIGH HUNT. Now Finally collected, Revised by Himself, and edited by his Son, Thornton Hunt.   1860
53. A SAUNTER THROUGH THE WEST END.   1861
54. THE CORRESPONDENCE OF LEIGH HUNT. Edited by his Eldest Son. 2 vols.   1862
55. THE BOOK OF THE SONNET. Edited by Leigh Hunt and S. Adams Lee. 2 vols. Boston.   1867
    100 large-paper copies printed at the same time appeared, with added portraits, at New York, 1885. Messrs Sampson Low were the English publishers.

Since 1867 no separate work by Leigh Hunt, so far as I know, has made its first appearance. The following selections and new editions should be mentioned:

1. A TALE FOR A CHIMNEY CORNER, and Other Essays. Edited by Edmund Ollier.   1869
    From the original *Indicator*. The earlier issue has some pages on L. H.'s monument at Kensal Green.
2. A DAY BY THE FIRE; and Other Papers, Hitherto Uncollected.   1870
    Edited by J. E. Babson.
3. THE WISHING-CAP PAPERS. Now first collected.   1873
    Edited by J. E. Babson.
4. FAVOURITE POEMS BY LEIGH HUNT. Illustrated. Boston.   1877
5. THE POETICAL WORKS OF LEIGH HUNT. "Moxon's Popular Poets."   1883
6. THE POETICAL WORKS OF LEIGH HUNT AND THOMAS HOOD. Selected. "The Canterbury Poets."   1889
7. LEIGH HUNT AS POET AND ESSAYIST. Edited by Charles Kent.   1889

8. ESSAYS BY LEIGH HUNT. Edited by Arthur Symons. 1889
9. ESSAYS AND POEMS OF LEIGH HUNT. Selected and edited by R. Brimley Johnson. 2 vols. 1891
10. TALES BY LEIGH HUNT. Edited by William Knight. 1891
11. DRAMATIC ESSAYS BY LEIGH HUNT. Edited by William Archer and Robert W. Lowe. 1894
12. LEIGH HUNT. SELECTIONS IN PROSE AND VERSE. Edited by J. H. Lobban. 1909
13. LEIGH HUNT. POETRY AND PROSE. Edited by Edward Storer. 1911
14. THE POETRY AND PROSE OF COLERIDGE, LAMB, AND LEIGH HUNT. Edited by S. E. Winbolt. 1920
15. THE POETICAL WORKS OF LEIGH HUNT. Edited by H. S. Milford. "Oxford Poets." 1923
16. PREFACES BY LEIGH HUNT. Edited by R. Brimley Johnson. 1927
17. SHELLEY–LEIGH HUNT. Edited by R. Brimley Johnson. 1928
18. LEIGH HUNT'S "EXAMINER" EXAMINED. Edited by E. Blunden. 1928

There are some pamphlets accredited to Hunt which I have not seen; and an American edition of Fairfax's *Tasso* should be in my list, for it contains by way of introduction an essay by L. H. But his American bibliography should be undertaken by an expert. "Many of Hunt's works," says Allibone, "have been republished in America by Wells & Lilly, Carey, Lea & Blanchard, Carey & Hart, Wiley & Putnam, the Harpers, W. P. Hazard, Ticknor & Fields, &c."

PERIODICALS EDITED BY LEIGH HUNT

1. THE EXAMINER, a Sunday Paper. 1808–21
2. THE REFLECTOR, a Quarterly Magazine. 1810–11
   Subsequently bound in 2 vols. as "The Reflector, a Collection of Essays on Miscellaneous Subjects," etc.
3. THE LITERARY POCKET-BOOK. Annually. 1819–23
   See Dr Mitchell's Bibliography.
4. THE INDICATOR. Weekly. 1819–21
   The numbers bound into one volume, 1822.
5. THE LIBERAL. 4 Nos.; 2 vols. 1822–23

6. THE COMPANION. Every Wednesday. 1828
7. THE CHAT OF THE WEEK. Every Saturday. 1830
8. THE TATLER. A Daily Journal of Literature and the Stage. 1830–32
9. LEIGH HUNT'S LONDON JOURNAL. 1834–35
   With supplements by L. H.
10. THE MONTHLY REPOSITORY. New Series. 1837–38
11. LEIGH HUNT'S JOURNAL. Weekly. 1850–51

Besides the above works edited by him, Hunt contributed widely and frequently to all sorts of periodicals. No adequate list of these has been printed; there is a useful attempt, by J. P. Anderson, appended to Cosmo Monkhouse's *Life of Leigh Hunt*. Perhaps the majority of Hunt's fugitive writings appeared in *The Atlas*, *The True Sun*, *The Morning Chronicle*, and *The New Monthly Magazine*; but this subject will not submit to brief treatment.

Appendix 2

A VIEW OF LEIGH HUNT'S INTIMATE CIRCLE
(from an unpublished work by Thornton Hunt entitled *Proserpina*)

LEIGH HUNT

A CIRCLE of which portions and connecting links were known to you exemplified the law of contrasts, although it might be supposed to command an unusual degree of common feeling. He who was the centre of it was, in every sense of the words, a gentleman and a scholar. Cadet of a family broken by more than one revolution, he inherited nothing more than the ambition to be a student and a patriot, but his uncompromising love of truth led him to be a questioner of dogma, even on his own side in politics or religion; while his indolence and still more his *indoles*—which we imperfectly call taste, genius, or natural bent,—led him to the lighter "humanities." A devoted idealist, he actually lived in the world of poetry, painting, and music; coming into the real world only to play his part, confessedly with very elementary knowledge, in the stern unprofitable business of constitutional politics; and mingling in the business of common life only to treat his affairs on bookish principles and to invest his personal friends with ideal attributes; the tangible results of his conscientious endeavours being party persecution, imprisonment, embarrassment, and disappointment. He seldom viewed anything as it really was, but as it looked under the atmosphere of poetry,

MARIANNE HUNT

by the light of classic illustrations. Fate joined him with one who shared his taste for plastic art, with a greater natural aptitude, but without culture or the power of acquiring it; with a childlike sense of verse, never matured; with an almost equally childlike sense of oeconomy which the bookworm long believed to be nearly perfect. United by strong affection and love for their progeny, what had this couple in common? He was regarded as a stranger to real life, and he learned to be content with a total ignorance of the sphere comprising "the butcher and baker"; she could follow a little way into the domain of sculpture or painting, a still less way into the English library; but could not, even from his full conversation, which seldom drew from her any stedfast attention, form so much as a conjecture of the fields around Parnassus which were his pasture and habitual haunt. The inevitable dictates of daily life, it is true,—instincts of affection, the call of hunger, the need for clothing and lodging, the attractions of society,—had a power over both, but in the most remarkably opposite degrees and modes; the same thing which to the one was aliment and grave delight, affording to the other no more than "amusement"; and of course with thoughts and sensations so diverse, they were actuated by motives so different, that lengthening years only made them, in the longer portion of their faithful and unsevered union, strangers. Another in the same household might have seemed a better companion for its head, for though coming with little better than a dame-school education, she had so much natural faculty for study as to master two languages, a wide range of history, fiction, and poetry, with a technical knowledge of woman's favourite science, botany; which she illustrated from the library by really graceful writing. Ambitious, of ardent affection, truthful, what "incompatibility of temper" it was, or what outward uncongeniality of taste, that set up an impassable barrier between the two I know not; but most of all I think it was a sort of masculine, predetermined and inflexible resolution in the sister on matters of conviction, of wilfulness or obstinacy on matters of personal liking, which made her insist too much, and which was the very opposite of the brother's nature; for though he could be a martyr, he never could be quite sure that he in particular was right, and always preached that "will is the Devil." The next in the family circle is a cousin, a pretty gentle girl with tender heart, and no more mind than a baby,—a born ancilla, never destined to be mistress of anything. Next another cousin, the firm uncompromising teacher; who risked her life for the head of the household, but never yielded to his patriotism or idealism one iota of her routine ideas—a model of virtue, whose thoughts seemed to be so exclusively those of duty, that duty itself was kept within the limits of a solitary life; which ended in nothing. Next to her the younger brother-

ELIZABETH KENT

VIRTUE KENT

in-law, the somewhat "fast" medical student,—a skilful manipulator and sharp-sighted observer who could not stick to his own profession, and wandered dubiously through life, now among uncongenial proprieties, then among utterly unintelligible aesthetics, until at last he found a nest of his own, apart. But MRS KENT I must not omit the mother-in-law—the widow of his fast father—who had brought up her girls so respectably. She had done it all by clear-sighted energy, clear management, and unflinching will. Uneducated, triply tried in schools of poverty, thrift, and trouble, untrained in modern ideas of discipline by force of influence, she was dogged, violent, at times almost cruel. A sincere and rather "serious" Christian, hasty to inflict chastisement for the first departure from "principle" as *she* interpreted it, she severely tasked the charity of her son-in-law's then unfashionable neo-christianity; who as readily threw the Bible in her face, morally, as she would cast it at one of her contumacious children's heads; and he long viewed her with a repugnance which she did *not* reciprocate. He thought that her goodwill was a sort of intellectual tuft-hunting, a feeling of vanity at her alliance with his repute; his repugnance to her combatant proprieties and inconsistent Christianity made him paint in her place an ideal hypocrite; and although he ultimately "moderated" his estimate, the fancy picture ever prevented him from knowing her as she was—strong in affection, with keen tastes that highly appreciated his powers, an active generosity that constantly broke through long enforced habits of care and penury, and a strength of heart-will that made her a thorough friend through all trials even of misconduct in some, or of misconception in others. But for all her natural tastes, which were rather of the positive or material order, save in religion, untrained in art, unlearned, without accomplishments, she was a bigoted realist; it was the "reality" part of his own writing or amateur art that she understood; the reality of his success; of her life he understood simply nought.

JOHN HUNT From this household let us go, as it were, next door in the same family,—to find the brothers; the first married to a most excellent housekeeper, himself a perfect gentleman with commercial education, a grave dignified resolve to do his duty, though it involved prison, ruin, or submission to unjust charges, if they could only be contradicted by accusing others; the second a lawyer, married to a lady with "a small inde- STEPHEN pendence," several daughters, and habits of ease,—himself a HUNT proud gentleman, indolent, indifferent to everything except "society," and growing callous even to that; and the third an artist, utterly devoid of any natural talent, except for digestion, ROBERT married to a pattern of conjugal worth and charitable affection. HUNT Family pride and hereditary patriotism formed common bond among all these men,—the man of calm deliberate integrity, the proud, indolent, generous lawyer, the thriftless, thoughtless, bookless, homely non-artist; but beyond that one idea, viewed by each in aspects wholly unlike, they were to each other so many unknown departments of life, in which the others "had no business"; while of their more eminent brother, who through the mirror of fiction had some idea of them and their existence, they could form not the faintest conception, save that they were proud of their brother as a successful author and a tried patriot.

But, quiet and homely as it is, there is something which attracts to the idealist's home a wide and still more varying circle of friends, bound to him in various ways by affection and esteem. Early among them is a commercial man and sub- T. ALSAGER sequently the monetary oracle; he finds in his value for honest conviction and refined taste, and also in his own violin, links which unite him to the connexion; next, the agreeable bass THE singer who is too nervous to be more than a chorus singer on ROBERT- his native stage, enters by right of music, and with him his SONS brother, the director of the musical evenings which bring round the fortepiano a real company of voices; the silent violin player, with Marcello's violin compositions; and the young pupil-performer and writer, who unites the concert-room, the library, the drawing-room and the tourist's inn. The one whom VINCENT I have called the Director hardly knows whether his family is NOVELLO Italian or German, French or English; he is attended by the shrewd, warm-hearted, clear, undemonstrative, sharp-eyed managing partner of his home, indulgent of Epicurean refinements until they thwart the main chance, but never forgetful of that idol-object. To the gathering comes the lovely A. G., whom the author of Amadis of Gaul prophetically described in Queen Briolanea,—a specimen of beautiful womanhood, fit to be, as she was, the Queen of a memorable Twelfth Night muster; by her side the silent faithful A. G., as perfect a piece of affection as ever wore man's fleshly dress, and loved accordingly by all who knew him, man, woman, or child. Comes too the unlearned, witty East India House clerk, the immortal essayist "Elia," and his sister, the sweet writer of fiction for children, to whose afflicted life his own is unrepiningly sacrificed; the earnest, eloquent critic, W. H.,—sensitive, captious, anxious to please, ready to fear that he is displeased, prompt to take offence; quick of insight into definite character and bookish qualities; half a genius in art, but only half; trained in a narrow dissenting school, conscious of deficiencies in the very alphabet of literature, at a loss in the world, perplexed by fanciful mistrusts that others are ridiculing him; jealous, bitter, eloquent, generous, confessing a weakness for rackets and tea, at war with himself against foibles he despises, but confident in honest purpose, and the permanent rule of intellect and beauty. Comes too the earnest living picture of a youthful poet, J. K., who *has* marked his place in fame, though he went to Rome to die before his time, attended by friendship, but not by the affianced love which punctilio held back. Comes the learned witty low-voiced "gentleman of independent property"—the satirist, who nurses a secret and unsuspected vanity of his personal appearance; the sceptic who stands out of all but a modicum of his own fortune that his mother and sisters may use it for their lives; the kind-hearted, self-indulgent Epicurean, who learns a hideous mistrust even of nature, through lack of sympathy forced on and additionally contracted by being in early life a sort of male "femme incomprise"; who can speak ancient Greek, but scarcely understands what any body means in his own day, and finds nothing certain but a good dinner and physical pleasure.

THE
GLIDDONS

CHARLES
AND MARY
LAMB

HAZLITT

KEATS

H. SMITH

Attracted to the same centre is N. B., whose whole biography BYRON is a moral tale. Orphan heir to title and fortune, "his own master" while a boy, of classic beauty yet a cripple, endowed by nature with wit, imagination, and the gift of numbers; accomplished in manly sports and literature, "emancipated" from every conceivable restraint, and burning to be the chief figure in many a successive tableau de théâtre, the young scion of a twofold aristocracy, in Westminster and in Parnassus, is held in merciless bondage by a triple daemon—love of pleasure, love of applause, and love of gold,—three several forms of the influence which makes him a devoted worshipper of "Number One." With genuine patriotic sympathies, he thinks more of the melodramatic effect of a patriotic coup, and half flinches from the mission he undertakes. With a real *storge* of generosity in his breast, he flings his gold broadcast for luxury or for friendship, and then haggles over his steward's items. With a true aesthetic sense of the beautiful, but an Eve-like curiosity, he will literally try profligacy "to the dregs." With a keen sense of folly in others,—and himself,—he writes magnificent metrical satires on the vices of the age, in which the hero is drawn from the looking glass,—and then he hides away from his own library those Italian models of romance and satire from whom he caught his first idea of the form for his own art; though Pulci or Fortiguerri might have wondered why the rival who excelled them both in wit and fertility could have dreaded the comparison. And finally, with a touching frankness of conduct as well as tongue—for he *cannot* know concealment,—he confesses that, victim to early lack of guidance, he never has yet done justice to his own nature, and attaches himself to a noble friendship just long enough to prove what that great school might have done for him, when death removes the teacher, and next takes away the pupil before he can fulfil his studies even alone. The sport of impulses retracted, familiarised with "the dregs" aforesaid, suspecting and suspected, beauty had become to him a painted sepulchre to be laughed at; friendship a "plant," patriotism Buncombe, à la Sadler's Wells; and yet, although he will scoff behind her back at this unconscious beauty who has abandoned all for him, he really craves affection, freedom for his kind, and exalting idealism; setting to learn his mission after he has sown even his middle-aged wild oats, only in time to see his master die, and to revoke his intellectual will, before his own demise, by a codicil implying that he does not bequeath to posterity a perverse admission that "all is vanity and vexation of spirit."

In what I have spoken of as a circle centring round one man, there were, you already know, those who were centres of yet larger circles, in which he was proud to be subordinate; and none was more emphatically *the* chief man than he whom I have just spoken of as the "teacher." His disciples have been many, among them men of commanding powers; but it has been only by degrees that the real scope and direction of his genius has been comprehended. Heir to fortune and title, while yet a boy he revolted against tyranny, dogma, and falsehood, so openly and uncompromisingly that his family disowned him as far as it might, society looked askance at him, and only they welcomed him who were at issue with the dominant idolatry of that period, now passed away. At first his vindication of intellectual freedom took the shape of antagonism; he went back from the doctrines which he found identified, for the time, with servility and corruption in politics, to classic models of virtue and ideal standards of beauty; and refusing a family condonation, a seat in Parliament, and higher honours in prospect, he sought his life in poetry made real; wedding the daughter and intellectual heiress of "Political Justice," and literally leading her clear mind into his own path of classic study and exalted speculation. As he advanced towards its midst he drew around him men older in years, more trained in the world; and more accustomed to embody their thoughts in definite aims, whether of social action or worldly success. Thus he formed a circle which included the faithful idealist whom I first spoke of, the ultra-emancipated romantic satirist of noble birth, the witty sceptical classicist, the tender-hearted Montaigne-like essayist-clerk, the sensitive critic who condescended to speak of Rousseau as his model, the worldly clever

SHELLEY

satirist, the picture-writing young poet, the aesthetical bookseller, and many more as various in nature. Each one understood some part of his genius, but not one the whole of it,—
for at that time the data were not accessible to any one man,
if all the elements of his truly great character will ever be
thoroughly known. Most he seemed to command the sympathy of the pure and thorough-going idealist; but that
congenial friend was perplexed to find so clear an accord between the self-sacrificing, devoted, pure-minded philosopher and
the melodramatic, self-indulgent, wavering "noble bard"; and
neither was prepared for the rational, plain, business-like,
practical manner in which their acknowledged leader now
grappled with hard problems, whether of primaeval antiquity,
working politics, abstract morals, every-day life, or even hard
cash. Nay, the deeply loving mate by his side, trained in MARY
antagonistic ideas of "independence," somewhat touched by a SHELLEY
peevish sickliness of temperament, only learned too late, from
retrospection, all her own sympathy and all the grand beauty
of spirit and conduct which commanded it,—no, not too late,
for love lives after death, and of such influences we can in
truth *never* discern the end.

*　　*　　*

Glance over what I have written, and add in some few points
of variety which I could not so well note in passing.—For SHELLEY
instance, the one of highest intellect and most poetical genius
had no ear for music; and the critic who was the half artist HAZLITT
lacked the sense of form. Remember how many in the circle
were wholly ignorant of languages, of arts, of whole fields of
literature, sciences, classes of society, incidents of life, which
were known to the rest; and tell me if I am not justified in
speaking of the diversity which separates original natures and
is still more widened by differences of training. In the household with which I began, the simple creature who was never
anything but a pretty girl put to pasture on this earth had not
the vaguest idea of scenes familiar to her "fast" medical
student, or the accomplished idealist; she did not know that
living creatures go through that which was daily pastime to

her young brother, nor could she guess at a hundredth part of the things present to the idealist, and constituting the reasons why he acted as he did. His wife did not know nearly half; and he only knew half of her life by report of printed books, most confusedly. [Virtue Kent] and the idealist's wife were familiar with the aspect of his more gifted friend the poet-philosopher, "knew him well"; but so little did they comprehend the thoughts that pressed upon his soul, the passions he felt, the motives on which he acted, or the real nature of the things...that, to speak the plain truth in short phrase, they actually did not know that such a being as he who was their house-mate actually existed.

*   *   *

To P. B. all the events of life are so many illustrations of natural forces, the course of which is never entirely absent from the thoughts, while the same events are explained by the laws they illustrate, with endless lessons in forbearance, patience, and guidance. Another submits to the same events blindly, undergoing each as an isolated visitation; is elated at the "luck" or downcast at the "ill-luck"; is indignant at the effect of deficiencies in companions who really suffer more than anybody else from their own shortcomings in perception. A third, duller in perception, is incapable of the same joy through others,—of the same sympathy, the same passion, the same sense of beauty in art, in nature. Of the party sitting in quiet

converse round the family table is the idealist, the whole range of his thoughts drawn from the library flocking round his head, and he is seeking to conjure up the fancy that the homely life of which he is centre is the parallel and counterpart of that ideal world, if he will but lend to it the associations which he draws from literature, and which he regards as ennobling and purifying what they idealize. At the same time in right reverent spirit he upholds the true nobility and beauty of God's world, but can best understand it by viewing it through the aggregate

intellect of the past. With faculties drawn forth and informed by the same library, but endowed with the powers of life in their fullest intensity, the friend whom the idealist specially and deliberately honoured, P. B., knows the beauties of nature by direct study; does not so much read life by the light of books, as those well-known books by the light of life; draws from the creation the raw material of thoughts the most sublime and lovely; feels in beating heart the sweet passion which poets have striven to utter, and follows the noblest motives of nature's aristocracy with a thorough understanding. In this group, one sits placidly grazing on the daily food of life, wholly untaught in the learning of the idealist, ignorant that such emotions, such ideas, such purposes as are familiar to P. B., have so much as an existence in the world of reality.

Appendix 3

LEIGH HUNT'S COLLECTION OF LOCKS OF HAIR

THIS, the principal show-piece of his study in later life, is catalogued thus:

Milton	1608–1674	From Dr Johnson to John Hoole, who gave it to Dr Batty
Swift	1667–1745	From John Hoole to Dr Batty
Johnson	1709–1784	From Mrs Hoole to Dr Batty in 1784
Keats	1796–1821	[There were two locks]
Shelley	1792–1822	Dec. 3rd, 1820
Mary Shelley	1798–1851	1820
Procter	1787–1874	March 26th, 1821
Lamb	1775–1834	July 7th, 1826
Hazlitt	1778–1830	
Coleridge	1772–1834	1839 From Mrs Gillman
Carlyle	1795–1881	1840
Wordsworth	1770–1850	1845
Maria Edgeworth	1767–1849	1845
Southwood Smith	1788–1861	1845
G. P. R. James	1801–1860	1850
Robert Browning	1812–1899	July 1856
E. B. Browning	1806–1861	1856
R. H. Horne	1803–1884	
Napoleon	1769–1821	From Lord Byron who had it from Augusta Leigh, who had it from Napoleon's valet.
Washington	1732–1764	From S. Adams Lee who had it from his cousin, Mrs Mary Curtis Lee, only daughter of G. W. P. Curtis, adopted son of George Washington.
Richard Henry Lee	1732–1799	
Lucretia Borgia		From Byron, or Trelawny?

The last, a solitary hair, "was given me by a wild acquaintance, who stole it from a lock of her hair preserved in the Ambrosian library at Milan. On the envelope he put a happy motto: 'And Beauty draws us with a single hair.' If ever hair was golden, it was this." The manner in which Hunt would talk to the sympathetic visitor over his relics is displayed by his essay in *Tait's Edinburgh Magazine*, January 1833: "It is Milton's! It was this and two others, which set us upon the plan of collecting as many as were not unworthy to keep them company; and the reader will see that we have been fortunate.

"This lock of the great poet is almost as beautiful, in a soberer way as Lucretia's is splendid. It is remarkable for its excessive and almost preternatural fineness—we mean the softness and slenderness of its individual hairs. It furnishes an interesting corroboration of what was said of his looks at the University, where he was called (not much to his liking) the 'Lady of the College.' Certainly, it is more like the hair of the most delicate girl, than what we should have expected from the tresses of him

'Who set the embattled Seraphim in arms.'

"This treasure was generously given us by Dr. [Batty] the physician, who had it from his father-in-law, who had it from Hoole the translator, who had it from Johnson. The link of evidence is here lost; but Johnson was famous for his veracity, and he would not have given it to Hoole as Milton's, had he not believed it genuine. The internal evidence of the hair itself is strong; and the colour is brown, which is known to have been Milton's. It should be added, however, that perhaps the extreme fineness of the hair is owing partly to age. Yet Lucretia's looks as strong as ever; and we do not remember that the hair of Edward the Fourth, taken out of his grave, had lost any of its thickness. There is no grey in the lock. It must have been cut when the poet was in the vigour of life, before he wrote 'Paradise Lost'; and we may indulge our fancy by supposing it was cut off as a present to his wife. Love and locks of hair, the most touching, the most beautiful, and the most lasting of keepsakes, naturally go together; and as Milton valued himself on his tresses, a woman who loved him would hold them of double value. In his mention of Bacchus and Circe in 'Comus,' he makes the god's hair, and the rest of his aspect, of equal importance:

'The nymph, who gazed upon his clustering locks,
    With ivy-berries wreath'd, and his blithe youth,
    Had by him, ere he parted thence, a son.'

"Milton must have been more delighted than most poets at the compliments paid to beautiful tresses by his brethren, particularly by his favourite Greeks. We say nothing about his portrait of Adam, supposed by some to have been drawn from himself, because we are ambitious in these papers of touching as little as we can upon what has been said before us.

"The hair of Milton in this our illustrious collection is followed in the order of time by that of Swift, consisting of two locks, one when he was young, a handsome brown; the other, a fine glossy white; which is affecting, from the circumstances of its having been cut off his head 'by Mrs. Ridgway, his housekeeper, after his decease.' This is recorded on the paper that wrapped the hair when it was presented to us. Swift's lock, and the one we shall next speak of, was also given us by the gentleman who honoured us with the bestowal of Milton's. From the thought of the white lock, we turn in pity and grief, knowing what Swift must have undergone while it was on his head. The other was cut, probably in the time of King William, when young men often wore their own hair. It argues nothing against the genuineness of the older lock of hair, either in this or the instance we shall mention next, that old people, in those days, wore wigs, and had their heads shaved—for the head was not always strictly shaved; probably when they stopped most in doors, it was not shaved for many days; the hair was some-times suffered to grow a good deal under the wig; and in Swift's case, his hair may have been suffered to grow consider-ably, a short time before he died; for he never stirred from home, and there was no reason for cutting it. We have not an elaborate life of him by us to consult; but we think we have read somewhere that his hair was very dark. The lock before us is brown, and not a very dark brown. Swift's eyes are known to have been blue, which is not a colour generally found in company with very dark hair. Pope described them as being as 'blue as the Heavens!' Swift's hair belonged to Mr. Hoole, and was given him by Johnson. We know not how the latter came by it. Probably it was a present to him as an author; or he may have had it from Sheridan the actor, father of Richard Brinsley, and son of Dr. Sheridan, the friend of Swift. The channels are many through which it might have come to him.

"The next lock is Johnson's own. It is old and coarse, of a whitish colour mixed with grey. Not the less reverently is it to be regarded. The very coarseness of it suits somehow the peculiarity of his pretensions—not as being coarse, but from a sort of unpoetical vigour and a disdain of things 'fine.' We are loth to call it horse-hair; but it may be styled a very good HOUYHNHNM lock. Hoole attended Johnson in his last illness.

"A mighty name ensues, with a minim specimen of hair attached to it—Napoleon. There is no doubt of the authenticity of the specimen. It was obtained for the gentleman who gave it us by his sister, who had it from the valet who cut the Emperor's hair. It is, in fact, nothing but such a shred or two as the valet might have hastily picked up with his fingers, when he was quitting his task, or even retained upon his coat. It consists of two or three small scratches of hair, kept together by a piece of sealing-wax. The sorry look of it would be an evidence of its genuineness, if evidence were needed. It adds to the impression upon the beholders, looking almost like a mockery of his fate. To complete its petty aspect, it is enclosed in a very small bit of paper. The late Mr. Hazlitt, who, from his hatred of the Allies, was a fond admirer of the man who has so knocked them about the head and ears, stood one day looking at it, wrapt in thought; and some burst of enthusiasm was expected from him; but, probably, on that account, he exclaimed with his usual sincerity 'I cannot get up a sensation about it.' He said, that memorials of this kind did not touch him; he supposed, from a 'defect of imagination.' He was struck, however, with the shining relic of Lucretia Borgia. The impression of beauty is instantaneous, and wants no aid from reflection.

"The names that close our list want none of the graces of fame, except those which time will bestow, and are far more affecting to us than the rest. They are those of Shelley, Keats, and Mr. Hazlitt himself.

"Shelley's hair is a delicate chestnut lock, dashed with grey. He was prematurely grey. His mind was a hundred years old, and had affected his body. The lock was cut off about three years before he died, and sent in a letter from Italy. Over what a world of thought, feeling, fancy, imagination, pain, playfulness, subtlety, universality, has it grown! But the tenderness caused in our minds by looking at it, surpasses even the wonder and the admiration.

"We pass to that of the next friend, admirable also for his genius and only less dear to us, because we had not had occasion to know him under so many endearing circumstances. How we loved him, need not be added. Mr. Keats' hair was remarkable for its beauty,—its flowing grace and fineness. It was a kind of ideal, poetical hair; and the locks we possess (for we have two) are beautiful specimens, calling up the instant admiration of the spectators. They are long, thick, exquisitely fine, and running into ringlets. The colour is brown, of that sort which has a yellowish look in it in some lights, and a darker one or auburn in others. They remind us of the love-locks of the cavaliers. Colonel Hutchinson might have had such, or young Milton. They are tresses—things rarely seen nowadays, of a natural growth, on the heads of young men: and remember the poet was a young man, and manly in spirit as his locks were beautiful.

"The lock of Mr. Hazlitt's hair is a good thick ring, smooth and glossy, and almost black. Those who remember this great writer, during his latter years only, have no conception what a fine head of hair he had at a period a little earlier. It rapidly degenerated; and he cut it off as if in spite, and suddenly appeared with a docked grizzled head, to the great resentment of his friends, and (what he would not easily believe, or pretended not to believe) of the ladies. He was always desiring the regard of women: and then, between complexional and metaphysical doubt, taking pains to prevent himself from having it. When we first had the pleasure of an interview with him, and he took off his hat, there fell from it about his ears a load of handsome dark curls, which alone would have furnished a favourable introduction of him to the fair sex. A lady, who was in the habit of seeing him, at an evening party sitting with these dark locks against some crimson window curtains, and who, like himself, was a connoisseur in the Fine Arts and their manœuvres, told him that he did it on purpose to set off the beauty of his hair. 'Oh, no!' he exclaimed, 'if I could have done that, it would have been the salvation of me': meaning, that if he could have been fop enough, he would have had enough self-sufficiency to act a less diffident figure in general."

Appendix 4

SOME AUTHORITIES ON LEIGH HUNT, BIOGRAPHICAL AND CRITICAL

ALLINGHAM, WILLIAM. Diary. Edited by H. Allingham and D. Radford. 1907.

BARHAM, R. H. D. The Life and Remains of Theodore Edward Hook. 4th ed. 2 vols. 1850.

BATES, WILLIAM. The Maclise Portrait-Gallery of Illustrious Literary Characters, with Memoirs. 1883.

BEAVAN, ARTHUR H. James and Horace Smith. 1899.

BESANT, WALTER. Fifty Years Ago. New ed. 1899.

BIAGI, GUIDO. The Last Days of Percy Bysshe Shelley. 1898.

BLANCHARD, S. LAMAN. Poetical Works, with a Memoir by Blanchard Jerrold. 1876.

"BON GAULTIER." Book of Ballads. 1875.

BONER, CHARLES. Memoirs. Edited by R. M. Kettle. 2 vols. 1871.

BREWER, LUTHER A. The Joys and Sorrows of a Book Collector. [Cedar Rapids, Iowa; privately printed.] 1928.

—— Some Letters from my Leigh Hunt Portfolios. With brief comment. [Cedar Rapids, Iowa; privately printed.] 1929.

BRITTON, JOHN. Autobiography. 2 vols. 1850.

BROUGHAM, LORD. Life and Times. 1871.

BROWNING, R. and E. B. Letters, 1845–1846. 2 vols. 1899.

BYRON, LORD. Works. A New, Revised and Enlarged Edition. Edited by E. H. Coleridge and R. E. Prothero. 13 vols. 1898–1901.

CAMPBELL, JOHN, LORD. Lives of the Lord Chief Justices of England. 2 vols. 1849.

CARLYLE, THOMAS. On the Choice of Books. Second Edition, with a New Life of the Author. 1869.

—— Reminiscences. Edited by J. A. Froude. 2 vols. 1881.

—— Letters, 1826–1835. Edited by C. E. Norton. 2 vols. 1888.

—— New Letters. Edited by Alexander Carlyle. 2 vols. 1904.

CHAMBERS, W. and R. Memoir of Robert Chambers, with Autobiographic Reminiscences of William Chambers. 6th ed. 1872.

CLARKE, CHARLES and MARY COWDEN. Recollections of Writers. With Letters of Lamb, Hunt, Jerrold and Dickens. 2nd ed. 1878.

CLARKE, MARY COWDEN. The Life and Labours of Vincent Novello. 1863.

—— My Long Life. 2nd ed. 1896.

CLAYDEN, P. W. Rogers and his Contemporaries. 2 vols. 1889.

COLERIDGE, SARA. Biographia Literaria, by S. T. Coleridge. [1847 ed. 3 vols. Appendix.] 1847.
—— Memoir and Letters. 2 vols. 2nd ed. 1873.
COLLIER, J. P. An Old Man's Diary. 1871.
COLVIN, SIDNEY. John Keats, his Life and Poetry, his Friends, Critics, and After-Fame. 2nd ed. 1918.
CONWAY, MONCURE D. Thomas Carlyle. 1881.
COOPER, THOMAS SIDNEY. My Life. New ed. 1891.
CRAIK, GEORGE LILLIE. History of Literature and Learning in England. 6 vols. 1844–5.
—— A Compendious History of English Literature. 2 vols. 1861.
CROSS, LAUNCELOT, i.e. FRANK CARR. Characteristics of Leigh Hunt, as Exhibited in..."Leigh Hunt's London Journal." 1878.
—— Hesperides. 2nd ed. 1885.
CUNNINGHAM, ALLAN. Biographical and Critical History of the last Fifty Years. 1834.
DALBY, JOHN WATSON. Poems. c. 1865.
[DEACON, W. F.] Warreniana; with Notes. 1824.
DICKENS, CHARLES. Bleak House. 1853.
DILKE, CHARLES WENTWORTH. Papers of a Critic. 2 vols. 1875.
DOWDEN, EDWARD. The Life of Percy Bysshe Shelley. 2 vols. 1886.
—— and others. Letters about Shelley. 1917.
ESPINASSE, F. Literary Recollections. 1893.
FIELDS, JAMES T. Barry Cornwall and Some of his Friends. Boston. 1876.
—— Biographical Notes and Personal Sketches. 1881.
FIELDS, MRS JAMES T. A Shelf of Old Books. New York. 1894.
FONBLANQUE, EDWARD BARRINGTON DE. The Life and Labours of Albany Fonblanque. 1874.
FORSTER, JOHN. Walter Savage Landor. A Biography. New ed. 1879.
—— The Life of Charles Dickens. Edited by B. W. Matz. 2 vols. 1911.
FOX, W. J. Lectures Addressed Chiefly to the Working Classes. 4 vols. 1845–49.
FROUDE, JAMES ANTHONY. Thomas Carlyle, 1795–1835. 2 vols. 1901.
GALT, JOHN. The Life of Lord Byron. 1830.
GARNETT, RICHARD. Relics of Shelley. 1862.
GILFILLAN, GEORGE. A Second Gallery of Literary Portraits. 1850.
GORDON, MRS. "Christopher North." A Memoir of John Wilson. 2 vols. 1862.
GRUNDY, FRANCIS H. Pictures of the Past. 1879.
HACKWOOD, FREDERICK W. William Hone, his Life and Times. 1912.
HALL, SAMUEL CARTER. A Book of Memories of Great Men and Women of the Age. New ed. 1876.
—— Retrospect of a Long Life. 2 vols. 1883.

HANNAY, JAMES. Characters and Criticisms. 1865.
HARE, AUGUSTUS. The Story of My Life. 6 vols. 1896–1900.
HARPER, GEORGE McLEAN. William Wordsworth, his Life, Works and
    Influence. 2 vols. 1916.
HAWTHORNE, NATHANIEL. Our Old Home. 2 vols. 1863.
HAYDON, BENJAMIN ROBERT. Autobiography and Journals. Edited by
    Tom Taylor. 3 vols. 1853.
—— Correspondence and Table-Talk. Edited by F. W. Haydon.
    2 vols. 1876.
HAZLITT, WILLIAM. Table-Talk. Select British Poets. 1824.
—— The Spirit of the Age. 1825.
—— Notes of a Journey through France and Italy. 1826.
—— Collected Works. Edited by A. R. Waller and Arnold Glover.
    13 vols. 1902–6.
HAZLITT, WILLIAM CAREW. Memoirs of William Hazlitt. 2 vols. 1867.
—— Mary and Charles Lamb. 1874.
—— Four Generations of a Literary Family. 2 vols. 1897.
—— The Hazlitts, an Account of their Origin and Descent. 1911.
HOLYOAKE, GEORGE JACOB. Sixty Years of an Agitator's Life. 2 vols. 1892.
HORNE, RICHARD HENGIST. A New Spirit of the Age. 2 vols. 1844.
—— Gregory VII. 3rd ed. 1849.
—— Letters of Elizabeth Barrett Browning.... With Comments on
    Contemporaries. 2 vols. 1877.
HOWE, P. P. The Life of William Hazlitt. 1922.
HOWITT, WILLIAM. Homes and Haunts of the British Poets. 2 vols. 1847.
HUNTER, JOHN. Miscellanies by N. R. 1843.
HUTTON, LAURENCE. Literary Landmarks of London. 1885.
INGPEN, ROGER. Shelley in England. 1917.
IRELAND, ALEXANDER. List of the Writings of William Hazlitt and
    Leigh Hunt. 1868.
—— Ralph Waldo Emerson: Recollections of his Visits. 1882.
JERROLD, DOUGLAS. Works. Vol. v. Containing Memoir by W. Blan-
    chard Jerrold. 2nd ed. 1860.
JOHNSON, R. BRIMLEY. Leigh Hunt. 1896.
—— Christ's Hospital. Recollections of Lamb, Coleridge, and Leigh
    Hunt. 1896.
JOLINE, ADRIAN H. Meditations of an Autograph Collector. New York.
    1902.
KEATS, JOHN. Complete Works. Edited by H. Buxton Forman. 5 vols.
    1900–1901.
KENT, CHARLES. Footprints on the Road. 1864.
[KENT, ELIZABETH.] Flora Domestica; or, the Portable Flower-Garden.
    New ed. 1831.

[KENT, ELIZABETH.] Sylvan Sketches; or, a Companion to the Park and the Shrubbery. New ed. 1831.

LAMB, CHARLES and MARY. Works, and Letters. Edited by E. V. Lucas. 7 vols. 1903.

—— Works. Edited by Thomas Hutchinson. 2 vols. 1908.

LANGFORD, J. A. Prison Books. 1861.

LEWES, GEORGE HENRY. Modern British Dramatists. 1867.

LINTON, ELIZA LYNN. My Literary Life. 1899.

LINTON, W. J. Memories. 1895.

LOCKER-LAMPSON, FREDERICK. My Confidences. An Autobiographical Sketch. 2nd ed. 1896.

LUCAS, E. V. The Life of Charles Lamb. 1905.

—— The life of Charles Lamb. New ed. 1910.

LYTTON, LORD. England and the English. 2 vols. 1833.

—— Quarterly Essays. 1875.

MACAULAY, THOMAS BABINGTON. Critical and Historical Essays. New ed. 1850.

MACFARLANE, CHARLES (1799–1858). Recollections of a Literary Life. 1917.

MACREADY, WILLIAM CHARLES. Diaries, 1833–1851. Edited by William Toynbee. 2 vols. 1912.

MAIN, DAVID M. A Treasury of English Sonnets. 1880.

MARSHALL, MRS JULIAN. The Life and Letters of Mary Wollstonecraft Shelley. 2 vols. 1889.

MARTINEAU, HARRIET. Autobiography. 1877.

MASSON, DAVID. Memories of London in the Forties. 1908.

MATHEWS, CHARLES. Memoirs. 4 vols. 1839.

MAYER, GERTRUDE TOWNSHEND. Women of Letters. 2 vols. 1894.

MEDWIN, THOMAS. Journal of the Conversations of Lord Byron. 1824.

Men of the Time. 1856.

MILLER, B. Leigh Hunt's Relations with Byron, Shelley, and Keats. 1910.

MITCHELL, ALEXANDER. Notes on the Bibliography of Leigh Hunt. In The Bookman's Journal, ser. 3, vol. xv, No. 1. 1927.

MITFORD, MARY RUSSELL. Recollections of a Literary Life. 3 vols. 1852.

MOIR, D. M. Poetical Literature of the Last Half-Century. 1851.

MONKHOUSE, W. COSMO. Life of Leigh Hunt. [With a Bibliography by John P. Anderson.] 1893.

MONTGOMERY, ROBERT. The Age Reviewed. 1827.

MOORE, THOMAS. The Life, Letters and Journals of Lord Byron. New ed. 1866.

MORLEY, F. V. Dora Wordsworth, her Book. 1924.

NOBLE, J. ASHCROFT. The Sonnet in England and Other Essays. 1893.

O'DONOGHUE, D. J. Life of William Carleton. 1896.

PATMORE, PETER GEORGE. Letters on England. 1823.
—— Imitations of Celebrated Authors; or, Imaginary Rejected Articles. 1826. 4th ed. 1844.
—— My Friends and Acquaintance. 3 vols. 1854.
PLANCHÉ, J. R. Recollections and Reflections. 2 vols. 1872.
PROCTER, BRYAN WALLER. Charles Lamb: A Memoir. 1866.
—— An Autobiographical Fragment. 1877.
QUEEN VICTORIA. Letters, 1837–1861. 3 vols. 1908.
REDDING, CYRUS. Fifty Years' Recollections. 3 vols. 1858.
—— Yesterday and To-day. 3 vols. 1863.
REID, T. W. Life of Lord Houghton. 2 vols. 1890.
RENTON, R. John Forster and his Friendships. 1912.
REYNOLDS, JOHN HAMILTON. Safie. 1814.
—— Poetry and Prose. Edited by G. L. Marsh. 1928.
ROBINSON, HENRY CRABB. Diary. Edited by T. Sadler. 3 vols. 1869.
ROSSETTI, WILLIAM MICHAEL. Life of John Keats. 1887.
SCOTT, WILLIAM BELL. Autobiographical Notes. Edited by W. Minto. 2 vols. 1892.
SHARP, WILLIAM. Life and Letters of Joseph Severn. 1892.
SHELLEY, PERCY BYSSHE. Complete Poetical Works. Edited by Thomas Hutchinson. 1912.
—— Letters. Edited by Roger Ingpen. 2 vols. 1912.
—— Letters to Leigh Hunt. Edited by T. J. Wise. 2 vols. 1894.
TAYLOR, BAYARD. Home and Abroad. 1862.
TENNYSON, HALLAM. Memoir of Lord Tennyson. 2 vols. 1897.
THORNBURY, W. and WALFORD, E. Old and New London. 6 vols. n.d.
TRELAWNY, EDWARD JOHN. Recollections of the Last Days of Shelley and Byron. 1858.
—— Records of Shelley, Byron, and the Author. 2 vols. 1878.
TREVELYAN, GEORGE OTTO. Life and Letters of Lord Macaulay. 2 vols. 1913.
VAN DOREN, CARL. Life of T. L. Peacock. 1911.
[WEBSTER, B.] Scenes from the Rejected Comedies, by some of the Competitors for the prize of £500, offered by B. Webster. 1844.
WILKIE GALLERY, THE. 1849.
WILSON, JOHN. Works. Edited by Professor Ferrier. 12 vols. 1855–58.
WILSON, JOHN ILIFF. The History of Christ's Hospital...to which are added Memoirs of Eminent Men Educated There. 1821.

Index

The initials "L.H." in this index represent "Leigh Hunt."